THE POLITICAL ECONOMY OF ISRAEL

SUNY Series in Israeli Studies

Russell Stone, Editor

THE POLITICAL ECONOMY OF ISRAEL

FROM IDEOLOGY TO STAGNATION

YAKIR PLESSNER

STATE UNIVERSITY OF NEW YORK PRESS

HC
415.25
P578
1994

Published by
State University of New York Press, Albany

© 1994   State University of New York

For information, address State University of New York Press,
State University Plaza, Albany, NY 12246

Production by M. R. Mulholland
Marketing by Nancy Farrell

Library of Congress Cataloging-in-Publication Data

Plessner, Yakir, 1935–
      The political economy of Israel : from ideology to stagnation /
Yakir Plessner.
           p.   cm. — (SUNY series in Israeli studies)
      Includes bibliographical references and index.
      ISBN 0–7914–1741–7. — ISBN 0–7914–1742–5 (pbk.)
      1. Israel—Economic conditions. I. Title. II. Series.
HC415.25.P578   1993
338.95694—dc20   93–203
                                                                                           CIP

10 9 8 7 6 5 4 3 2 1

THE RESEARCH THAT LED TO THE WRITING OF THIS BOOK, CARRIED OUT UNDER THE AUSPICES OF THE JERUSALEM CENTER FOR PUBLIC AFFAIRS, WAS MADE POSSIBLE BY GENEROUS GRANTS FROM THE LYNDE AND HARRY BRADLEY FOUNDATION AND THE EARHART FOUNDATION. THEIR GENEROSITY IS GRATEFULLY ACKNOWLEDGED.

CONTENTS

PREFACE

My fascination with what I learned about political economics during my stint in the public sector led me to write this book. From the end of 1981 to early 1985, I served, first as economic adviser to the minister of finance and then as deputy governor of the Bank of Israel. Many of the observations and analyses that inhabit this volume were formed, at least partially, during those years. With them, my distrust of government meddling in the economy grew by the day.

I started the systematic research of the existing material on the Israeli economy in 1986, working my way backwards in time. During my progress I became increasingly fascinated as I realized that the story of the Israeli economy was a natural extension of the story of Zionism. The story of the Israeli economy thus turned into the story of the economy of the Jewish people in *Eretz Yisrael*—the land of Israel. The roots of what I call Israel's economic culture were to be found, as I gradually discovered, as early as in the last quarter of the nineteenth century, which is when practical Zionism began.

The search and research took a lot longer than I had anticipated, because nobody had ever attempted to write a comprehensive history of the Israeli economy, which meant that I had to go back to the original documents to find enough material to corroborate my emerging hypotheses.

I did my best to present the material in a form that does not require the reader to be a professional economist, nor even to have attended economics courses. The little technical material contained in the book is relegated to the appendices of chapters and may be safely skipped by the uninitiated.

The story told is of why Israel's economy grew vigorously during the first quarter-century of the state's existence and why it has virtually stagnated since. The obstacles to growth are identified and analyzed, and then their origins in Zionist history are unearthed. Wherever possible and instructive, comparisons are drawn between Israel's economy and other economies, both in the free world and in the former communist domain.

Being a novice in searching through historical material, I needed guidance. This was generously extended to me by my sister, Hagit Lavsky, who is a historian specializing in the Zionist movement. My search was aided by Sara Ben-Amy and Hagit Sten, both of whom did a marvelous job in going through the thousands of documents, articles, and collections of papers. In this context I owe a debt of gratitude to the Zionist Archives, where I was extended courteous help and patience during many months of search.

My thinking about the problems and the development of the various hypotheses benefitted greatly from conversations with David Levhary of the Hebrew University, Steve Hanke of Johns Hopkins University, Meir Kohn of Dartmouth College, Alvin Rabushka of the Hoover Institution, and Joe D. Reid, Jr., of George Mason University. But most of all I owe a great intellectual debt to Pinhas Zusman of the Hebrew University, whose profound insights, gained partly during his tenure as director general of Israel's Ministry of Defense, enhanced my thinking to a considerable degree. I also benefitted tremendously from my conversations with Yoram Aridor, former minister of finance of Israel, who was the first occupier of the job with extensive training in economics.

Yoram Aridor, Steve Hanke, Alvin Rabushka, and Joe Reid read earlier drafts of the manuscript and provided me with valuable comments.

Daniel Elazar and Zvi R. Marom, president and director, respectively, of the Jerusalem Center for Public Affairs, were extremely helpful in every respect, making my toil that much easier. Part of the work was done while I was a visitor at the Department of Economics at Dartmouth College, whose hospitality I greatly appreciate. Mark Ami-El of the Jerusalem Center for Public Affairs performed a marvelous editing job, for which I am grateful. Andrea Arbel prepared skillfully the camera-ready figures.

Russell Stone of SUNY played a key role when, on having been told by me about the project, suggested that I submit the manuscript to SUNY Press. When I followed his advice, I had the good fortune of dealing with Rosalie Robertson, editor of SUNY Press, whose efficiency and swiftness in handling the process that led to the book's acceptance by the publisher are admirable. Finally, I am grateful to two anonymous referees for SUNY Press for comments that helped a lot in the final editing of this volume. After this volume started its journey through the production process, I discovered the new book by Yair Aharoni, *The Israeli Economy: Dreams and Realities* (London: Routledge). I regret not being able to refer to it.

INTRODUCTION

The description of an economy, if it is to constitute more than just a compendium of facts and statistics, must be based on some conceptual framework, which serves as a guide in straining the wealth of data and organizing the data chosen along some logical lines. Needless to say, the chosen conceptual framework presents, in a sense, a biased picture, if only because it determines which data will constitute the evidence and which will be ignored or assigned secondary importance. Hence, the resulting description of the economy cannot be called neutral in the sense of a catalogue.

That the Israeli economy has failed, on any number of criteria, for roughly the past two decades is not a subject for debate. The evidence is beyond dispute. What may be hotly contested is the question why. The basic hypothesis advanced here is that the failure can be explained by the extent of the economy's departure from the institutions and rules that govern predominantly market economies. Israel's economy operated on principles too far from liberalism (in the European sense; neo-conservatism in the American sense) and too close to socialism.

Liberalism in the present context is not meant in the ideological sense. It could be: many liberals argue that individual freedom is impossible without economic freedom, and that for this reason alone people should aspire to market economies. Not that I deny the connection, but my critical study of the Israeli economy is not motivated by the observation of lack of individual economic freedom per se. Rather, the motivation here is completely pragmatic: at the end of the day, could an economy that did not conform to the rules of a market economy perform as well, or even better, than one that does? Can one tell a coherent story of the Israeli economy on the supposition that what happened, and what did not happen, can be traced to the economy's lean toward socialism?

The temptation to tell the story of Israel's economy on this basis is not surprising. One did not have to await the collapse of the communist block in Eastern Europe to suspect that socialist, centrally planned economies do not fare well in comparison with capitalist, market economies. Not one of the prosperous economies in Europe and North America came to prosperity on the strength of government plans. No government-built economy ever allowed the members of a society to become affluent.

Although ideology is not at issue here, there is no way one can completely divorce oneself from value judgments when dealing with economics.

Without ideology of any sort, one would be unable to identify goals that an economy is supposed to strive for. Hence, it would be impossible to tell whether or not an economy is successful. Nor would it be possible to formulate economic policies, if objectives are not set first. But this cannot be done without a measure of ideology.

Liberal ideology enters the framework in the following way. First, there is the fundamental working assumption that people are motivated by the desire to improve their economic lot. The value judgement lies with the postulate that the economy should be designed in such a way as to create the best environment for people to do so. This implies, among other things, efficiency and the desirability of economic growth. It is not, of course, the only possible postulate. One could pursue instead, guided by a different set of values, an economy that provides as equal a distribution of claims to consumption as possible. Or one could base an economy, as has been attempted at various times in various places, on the premise that the pursuit of a high standard of material living is evil, and the economy should therefore be geared to the provision of "necessities" only.

Why should one expect a market economy to work so much better than any known alternative? It seems that the basic reason for its superiority is the discipline which the market imposes on economic agents. A competitive market is the only one in which survival depends exclusively on economic success. A firm which is not good at what it is doing, or which produces something which society no longer wants, is guaranteed to fail only if it operates in a competitive environment, where it cannot receive favors or bribe its way to survival.

One exceedingly important consequence of this is what Hayek calls the *process of discovery* that is facilitated by competition.[1] The need to survive provides a constant impetus to excel. This, in turn, causes existing and potential producers to be constantly on the outlook for new, better methods of production, better quality of goods and services, and newly generated wants for whose satisfaction new goods must be created. This, in turn, fuels the research that generates innovations, without which growth would be impossible. Hayek likens the competitive form of market organization to a scientific methodology. The only way to judge the superiority of a scientific methodology is by comparing its record to that of alternative approaches. The same is true for the competitive market system.

In the absence of market discipline, there is always the threat to growth that emanates from the moral hazard that all but the competitive environment create. Arrangements other than competition create opportunities for getting financially ahead without being efficient and without innovation. Monopolies or cartels that can deny entry to new firms need not run scared and therefore can indulge in the luxury of not being constantly on the alert for innovation.

The car industry in the United States provides an excellent example in this respect.

Industries regulated by the government automatically come to expect one kind or another of government handouts. The reason is very simple: when the government intervenes, it cannot but come to be regarded by the subjects of the intervention as assuming part of the responsibility for their survival. The underlying rationale is that, if you tell me what to do and I obey, you are responsible for the outcome of whatever you told me to do. And if the outcome is adverse, you should bear the consequences by compensating me. And because it is never possible to tell which part of the outcome must be ascribed to regulation and which to failures by the regulated, moral hazard is created.

Similar, if potentially more damaging, ramifications obtain where government itself owns economic enterprises. Government ownership of firms promotes inefficiency because governments are reluctant to admit failure. If a firm fails in the competitive market, it has no recourse. It must either shape up or get out. Governments command the wherewithal to perpetuate failures, or at least keep them alive for a long time. Pre-Thatcher Britain provides a prime example of this.

In addition to the direct consequences of inefficiency of government enterprises, such practices have economywide adverse effects. For example, if the government helps keep alive an inefficient steel mill, a private entrepreneur, efficient as he or she may be, will be very hesitant about entering the steel-milling business.

The Israeli economy constitutes a laboratory case for the study of inefficient economies. First, it is unique in that in some important aspects it features the most socialized economy of any politically free country except, perhaps, India. This implies that the observer need not worry about whether a particular attribute of economic performance is the result of the economic form of organization or could possibly be generated by political oppression. This sort of doubt is always associated with socialist countries in, for example, Africa, because they are also dictatorships. Not so in Israel, which actually has a quite fragmented political structure with proportional representation. It has complete freedom of the press, save for the fact that the electronic media are still wholly owned by the government. But this is changing, as pay-television cable networks have begun to operate.

But Israel never went so far as obviating the pricing mechanism itself. Instead, it devised a plethora of institutions and rules whose purpose is to change the outcome of the pricing system. The degree of public involvement in the economy, both before and after the establishment of Israel, educated the population to systematically ignore economic efficiency considerations. First there was the ideology, which viewed private profit and social welfare as contradictory. Second, because the population got used to not having to bear the consequences of its financial decisions, it could afford to become economically ignorant. When the outcome of one's decision does not depend on whether the decision was correct, why bother about collecting information? In addition, there was the relegation of economic considerations to a position of secondary importance because of what was perceived as national imperatives that ran contrary to economic efficiency. This last rationale is the hardest to set aside. In essence, it held that the state would have never been born if its founders had allowed efficiency considerations to bother them.

At its most eloquent, the argument goes something like this. History opened for the Jewish people a very small window, which stretched from after World War I to a little after World War II. Within that time span, only a shade over a quarter-century long, Jews in Palestine had to take the actions that would secure, first, the eventual establishment of a Jewish state and, second, its physical survival in the face of overwhelming odds. This implied, in the first place, the physical settlement of as many parts of the land as land ownership and personnel availability would allow, regardless of whether the established communities could be made economically viable.

It was not just that the founders decided to set economic considerations aside whenever a situation required such an approach. They definitely believed that the investment required to achieve the larger national objective could not be expected to be profitable in the usual sense. In consequence, they assumed that private capital could not possibly be relied on to provide the resources for the construction of the National Home. The conclusion was that if a Jewish state was going to be built, it would have to be financed by public funds, invested for national reasons, and not for the sake of profit.

It is, of course, impossible to refute the reasoning behind this national strategy. What happened can be judged only in the light of what could have been, and the latter inevitably involves a degree of speculation. It must therefore be admitted that, had the entire Zionist effort relied on investment motivated by business considerations, Israel may never have been established.

The national imperative as a reason for ignoring economic considerations prior to the establishment of Israel cannot be dismissed, but what about after the creation of the state? First came fifteen months of the War of Independence, which required the mobilization of the entire community. Then, in the course of the three years 1949 to 1951, the new Israel was inundated by an immigration wave that tripled the population. Absorbing the mass of immigrants required an economy much like a wartime economy. But by the time Israel settled into a more normal state, the national argument for ignoring economic considerations became such an integral part of the national philosophy that it was hardly ever questioned. Governmental domination of the economy was therefore accepted quite naturally even as the independence of Israel was becoming secure.

Not only the time dimension of government domination of the economy cannot be justified by national considerations, also the scope of intervention. For example, although the national argument may not be denied as concerns agricultural settlements in pre-state years, most of the de facto nationalization of the capital market occurred after the immigration wave was receding.

The trouble with economic strategies that get governments, or in the case of pre-Israel Palestine, governmentlike bodies involved "temporarily" in an economy, is that the transitory becomes the permanent. Moreover, as the saying goes, with each progressive course of the meal, the appetite increases. Examples of makeshift methods that turned into permanent fixtures abound. Agricultural settlement is again a case in point: in the pre-Israel years, financial support of farming communities could be justified by the need to keep settlers on the land. But what is the justification for bailing such communities out of a financial mess with public funds seventy years later?

This book tries to describe the Israeli economy and understand it in light of the systematic exclusion and distrust of, and the squeezing of operating space for, private enterprise. The implication is that as long as the economy will not be reformed in a way that will create a hospitable climate for truly private investment, the economy will not extricate itself from stagnation.

The book traces these general assertions through the Israeli economy, thus tying the facts and figures into a story of how the economy evolved and why. The first chapter describes how Israel slid into the economic stagnation in which it has languished since 1973. The next seven chapters deal with the four main categories of obstacles to the resumption of economic growth: the government's domination of the capital and credit markets, the artificial economic environment surrounding Israel's citizens, the absence of a really independent private sector, and the turning of the government into little more than an instrument in the hands of groups that have evolved due to excessive government intervention in the economy.

The next two chapters describe the way in which the various obstacles to growth combined to produce Israel's bout with near-hyperinflation and the consequences of the inflationary process. The final chapter deals with the stabilization program of 1985 and its aftermath and tries to provide a prognosis for the near future. Through it all, the reader is introduced to the main descriptive features of the economy, including the institutional and legal framework within which it operates. In some cases there are technical appendices, which readers who are not economists are invited to skip.

1

THE ROAR THAT BECAME A WHISPER

Soon after the state of Israel was established in 1948, its economy took off, with vibrant economic growth continuing for twenty-three years (Table 1.1). After 1973, however, this vigorous growth was replaced by sluggishness and a very disappointing rate of economic expansion, barely sufficient to sustain the rate of per-capita production attained in 1973.

The story of how growth was replaced by stagnation is the story of the past two decades of Israel's economy. We will see that the roar became a whisper largely because of the semisocialist arrangements on which the economy was founded, many of which survive to this day.

The term *socialism* is used here in its strict sense: the collective ownership and allocation of an economy's means of production.[2] According to this definition, Sweden, often referred to as *socialist,* is not: it has the highest incidence of private ownership of any Western economy.[3] *Socialism* is used interchangeably to describe the ideology and to identify the organizational setup within which the norms laid down by the ideology are being pursued. This semantic problem does not exist with capitalism, which is the institutional setup spawned by liberalism.

TABLE 1.1

Growth of Real GDP,* Annual Averages

Period	Percent	Period	Percent
1950–55	12.6	1971–75	7.1
1956–60	8.8	1976–80	2.6
1961–65	9.8	1981–85	2.8
1966–70	7.7	1986–89	3.1
1950–73	9.7	1974–89	2.8

*Gross Domestic Product.
Source: Central Bureau of Statistics,[1] *National Accounts,* various years.

These distinctions are important, since the institutional setup is crucial in determining the functional efficiency of an economic system. This can be most sharply demonstrated by noting that in the Soviet version of socialism, the institutional system tried to replace the market institution. This has probably been the most important factor in the spectacular collapse of the communist economic system, and it is also what made Western economists so confidant that the communist system could not ultimately deliver on its promises.

In contrast, the Israeli system recognizes the forces of supply and demand. Hence, to a casual observer it looks as though the Israeli economy works like a capitalist one, except that the government is more heavily involved. The task of attributing Israel's economic failure to socialism is thus made more difficult. Israeli socialism is, as one might put it, more subtle.

The use of the adjective *socialist* in the description of the Israeli economy hinges on three central attributes of the institutional system. First, there has been virtually no free access to the capital market. For many years, there was almost no way to raise capital in Israel except through the government. Hence, even though a substantial share of capital is not collectively owned, almost all of it has been collectively allocated. Second, a substantial proportion of the means of production has been owned either by the government or by the Trade Unions Federation—both forms of social ownership of the means of production. This is true of much of the capital, but most particularly of the land, which is 94 percent socially owned. Third, the wage structure reflects the attempt to implement the basic socialist welfare criterion.

This is, then, the sense in which the term *socialism* is being used throughout. As we shall see, some of the more important consequences of this structure resemble the obstacles that the ex-communist world confronts.

The Bumpy Road of Political Economy

The task of identifying certain traits in an economy as the causes for longstanding problems is a very treacherous one. The difficulty emanates from the fact that it is impossible to *prove* assertions in this field in the usual, scientific sense of the word. Propositions in economics, other than in the context of pure economic theory, are not prone to proofs in general, for the simple reason that virtually no experimentation at all, and certainly no controlled experimentation, is possible. In this respect, economics is in much the same position as meteorology. A meteorologist cannot create in the laboratory mini-weather systems that exactly duplicate natural ones. And because weather patterns are quite varied, no clear rules can be established other than in extreme situations. For example, it can be stated with certainty that wherever a hurricane will pass, it will rain. But the spectrum of weather patterns that involve cloudiness is so wide that definite statements about the relation between clouds and rain are virtually impossible. Instead, meteorologists rely on statistical analysis of past, observed weather patterns, which allows them to produce probabilistic forecasts, such as "a 70-percent chance of rain."

Like meteorology, economics can also use statistical observations to try to establish relations between various events. But in only very few cases can the results be stated as a rule or theorem, and no amount of statistical analysis can "prove" anything. It merely helps investigators to strengthen their beliefs. Even statistical analysis is limited to those phenomena that are relatively narrow in scope, such as specific supply or demand relations, cost of production, and so forth. In particular, no statistical analysis can be expected to do any good when it comes to assessing or comparing entire economic systems.

To help clarify the point, consider the following assertion that concerns an entire economic system: *the Soviet economy has performed poorly because of its communist form of organization.* If one believes this statement to be true, it is probably not due to the refined results of statistical regression analysis. Rather, it is based on casual observations of living conditions in the Soviet Union and basic notions concerning the incentives that drive individuals to be industrious; that is, those that create the circumstances for the existence of a productive economic system.

The diagnosis of the communist form of economic organization as the cause for the Soviet Union's economic troubles is by no means the only possible one. For example, one might suggest that the Soviet economy faces a variety of difficulties unique to the Soviet Union and that have nothing to do with communism. Such difficulties might be the lack of access to a warm-water port, a harsh climate, a large population with cultural and religious backgrounds that are not particularly conducive to rapid economic growth, a war that devastated large parts of the economy, a dictatorial form of government. Yet even if statistical analyses were to be presented to back up these latter explanations, it is unlikely that anyone who had been initially convinced by the argument that ascribes the Soviet economic failures to communism will have changed his or her mind in light of such analyses.

This demonstrates both the strength and weakness of the way by which we form opinions about economic systems. The strength lies with the fact that we have to refer to a basic conceptual framework and a broad body of knowledge concerning human behavior. The weakness concerns the temptation to select from the observed facts only those that support our preconception. This selectivity is facilitated by the fact that, in the absence of methodical statistical analysis or experimentation, we are not subject to the discipline imposed on us by the procedure of these methodologies.

Given the history of the Israeli economy, the task of establishing a causal relationship between the socialistlike structure of the economy and its poor performance for the past two decades is far from easy. What makes it possible to pass unequivocal judgment concerning the performance of the Soviet economy, for instance, is its very long history of stagnation. While the free world had its share of crises, it always rebounded. The Soviet economy, on the other hand, slowly grinded to a halt, producing in the end the Gorbachev revolution. Israel, in contrast, does not feature such clear-cut evidence. In broad terms, the length of time during which the economy grew vigorously still exceeds the period of dull performance. If Israel had failed to grow all along, the sort of statement made about the Soviet economy could have been applied to Israel as well. All one would have to do is convince the reader that Israel's economy does indeed feature many attributes that render it incapable of economic growth at rates common in the free world. However, given the brisk pace of growth during the first twenty years following Israel's War of Independence, the task of justifying the diagnosis is greatly complicated. As we shall see, the very features of the Israeli economy that will be blamed here for the poor economic performance since 1973 had been present all along. Yet for two decades the economy managed to perform very nicely despite that presence.

This is not the only difficulty. Another problem emerges in the fact that growth declined abruptly around 1973. This precludes the possibility that the obstacles to growth had been gathering momentum until they finally became strong enough to depress growth rates. For such a story to be credible, one would expect to observe gradually declining growth rates, rather than a sudden death. The reason is simple: mounting obstacles are likely to affect some parts of the economy sooner than other parts, and there are also likely to be differences in the intensity of the obstacles' impact.

The suddenness with which growth rates declined, combined with its timing, has produced an explanation viewing the entire development as a consequence of wrong policy reactions to the twin crises of 1973—the Yom Kippur War and the Oil Crisis.[4] This, it is argued, both stifled growth and created the decade-long inflationary process that brought the country's economy dangerously close to collapse. It also created the vocabulary economists frequently use when talking about recovery. The key phrase here is *resumption of growth*, which suggests what the country must do is return to the pre-1973 path in terms of the structure of priorities and the policies engineered to achieve them. The implication is that nothing had been fundamentally wrong with the pre-1973 economy. If this is true, then it cannot be argued that the economy has contained all along some basic faults whose presence stymies growth.

An argument that places the blame for Israel's failure to grow on a fundamentally flawed structure must therefore establish that things were not all right prior to 1973. It must be demonstrated that the fast growth rates that the economy had experienced for two decades happened despite the flaws and were facilitated by special circumstances.

The essence of the argument offered here is this: during the early stages of development there are opportunities for large-scale investment that are easy to identify. Prime examples are infrastructure, such as roads and electricity, and residential construction. Massive investment in these and other projects generates rapid growth not only in those sectors of the economy at which the main thrust of investment is aimed, but also in related sectors. For example, a rapid growth in residential construction generates growth in the construction-equipment economy, in the cement industry, and in the industries that specialize in housing fixtures, such as glass and plumbing fixtures. Similarly, road construction spawns an expansion in quarrying and road-construction equipment.

Industrial investment, too, comes relatively easily. In the early stages of development, when wages are low, large numbers of workers can be employed in traditional industries, such as textiles, steel, and shipbuilding.

During early development, the ease with which projects can be identified, and the relatively large chunks of capital that each such project can absorb, make it possible for governments to become the major investors. This means that during the early stages, the availability of private entrepreneurs is not that crucial to generate growth. Their ability to spot opportunities and exploit them is not sorely missed because it does not take their special capabilities to identify opportunities. Put differently, the difficulties into which centralized economic planning and management are bound to run eventually are not serious enough during the first stages of development.

But as the economy becomes more complex, and investment opportunities become less obvious, the economy must rely on the private entrepreneur to discover the niches of relative advantage, a discovery process in which a cumbersome bureaucracy has a distinct disadvantage. It is also the stage when an increasing part of investment takes the form of relatively small initial outlays, magnitudes of little interest to bureaucrats. When the required class of entrepreneurs does not exist, or is relatively small, or if private enterprise finds it hard to pick up where the government has left off because of the institutional rigidities it left behind, the economy will stop growing. This is when the major drawbacks of central planning show. As we shall attempt to show, the dominating role played by the government during the first two decades created an environment hostile to private enterprise, so when the government could no longer play the role of the major entrepreneur, there was no one to replace it.

Centrally planned economies do indeed grow fast in the early stages of development. Table 1.2 contains data concerning Israel and three Eastern European countries whose economies were completely centralized during the period covered by the table. The table also contains data for West Germany, which is ideal for comparison with its eastern neighbor, as both started from roughly the same ruinous state after World War II.

TABLE 1.2

Early Development Growth Rates, Percent per Year

Country	1950–55		1955–60		1960–65	
	GDP*	NCF**	GDP	NCF	GDP	NCF
Israel	13.0	10.2	9.2	6.4	9.9	10.2
West Germany	9.1	12.7	6.0	7.3	5.0	7.1
East Germany	13.0	36.6	8.0	20.9	2.7	3.1
Poland	8.8	13.2	6.7	10.1	6.0	7.9
Yugoslavia	11.2	8.2	9.7	14.0	7.6	6.7

  * Gross Domestic Product; for Eastern European countries, Net Material Product.
** Net Capital Formation

Source: Data except for Israel: United Nations, *Yearbook of National Accounts Statistics*, 1969, vol. II, Tables 4A, 4C. See also Table 3.1 in Alan H. Smith, *The Planned Economies of Eastern Europe* (New York: Holmes and Meier, 1983). The growth rates he quotes for Poland are almost identical to the U.N.'s, and the rates for East Germany are higher, especially for 1960–65, where he reports a growth rate of 5.8 percent. But see also U.S. Bureau of East–West Trade, *Selected U.S.S.R. and Eastern European Economies Data* (June 1973), where the GNP of East Germany is estimated to have grown an average 3.3 percent from 1960 to 1965. The rates for Poland and Yugoslavia are also quite close to the U.N.'s for 1960 to 1965.

The salient feature of the table is the rapid growth experienced by the three communist countries during the early stages of their development. East Germany grew even faster than its western counterpart. The very rapid rate of capital formation is also common to the countries considered, as is the marked tapering off of both capital accumulation and economic growth.

Similarly, early fast growth in Israel was indeed generated to a very substantial extent by the government. Therefore, early economic growth at reasonable rates is not inconsistent with central planning or heavy government involvement.

This does not mean, of course, that a strategy of early development led by the government necessarily yields good results. Such a strategy has failed miserably in virtually all of the newly enfranchised African states.

Early Growth in Israel

Figures 1.1 and 1.2 contain the facts asserting that growth during the first twenty years occurred because it was easy to grow, more or less regardless of the institutional setup of the economy. Figure 1.1 summarizes the characteristics of investment in residential construction, whereas Figure 1.2 does the same for all nonresidential investment in fixed assets.[5] Both figures depict variations in the rates of change of investment. That is, rather than plotting the absolute rate of investment against time, they plot the rate of change of investment against time. The reason is this. Let us assume that economic growth depends on the net stock of capital at the disposal of the economy. The net stock is the outcome of gross investment over the years, less depreciation of the existing stock, which we shall suppose to proceed at a fixed rate (e.g., 10 percent of the capital stock available at the beginning of a year depreciates during the year). Then it can be shown that if the net capital stock is to grow at a sustained given rate, then investment must grow at the same rate. The significance of this becomes obvious when we think of the net capital stock per person or per employed person. If we wish to at least keep the standard of living from sliding, then the net stock of capital per capita must remain constant, which means that it must grow as fast as the population, which implies that investment must grow at the same rate. Indeed, per-capita growth of Israel's economy has been negligible between 1973 and 1989. It is important to note that points in Figures 1.1 and 1.2 that lie below the horizontal axis represent absolute declines in the rate of investment.

Let us concentrate first on the period up to 1967, starting with residential construction. Immediately after Israel gained independence, immigrants came

FIGURE 1.1

Investment in Residential Construction: Percentage Change and Shares

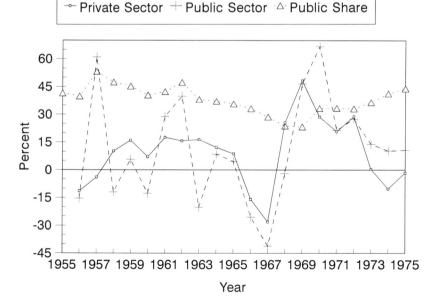

FIGURE 1.2

Investment in Fixed Capital: Percentage Change and Shares

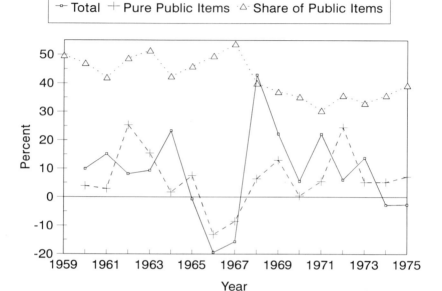

flooding into the country. But by 1952 the tide had subsided, and another surge came only in 1955–57, albeit a much smaller one than the first. The rapid expansion of the population required considerable investment in housing, and throughout the period 1955–66, such investment hovered around one-third of all investment in fixed assets. Because gross domestic investment grew over those years at an average annual rate of over 8 percent, residential construction maintained its place as a generator of growth. It did not require sophisticated capital equipment, and labor was abundantly available as a result of all that immigration. Construction spawned, in turn, investment in construction equipment and high rates of growth in the cement industry, quarrying, and transportation. For example, from 1960 to 1966 the gross capital stock in the construction industry grew by an average annual rate of 13.5 percent.[6]

The 1955–57 surge in immigration is clearly manifested in Figure 1.1 by a large increase in the rate of change of investment in construction by both the public and the private sector. The figure also reveals that, except for a blip in 1961 and 1962, the share of public investment in residential construction declined continuously from about 53 percent in 1957, to less than 24 percent in 1968, a cut of more than one-half in the government's share in only ten years. The blip coincides with another surge in immigration, which lasted from 1961 to 1965, with the peak years being 1962 and 1963. By 1965 immigration declined to less than half the 1964 level. As is evident, the private sector reacted in an entirely reasonable way. From 1961 to 1965 the curve representing the private sector is very smooth, but the curve representing the public sector indicates violent fluctuations.[7]

The steady decline in the government's share in residential construction occurred because the reason for its intensive activity no longer existed. In fact, by 1964 an excess supply of apartments was beginning to accumulate, after a hefty increase in construction. Ironically, part of that increase was attributed to rumors concerning a pending government decree intended to limit new housing starts.[8] Naturally, the prolonged construction boom brought about a considerable upgrading of the standard of housing: whereas in 1957 some 25 percent of the population resided at a density of three or more to a room, by 1967 only 10 percent lived that way.[9]

Figure 1.1 also suggests that 1962 constituted a turning point in the growth of investment in housing. The general trend of both the rates of change of total investment and government investment in housing turned downward. Indeed, although over the period 1956–62 investment in housing grew annually at an average of 8.4 percent, over the period 1963–67 it declined by about the same percentage. Although government investment grew at an average of 10.4 percent over the first period, it declined at an average annual rate of almost 17 percent over the second. The more rapid decline in government investment in housing explains, of course, the decline in its share of the activity. The importance of this half-decade-long decline will soon become evident.

By 1965 it had become clear that immigration rates were rapidly declining: net immigration dropped from about 48,000 in 1964 to roughly 23,000 in 1965, and then plummeted to a little over 8,000 in 1966. Although the rate of investment in housing still increased in 1965, a surplus of housing was already evident. The reaction in 1966 was very sharp: total investment in housing plunged by almost 20 percent and the government reduced its investment by over a quarter as compared to 1965.

Turning to investment in nonhousing fixed assets, one encounters an even greater extent of government involvement than in housing. Over the period 1959–67, the public sector (including nonprofit organizations—mainly universities and hospitals) either carried out or initiated, on the average, 54 percent of total investment in plant and equipment. That vastly underestimates the government's role, because much of the means that flowed from savers to investors directly were directed by the government. This aspect of how the government dominated the allocation of investment resources will become clear in Chapters 2 and 3.

Figure 1.2 describes the rate of change of investment in fixed assets other than housing and the rate of change of investment in those sectors in which the government was virtually the sole investor. These include agriculture, water transportation and irrigation systems, mining, electricity, construction for public services, construction for government-run communications such as the postal service, and construction of roads and ports. The third line in the figure depicts the share of these pure government items in total investment in fixed assets other than housing.

Some of the items listed as pure government ones typically belong to the infrastructure category, where governments all over the world are heavily involved. Of the items that cannot be classified as infrastructure, agriculture and mining stand out. The preponderance of the government in the financing of the agricultural sector stems from ideological and political reasons, which will be given wide attention in the proper context. Suffice it to say here that the government has undertaken to settle Israel's lands, more or less regardless of profitability.

All natural resources in Israel are either nationally owned, as in the case of phosphate deposits and part of the water resources, or subject to government control by law, as in the case of privately owned water wells; again, this is ideological.

As in Figure 1.1, we note first that the share of the pure government items displays a declining trend, which this time stretches all the way to 1971. Still, we shall concentrate first on developments up to 1967, as we did with regard to housing. It is also evident that, just as in the case of housing, the rates of change of investment in the pure government items declined after 1962, and in 1966 and 1967 even the absolute rate of investment declined.

The reason for the decline is that several large projects, of the sort that are easily identified and can swallow large chunks of capital, came to an end. The first part of the curve, from 1959 to 1962, which shows an upward trend, coincides with the start or continuation of these projects.

Included are the Haifa 2 and Ashdod 2 power plants together with power transformation stations, the copper and phosphate mines and especially the Dead Sea Works and the Eilat–Be'er Sheva oil pipeline. The Ashdod port was constructed, the port of Haifa expanded, and a lot of investment in the construction of schools and hospitals took place. One of the more ambitious projects was the construction of the National Water Carrier. This is a system of pipes, canals, tunnels, and reservoirs that transports water from the Sea of Galilee to the arid southern parts of the country. In contrast, the farm sector began to produce surpluses in certain areas, and so investment in agriculture was on the decline.

The three years 1959–61 also saw considerable activity in the construction in Jerusalem of the new campus of the Hebrew University, the Hadassah Hospital, and the Ben-Gurion government offices complex. The World Bank financed a road construction project. There was also considerable investment in the postal service and the telephone system.

In 1964 the National Water Carrier was completed, and investment in water systems dropped sharply. The farm sector generated surpluses in an increasing number of products, which meant curbs on further expansion of production and hence slower investment. Procurement of equipment for the telephone system constituted 80 percent of all purchases of equipment for the transportation and communication sector (excluding vehicles). There was also a large increase of investment in industrial structures commissioned by the public sector. In its 1964 report, the Bank of Israel (the Bank, Israel's central bank) noted the bulky nature of much of the government's investment activity, but it did not draw any conclusions from this observation. As more and more projects were completed, investment continued to drop in 1965 and 1966.

The story of this first period would be incomplete without reference to the growth of industry. Over the five years from 1960 to 1965, investment in industry grew at an average annual rate of 6.6 percent. Much of it was government financed, either directly or through intermediaries getting their instructions from the government. However, this does not constitute a sufficient explanation for industrial growth. What does provide at least a partial explanation, as has been pointed out previously, is that in early stages of industrial development labor is cheap, and the sorts of industries that emerge are labor intensive. One typical member of this category is the textile and apparel industry. Indeed, much of the newly created industry in Israel came in the form of textile factories as well as diamond-polishing plants. Almost a third of all growth in the number of people employed in industry from 1958 to 1965–66 is accounted for by these two industries.[10]

The heavy involvement of the government in industrial investment was manifested, in part, in the construction of industrial buildings by members of the public sector, such as municipalities. By 1965 an excess of such structures emerged. This could happen because construction took place without firm plans as to how the structures would be used. Buildings were being erected in the hope that their existence would attract industry.

Figures 1.1 and 1.2 indicate very clearly the recessionary nature of 1966 and 1967. In both years there were sharp declines in all categories of investment, both private and public. The important role played by big government projects was obvious to at least some observers at the time. One of them pointed out clearly that an important factor in the slump was the winding up of major government projects in 1965, without new ones to take their place. However, he failed to realize that the development was more than temporary. In fact, he expressed surprise that even at the start of 1968 there were still no plans for new government projects.[11]

We shall return to the question of the 1966–67 economic period, but first let us look at the period from 1968 until the 1973 war. In Figure 1.2, one observes a clear rising trend in the rates of change of investment from 1968 to

1972 and a clearly declining trend thereafter. What stands out is that the share of pure public investment items continued to decline until 1971. This implies that investment in those categories not purely public in nature increased faster than investment in public items. It thus looks as though the private sector, or at least the less public sector, picked up the slack left by the termination of a host of government investment projects.

In reality, something very different was happening. In June 1967 the Six Day War erupted. Within less than a week the Israel Defense Forces captured all of the Sinai peninsula, Judea, Samaria, Gaza, and the Golan Heights. These newly acquired territories exceeded in size the land area of Israel proper. This meant a concentrated effort of both military and civilian construction, implying both stepped-up public investment and increased consumption for defense. The latter included military camps, fortifications (among them the Bar-Lev Line along the Suez Canal), and roads. Thus, even though the war itself, and the preceding gestation period, caused a 57-percent increase in domestic procurement for defense (i.e., excluding imports of defense materiel), a further increase of almost 50 percent took place in 1969, with 1970 and 1971 each registering a 20-percent increase.

The construction-equipment sector can again exemplify the magnitude of the change. Although in 1967 investment in construction equipment all but vanished, in 1968 it almost returned to its 1965 level (a rise of 725 percent compared to 1967) and continued to increase at an average of 13 percent until 1972. But as far as investment is concerned, developments surrounding the war have been even more important than the war itself. First, France, which had been Israel's chief arms supplier, put an embargo on further shipments. This placed Israel in the intolerable position of being cut off from the supply source of the two most important weapons systems: combat aircraft and tanks. The government responded with an ambitious program designed to acquire the capability of producing both of these systems. Thus came into being the Merkava (literally Chariot) main battle tank and the Kfir (literally Lion Cub) fighter plane, for which the French Mirage served as a basis. The need to carry out these projects in as short a time as possible required considerable industrial investment by the public sector, including government corporations, who own the most important defense industries. Such investments always spawn secondary investments, and so private sector investment also rose sharply.

The main beneficiaries from the government's defense production program were the metal and electronics industries. Over the five-year period from 1968 to 1972, the real product of manufactured metal goods grew by 142 percent, or 19 percent per year. In 1972 the electric and electronics industry produced 232 percent more than in 1967, an average annual increase of 27 percent.[12]

However, the investment that made all this possible is not included in the categories classified as pure public investment. Hence, the continued decline in the share of these categories after 1967. Nevertheless, the stepped-up investment was clearly the result of government initiative, which had to do with all sorts of considerations other than economic ones.

By 1972 the wave had began to subside. The Bank of Israel observed that[13] "The reason for the stabilization of investment [in the metal industries] is mainly the slowdown in defense procurement from these industries. It was the demand of the defense system for the products of the metal industries which accelerated their development and the big investments in them." For this reason the share of pure public items increased again after 1971, and particularly so in 1974 and 1975, years in which investment in some of the other categories declined considerably. For example, purchase of ships and aircraft declined by 55 percent in 1974 and by another 73 percent in 1975.

In addition, investment in some pure public items increased, especially in agriculture, irrigation, and electricity. This was the result of a renewed settlement effort, directed at the newly acquired Golan Heights and areas south of Rafah, where the Gaza Strip joins the Sinai. Again, the settlement activity was hardly motivated by economic considerations. Politics and security had a lot more to do with it.

To complete the story, one must explain why even after 1973, investment in industry continued to grow quite considerably. As the data in the appendix reveal, investment in industry and mining grew by a healthy 14.2 percent in 1975. Even though this seems to contradict what has been argued, government behavior is again the cause. The rate at which the government subsidized new capital formation increased steadily over time. According to one estimate, the rate at which capital formation was subsidized increased from just 3.2 percent of all capital formation in 1964 to 35 percent in 1977. This means that, by 1977, many approved investments were actually subsidized at more than 50 percent, because the overall subsidization rate includes investments that received no subsidy at all. Most important, there was a real jump in subsidies during the period 1970–72, the last years of vigorous growth.[14] The average rate of subsidization leaped from 6.4 percent in 1969 to 11 percent in 1970 and 18 percent in 1971 and 1972.

Subsidization alone does not prove the point. What does is that it proved to be unproductive, as it created excess capacity in the industrial sector:[15] "[The increased investment] is surprising in view of the gap which exists between the required industrial capacity and the actual one, as reflected in the industrial stock of capital. Since 1972, industrial capital has increased much faster than necessary to facilitate output." It follows that part of the investment took place not because of the availability of good opportunities, but rather because it came cheap to the investors.

One possible corroboration of this view is lent by gross investment figures. Throughout the period 1971–75, gross domestic investment constituted around 30 percent of GDP. Its weight in the GDP started to decline seriously only in 1976 and 1977. Yet, the growth rate of the GDP was down from 12.1 percent in 1972 to 3.4 percent in 1975. How could this be explained without the observation that much of the investment, in both housing and industry, simply did not bear fruit?

Certainly the heavy investment in defense industries contributed greatly to Israel's capabilities in the design, engineering and manufacturing of metal and electronics products; and thus put Israel in a position to compete in the modern world, at least as far as human capital is concerned. However, this is largely a fortuitous outcome, and it comes at a heavy price because the fortunes of the defense industry depend on developments that are mostly political and not economic. Political events are hard to foresee, which makes it difficult to adjust in a gradual manner. Events in Eastern Europe during 1989, for instance, came largely as a surprise. The upshot is a considerable decline in demand for armaments, putting a squeeze on defense-based manufacturers. It is a very shaky proposition to base a substantial part of a country's industry on defense.

Turning to residential construction, Figure 1.1 indicates that in 1968 only the private sector increased its activity, whereas public investment was still declining and its share hit bottom that year. Then in 1969 there was a huge increase in investment, by both the private and the public sectors. At that point the housing market had been showing clear signs of excess demand, as the unsold stock of apartments disappeared. There was also an increase in immigration. After almost no net immigration in 1966–67, numbers began to pick up again, increasing steadily until 1973.

In 1970 the rate of increase in residential construction declined, as houses started in 1969 were being completed and the pressure of excess demand was beginning to subside. Still, the level of investment was on the increase. It seems that by 1972, as a result of the intensive activity since 1968, a stock of unsold apartments began accumulating once again.[16] In fact, a good deal of the construction activity in 1972 was due to housing starts that had taken place in the latter half of 1971.[17] The private sector was therefore simply reacting to economic developments, as it should have done. The government, on the other hand, kept on increasing its housing investment as though nothing had changed. As Figure 1.1 indicates, not only did the government increase its activity in 1973, but it kept doing so in 1974 and 1975 as well. This behavior prompted the Bank of Israel to remark that[18] "in 1974 public building starts took place on a wide scale although it was known that an unintended stock of apartments was accumulating, following the continued slowdown in sales of apartments to the public and the steep decline in net immigration."

Why did the government increase its residential construction activity despite the evident accumulation of unsold housing? The Bank of Israel speculated that the government was reacting to pressure from construction companies, who clamored for replacement of falling private business. More likely, the pressure was generated not because of declining private investment, but because of reduced construction for defense. A situation of this kind is typical, as we shall see later on, of economies with excessive governmental involvement. Another possible explanation is that the government, faced with lackadaisical private economic activity, was trying to keep the economy going by other means. This could be accomplished by a combination of increased public consumption and public investment. The latter course was preferred, because the tendency to increase government consumption expenditures had been under criticism since 1970. But the government was in no better position to identify new investment projects than it had been in on the eve of the 1966–67 slump. Having run out of defense-related investment opportunities as well, the government opted for the quick fix and continued to pour concrete.

One other aspect of Table 1.2, comparing Israel with some other economies, requires explanation. As is evident, the rate of capital accumulation during the third five-year period remained exceptionally strong in Israel, although declining considerably in the communist economies that serve for comparison, especially in East Germany. This may be explained by the fact that Israel continued to have access to sources of capital of a kind denied all the communist countries shown in Table 1.2. Whereas these countries depended almost exclusively on domestic savings for the finance of further investment, Israel enjoyed sustained, large capital imports. That is, Israel could rely on external financing of investment.

A good idea of the extent to which capital imports facilitated domestic investment can be obtained from Table 1.3.[19] The deficit in the goods-and-services account (henceforth referred to occasionally as *excess imports*) exceeded two-thirds of domestic investment throughout. It is also evident that during the half-decade containing the slump of 1966–67, the share of excess imports in domestic investment was particularly high.

On the basis of what has been said, it must be concluded that the engine that powered Israel's growth ran out of steam in 1966, because the government ran out of obvious investment opportunities. Only the aberration of the Six Day War and its aftermath gave the economy a temporary reprieve, as the government once more found obvious investment opportunities. And once the government ran out of those, too, the economy slid inexorably into its present lackluster economic performance.

This summary of developments contrasts sharply with the accepted view. According to conventional wisdom, what happened in 1966–67 was a regular recession, partly engineered by the government, from which the econ-

TABLE 1.3

The Deficit in the Goods and Services Account as Percent of Domestic Investment

Period	1951–55	1956–60	1961–65	1966–70	1971–72
Percent	82.9	72.0	69.3	87.6	74.3

omy recovered after 1968.[20] In this view, the government was forced into a recessionary policy by what it perceived as a worsening balance-of-payments situation and inflationary pressures.

If the conventional view of the 1966–67 episode as a recession is to be defended, then its proponents must change their story. For assuming that the government really did intend to create a recession, were its fears founded? The question is examined in Table 1.4, which reveals that none of the indicators often used showed significant, or indeed even any, deterioration in 1965. Excess imports as a percentage of GDP continued to decline in 1965, after a slight increase in 1964. The same holds for the ratio of imports to exports. In fact, in 1965 exports paid for a higher percentage of imports than in any other year represented in the table. True, unilateral transfers paid in 1964 for only 58 percent of excess imports, after having paid for over three-quarters of excess imports a year earlier. But the share of transfers in the finance of excess imports increased again in 1965. Finally, the current-account deficit, having more than doubled from 1963 to 1964, declined again in 1965.

As for inflation, the consumer price index increased by more than 4 percent during 1964 and by about 7 percent in 1965. This rise in the rate of infla-

TABLE 1.4

Balance of Payments Deficit Indicators

Year	Percent			Current Account millions of dollars
	Excess Imports of GDP	Imports of Exports	Unilateral Transfers of Excess Imports	
1962	22.4	205.7	70.6	-135.9
1963	20.1	191.4	76.9	-102.0
1964	21.8	199.2	57.9	-237.6
1965	19.1	187.5	62.6	-191.8

Source: CBS, *Statistical Abstract of Israel, 1969* and *1982*. The first two indicators are in terms of national accounts, whereas the last two are in terms of balance of payments.

tion could constitute a legitimate cause for concern. But monetary developments during 1966 put in doubt the degree to which the government had been concerned with inflation, as the money supply grew by about 109 percent.[21] The question of why the decline of growth rates was, relatively speaking, so abrupt, is left to the last section of this chapter.

Growth Does Not Mean Efficiency

The observation that Israel's economy grew for a while at respectable rates is not the same as saying that the economy performed efficiently. To establish efficiency, one would have to demonstrate that the realized growth rates justified the capital investments that produced them. For the condition to hold, those investments in fact undertaken must have proved capable of producing a rate of return at least as high as could be secured in alternative uses of the capital. In a market economy, it is the market mechanism that imposes a selection process favoring the best investment opportunities. Furthermore, if an enterprise, albeit profitable, could be made even more so, there is always the possibility of takeover by entrepreneurs who believe that they are capable of realizing the full potential of an existing capital stock. In a market economy, therefore, there is no reason to believe that the existing capital stock is invested in a pattern that deviates sharply from the most efficient pattern.

In Israel, the market test hardly applies. Free access to capital has been virtually nonexistent, a topic with which Chapter 2 deals in detail. There has been very extensive protection, in the form of both subsidies and import duties, and there has been a lot of cartelization and monopolization. It is therefore quite possible that at least part of the capital invested has been allocated suboptimally.

Data are only partly capable of substantiating this assertion. The degree of distortion in the economy may be such that a reallocation of capital expenditures could prove to affect the economy more than marginally, in which case we would have to consider comparing two different economies. If this were the case, then even if we had found, for instance, rates of return on the existing capital stock to be quite high, this still would not have proven efficiency, for these rates already reflect, for example, the artificially high prices brought about by import restrictions. More generally, rates of profit do not reflect general economic welfare. Rather, they may reflect a very skewed income distribution. As an example, consider the carpet industry, dominated in Israel by Carmel Carpets. The duty levied on imported carpets has been exorbitant—upward of 150 percent on many kinds of carpets. Consequently, Israelis have been paying outrageous prices for domestically produced carpets. It thus stands to reason that domestic carpet production has generated a handsome return on the capital invested in it, but this certainly does not imply an efficient allocation of capital. In the absence of a methodology that would allow us to examine the degree of efficiency of capital investment, the only alternative is to examine critically whatever data exist and evaluate individual incidents.

Armed with the various caveats, let us consider the existing evidence, beginning with the data in Table 1.5. This table constitutes an attempt to indicate the sort of impact that government intervention may have had on the allocation of investment capital. The table is organized by rate-of-return categories, the industries with the highest rates being the most profitable ones. Approved establishments are those that qualify for the privileges granted under the Law for the Encouragement of Capital Investment (henceforth LECI; see Chapter 2 for details). The premium per dollar's worth of exports represents the excess of the exchange rate granted exporters over and above the official rate of exchange.

As the table indicates, the government had a tendency to provide especially generous assistance for the less profitable enterprises. In fact, in the period 1965–72, the degree of public finance of investment bears an exact inverse relationship to the degree of profitability. Thus, although in the most profitable category the government provided only 17.9 percent of the finance, it provided fully 42.5 percent of the finance in the least profitable category. One item stands out: from 1965 to 1972 the government provided 79 percent of the finance for investment in mining and quarrying, almost double the next highest rate (and almost three times the industrial average). Yet the rate of return on capital in mining and quarrying has been the lowest of all. The proportion of approved plants in this sector was also one of the highest. The impression that the government has tended to support the less profitable enterprises is confirmed by the negative coefficient of correlation (-.5) found between the rate of return on capital and an index of government intervention.[22] In addition, no positive relation between the proportion of output destined for exports and the rate of return could be discerned.

TABLE 1.5

Investment Returns and Government Involvement

Rate of Return Category, % 1965–80	% Approved Plants, 1975	Premium per Dollar of Exports, % 1973–80	Index of Government Finance, % of Investment	
			1965–72	1973–80
22.5–27.8	48.6	30	17.9	34.0
17.9–21.5	33.6	31	20.4	55.0
15.8–17.6	38.2	34	30.8	47.0
10.7–14.8	40.9	27	42.5	34.0

Source: Bregman, *Industry and Industrial Policy in Israel*, p. 13.

Concerning the actual average rates of return, the Bregman study which provided much of the basis for this discussion, quotes two estimates. The first, based on a representative sample of Israel's industry, reports the average annual industrial rate of return on capital over the period 1960–68 to have been 13.3 percent.[23] The second estimate, which is based on national account data for the entire industrial sector, combined with capital stock estimates, reported that the rate of return on capital for the period 1965–72 was 17.1 percent per year, considerably higher than the first figure.[24]

The caution with which these numbers must be treated is exemplified by another study, which also took the sample approach. There, the cost of equity capital for the period 1964–77 is estimated to have been an average annual 9.7 percent.[25] One piece of somewhat unsettling evidence emerges from a comparison of rates of return on equity shares and on bonds. Between 1952 and 1969, the average annual real rate of return on all shares traded was 6.9 percent, whereas the comparable rate on exchange-rate indexed bonds was 7.4 percent.[26] One could use still another indicator, the national account data for the business sector as a whole. Such data, concerning the evolution of capital stock, product, labor input, and wages, indicate that between 1960 and 1972, the rate of return to capital had been on the increase, and this is particularly true for the period 1966–72, when the business sector product grew an average 9.2 percent annually, although the capital stock grew only at an average annual rate of 7.5 percent.[27]

Another way of assessing the economy's performance during the years of high growth rates is to consider individual episodes of prominent failure, which indicate that the government was incapable of distinguishing good investment opportunities from bad ones. Some may object to this approach on the grounds that high rates of failure among businesses during the first years of existence are quite common. For instance, in the United States it is estimated that three out of every five new enterprises fail during the first five years. Although there can be no exception to this objection in general, the situation is somewhat different when the government is involved, for government involvement eliminates a good deal of the uncertainty and so allows the investor to start at the outset on a much larger scale than would have been dared otherwise.

The contribution of productive assets constructed in any particular year to the national product is evaluated not by the future return to these assets, but by the cost of constructing them. If a business collapses before the cost of the investment has been recovered, the implication is that growth had been overestimated at the time of investment. But in practice such corrections are not being made. Rather, the collapse of an enterprise is charged against growth during the year in which the debacle occurred. It follows that past, overestimated growth rates are offset by present, underestimated growth rates. This implies that what appeared as spectacular growth rates in Israel during the 1950s and 1960s were not quite that spectacular after all. Some examples follow.

The first two fiascos considered concern adventures in the assembly and production of cars in Israel. Of the two auto plants, the first was opened in 1951, with the majority shares held by the Ilin family. The opening date is not a coincidence: the project had started right after the passage of the Law for the Encouragement of Capital Investment (see chapter 2), and Ilin was one of the first to enjoy its benefits. The plant assembled Kaiser-Fraser cars, and when the American company went out of business Ilin switched to assembling Studebaker cars. When that company, too, ceased operations, Ilin began to assemble another car, Contessa, whose original producer also went bankrupt later on. Through it all Ilin expanded, obtaining considerable government finance in the process. It even managed to export cars. This was made possible by the exorbitant duties imposed on imported cars, which enabled Ilin to continue its very inefficient operation, but also granted it a clear advantage in the domestic market, as prices of imported cars exceeded even the prices of its own costly product. The extent to which the company enjoyed a preferred status in the Israeli market could be easily discerned from the highway scenery. When Ilin assembled Henry J cars, the roads were full of those; later Studebaker became the dominant model on Israel's highways and so on.

One of the more comic events in Ilin's story is the exclusive concession it received from the government to import Colombian coffee, a move designed to ease its financial difficulties.[28] The government went on providing Ilin with all sorts of assistance until it became clear that the company could never be made profitable, so it was sold in 1969 to Autocars, the second car producer destined for failure, with money provided by the government.

Autocars differed from Ilin only in that the latter assembled cars solely from imported parts, whereas the former also produced some of the parts. The company entered a partnership with British Leyland, itself a troubled behemoth, to supply buses and trucks to the Israeli market, with a government guarantee of monopoly. Consequently, for several years Israel's entire bus fleet was made up of Leyland Tiger buses. Moreover, the financial arrangements accompanying the deal were decidedly inferior to what could have been obtained from alternative sources of supply.[29] The Autocars scandal reached such proportions that in March 1971 it was taken up by the Knesset, which hastened the demise of the company at the end of that year.

Whereas in the two auto stories there is no way to tell how much public money went under when the companies did, the next story, which concerns shipping, provides a better idea as to the magnitude of the disaster. In 1959, Meir Halevi convinced the Israeli government to join with his Swiss company, Somerfin, in building a versatile seagoing fleet, comprising passenger liners, oil tankers, deepwater fishing boats, and tramp steamers. His claim to expertise had been that, after World War II, he had traded in ships built in Japan. In effect, his experience concerning shipping consisted of buying cheap and selling dear. That had been enough of a credential for the government, who put up no less than $17 million in loan guarantees towards the $34 million needed to build the ships. By the time the company went under in 1966, it had assets of $26 million and debts of $34 million, half of which were guaranteed by the government of Israel. Said the accountant general at the Ministry of Finance:[30]

> Every bank that contacted Swiss banks concerning [Halevi] was given very positive information and excellent references concerning Mr. Halevi and Somerfin. Only now does it turn out that he was losing money even while expanding. The 20 percent that he had been required to invest as his equity, and the 13.3 percent of bank guarantees that he was supposed to obtain, had been actually obtained by him as loans from other banks. He had no equity.

The state comptroller commented extensively on the fiasco. His findings include the fact that no one ever took the trouble of running a check on Halevi's concern to find out whether he really had the financial backing he claimed. The comptroller also found that, given the amounts the state was going to invest in the acquisition of new ocean-going vessels, very little was done to ascertain the reasonableness of the prices of the new ships. Significantly, the report found no wrongdoing in the sense of personal corruption. This is important, because it allows focusing on the general inaptitude of government in matters of this nature, even when intentions are all good and the conduct is blameless.[31]

There were other spectacular failures involving huge public sums of money. Among the most prominent are the Timna Copper Mines, just north of Eilat, at the tip of the Red Sea, and the passenger division of Zim Lines, which never made money and was ultimately discontinued at considerable loss.

None of the data and individual episodes constitute positive proof of gross misallocation of resources by the government. As has been pointed out, it is impossible to prove anything in a situation where the alternative is in the nature of "what might have been." However, the body of data seems to be rich enough to lend credence to the explanation of Israel's ability to grow at a considerable pace, despite adverse institutional setups and to the assertion that capital had been inefficiently allocated, so that the same growth rates could have been achieved more cheaply under different institutional circumstances.

Other Factors

The subsequent chapters describe those features of the economy blamed here for the absence of the sort of entrepreneurial activity that might have replaced the government's investment activity. However, as concerns developments during the mid-1970s, one should not ignore the adverse impact of some of the events following 1972, events that undoubtedly reinforced the decline of growth rates. In this context, the swiftness with which growth rates declined will also be analyzed.

The first development, although not necessarily the most important one in its quantitative impact, concerns Israel's position in world markets. The continuous improvement in Israel's competitiveness in the international market, which had started in 1967, was apparently slowing down.[32] The competitiveness index used by the Bank of Israel indicates an increase of over 68 percent between 1966 and 1972, but in 1972 the increase in competitiveness slowed down markedly, as the average for 1973 shows no improvement at all over 1972.[33] This is reinforced by the fact that the chief reason for the halt in the improvement of export profitability had been an increase in domestic wages far exceeding that which occurred in competitor countries. This is important because, unlike changes consequent on exchange rate movements—changes that might not be foreseen by employers—wage changes usually are anticipated. That holds in particular for 1972, as new national wage agreements were signed at the beginning of the year,[34] so employers must have had an inkling as to what would happen to their profits.

Average wages increased in the first nine months of 1973 by 5.5 percent in real terms, in line with the 1972 wage accords.[35] The wage development is complemented by another figure: industrial exports increased in 1972, in real terms, by only 9 percent, after they had been growing at an average annual rate of about 20 percent from 1967 to 1971.[36]

Another explanation for the behavior of the private sector in 1972–73 concerns inflation. As will be stressed later on, inflation in Israel was not merely a natural part of the ordinary trade cycle. Rather, it was generated by the very same institutional arrangements responsible for the miserable economic performance of the past two decades. Inflation was the most dramatic manifestation of these traits. Hence, by blaming inflation for some of the unfortunate developments that have taken place since 1972, blame is also placed on these more fundamental components of Israel's economic setup. For now, however, we concentrate on the bare facts of the early 1970s.

The first signs that inflation might be brewing came in 1970, when the consumer price index increased by 6 percent over the previous year.[37] This price increase was definitely read as a warning sign, for the government reacted with increased taxes and reduced expenditures, particularly as far as nonhousing investment was concerned. The 1971 figure was double: close to 12 percent. During 1971, that is, from December 1970 to December 1971, the consumer price index rose by 13.4 percent. Inflation intensified in 1972: the average consumer price index for the year was almost 16 percent higher than it had been in 1971. Furthermore, during the first half of 1973 there were no signs that inflation was going to abate any time soon, as prices increased from December 1972 to June 1973 at an annual rate of 24 percent. All this, we recall, was before the 1973 war and before the oil price shock.

Such rates of inflation, exceeding as they were the world inflation by a considerable margin, must have caused consternation among producers. The reason is that employers were bound to expect wages to increase in the wake of price increases, because of wage indexation. But that meant a prospective deterioration in export profitability, because the exchange rate had not been expected to change in tandem with wages. Inflation is thus seen to have deterred investment, at least insofar as exports are concerned.

It is common to blame the precipitous decline in economic growth rates on wrong economic policy responses to the events that hit Israel in 1973 and 1974. This line of reasoning has been rejected earlier, but it should be clear that the rejection concerns only the central role attributed to these events. The responses were indeed wrong and must have contributed to the process of declining growth rates. In fact, they are probably responsible to a large extent for the abruptness of the decline, as they might be compared to a blow to the head of somebody who was already faltering.

First came the Yom Kippur War that, in addition to the horrible death and injury toll it inflicted, wreaked havoc on the economy by mobilizing a substantial part of the labor force for an extended period of time—up to six months. The uninitiated reader should be made aware that Israel's defense strategy calls for a relatively small standing armed force, combined with a constant training of reserves that include virtually every able-bodied man under the age of 55. In the event of a high state of alert or actual war, these reserves are mobilized, causing a very significant decline in civilian employment. In fact, production in many instances is so disrupted as a result that it must be temporarily halted altogether.

Of the data officially available that reflect the magnitude of the damage caused by the war, the most telling is the wage component of domestic consumption for defense, which increased by more than 53 percent relative to the 1972 level. Total domestic consumption for defense increased by 29 percent, with defense imports increasing by a staggering 127 percent as compared to 1972. Consequently, although in 1972 public consumption claimed a little over 30 percent of the GDP, not a small percentage in itself, it increased to over 42 percent of the GDP in 1973. This means that the share of public consumption grew by more than a third. A change of this magnitude over so short a period constitutes nothing less than a severe shock. It is no wonder then that as a result the net domestic product of the business sector failed almost entirely to grow in 1973, after seeing growth rates of about 13 and 14 percent in 1971 and 1972, respectively.

The next blow was the oil price shock, which compelled Israel to pay almost $600 million for energy imports in 1974, compared with $211 million in 1973. Relative to the size of Israel's foreign trade that was by no means negligible: energy imports, which had constituted about 7 percent of nondefense imports of goods in 1973, doubled to 14 percent of goods imported in 1974.

Another international development that affected Israel adversely in 1973 was the sharp rise in world prices, particularly for raw materials. Because Israel is very poor in natural resources, it imports virtually all the raw materials it uses, except some that are produced by the agricultural sector (e.g., cotton) and some minerals mined in the Dead Sea and the Negev desert. It also imports all its energy. The worldwide rise in prices caused the prices of Israel's imports to rise sharply: in the last quarter of 1973 they exceeded the average for 1972 by 52 percent. True, export prices had risen as well, but by appreciably less: in the last quarter of 1973 they exceeded the annual average for 1972 by only 31 percent. The upshot was a significant 13.5-percent decline in Israel's terms of trade in the last quarter of 1973 as compared to 1972.[38] We shall come back to this fact, because a decline in a country's terms of trade constitutes a decline in that country's income, a development that must be reflected in the incomes of the citizens of the country. A failure of private income to so adjust will result in increased excess imports and, unless compensated for by increased unilateral transfers from abroad, will lead to increased international indebtedness. The failure of private incomes in Israel to reflect the decline in the terms of trade will be seen to have constituted a major factor in the ongoing poor performance of the economy. And government policies are largely to blame for the failure to adjust.

Another harsh development that hit Israel in 1974, perhaps partially as a result of what had happened in 1973, was the precipitous decline in net immigration. Whereas immigration had exceeded emigration by 46,000 and 50,000 in 1972 and 1973, respectively, net immigration declined to only about 14,000 in 1974 and almost nothing in 1975. The main source for these changes was a dramatic decline in Jewish immigration, from over 55,000 in 1972 to less than 20,000 in 1975.[39]

It is impossible to say with any degree of certainty whether the speed with which growth rates declined can be attributed solely to these events. The sharp decline may also have been the result of the relative suddenness with which the government ran out of productive investment opportunities. One possible piece of evidence lies with the sharp sinking into the 1966–67 slump. From a GDP growth rate of 9.3 percent in 1965, the economy plunged to virtually no growth in the following year, and there were no salient external factors then. Further aggravation was caused by the recession that hit the industrial world in 1975. Combined with much higher energy prices, it produced a virtual standstill in the development of exports from Israel, which hardly grew at all in comparison with 1974.[40]

Perhaps the most important manifestation of the failure of the government to respond rationally to the events that profoundly affected the economy was its embarkation on a speedy transformation of the country to a classic welfare state. The evidence is unmistakable: in 1972 transfer payments, not including credit subsidies, constituted 14.5 percent of the GNP; by 1977, they had grown to almost 24 percent. In other words, the share of transfer payments in the GNP grew by 65 percent over a five-year period. While GNP grew from 1972 to 1977 at an average annual real rate of only 2.9 percent, transfer payments grew at an average of 13.7 percent annually in real terms. It would thus come as no surprise that taxes had to be hiked, and so they were. Although taxation made up 39 percent of the GNP in 1972, by 1976 and 1977 it hovered around 50 percent of the GNP. Again, this is an increase of over 27 percent in the tax burden, as measured by its share in GNP. No less significant is the fact that, as far as direct taxes are concerned, the tax burden on nonwage income grew at a particularly stiff pace: from 20 percent of such income in 1972 to 32 percent in 1977. This constituted a 60-percent increase in the burden.[41]

No less important was the increase of many of the marginal tax rates. The increases comprised the first seven tax brackets and the highest bracket, the top marginal rate was increased from 63 to 65 percent. The eighth bracket enjoyed a rate reduction, and the next two brackets were broken up into two brackets each, with more graduated marginal rates.[42] After the changes, a single wage earner receiving the average wage for the first quarter of 1974 was paying a marginal rate of 48 percent.[43]

In addition to these developments, the government in 1975 made two landmark decisions: it adopted a crawling peg regime for the exchange rate and it sanctioned a change in the rules for linking wages to the consumer price index. As we shall see, these steps can be properly viewed as encompassing or representing the fruition of many of the attributes of the economy that prevented it from growing as it could have. Furthermore, these twin policy changes provided the engine that powered Israel's journey to near-hyperinflation, with its growth-retarding effects.

We shall return to all of these developments in more detail in the last three chapters. At this point, however, having explained the apparent contradiction between the early high growth rates and the possibility of a presence of fundamental flaws in the structure of the economy, we turn to the description and analysis of these flaws, and try to support the assertion that the presence of these flaws has and still does prevent the Israeli economy from performing satisfactorily.

Appendix

TABLE 1.6

The Data Underlying Figure 1.1

Year	Percentage Change in Residential Construction			Share of Public Construction, %
	Total	Private	Public	
1955	—	—	—	41.5
1956	-13.1	-11.5	-15.4	39.9
1957	22.3	-4.0	61.0	53.2
1958	-1.6	10.2	-12.0	47.5
1959	11.1	16.0	5.7	45.3
1960	-1.9	7.1	-12.7	40.5
1961	22.1	17.6	28.8	42.4
1962	26.0	15.7	39.9	47.3
1963	-.9	16.4	-20.2	38.1
1964	10.8	12.2	8.5	37.1
1965	7.2	8.7	4.6	35.7
1966	-19.4	-16.0	-25.5	33.1
1967	-32.4	-28.1	-41.2	28.6
1968	17.6	25.5	-2.1	23.8
1969	47.9	48.3	46.6	23.3
1970	39.2	28.6	66.7	33.3
1971	21.0	20.8	21.4	33.4
1972	28.4	28.8	27.6	33.1
1973	4.8	.2	13.9	36.5
1974	-2.8	-10.3	10.3	41.3
1975	3.4	-1.7	10.7	44.0

Sources: Figures for the government's share of residential construction were obtained from BOI, *Annual Report 1967*, p. 293, for 1955–64; *1968*, p. 78, and *1970*, p. 87, for 1964–69; *1972*, p. 103, for 1969–70; *1974*, p. 162, for 1970–71; *1975*, p. 164, for 1971–72; *1976*, p. 153, for 1972–75. The rates of change of investment in total residential construction were obtained from CBS, *Gross Domestic Capital Formation in Israel 1950–1978*. The rates of change of private and public residential construction were then computed from the two series of data.

Because the series of government shares has been updated from time to time with the updating of the national accounts, overlapping parts of the series published in different reports are not always identical. To make the set of data in Table 1.6 consistent, the series of shares of the public sector has been recomputed from the rates of change of the investment by the two sectors. However, any deviations of the numbers in the last column of the table from the ones reported by the Bank of Israel are marginal and affect the picture in no important way.

TABLE 1.7

Data Underlying Figure 1.2: Percentage Rate of Change of Investment
in Each Category

Year	Agriculture	Irrigation	Industry[*]	Mining[**]	Electricity	Commerce and Services[†]
1960	-8.4	35.2	-2.6	5.0	-3.5	27.1
1961	-6.3	14.6	15.2	78.3	-1.7	14.7
1962	-5.6	37.2	-2.0	82.9	49.1	2.7
1963	-11.3	5.4	13.8	12.0	-21.6	20.3
1964	9.4	-36.8	10.3	2.4	-4.3	17.7
1965	-11.7	-12.8	1.9	-41.9	69.7	11.8
1966	-6.9	0.0	-31.9	-28.0	-21.4	-10.9
1967	1.7	-5.6	-25.7[††]		-34.8	-12.8
1968	6.0	-17.9	106.0		23.3	16.1
1969	8.0	-29.1	32.8		30.0	25.1
1970	16.5	5.4	12.5		11.5	4.9
1971	0.0	11.4	11.7		-17.6	9.9
1972	22.7	20.4	10.9		96.0	17.2
1973	-10.0	-15.9	-3.9		-7.9	12.7
1974	11.5	-5.2	3.8		4.5	8.1
1975	13.4	32.7	14.2		20.4	.8

[*] Including construction equipment.
[**] Including quarrying.
[†] Including public services
[††] As of 1967 investment in mining became so small that the Bank of Israel
stopped reporting it separately and included it in industry.

Source: (Tables 1.7–1.10): Bank of Israel, *Annual Report 1964*, pp. 72–73, for
1959–60; *1965*, pp. 70–71, for 1961–63; *1966*, pp. 88–89, for 1964–66; *1970*, p. 88,
for 1967–68; *1972*, p. 105, for 1969–70; *1974*, p. 182, for 1971–72. CBS, *Gross
Domestic Capital Formation in Israel 1950–1978*; this publication also provided the
data on investment in public construction for services and for transportation and communication.

TABLE 1.8

Data Underlying Figure 1.2: Percentage Change of Investment in Each Category

Year	Transportation and Communication			Public Construction for			Pure Public Items
	Vehicles	Ships and Aircraft	Total	Public Services	Trans-portation and Commu-nication	Total	
1960	37.8	140.0	27.0	5.3	12.8	9.9	3.9
1961	57.4	54.6	46.8	-1.3	44.1	15.2	2.9
1962	24.7	-60.5	-11.5	10.3	26.8	8.1	25.3
1963	39.6	-24.2	14.3	26.5	36.9	9.3	15.4
1964	27.0	250.0	84.4	18.3	46.1	23.3	1.7
1965	-2.1	-47.4	-10.0	15.0	28.1	-.7	7.5
1966	-23.6	-47.8	-26.6	-11.2	-12.0	-19.5	-13.2
1967	-40.5	-3.6	-14.7	-11.4	-1.2	-15.7	-8.5
1968	93.6	258.5	66.9	11.0	6.6	42.9	6.4
1969	74.2	-50.2	18.1	23.0	-1.3	22.2	13.0
1970	-4.0	109.7	-3.0	-3.8	-10.9	5.5	.4
1971	1.3	219.0	57.6	6.1	30.2	22.1	5.5
1972	22.8	-73.4	-16.1	18.5	6.7	6.0	24.5
1973	26.3	222.0	40.3	11.6	10.5	13.8	5.2
1974	9.2	-54.9	-19.3	9.2	-7.9	-2.8	5.2
1975	-43.3	-73.0	-29.3	4.9	-9.7	-2.7	7.1

TABLE 1.9

Shares of Total Investment, Percent

Year	Agriculture	Irrigation	Industry	Mining	Electricity	Commerce and Services
1959	18.7	5.3	29.7	2.0	5.6	21.4
1960	15.7	6.8	24.9	1.9	4.9	26.2
1961	12.4	6.6	24.3	2.9	4.1	25.5
1962	11.3	8.7	23.0	5.1	5.9	25.3
1963	9.1	8.3	23.8	5.2	4.2	27.7
1964	8.1	4.3	21.3	4.3	3.3	26.5
1965	7.2	3.8	21.8	2.5	5.6	29.8
1966	8.3	4.7	18.5	2.2	5.5	33.0
1967	10.2	4.7	16.8		4.8	35.9
1968	7.6	2.7	24.2		4.2	29.1
1969	6.5	1.6	26.4		4.4	29.8
1970	7.2	1.6	28.1		4.7	29.6
1971	5.7	1.5	25.6		3.0	27.1
1972	6.6	1.7	26.8		5.6	30.0
1973	5.9	1.2	22.4		4.6	30.2
1974	6.8	1.2	23.9		4.9	33.5
1975	8.0	1.6	28.0		6.1	34.8

TABLE 1.10

Shares of Total Investment, Percent

Year	Transportation and Communication			Public Construction for		Pure Public Items
	Vehicles	Ships and Aircraft	Total	Public Services	Trans- portation and Commu- nication	
1959	3.6	4.4	17.4	14.7	3.4	49.7
1960	4.5	8.9	19.5	14.1	3.6	47.0
1961	5.9	11.6	24.3	11.7	4.3	42.0
1962	7.1	4.4	20.7	12.3	5.4	48.7
1963	9.1	3.1	21.6	17.8	6.8	51.4
1964	9.4	8.7	32.3	4.3	8.1	42.4
1965	9.2	4.6	29.3	16.5	10.3	45.9
1966	8.4	3.0	27.8	18.2	10.6	49.5
1967	5.3	3.0	27.6	21.5	12.5	53.7
1968	7.1	7.5	32.2	16.4	9.1	40.0
1969	10.7	2.9	31.4	16.8	7.3	36.6
1970	9.7	5.8	28.8	15.5	6.2	35.2
1971	8.0	16.0	37.0	13.5	6.7	30.4
1972	9.2	4.0	29.3	15.1	6.7	35.7
1973	9.9	11.2	35.8	14.8	6.5	33.0
1974	11.1	5.2	29.7	16.6	6.2	35.7
1975	6.5	1.5	21.6	17.9	5.7	39.3

2

OBSTACLES TO GROWTH:
THE ABDUCTED CAPITAL MARKET

The Absence of a Free Capital Market

Not all economies embedded in political democracies are alike, but it would be hard to find an economist anywhere who would dispute that they are basically capitalist economies. For, although they certainly feature various degrees of institutional restrictions on their market systems, they all have in common the basic ingredient of a capitalist system: a free capital market. This means both free access to capital and the right to own capital assets. On the strength of this test, Israel's economy has been unlike that of any other free country's.[1]

The central feature characterizing Israel's capital market for as long as Israel has existed is the government's domination of the capital market. The government's involvement transcends anything that is known in politically free countries. The main expression of this involvement is the fact that most of the finances that accumulate in the various savings schemes . . . are channeled to the state's budget or allocated by it. The government sets, for every financial instrument, its term, rate of interest, and tax regulations. Since the government is the chief mobilizer of savings, it is also the main allocator of credit. The lion's share of long, and medium-term credit to households (mortgage loans) and the business sector (finance of investment in industry, agriculture, tourism etc.) is allocated by the government through its budget or by other means.[2]

The focus here will be on the impact of the economic form of organization on the system's ability to perform in the sense of providing the environment for the production of economic well-being.[3]

The Basic Features of the Financial System

The Capital Market

The basic fact of the capital market in Israel is that the government has undertaken to act as the principal capital-market intermediary and to ensure its dominance has imposed very stringent restrictions on the other intermediaries.

Considering first the government as an intermediary, let us assume for simplicity that the public employs four channels of saving: deposits in saving accounts with banks, shares in pension funds, purchase of shares of stock, and purchase of corporate or government bonds. When a government sells bonds and uses part or all of the proceeds to finance lending to the private sector, as the government of Israel has indeed been doing, it becomes a capital market intermediary. In this case the government has gone much further. It forced banks and pension funds to use most of the funds raised from the public in either of two ways: purchase non-negotiable government bonds or finance private-sector loans earmarked by the government. For example, as of May 1992, commercial banks still had to use anywhere from 30 to 100 percent of funds deposited in indexed time deposits, depending on the type of the account, on government instructions.[4] In other words, banks and pension funds are being told by the government what to do with a significant part of the public's savings.

To assert its role as allocator of savings, the government had to suppress potential competition from the private sector. To that end it created the overseer of the capital market and insurance in the Ministry of Finance, without whose approval no new security could be issued.

The Banking System

Israel's commercial banking system has been shaped overwhelmingly by its subordination to the government, which has controlled the lion's share of both the assets and liabilities of the banks. In the first place, the banks have not been free to offer saving schemes to the public. Every saving plan has been subject to approval by the Ministry of Finance's overseer of the capital market. This was, of course, logically consistent with the fact that, once a scheme was approved, the bank had to use most of the funds generated by the new instrument according to government instructions. It follows that most of the profit made by the bank would be the result of the interest-rate spread between what the bank pays to the *public* and what the *government* pays to the bank. This contrasts sharply with banking operations in normal, free economies, where the bank both receives interest payments from the borrowing part of the public and makes interest payments to the lending part of the public. When the government sets the terms of savings schemes, it determines the interest-rate spread, thereby effectively dictating an important part of bank profitability.

Another important distinguishing characteristic of the Israeli banking community has been its ownership structure. Namely, out of the four largest commercial banks, three have not really been privately owned. After the collapse of the bank shares in 1983 (an event to which we shall return), the three banks have been owned, albeit in a disguised fashion, by the government. Previously, Bank Leumi, was owned by the Zionist movement, which had founded it shortly after the turn of the century; Bank Ha'Poalim was controlled by the Histadrut, the Israeli Labor Federation; and Bank Ha'Mizrachi was owned by the world Mizrachi movement, an organization of Orthodox Jews that also forms one of Israel's political parties.

The main trouble in all of these cases was not the mere institutional ownership of banks. Rather, the institutions that controlled the votes on the boards of directors have done so on the strength of "founders' shares," while owning a negligible part of the equity, which had been owned by the public at large. Consequently, those who were the most interested in the profits had no say in running these banks, and those who ran the banks (and under the present ownership still do) were not guided by profitability because they did not stand to share in the profits.

Another very important feature of the Israeli credit market is the linkage of saving instruments to some price index. All government bonds are indexed to either the consumer price index or rate of exchange of the domestic currency for the dollar. So are all time deposits whose term to maturity exceeds two years. Likewise, all long-term commercial loans have been indexed since 1980. The same was true until recently for life insurance policies and is still true for pension funds. Israel did not invent indexed saving instruments, nor is it the only country in which they exist, but the all-embracing extent of indexation in Israel is quite unique and will be seen to have played a major role in the shaping of Israel's economy and its peculiarities.

The Background

Why did Israel's government set out to dominate the capital market after the creation of the state? First, there was the ideology, to which we turn in the next chapter, because the ideological story has its origins long before Israel was established as an independent country. Second, the early framers of Israel's economic thinking, with astonishing unanimity of opinion, believed that a government could allocate capital more efficiently than could the market. For example, some prominent economists of Tel-Aviv University and the Bank of Israel stated the following in the course of explaining the merits of government allocation of investment:[5]

Government intervention, if carried out consistently and efficiently, will reduce the risk premium demanded by investors. . . . Undeveloped capital markets make it necessary for the government to intervene. . . . In practice, most of the advantages [of government intervention] are connected with government influence on the level of investment and saving, while all the disadvantages derive from government influence on the composition of investments. In order that government intervention may lead to increased economic efficiency while causing minimum waste, suitable methods of intervention must be chosen to effect the volume of saving and investment without distorting allocation. Such a method of intervention is proposed in Chapter 16.

The third impetus for heavy government involvement in the capital market was the view that the most profitable projects are not necessarily those that are most preferable from a national standpoint. Providing an explanation as to why government control of credit is required, the Bank of Israel asserted that:[6] "Because of the incompatibility which sometimes exists between business objectives and long-term national needs, the government has to direct the limited resources to conform to the economy's priorities. Credit constitutes in many cases a key instrument in the activation of resources, and therefore qualitative direction of credit exercises considerable influence on resource allocation."

Cases where economic activity powered purely by the profit motive comes into conflict with overall economic welfare are called *externalities.* These are cases where the actions of business impose costs on society as a whole that are not reflected in the cash flow of the business; for example, pollution. There is also the case of public goods and services, such as defense, for which there is demand, but private enterprise will not initiate production because no profits are to be made. But the preceding quote goes far beyond these special circumstances in advocating government intervention in the allocation of investment. It says that profits are not a sufficient barometer of the desirability of any given investment even in those cases where externalities or public goods are not at stake. It alleges a class of benefits associated with neither of these cases and yet cannot be reflected in profitability.

This philosophy is also echoed in the Bank of Israel's assertion that[7]

Public finance of private investment fulfills several functions simultaneously: whereas finance through the private capital market is negligible, it is government finance which enables entrepreneurs to accomplish the very accumulation of the capital required for investment. Second, extending or refusing to extend public finance, facilitates the direction of new investment to those ends which are preferred from the national standpoint.

But the Bank did not think that the government should be the only arbiter of investment, arguing that "Experience proves that the most important limitation to qualitative direction [of credit by the government] is the opportunity given to banks to extend credit from their means to ventures that are not at the top of national priorities, but are more profitable, knowing that credit for the more essential purposes will be extended through the special arrangements."

This brings us to the fourth reason for intervention. Whereas the previous three reasons were grounded in principle, this one is practical in nature. It is associated with the fact that the first years of Israel's existence had been marred by high rates of inflation. During the four-year period 1950–53, inflation as measured by the consumer price index averaged 26 percent annually, hitting 66 percent in 1952. Under these circumstances, the capital market found itself all but paralyzed. For example, the General Mortgage Bank, which had been very successful in its bond issues, found it impossible to raise any new debt. As a result, it was forced to lend from funds that the government had on deposit with it.[8]

The fifth reason for the government's involvement in the capital market resulted from Israel's external economic relations. From the very beginning, Israel enjoyed unilateral capital transfers as well as loans from abroad. Both types of capital imports were of a largely intergovernmental nature. Thus, in Fiscal 1951, 63 percent of the funds earmarked by the government for investment were obtained from foreign sources not directly accessible to private investors.[9] Imported capital, most of it brought in by the government, remained important in the 1960s. It is estimated that between 1960 and 1965, imported capital channeled through the government amounted to 31 percent of total private savings.[10] The implication is that imported capital constituted a very important source of investment finance. However, one should not conclude from this that the circumstances surrounding capital imports were totally innocent. In fact, capital imports by private enterprise were expressly discouraged by the government. The reason is that the government did not want private enterprise to compete with its own efforts, or with the efforts of government corporations, to raise money abroad.[11]

Although the domination of the capital market by the government has been slowly declining recently, the treatment of the subject here is coached in terms of the 1950s and 1960s, as these two decades constitute the period over which the government set about the virtual nationalization of the capital market, without formally nationalizing the financial intermediaries, such as banks and other financial institutions.

The Interest Rate Law

The Interest Rate Law, the first instrument of government control, was not invented by any of Israel's governments, but had first been promulgated by the Ottoman Empire in 1887. It stipulated a ceiling of 9 percent on interest rates on all manner of financial transactions. And, although charging a higher rate did not constitute a punishable offense, rates in excess of 9 percent were not enforceable by a court of law. The British Mandate made some minor changes in the law in 1929, but the essential part of it, the ceiling, was left intact.[12]

When the state of Israel was established, no steps were taken to change the law. However, when the Bank of Israel was created as the central bank in 1954, its governor was given the power to revoke the legal ceiling on bank loans, replacing it instead with a decree issued by the bank itself. What the first governor chose to do is symptomatic of the relations between the Bank and the government: he did nothing. The real reason for this decision was that the Bank had always been dominated by the government to the extent of being deprived of any real power, a topic that will occupy us a great deal in Chapter 9. But the reasons given for not repealing the interest rate ceiling were that an increase in the rate of interest would cause an increase in business costs, and that the public in Israel had been accustomed to a legal ceiling. The Bank elected to desist from repealing the ceiling even though it was aware that enforcement would be difficult to achieve.[13]

It is also clear that the governor of the Bank was fully aware of the consequences of an artificially low interest rate. He explained that the first years of statehood had been marked by inflation, so that at the maximum rate of interest an excess demand for loanable funds had developed. A government's natural response to such a condition is to ration. A market's natural response is the spawning of a "black market," in which the rate of interest exceeds the legal one.[14]

In 1957 the old 9-percent ceiling was replaced by a progressive set of maximum rates: 11 percent for "ordinary" loans, meaning loans in which the government had no interest; 10 percent on loans to agriculture and industry, and 6.5 percent on loans indexed to either the rate of exchange or the cost of living, indexation methods that are explained later.[15] Only thirteen years later, after the credit market had undergone a convulsion that, among other ramifications, caused the collapse of a bank, did the government finally abolish all legal restrictions on interest.[16]

The Process of Domination

It will prove convenient to divide the description of the origins of the de facto nationalization of the capital market to correspond to the two markets involved: the long term and the short term. The former is the market where investment capital is raised. The latter is the one where working or revolving capital is raised.

Long-Term Capital: The Law for the Encouragement of Capital Investment

The government's massive intervention in the capital market could be said to have begun with the passage of the Law for the Encouragement of Capital Investment in 1950. The original version stipulated that the privileges conferred by the law would be accorded only to "approved" investments. To be approved, an investment had to be deemed beneficial to Israel's economy, in terms of what the government defined to be beneficial, as follows:[17]

(1) The development of the productive capacity of the national economy, the efficient utilization of its resources and economic potential and
full utilization of the productive capacity of existing enterprises; (2)
The improvement of the balance of payments of the state, the reduction
of imports and the increase of exports;(3) The absorption of immigration, the planned distribution of the population over the area of the state
and the creation of new sources of employment.

The law underwent several modifications, and its reformulated version, still largely in effect, was adopted in 1959. On the basis of its objectives, the law specifies three criteria for the eligibility of a project to be recognized as "approved": the kind of product to be produced, the percentage of exports out of total output, and the location of the plant.

The significance of the law in the present context lies with the concep-tual deviation from similar laws in some of the more successful economies. Laws designed to achieve similar objectives in such fast-growing economies as Taiwan focus on rewarding success. They confer benefits on those who have already proven their contribution to the economy. For example, they grant various tax breaks and accelerated depreciation. The idea is that, to be able to enjoy the benefits, a venture must be profitable; losing enterprises can-not enjoy tax breaks, because they do not pay taxes to begin with.

In contrast with this philosophy the Israeli law grants, in addition to a plethora of benefits that accrue on the generation of income, considerable up-front benefits. The clearest rule for obtaining approved status concerns the location of the project. The law defines development zones by order of gov-ernmental preference. The exact boundaries of the various zones can be set from time to time by the ministers responsible for the law's implementation. In general, the most preferred development zones are the least developed regions of the country; for example, the Negev (the desert that constitutes the southern-most region), which reflects the law's emphasis on population dispersal. But Jerusalem, for example, is also most preferred, largely for political reasons. The rate of up-front benefits changes from time to time. In 1967, for instance, an approved project in Development Zone A could obtain up to 80 percent of the cost of investment in government finance: 30 percent in the form of a grant, and the rest as a loan.[18] As recently as 1986, a similar project was eligible for a 39-percent grant.[19]

The other two criteria are much looser and are largely left to the discretion of the bureaucracy. This is certainly true concerning the type of product to be produced by the proposed enterprise. As for the percentage exported, guidelines have been published occasionally. For example, in 1986 a project located in Development Zone A had to export 35 percent of its output to be eligible for approved status and in Zone B it had to export 45 percent of its output.[20]

Until 1980, the loan component of government assistance under the law was extended unindexed. In the presence of inflation, particularly in the second half of the 1970s, that meant a subsidy over and above the grant component. The subsidy reached a peak in 1977, when it amounted, on the average, to about 70 percent of the cost of investment.[21] With the grant, this means that in some cases the government presented the entire project as a present to the "entrepreneur."

The conferring of up-front benefits has three categories of consequences, all of them adverse to the process of economic growth. The first obvious consequence is that the law opens the door for unintended allocation of resources. This is so because, out of the three criteria for eligibility for the law's benefits, only two are verifiable at, and immediately following, the construction phase: the location of the plant and the type of product to be produced. But the share of exports is not, nor is there any time span within which the export target must be achieved. And although compliance with the conditions on which grants were extended has been monitored occasionally, the law does not specify any criteria for deciding that a particular project has not delivered on its promises. So the granting of benefits on the basis of the investor's export performance is based on expectations that can be influenced in various ways. The contingent adverse effect which this may have may be avoided only under rigorous enforcement of the terms of the agreement under which government favors were obtained. Such rigorous enforcement has never been practiced. This is very important, because a project with a high export percentage used to receive almost full benefits even if located outside of the most preferred development areas.[22]

The second consequence, and conceivably the most important one, is that the law obliges the government to become involved in the capital market. Because the government confers grants and loans, it needs financial resources for the implementation of the law, and these are obtained by raising capital. Put differently, the law renders the government a capital market intermediary.

The third consequence is related to the second one. Given that the government provides grants and loans, it may very well happen that more applicants will be found to qualify for these benefits, in principle, than the resources at the government's disposal allow. There will then be a need for rationing, and to do it a bureaucracy is required. True, the law used to be an open-ended proposition: there was no definite budget to whose limits the law had to confine itself, but in recent years this is no longer true. The mechanism for the implementation of rationing is also provided for by the law, which authorizes the government to set up an executive body entrusted with gauging benefits, called the *Investment Center*. By selecting the "approved" investment projects the Investment Center actually determines which projects will be carried out and which will not. Thus, the law makes the government not only a capital market intermediary, but also an allocator of resources for investment.

There are several ways in which the adverse effect of the bureaucracy on growth expresses itself. To begin with, in its decisions and recommendations, the Investment Center was to be guided by little more than the preceding principles. Because the law provides no detailed rules for the determination of eligibility, much room is left to the discretion of the ministers who oversee the application of the law, and very considerable latitude is left to the Investment Center in its day-to-day operations. A lot of discretion leads virtually unavoidably to a lot of discrimination, as it is impossible to be even-handed without adhering to set rules. And discrimination, as we shall see, does not constitute a very good prescription for growth.

To exemplify the extent of discretion under the law, consider the agreement signed between the government and Israel Polak, who founded Polgat, one of the country's largest apparel firms. The agreement, concluded on July 12, 1960, calls for the government to provide 85 percent of the cost of the land and buildings in the form of a loan for twenty years at 5 percent interest and 70 percent of the finance for all the other sorts of fixed investment in the form of a loan for thirteen years at 6.5 percent interest.

The philosophy guiding the Investment Center was clearly enunciated upon its establishment by the director general of the Ministry of Trade and Industry, under whose jurisdiction it functions.[23] In general, "The Investment Center . . . desires to manage a positive investment policy and try, if not to plan, at least to direct, suggest, set in motion, and encourage investments that are desirable to the Israeli economy and prevent the ones which are not." The director goes on to say that there will be in the main two criteria for conferring the privileges of the law. First, a project would have to earn foreign exchange through exports, or save foreign exchange through import substitution. Second, a project would have to provide a lot of employment. Clearly, neither criteria need be correlated in any positive way with profitability.

Because the allocation of resources is carried out by a body whose rewards do not depend on the outcome of its decisions, it is liable to be guided by considerations other than the viability of the projects it approves. For example, it stands to reason that, in general, only relatively large projects will be considered. The motivation is simple: when individuals make investment decisions, each prospective investor considers only those projects in which he or she contemplates to invest. One's entire attention can thus be devoted to what one is interested in. But in the case of the Investment Center, its employees must consider all the projects that apply for approval. This is, of course, a very time-consuming process. Consequently, they will strive to maximize the dollar-value of proposals scrutinized per unit of time. This implies that, rather than considering hundreds of small projects, attention will be focused on large investment projects, which are not necessarily the most promising ones.

The fact that Israel's economy is dominated by a few large concerns (more on this in Chapter 6) is probably partly a result of the bias for big over small. South Korea, too, is typified by such a structure, and there, too, the government intervened heavily in the allocation of financial resources.[24]

There is another motive for favoring large over small projects. Governments are biased toward large projects because these are more visible. That way it is possible to demonstrate to the public that the government is working hard at promoting the economy. It is well known, for example, that loans extended by the World Bank to governments over the years have been directed primarily at very large and visible projects. But favoring large projects may have very little to do with the optimal route toward economic development. Oftentimes smaller projects prove later on to be the more successful ones.

The temptation to select large projects is also related to the fact that such a strategy minimizes the bureaucrats' risk. If benefits are awarded to well known companies, it would be much harder to reprimand the bureaucrats for any error of judgment. And established firms usually invest larger amounts than fledgling entrepreneurs.

There is yet another reason for expecting a bias toward big projects. Investors who wish to qualify for the law's benefits have to solicit the services of lawyers, gobetweens, and accountants in their dealings with the bureaucracy. This requires considerable expenditures, which are unlikely to be undertaken by people who have relatively small projects in mind.

Moreover, because of the considerable degree of discretion the officials administering the law have, there is ample room for lobbying and influence peddling. The people who are good at this sort of thing are not necessarily the best entrepreneurs. It is therefore unlikely that the really good entrepreneurs will elect to traverse this tortuous road. On the other hand, they are unlikely to simply ignore the law and invest their own resources, thus sparing themselves the dealings with the bureaucracy. The reason is that an investor who elects to undertake a project unassisted by the government will be at a competitive disadvantage relative to an investor who does enjoy government assistance. It follows that the law may actually reduce the chances of business success, rather than enhancing them.

The deterrent effect of the law on potential investors who elect not to seek the approved status implies that government bureaucrats not only control investment under the auspices of the law, but also influence investment outside it. They thus determine to a very substantial degree the allocation of investment capital in general. Once again, history does not provide evidence that this is a good prescription for growth.

The law also has built into it some mechanisms that defeat its own purpose, even without reference to the bureaucratic process associated with it. One such curiosity emanates from the fact that the law subsidizes capital, while proclaiming population dispersal as one of its objectives. It thus encourages investors in development zones to tilt toward a capital-intensive technology, which is certainly not the way to attract people to these areas. Another twist of this nature is generated by the fact that a smaller share of the output of an approved project must be exported if the project is located in a development zone, than must be exported if the plant is located elsewhere. Because more exports means more exposure to international competition, it requires higher sophistication. This implies employment of more highly educated labor. Once again, then, the law not only encourages capital over labor, but it attracts the relatively lower grade of labor to the development zones.[25]

To finance investment under the law, as well as investment by government corporations, a special development budget was implemented, financed by borrowing at home and abroad and by unilateral governmental transfers from abroad. It existed alongside the ordinary budget, from which government consumption and transfer payments were financed. For example, in Fiscal 1951, the government operated a development budget that came to over 80 percent of its ordinary budget. At that point, more than half of the financing of the development budget came from abroad.[26]

In terms of the objective of attaining a position of dominance in the capital market, the government's success was instantaneous. As early as 1951, government finance accounted for 54 percent of all fixed capital formation. The government's share climbed to 80 percent in 1954, a peak from which it has been declining ever since, yet never losing the lion's share.[27] Thus, for instance, in 1956 public finance accounted for 75 percent of investment in agriculture, 30 percent in industry, 65 percent in mining, and 85 percent in transportation.[28] One indication as to where all this could lead can be demonstrated with the following: in 1952 and 1953, government grants to public sector enterprises *exceeded* the total amount invested by these enterprises in those years.[29] In effect, the government was financing the acquisition of nonproductive assets.

The story of economic growth through legislation would be incomplete without mentioning the case of the Israel Corporation, although it occurred much later, in 1969. Here, the government actually managed to get through the Knesset a law tailored to a particular corporation. What the government asked for, and got, was a law conferring on this one corporation benefits not accorded anyone else. In return for raising an initial amount of at least $30 million, 80 percent of which had to be in foreign exchange, the Israel Corporation was granted, among other benefits, complete exemption from capital gains taxes, a thirty-year exemption from income taxes, and a reduced corporate tax rate for eleven years following the first profitable year. There was also a complete exemption from taxes on dividends for a period of fifteen years.[30]

As we have seen, the government was able to achieve primacy in the capital market simply by offering to assist investors. The effect this had on the incentive structure was sufficient to render the government chief allocator of capital without having to nationalize any part of the institutional framework of the capital market. However, to carry out this scheme, the government needed the wherewithal to finance grants and loans to approved investors. This meant mobilizing a sizable portion of personal savings, but without nationalizing the institutions in which such savings are deposited.

Long-Term Capital: The Institution of Indexation

To become the chief mediator in the capital market, the government had to set the rules for both sides of the market. It had to decide under what terms it would raise capital from the public and under which rules it would lend it to both business and consumers. The solution was indexation.

As early as 1951, the Histadrut's financial affiliate, Gmul, which served as a financial intermediary for the pension funds managed by the Histadrut, had been extending indexed credit. Indexation was either to the consumer price index or to the price of the product produced by the borrower. By 1956, 65 percent of all credit extended by Gmul was indexed.[31] In 1955, the Electric Corporation of Israel offered I£10 million in indexed bonds, fully guaranteed by the government.[32]

In general, there are three principal ways by which the savings of the public are transmitted to business enterprises for the purpose of investment. First, businesses may mobilize equity capital by issuing shares of stock. Second, they may borrow by issuing bonds. In both of these cases the investor comes into direct contact with the saver, or the original lender, in the sense that there is no financial intermediary. The broker is merely an agent who carries out instructions, and therefore no real financial mediation is present.

The third principal way involves the services of a financial intermediary who acts as an independent decision maker. The intermediary can be either a mutual fund acquiring shares of stock or bonds or it can be a financial institution such as a savings and loan institution or a pension fund. Here, the savers put their savings at the disposal of the intermediary, who in turn uses the funds at its discretion, under the terms agreed upon with the saver. For example, if the saver bought a bank's certificate of deposit, the bank is obliged only to redeem the certificate at maturity and pay a prespecified interest. Otherwise, the bank is free to use the proceeds as it sees fit.

The details of this description are needed to lend clarity to the story of how Israel's governments proceeded in the capital market from 1956 onward, for it enables us to identify the actions that a government would have to take in principle if it wanted to neutralize an independent capital market.

Let us consider first the obvious instrument: government debentures offered on the free market. The purchase of treasury bonds is, in any free economy, the main avenue for lending money to the government. By selling bonds, the government enters the capital market as a borrower. Such entry causes an increase in the demand for loanable funds, pushing interest rates up, and thereby "crowding out" potential private borrowers. The funds that private borrowers forego and the incremental saving induced by the higher interest rate, constitute the funds the government is able to mobilize.

The one disadvantage that this system engenders is that the government, too, has to pay the higher interest rate. So in 1956 Israel's government came up with the idea that it could crowd out private borrowing not by hiking the rate of interest, but by providing a risk so much smaller when compared with private debentures that the public would shun nongovernment bonds, even at existing interest rates. This was accomplished by issuing indexed bonds, that is, bonds whose value was linked to either the exchange rate or the cost of living index.[33] This meant that the government insured its bonds against inflation, something private business seems unable to afford on a regular basis. Insurance against inflation was received warmly by a public having vivid recollection of the rampant inflation of the early 1950s. Thus, the government made it effectively impossible for private business to offer bonds, because the rate of interest that would have to be offered on such bonds if they were to compete with the indexed instruments would be prohibitively high.

The unwillingness or inability of firms to offer indexed bonds is not fully understood on theoretical grounds. At first glance, the reason seems obvious. The public, whose object is consumption, measures the safety of an indexed bond in terms of its ability to preserve purchasing power relative to consumer goods. The issuing firm, on the other hand, is more interested in its ability to service its debt, an ability that depends on how well the firm is doing, which in turn depends on the price of the goods it produces. In other words, for the firm it is riskier to index a bond to the consumer price index than to index it to the price of its products, whereas the opposite holds true for the prospective buyers of such a bond.

But however appealing this explanation is, it involves a difficulty, because from the formal standpoint the description holds by default under price stability. The firm's reluctance to issue debt indexed to the consumer prices under inflationary conditions emanates from the possibility that the price of the firm's own product will escalate more slowly than the consumer prices. In that case profits will also grow at a slower rate, declining in real terms. Under these conditions, the firm's situation would be even worse if it held debt linked to the consumer price index.

Now consider an inflation-free environment. The absence of inflation does not mean complete price stability. Prices do fluctuate, and the price of any particular good might decline relative to the consumer price index. Yet the market rate of interest will be determined on expectations concerning the overall price-level movements and not the price changes affecting the particular good. Hence, the firm producing that good will find itself paying, in terms of the purchasing power of its product, a real rate of interest that exceeds the market rate. This is precisely the same thing as paying an indexed rate under inflation, when the rate of price increase of the particular good under consideration falls short of the overall rate of price increase. So why are firms willing to offer unindexed bonds when there is no inflation? Does this contradict the previous explanation?

The answer lies, apparently, on the practical side: it seems that the probability of synchronization between individual prices and the overall price level declines when inflation increases.[34] This means that although the firm does face a risk of price variability even under price stability, that risk increases under inflation, which is why firms abstain from offering bonds linked to the consumer price index.

In 1957 the Knesset adopted the new Interest Law, which made sure that indexation payments did not come into conflict with the interest-rate ceiling. This was accomplished by classifying indexation payments as noninterest for all instruments with a term to maturity in excess of two years.[35] Because the private sector could not compete with the indexed instruments, the newly instituted government bonds swept the market, so much so that in 1956, the first year in which indexed bonds were offered, they constituted fully 92.6 percent of all new issues.[36]

The inevitability of this outcome could be anticipated by considering the effects that indexed bonds had on alternative ways of channeling savings to investors. First, the indexed bonds obliterated not only private corporate bonds, but also saving deposits with banks. The latter could no more afford indexation of certificates of deposits than corporations could afford to offer indexed bonds. Said the Bank of Israel:[37] "The reason for the stagnation in [approved nonindexed] savings accounts between mid-1961 and mid-1962 is to be apparently blamed on the fact that all these accounts had been unindexed, and when expectations for price rises increased, so did withdrawals from these accounts."

Next, consider shares of stock. In many instances, tax laws make the mobilization of equity capital more costly than debt capital because interest on debt is classified as cost, hence tax deductible. On the other hand, dividends are not, which makes equity more costly than debt. With the government subsidizing long-term loans, the advantage of debt over equity became even more pronounced, so that firms had very little incentive to issue shares of stock. The government thereby succeeded not only in discouraging the demand for shares, but also their supply:[38] "Businesses do not tend to mobilize equity capital as long as they can obtain debt capital on reasonable terms. . . . One should not ignore demand factors that have not encouraged new issues of stock either. The rate of return offered to investors in bonds was high enough, so that their willingness to purchase the riskier shares was conditioned on prospective rates of return that issuing firms were unable to offer."

Given the overwhelming advantage of indexed government bonds, it is impossible to explain why the government found it necessary to compel pension funds, usually the largest capital-market intermediaries, to channel most of the funds at their disposal to government-approved instruments. This would be understandable if long-term credit to borrowers other than the government had been unindexed, but in fact it was indexed. Moreover, in light of the fact that the public's savings through pension funds had already been indexed, the funds could hardly afford to extend nonindexed credit. Indeed, by the end of 1962 the nonbank financial institutions (including mortgage banks) had, in addition to I£252 million outstanding to the government, a total of over I£1.4 billion outstanding to other borrowers throughout the economy.[39] Yet despite all this compelling reasoning the government sharply curtailed the discretion of pension funds. As of 1957, they were instructed to invest 65 percent of their means in approved indexed instruments, and in 1960 this was increased to 75 percent.[40] In subsequent years, the percentage of funds that had to be invested on government instructions continued to increase. In 1970 it was set at 85 percent,[41] and ultimately reached a peak of 92 percent in 1976.[42]

The evidence provides considerable support for the contention that all that regulation was superfluous. Thus, in 1961, the year in which the percentage of approved investment was raised to 75 percent, the pension funds devoted 98 percent of all new purchases of debentures to government-sanctioned instruments.[43] When the required percentage was raised to 92 percent of resources, pension funds already held 94 percent of their total assets in indexed instruments.[44] And in 1987, after the percentage that had to be allocated to approved investment had already been reduced, pension funds held over 96 percent of their assets in government securities.[45]

Of particular note is the fact that, on the basis of an agreement reached in 1960, the government allowed special latitude to the Histadrut's financial intermediary, Gmul. According to this arrangement, Gmul could use a substantial portion of money acquired from Histadrut pension funds (the percentages varied over time: in 1970, for instance, it stood at 50 percent[46]) to make loans to the latter's industrial enterprises. That is to say, it received a blanket approval from the government, thereby being able to allocate finance more freely among Histadrut corporations. This constituted a specific kind of discrimination, because it granted the Histadrut economy a greater freedom in the allocation of funds than was generally available. The confinement of these funds to the Histadrut economy made it even less likely that capital would be allocated to the better investment prospects.

Had the government left it at that, the Israeli banking system would have, for all practical purposes, ceased to exist as a provider of all but short-term credit. As long as the public had access to indexed government securities, it could hardly be expected to deposit its money in unindexed bank accounts of similar terms to maturity. The banks would thus be deprived of all but short-term deposits, so something had to be invented to prevent indexed government bonds from completely displacing the banks.

The legal framework for shoring up the banks was provided by the Encouragement of Saving Law of 1956 (the year when indexed bonds were offered by the government for the first time), which empowered the Minister of Finance to provide state guarantee to debentures offered by companies and institutions designated for this purpose and to grant income-tax concessions to savers.[47]

Based on the new law, banks were allowed to offer savings plans as approved by the government, which meant primarily that interest earned on such plans could enjoy tax breaks. Yet by 1961 it had become clear that this was not going to be enough if the banks were to be able to compete with indexed bonds.

So in mid-1962, banks began offering indexed saving accounts. In essence, these plans allowed depositors to have their deposits linked to the cost of living index in a progressive fashion: the principal of a saving plan with a term of three years to maturity was 50 percent indexed; that is, the depositor received compensation for half the rise in the cost of living index. For a four-year plan indexation coverage was 70 percent, and in plans stretching five years or more, both the principal and interest were fully indexed. Of course, a bank could hardly offer such protection from inflation on its own. To be eligible for indexation, therefore, banks, like pension funds, had to agree to use a specified percentage of the funds deposited by the public on government instructions. Thus, 60 percent of deposits in approved plans had to be used for the purchase of nonnegotiable, indexed, treasury bonds, and another 25 percent had to be extended as development loans approved by the government. Only 15 percent of sums deposited in approved saving plans could be disposed of by the banks at their own discretion.[48]

Although the government wanted to have a dominant say in the allocation of credit, it did not want to bother with the day-to-day administration of credit extension. It therefore devised the scheme known as *earmarked funds.* Money raised by banks by selling debentures to pension funds and money raised by the government by selling non-negotiable treasury bonds to the banks themselves was deposited with these same banks. The banks, in turn, were obliged to extend credit out of these funds on government instructions. The government not only selected the recipients of such credit, but also set the terms. It determined the interest rates earned by the savers, both through banks and pension funds, those the bank earned on bonds, and the rates paid by borrowers to the banks. In this way the government acted not only as the allocator of most of the funds, but also determined the interest-rate spread and so the banks' margin of profit.

The question of why a person would prefer to purchase a government bond through a saving account rather than directly is a valid one. The answer must rest on some discriminating features as between the two saving instruments. Indeed, bonds bought directly were negotiable and could be sold any day, but the yield was not guaranteed unless the bond was held to maturity. That is, bonds could be turned into money quickly, but they involved interest-rate risk. Saving accounts, on the other hand, offered slightly higher interest rates, but were for fixed terms, with penalties imposed for early withdrawal. The two instruments thus offered different mixes of yields, risk, and liquidity, which is all that is required for coexistence. Just to make sure that savings would flow almost exclusively into its instruments, the government also instituted a tax discrimination: interest on government bonds was exempt from income tax, but interest on corporate bonds was not.

Long-Term Capital: Loan Indexation Is Abolished

Although the government succeeded in gaining virtual complete domination of the long-term capital market, subsequent developments caused it to get even more involved, perhaps partly unintentionally. The currency depreciation of 1962 changed the official exchange rate of the Israeli lira from I£1.8 to I£3 to the U.S. dollar. Prior to the devaluation, most mortgage loans and many other long-term loans, including those made by the government through the development budget, had been indexed to the exchange rate. That meant that the dollar-value of the loans was to be sheltered from inflation. For example, the foreign-exchange value of a mortgage loan of, say, I£9,000, issued on January 1, 1961, was $5,000. Suppose the loan had been for ten years, at 4 percent interest. If the loan was to be discharged in ten equal end-of-year installments, then at the end of 1961, I£1,110 was due. Of this, I£750 was amortization of the principal, so that after the payment the remaining debt was I£8,250, or the equivalent of $4,583.30. At this point the depreciation to I£3 to the dollar took place. Our borrower, the value of whose debt had been indexed to the dollar, was still viewed as owing the equivalent of $4,583.30, but now he or she owed in domestic currency I£13,750, a sum that exceeded the initial loan by more than 50 percent.

The furor generated by this development caused the government to embark on what must be seen as a landmark in Israel's economic history: it changed, *retroactively*, the terms of the mortgage loans. Henceforth, these loans were to be linked to the cost of living index, rather than to the exchange rate.

Once the government made an exception to the rule that people ought to be held to their contractual obligations, the door for more concessions was open. In the years following 1962 more retroactive scrapping of indexation took place, until by 1967 almost all manner of loan indexation was repealed, not only in respect of mortgage loans, but also for business loans.[49] This ushered in a new era, for from then on the long-term credit intermediaries, including the government itself, had to borrow indexed and lend unindexed funds. Of course, such a system could not be made viable without government assistance, because pension funds and other intermediaries would have gone bankrupt in a short period of time. Specifically, the government had to stand ready to cover the inflationary losses incurred by the financial institutions. It proceeded to do so by instituting an arrangement called *indexation insurance.* For a small premium paid to the government by the financial institutions, it agreed to cover any losses caused by inflation. Because the "premiums" had not been based on any actuarial calculations, the consequences were disastrous. Said the Bank of Israel:[50] "This arrangement of abolishing indexation for the borrower without doing the same for the lender (the purchaser of the bond) intensifies the government's control over the financial institutions in particular and over the capital market in general. . . . The abolishing of indexation increased the gap between the effective rate of return to the lender and the real cost of capital to the borrower." The Bank also pointed out that this arrangement completely obfuscated the rate of interest as a signalling device in the capital market.[51]

One can safely assume that when these words were written, no one suspected the magnitude of the problem the scheme would generate. As it turned out, two sets of growth-retarding consequences emanated from the new arrangement.

The deindexation of loans set the stage for an unintended inflationary subsidy to borrowers, both producers and consumers, of the kind already mentioned in connection with credit extended under the LECI. In time, the advent of inflation was to drive real rates of interest on borrowed funds down so far that investors found it profitable to borrow and invest such funds, even in enterprises that yielded negative rates of return. A rate of return of, say, minus 5 percent is very profitable to the investor if the investment capital is mobilized at a real cost of, say, only minus 15 percent, but this is hardly the way to promote growth.

As for the other consequence, with the government intermediating most of the lending, it assumed a huge position in terms of inflationary risk. Therefore, when inflation hit, it eroded the real value of government claims, but left government obligations intact. The government thus incurred a rapidly growing net debt, compelling it to both raise taxes and get even more involved in the capital market to acquire the wherewithal for financing the growing debt-service needs.

At the end of 1988, domestic government debt stood at about 111 percent of the GNP, after having reached a peak of 133 percent in 1985. The external government debt at the end of 1988 amounted to another 29 percent of the GNP, down from a peak of 51 percent in 1985. On the other side, total net wealth, financial and physical, held by the public at the end of 1988 came to 224 percent of the GNP. The conclusion has to be that the deindexation of loans resulted in a huge net transfer of wealth from the government to the public.[52]

Even if the government refrains from reducing the debt, which requires only the recycling of existing savings (as opposed to the mobilization of new savings), the burden of servicing interest payments alone constitutes a significant addition to the obstacles for growth. If we assume the average real rate of interest on the debt to be 6 percent, then annual interest payments require an amount equivalent to over 8 percent of the GNP. This is, then, the tax burden that must obtain even if the government ceased operations. The implication is that, relative to the changes sweeping the Western world, the tax burden in Israel will have to remain heavy for years to come, which does not bode well for growth.

Short-Term Capital

Our discussion has centered on the market for long-term capital, but what about the short term? Although government domination of the working-capital market has not been as overbearing as in the investment-capital market, the government has been exerting considerable influence over it. As noted earlier, the government's failure to remove the interest-rate ceiling meant that it would have to ration credit whenever the maximum allowable rate of interest fell short of the market equilibrium rate.

This is precisely the course the government has chosen, beginning in 1951 when it asked the banks to abstain from certain kinds of lending. Because three of the four most important banks were controlled by public institutions, they could not refuse the request. But the real turning point came in 1953, when the government instructed the banks to extend at least 20 percent of new lending to the agricultural sector. This marked the birth of "directed credit," which was to be refined and become the main vehicle for government control of the short-term credit market. At the beginning of 1954, the government instructed the banks to freeze the volume of credit at its November 30, 1953, level.

The establishment of the Bank of Israel in 1954 did not engender any break in the continuity of credit policy. In addition to leaving intact the credit allocation edicts already in place, the Bank, for all practical purposes, continued the freeze on credit by requiring that commercial banks maintain a reserve ratio of 90 percent on all deposits acquired after December 31, 1952. This meant that banks could lend out only 10 percent of the money accumulated in new deposits. The Bank then proceeded to exempt certain amounts of credit from the reserve requirement, provided the credit was extended according to government priorities.[53]

The system worked as follows. Generally, when calculating reserve requirements, the ratio of total reserves to total deposits is computed. When a certain amount of credit is being exempt, this amounts to applying a lower rate of reserves to part of the deposits, so that the average ratio of reserves to deposits decreases.

As in the case of long-term credit, short-term credit allocation was also effected partially through the use of government deposits. The government would deposit certain amounts with banks and then direct them in how to use the funds. This form of credit direction played a significant role: at the end of 1955, government deposits made up 26 percent of total banking liabilities,[54] and over 36 percent of credit outstanding at the end of 1955 was given out of government deposits. That credit out of government deposits as a proportion of total credit could exceed the proportion of government deposits out of total deposits was made possible by differential reserve requirements. Government deposits were subject to less stringent requirements, so that a larger share of overall credit could be channelled toward those borrowers who were favored by the government. Another 4 percent of outstanding credit came from the Bank of Israel.[55]

At the end of 1956, the government and the Bank accounted for 45 percent of total outstanding short-term credit. Their share reached a peak of 47 percent in 1958, declining thereafter. But this does not mean that the public sector's influence over credit allocation declined; only the means changed. One might get a better feel for what *direction of credit* meant on a day-to-day basis by considering credit directed at the farm sector. At the end of 1958, the public sector's share of total short-term credit outstanding to the farm sector stood at about 60 percent. But *direction* did not just mean direction to the sector as a whole. The government actually allocated credit separately to the cotton-growing industry, citriculture, peanuts, grains, supply cooperatives (cooperatives established on a regional basis by associations of farm communities), and new settlements.

In addition to controlling a substantial share of the domestic credit market, import of foreign credit was also strictly policed and discouraged. Although in theory foreign investment was welcomed, in practice all manner of foreign credit was disallowed. Purchase of corporate bonds by foreign investors was discouraged because it was feared that this might compete with the sale of government bonds abroad. Long-term lending to Israeli corporations by such institutions as the Export-Import Bank was discouraged because the government feared that this would make it harder for government corporations to borrow. Short-term borrowing abroad was discouraged because short-term capital movements were deemed to hamper control of the money supply.[56]

One of the more prominent arrangements was credit directed for export. Primordial forms of this institution had already existed by the time the Bank of Israel was established. At that time, the government had been operating special export-credit funds in association with the larger banks. The Bank joined the arrangement flawlessly, and in its first full year of existence, 1955, was already providing finance to the export fund at subsidized interest.[57] By the end of 1963, this special export credit fund grew to the extent that it dispensed almost a quarter of all directed credit, or over 9 percent of all banking credit. The public sector's share in the fund was 70 percent, and that share was extended at a heavily subsidized rate of interest. The methodology employed was not unlike that used for long-term credit; namely, the scheme under which the government borrowed indexed and lent unindexed funds, covering the difference from its budget. Here, too, the government extended its part of the credit at an interest rate of only 2 percent, enabling the banks to charge only 6 percent on the loans to exporters. The funds extended by the government had to be borrowed, of course, at interest rates considerably in excess of 2 percent (recall that at that point the government had already been selling indexed bonds),[58] with the difference constituting a subsidy.

Government support for exports through subsidized credit developed into a full bloom of *seven* different credit funds, which still existed in 1983. The five funds that extended foreign exchange credit were Import for Export, Consignment (ordinary), Long-Term Export, Diamonds, Overseas Marketing. The function of most of these funds is evident from its name. The Consignment Fund financed customer credit, whereas the Overseas Marketing Fund provided finance for sales promotion. The Diamond Fund was essentially an import-for-export fund, used to finance imports of uncut diamonds. Its separation from other, similar funds was motivated by the special nature of the diamonds trade.

The money for all five funds was extended, through the commercial banking system, by the Bank of Israel, except that the Diamonds Fund was financed by exemption from reserve requirements. The arrangements not only sound complex, they really were, and in the Bank an entire department existed whose sole function was the administration of the various credits.

Apart from the five foreign exchange funds extending credit for exports, in 1983 two more such funds extended domestic currency credit: Production for Exports and Indirect Export. The first financed that part of short-term credit which did not qualify under the Import for Export Fund; namely, the credit needed to finance the purchase of domestically produced inputs, chiefly labor services. Finance in this fund was expressed in terms of shekels per dollar's-worth of exports. The second fund was almost comical: it provided finance to those producers whose outputs are utilized as inputs in export-producing processes. For example, the domestic producer of fertilizer was entitled to credit because that product is used by citrus growers, whose product is exported.

The most obvious adverse effect of this system on growth was that credit allocation was based on past performance. Exporters got in any given year a credit allocation based on exports in the preceding year. Even if one ignores the incentive to cheat that this arrangement generated, it is still damaging because it tends to freeze the sectoral structure of the economy. Because it slows down change, it impedes the exploitation of new opportunities and evolving comparative advantages.

Directed credit has not been confined to exports alone. Directed credit for non-export-related activities comprised, until 1983, the following funds: Special Loan to Agriculture, Aid to Industry, Aid to Agriculture, and Conversion Loan to Agriculture. Discrimination was effected not only by who could or could not belong to these credit clubs. Further discrimination was based on interest-rate differentials. Interest rates differed even within the same general category. In fact, as far as the export-oriented funds were concerned, no two rates were the same. Thus, in 1983, interest rates were 6 percent on Import for Export, Eurodollar rate plus 1.5 percent on Consignment (Ordinary), 7.6 percent on Diamonds, 10 percent on Long Term Export, and 80 percent of the Eurodollar rate on Overseas Marketing.[59]

At the end of 1978, directed credit in the various export funds constituted a quarter of total credit, both short and long term, outstanding to the Israeli public through the commercial banking system. Altogether, the government controlled over 68 percent of all credit extended through the commercial banks and that excludes all mortgage credit and long-term funds extended through investment banks, two items almost totally controlled by the government.[60] This means that the government controlled the credit sector almost as fully as it controlled long-term capital.

The government's complete domination of the credit market has not only stifled it in the same way in which it has stifled the capital market, it has actually shattered it. The evidence is presented in Table 2.1. Two important facts concerning the loanable funds market are reflected in the table. The first is the total separation of the long-term and short-term markets, as indicated by the tremendous difference between interest charged on bank loans and interest earned on bonds. A situation like this can come about only if the credit market is completely splintered, so that no movement between the various segments is possible. Under normal circumstances, the high interest rates charged by banks could not be sustained, as bond holders would have dumped them on the market rather than borrow at these astronomic rates. But in Israel, the holders of bonds and the borrowers are two distinct groups, mainly because a substantial proportion of government bonds is nonnegotiable.

The second feature is the enormous spread between interest rates charged on loans and interest rates granted on deposits. A situation like this comes about when the central bank uses as its main monetary instrument the reserve ratio requirements imposed on commercial banks. In the event, some reserve ratios were required to more than double, exceeding in some cases the 50-percent mark. Under these circumstances, deposit rates cannot grow alongside the lending rates, because the banks' income base shrinks as a result of the fact that less can be lent out of each shekel deposited. This is why the increase of reserve ratios is sometimes viewed as the imposition of a tax on the financial system.

In Chapter 9, we shall have an opportunity to discuss monetary policy in Israel more comprehensively. In Chapter 11 we shall return in more detail to Israel's bout with skyrocketing interest rates.

TABLE 2.1

Real Interest Rates* and Yields, Annual Terms

Year	Working Capital (revolving) credit) Accounts (nondirected)	Certificates of Deposit	Average Yield on Bonds Indexed to	
			CPI	Foreign Exchange
1984	60.0	-7.1	9.3	12.7
1985	93.8	-8.2	-6.7	-19.9
1986	33.6	3.3	-1.3	-21.5

*Interest rates after adjustment for inflation.

Source: Interest rates for 1984, Bank of Israel, *Annual Report 1984,* p. 274; for 1985 and 1986, Bank of Israel, Research Department, *Recent Economic Developments* 42 (1987): Table 21. Yields, Bank of Israel, *Annual Report 1986,* p. 273.

3

THE CAPITAL MARKET: THE ORIGINS

First Steps

As we have seen, the virtual nationalization of the capital market was underpinned by the perceived need to allocate investment in a manner that would enhance national objectives. Stated in this fashion, governmental involvement could be interpreted as an ad hoc means, designed to deal with Israel's extraordinary difficulties. Yet regardless of the special circumstances, it came naturally, because the ideological makeup of the early proponents of Israel's economic framework, their experience in pre-Israel Palestine, and their beliefs about how the economy of the Jewish community had developed were all conducive to the seizure of the capital market.

The first political nucleus that was organized enough to advance its ideological agenda in a systematic manner consisted of immigrants from Eastern Europe, who held both Zionist and socialist views. These views were forged by the terrible plight of the Jews, especially in Czarist Russia, and it was quite natural for the immigrants to associate the longings for a socialist revolution with a liberation of the Jews from their bondage, so much so that they came to view national and social liberation as inextricably intertwined. This is how socialist Zionism came into existence.[1]

The first socialist Zionists came to Palestine in the years between the turn of the century and World War I, in what came to be known as the Second Aliya (immigration wave). Upon arrival, they found a Jewish community made up of city dwellers and, more important, individual Jewish farmers. These farmers lived in farm communities that had been established during the last quarter of the nineteenth century and derived their livelihood primarily from the cultivation of citrus groves and vineyards. These activities were labor intensive, and the farmers therefore employed a lot of hired workers, the overwhelming majority of whom were Palestinian Arabs. The picture of Arab laborers who toiled at dirt cheap wages for the capitalist owners of the groves correlated beautifully with the new immigrants' image of the very economic setup they had come to hate in Russia. It was not the kind of economy they were dreaming about, and they were resolved to mold it to their own liking.

The first opportunity to direct funds collected by national bodies to what would otherwise be purely the domain of the private sector came when the Zionist Organization established its Palestine Office in 1908. It had at its disposal three financial instruments. Two had been founded earlier: the Jewish National Fund, founded in 1901 as a land-purchasing organ, and the Anglo-Palestine Company (APC, later referred to as the Anglo-Palestine Bank, or APB) founded in 1903 as a subsidiary of the Jewish Colonial Trust (JCT), which had been the first financial organ of the Zionist Organization and was established by the founding father of the movement, Theodor Herzl (1860–1904), in 1899. The shareholders were the founders of the movement, and they were guaranteed a majority vote. The JCT also founded a bank in Poland. The third institution was the Land Development Company, established together with the Palestine Office.

The director of the Palestine office, Arthur Ruppin (1876–1943), came from a background very different from that which produced the socialist component of the movement. He was a Central European, educated in the German tradition, and did not share socialist convictions. Yet he absorbed enough of the socialist rhetoric to skew his actions, and his views, away from a capitalist frame of mind. His extensive writings provide a fairly clear picture of the beginnings that ultimately led to the abduction of the capital market.

Very early on, Ruppin expressed his conviction that the colonization of Palestine often was at odds with the profit motive:[2] "I can say with absolute certainty: those enterprises in Palestine which are most profit-bearing for the businessman are almost always the least profitable for our national effort; and per contra, many enterprises which are least profitable for the businessman are of high national value" and[3] "In our agricultural work, which is connected with the training and adaptation of human material, we must be prepared to relinquish the idea of profit." That Arthur Ruppin had not been led to these utterances by socialist ideology is demonstrated by his apparent agonizing over the problem of incentives. His primary concern was to create a situation whereby new settlers would have a stake in their farms. He went to great lengths to devise a mechanism that would allow even settlers without any means whatsoever to feel as though they were investing something of their own.[4]

With the profit incentive taking a back seat, it was obvious that the settlement effort would have to be financed with money that could be allocated on considerations other than economic, and this could be done only through the various organs of the Zionist Organization, which meant that the national movement was engaged from very early on in the business of raising capital and allocating it. Of no less importance is the fact that the bulk of this capital was being allocated to the two socialized forms of settlement: the *kibbutz* and the *moshav*. The first featured a collective ownership of the means of production, together with strict equality on the consumption side. The second was a cooperative society, where each family cultivated its own farm, but where marketing, credit, and procurement, both for production and consumption, was done cooperatively, and individual farms of a given type were of identical sizes.

The Foundation Fund (Keren Hayesod)

Until 1920, the methods employed by the Palestine Office were based on an ad hoc approach, with Ruppin providing both the leadership and the conceptual framework, but in 1920 and 1921 events took a decisive turn. In July of 1920, the London Conference was convened to debate the economic activities of the Zionist Organization. The conference adopted the proposal, to be presented before the subsequent Zionist Congress, to found the Foundation Fund (Keren Hayesod), to finance immigration and settlement. The fund was to have a capital of £25 million, to be raised through contributions from Jews the world over. Of the money raised, 20 percent was to go to the Jewish National Fund (JNF), and none of the money was to be allocated to private business, unless such business also demonstrated the ability to enhance the "public well-being." The bulk of the money was intended for economic purposes; that is, the Foundation Fund was to act as a major source for investment capital.[5]

The adoption of this resolution came in the wake of a heated debate that pitted the European leadership of the Zionist Organization against the American Jewish delegation, under the leadership of Justice Louis Brandeis (1856–1941).[6] The Americans came down firmly on the side of a clear distinction between what was normally the domain of private enterprise and what could be viewed as legitimate public finance of the provision of public goods and infrastructure. Brandeis had been very much aware of the fact that the conditions in much of Palestine were such that some basic investments would have to precede regular business investment. In particular, Brandeis included investment in improving the land to the point where it could be considered fit for settlement, for much of the land available at that time was under swamp and plagued by malaria. Brandeis did not think that even under these adverse circumstances the source of capital should be philanthropy. He did argue, however, that this sort of investment should not be financed with debt capital, because conditions would not permit the payment of interest for a long time. Rather, he advocated the issue of stock, reasoning that, although profitability would be a long time in coming, it would arrive eventually and that therefore, in the long run, the settlement of Palestine was a sound business proposition.[7] The approach of Brandeis was reflected in the resolutions adopted by the Zionist Organization of America in its convention in Buffalo. The very first resolution stated that[8] "In appealing in the United States for

funds for the upbuilding of Palestine there shall be no commingling of investment and donation funds." Brandeis elaborated on some of his thoughts in an
address to the members of the Palestine Development League in New York,
when he stressed over and over again the need to create a self-supporting population in Palestine. He also made the point that to achieve this goal, it was
necessary to keep business management separate from political management.[9]

The views expressed by the American Zionists were firmly opposed by
the Zionist Left. The opposition is not surprising in itself, given the ideological hue of the socialists. What is interesting, though, is their partial resort to
nonideological arguments, based on the "special conditions" prevailing in
Palestine. For example, it was argued that the concentration of financial
power needed to cope with the desolation of Palestine could not be mobilized
by private enterprise. The proof was to be found in Brandeis's own assertion
that preparatory investment, financed through a national trust, would have to
precede individual investment. It showed that the country was devoid of the
conditions required to attract private capital. There was also a historical argument, advanced by C. Arlosoroff (1899–1933):[10]

> From the point of view of the Jewish settlement effort, private enter-
> prise has been, to date, disappointing all the way, in agriculture as well
> as in industry. This holds without even touching on the more far reach-
> ing question: what is the value of the individual proprietor during cer-
> tain stages of development of the private ownership society and econ-
> omy. Even if his historical achievements in general should shine like the
> heavenly aura, in the annals of the Jewish settlement of Palestine to date
> they come practically to nought.

The approval of the Foundation Fund by the Twelfth Zionist Congress in 1921
meant that politicians would make business decisions and exert considerable
influence on the shaping of Palestine's economic environment. The politicians
became investment managers.

The failure to separate investment in infrastructure from business
investment along the lines suggested by Brandeis and the concentration of the
financial source for the entire settlement effort in the hands of a political organization produced a historic and very basic contradiction that continues to
plague Israel to this day. It produced the view that settling Palestine could not
possibly be viewed as an economically sound proposition.[11] The contradictory
element came through very clearly in the debate over the National Loan, proposed by Arthur Ruppin in 1925. His plan called for borrowing up to E£10
million,[12] with which he proposed to settle 30,000 new immigrants, two-thirds
of them in agriculture. The idea was to extend to each settling family the
entire sum—about E£1,200—as a loan. Because it was doubtful that the set-

tlers could abide by the terms of the loan, a guarantee trust financed by world Jewry was to be established. What was formulated in terms of a loan thus had a subsidy element built into it.

The contradiction is exposed by observing that a business proposition is either economical, or it is not. If it is profitable in the long run, then it is profitable. Time enters into it only in relation to how long it will take before the project begins to generate profits and therefore for how long debt financing is necessary (assuming the project cannot be completely financed with equity capital). It follows that, if a project is economical, it never requires subsidies; and if it needs them, then it is unprofitable.

Not everybody was oblivious to these critical considerations. One who pointed out the inconsistency was Heinrich Margulies, one of the top executives of the APB. Like Brandeis, he believed that a clear distinction should be made between investment in infrastructure, such as clearing swamps, and investment in agricultural equipment, livestock, and so on. Such a distinction was inconsistent with the operations of the Foundation Fund, whose loans to settlers were designed to finance everything. What Margulies argued was that there was no way for the settler to be able to service all of this debt. The financial burden imposed on the settler in this way would make it impossible to ever stand on his or her own financially, creating the prospect of making settlers dependent on public finances forever. How, asked Margulies, could any public body undertake such a responsibility?[13]

The unbusinesslike approach was also seen as creating a moral hazard. Brandeis expressed his fear that too much pampering of the new settlers would destroy their morale and bring about an adverse selection process, which he described as the development of a population of undesirables. The same line of reasoning was advanced by Z. D. Levontine (1856–1940), who was the chief executive of APB until 1924 and the most vocal and consistent critic of the methods adopted by the Zionist Organization.[14] He stated that[15] "The land can be built only by those who invest their money in it, make profits, and live at their own expense and absolutely not by those who arrive without any means and are supported from the outset throughout." Being aware, however, that not many settlers could raise the means on their own, he proposed that the money be advanced as loans along strict business lines. This could be accomplished only through regular bank loans, not through loans from the Foundation Fund. His reasoning was that money advanced by public institutions, even if it were advanced as a loan from the formal standpoint, is likely to be viewed as charity, and settlers would not feel the same obligation to pay it back as they would with a regular bank loan:[16] "By now all the inhabitants of our country know that there are two sources for loans: APB and the Foundation Fund. A loan from the first source, the borrower must repay; failure to fulfil the obligation means civil death. A loan from the second source you have a right to repay." He thus clearly recognized another aspect of the moral hazard associated with public finance of business activity.

Land Ownership

The London Conference of 1920 also adopted the guiding principles of the land policy of the Zionist Organization. It was resolved that the JNF would not only purchase as much land as possible with a view to keeping it forever under national ownership, but would also help to facilitate private land purchases under the condition that such land be transferred to public ownership at a later date. The desirability of public ownership of land was universal:[17] "In the course of the twenty-seven years' existence of the [Jewish] National Fund the principle of the collective ownership of all land acquired by the Zionist Organization has become a fixed idea in the minds of all Zionists, a cardinal point in the whole Zionist conception of things." Land is not capital, but the considerations that affected national attitudes toward it were in many respects very similar to those that governed the views concerning capital. It therefore seems appropriate to consider the land story in the present context.

The desire to put as much land as possible under national ownership seems to have been based on three categories of considerations. The first was entirely nationalistic in character; that is, devoid of social ideology: the desire to prevent resale of land to the Arabs. Settlement on the land constituted the top priority of the national agenda. Assuming that individual landowners would not be driven by the same national zeal as the Zionist Movement, its leaders were afraid that such owners would not resist the temptation to profit by reselling land to the Arabs, if propitious circumstances for such profits arose.

The second category of reasons for preferring public ownership of land was ideological in nature, although in presenting it some purportedly practical concerns were voiced. It can be summarized by the observation that private ownership of land was deemed to have evil consequences. In describing the debate at the 1920 London Conference as to whether private ownership of land, in addition to collective ownership, should be viewed favorably or not, Granovsky elaborates the arguments of the opponents of private ownership as follows:[18] "The champions of the first alternative argued that the evils of private property in land are so outrageous that it must be done away with by every available means. They pointed to its pernicious results—high ground rents, undeserved enrichment of small groups by automatic rises in value, land speculation, concentration of large areas in the hands of a few landlords, land hunger on the part of the working population." Later on, Eliezer Kaplan (1891–1952) rendered the following admonition:[19]

The speculation disease struck every part of the country . . . and endangered the very possibility of increasing our land holdings. And among us there are still those who are enthusiastic about the great ideal of a Tel-Aviv sprawling all the way to Hadera in the north, Rehovot in the south and Ramla in the east; and if two years ago the talk was of citrus Zionism, nowadays it is of a Zionism of an urban plot. And this despite the fact that in the Diaspora we saw with our own eyes cities inhabited by hundreds of thousands of Jews who found their livelihood there, but the farmland was in the hands of strangers. And the fate of these Jews is well known.

The arguments contained in the two foregoing passages may be summed up as follows: first, private ownership leads to the unjustified enrichment of the few; second, it causes hunger for land among the working people; third, it brings with it land speculation, which causes real estate prices to rise; and fourth, it leads to overurbanization, defeating the struggle to return the Jews to the land.

The view of land speculation as inherently evil runs like a central theme through the annals of the Zionist efforts. Because speculators were regarded as contributing nothing to the economic process, any realization of profits on their part was deemed unjustified. As far as one can tell, speculative profits were seen as stemming from the speculators' ability to hold on to land for long periods of time, during which land appreciated in value, thus generating gains. Not only were these gains seen as unjustified, but the fact that the land which was the object of speculation lay idle caused land shortages. In consequence, flats built on the land were small and oppressive, and even these tiny apartments cost a fortune to rent, hurting mainly the working class.[20] It was therefore to be regretted that the JNF failed to purchase land in the vicinity of Tel-Aviv, which was becoming the most dynamic urban center and all of whose land was privately owned.[21]

The failure to purchase more land, especially in the vicinity of urban centers, was itself blamed on speculation, which had driven prices beyond the means of the JNF. Thus, the JNF failed to buy large blocks of land near Netanya because, as was argued, speculators drove prices to such levels that the JNF could purchase only small plots. This was viewed with particular consternation, because the land in this region was especially suited for the coveted citrus business.[22] A more clearly stated observation concerning land prices was that, if land acquisition were made through a monopsony, the single buyer being the JNF, purchase prices could be made lower than otherwise.[23]

One result of the widely held view of urban landowners as speculators who were getting rich at the expense of the community was that landlords came to be regarded contemptuously, as though they constituted a class of parasites.[24]

The third category of reasons for advocating collective ownership had its origins in both social and national considerations. The social component was the socialist principle of preventing exploitation of labor. The national one was the transforming of as many Jews as possible to farmers. Why was it necessary to accomplish the twin objectives through collective ownership of land? Because in this way one could ascertain that the size of the plot given to a settler was to be kept to the maximum that the settler could cultivate with his family; that is, without hired labor:[25] "Undoubtedly 'own work' would be the best test in the distribution of national land, for only in this fashion can a fully productive community be established. 'Own work' is the ideal . . . " So important was this principle, that the JNF sought to retain the right of reducing the size of plots even after the land had been settled. One such episode actually occurred in Kfar Malal, north of Tel-Aviv on the coastal plain. It was settled in 1913 by forty grain-growing families, who cultivated jointly 600 acres, or 15 acres per family. By 1934, upon the introduction of citrus groves, the number of settlers was increased and the average plot cut to 5 acres.[26]

The nationalist component of the objection to hired labor in agriculture was prompted by the disadvantage Jews suffered in their competition with Arab hired labor, as they had to compete with cheaper and better trained Arab labor. Direct ownership constituted a way of beating the competition. For in this way as many Jews could become farm workers as would have if they could beat the Arab competition and become hired hands:[27]

Concentration of several farm parcels in one hand is not permitted, since such estates would be too large to be worked by the settlers and their families. They would be forced to employ cheap labor, and such labor would almost always be non-Jewish—a situation that must by all means be avoided. Self-Labor, without hired assistance of any kind, is a basic principle in the Reconstruction of Palestine as the Jewish Homeland. The underlying idea of Self-Labor is to prevent the compulsory lowering of the higher standard of life of the Jewish worker.

The method chosen for both keeping the land in public hands and letting individual farmers work it was the long-term lease. The term of the lease was forty-nine years, and it was hereditary. It could also be sold, but such a transaction could be carried out only with the consent of the JNF. And such "Consent is withheld if anti-national or anti-social factors are involved in the transfer, if the successor be a non-Jew, or unfitted for farming, or if there be a speculative motive."[28]

The prevention of private ownership was also motivated by what the Jewish immigrants found in Palestine on their arrival, a situation still apparent nowadays in Arab villages. In the absence of appropriate laws, landowners habitually divided up their land among all eligible heirs. When this happens generation after generation, plots become smaller and smaller, making it ever harder to exploit economies of scale, thus reducing the chances for continued profitability.

When the state of Israel was established, all the non-privately-owned land gained as a result of the War of Independence became national land subject to the principles that guided the policies of the JNF. These principles were incorporated in the Basic Law of Israel's Lands, adopted in 1960 and providing that "The ownership of Israel's lands . . . shall not be transferred either by sale or in any other manner."These principles were reaffirmed recently by a public commission appointed to evaluate the objectives of Israel's land policy. It stated that "The principle which was set in the Basic Law of Israel's Lands, 1960, according to which national land will not be sold other than in limited circumstances, seems to the commission right and just and should be retained."[29] State ownership is exercised through the Israel Land Authority, under the auspices of the Ministry of Construction and Housing (until recently under the Ministry of Agriculture), which owns about 75 percent of the land in Israel, and through the JNF, which owns another 18 percent of the land.

A systematic evaluation of the reasons given for national ownership of land reveals either the absence of any economic analysis or fallacious economic reasoning. True, the main motivating factor behind land purchases by the JNF had been national and not economic in nature, but the absence of economic considerations was crucial, since if they had been present, the fear of the resale of land to Arabs could have been easily shown to be unfounded.

The reason is simple: if a private land deal is to take place, it must be regarded as profitable by both sides. An Arab landlord selling his holdings to a Jewish newcomer must assume that what he can get by selling the land is at least equal to the capitalized value of the expected stream of income from holding on to the land. The buyer, on the other hand, must assume that the capitalized expected stream of income from the acquired land must at least equal the price he or she has to pay for it. Under these circumstances, the reverse transaction cannot possibly take place. Indeed, under Jewish cultivation the land yielded considerably more than under Arab cultivation, and so there was no chance that Arabs would want to buy back the land. The same held true if the land under consideration was urban. The Arabs quite simply could not afford to repurchase the land.

Luckily, this is one instance in which one does not have to rely solely on "what if" reasoning: prior to independence, practically no privately owned land had ever been sold back to the Arabs, whether farmland or otherwise. So from this standpoint, collective ownership was simply unnecessary. After independence, the question became moot, because with sovereignty the Arabs could no longer use land transactions to block Jewish development.

The monopsony idea was, of course, naive. If a monopsony could be established for a moment, land prices would have declined. This would have attracted many more buyers to the market, thus causing renewed competition. And if the JNF could have obtained funds at the rate it would have liked to, its own demand for land would have increased, causing land prices to increase.

The speculation story could be credible only if the possibility of cornering the land market had existed, which, of course, it did not. The very descriptions on which the speculation stories were based indicate the existence of a very competitive land market. Speculation in a market of this nature involves a high degree of risk. What is more, given the relatively high interest rates that prevailed in Palestine, any hoarding of land involved a considerable cost. It is, in fact, quite possible that the land shortage in the important urban centers would have been mitigated had farmland been privately owned. Private owners of farmland would have been more responsive to market trends, which would have made it easier to expand the supply of urban land by reclassifying it. Public owners could afford not to respond to market signals, thereby aggravating the situation. There is empirical evidence for this supposition: after independence, new towns were established on publicly owned land. The jealousy with which the Commission for the Preservation of Farmland (a statutory body) guarded its empire is at the root of much economic mismanagement in these new towns.

The one argument that must be judged as having been valid is the settlement argument. Given that the Jewish newcomers could not have competed with Arab labor, the only way to return them to the land was by making them small-time owners. However, none of the reasons for national ownership apply to urban land.

The Private Sector Flourishes

Another step toward basing the capital economy of Israel on uneconomic foundations was taken in 1921, when Bank HaPoalim, the Workers Bank, was founded as the financial arm of the Histadrut economy[30] *with national funds*, largely due to Ruppin's efforts. The Foundation Fund invested in the bank about E£40,000, which at the time constituted a significant proportion of the total finances at the fund's disposal. The objective of the new bank was described as augmenting the number of Jewish workers in Palestine and assisting cooperatives in whatever trade they may be engaged.[31] The Histadrut received 100 founders' shares, which guaranteed control of the board, and the Zionist Organization bought 15,000 preference shares. The fact that public funds provided a good deal of the new bank's resources prompted Levontine to express his fear that loans extended by it would be treated by the borrowers much like loans from the Foundation Fund.[32]

Not long after the Foundation Fund was created, the Fourth Aliya was bringing to Palestine Jews from Central Europe, who brought with them considerable amounts of capital. It was during that period that the first genuine industrial plants were constructed, chiefly the Shemen edible oil concern and the Nesher cement factory, both on purely private capital. This buoyed those in the Zionist Organization who had been unhappy with the official financial policy to the point where, in the Fourteenth Zionist Congress (1925), they mounted a frontal attack on Labor. The most interesting fact about this confrontation consists, however, of the abstention of some of the more prominent nonsocialist leaders from joining the forces of the political Right. Kurt Bloomenfeld, a leader of the German Zionists, even defended the principles that guided the socialist effort in Palestine.[33]

In the Fifteenth Zionist Congress (1927), the political Right managed to elect an executive committee in which Labor was not represented and pass a series of resolutions indicating preference for private enterprise. Unfortunately, these remained on paper, since no concrete steps were taken to dismantle the institutional apparatus, like the Foundation Fund, through which policy was being implemented.

The debate surrounding these resolutions provides excellent insight into the attitudes that prevailed in the end. Even as the boom in the import of private capital was occurring, its efficacy was strongly doubted by one of the leading exponents of the socialist ideology. According to this line of reasoning, private capital was excessively concentrated in urban areas, chiefly Tel-Aviv, which was founded by private capital and continued to grow without the assistance of national funds. It was also argued that private capital was invested mainly in urban real estate and was therefore "unproductive." Furthermore, it created a huge balance-of-trade deficit, as it supported a high standard of living without at the same time increasing productive capacity.[34] The latter argument is especially interesting, because it set the stage for the oft-repeated rhetoric concerning what the leaders of the Jewish community saw as excessive living standards. As we shall see, they apparently never understood that it is impossible to found an economy on uneconomic principles and then expect the agents in the economy to behave as though it were.

In 1927 Palestine was hit by a severe recession. The ideologues of Labor seized the occasion to pounce on private capital, arguing that the recession proved its inability to cope with economic difficulties. There was also the reiteration of the belief that investment in agriculture could not possibly be undertaken by private capital and even industry could not develop without considerable investment of public means. Industrial settlement had to be regarded, in this view, just as much of a "national settlement" as agricultural settlement had been.[35]

The unleashing of a renewed attack against private capital came against a background of very sobering statistics concerning the prospects of national capital. During the Fourth Aliya (1924–29), the Foundation Fund spent an average of £163,500 annually for agricultural settlement.[36] The costs for settling one family was estimated at £1,500–1,800.[37] This implied that the Foundation Fund could finance the settlement of between 90 and 110 families per year—not very impressive. Not surprisingly, Foundation Fund agriculture constituted only one-fifth of the total agricultural sector, when measured by population or cultivated area.[38] Private capital invested in Palestine over the years was three times the amount invested by all public sources combined.

The next few years proved the socialists, once again, quite wrong. While the Western world was in the midst of the deepest depression on record, Palestine was enjoying a tremendous economic boom. It was largely powered by immigration, especially from Central Europe, created largely, but not only, by Hitler's accession to power in Germany. The new immigrants brought with them considerable amounts of capital: between 1932 and 1937 investment of private capital in Palestine made up more than 87 percent of all investment. During that period private entrepreneurs constructed such pioneering enterprises as the Vulcan Foundries, Phoenicia Glass Works, and the Ata textile company. However, as we shall see in Chapter 5, the environment they encountered made it impossible for some of them to survive. Another important event was the founding in 1935 of the Discount Bank, with private capital imported by Greek Jews. In time, it was to become the only privately owned bank among Israel's four largest.

A story of private enterprise that deserves prominence in the Zionist economic hall of fame is the creation of Palestine Potash, whose successor is the successful Dead Sea Works. The idea of extracting the Dead Sea minerals occurred to Moise Novomeysky (1873–1961), an engineer at the Russian works on Lake Beikal in Siberia as early as 1906. He carried out the first survey of the Dead Sea in 1911. Between the years 1920–30 he carried out experiments financed largely out of his own pocket. Later on, as expenses mounted, he raised considerable private capital and received some public assistance as well. But what enabled the company to start operations in 1930 was a sizable investment made by the Palestine Economic Corporation (P.E.C.), a business enterprise founded by the Brandeis-Mack group in the United States, after their approach was rejected by the Zionist Organization. Public funds constituted less than 10 percent of the initial investment.

The story is important because it is hard to imagine a more tortuous road for private initiative. The climatic conditions at the Dead Sea are inhospitable. Access was hard and dangerous. In addition, the British Mandate government was not eager to extend the concession for exploiting the Dead Sea to, from its standpoint, a foreign (i.e., non-British) company, and therefore raised a multitude of obstacles. The Dead Sea Concession had to be negotiated with two governments: the British, and the Transjordanian. Experts from around the world offered their opinion that no Dead Sea venture could become profitable. On the operational front, there were no qualified personnel in Palestine, and the company had to train all the personnel on its own. As the company started operations, the German potash cartel, which at that time reigned supreme, tried to strangle the fledgling Palestine Potash by dumping its potash on the market at below-cost prices. Despite all of these difficulties, the company managed to turn its first substantial profit in its fifth year of operation, 1936. The following eleven years were all profitable, with 1947, the last full year of operations, yielding 16 percent on equity.[39]

The company's operations came to an abrupt end in 1948, as a consequence of Israel's War of Independence. The site of the northern half of the production facilities, at the northern tip of the Dead Sea, was occupied by the Jordanian Legion, which destroyed the buildings and looted the machinery. That left only the works at the southern end of the Dead sea, which had also been idled for the duration of the war and had to be doubled in capacity if they were to replace the lost northern plant.

The company had to face a new reality in two respects. First, because the concession had been granted by two governments, Palestine and Transjordan (today's Jordan), the Israeli government was not subject to any continuity: it inherited only part of the concession area. Hence, it could revoke the concession.[40] Second, there was practically no access to the southern plant, because the only road that led to it stretched along the Dead Sea, whose northern half was under Jordanian occupation. This meant that a considerable investment had to be made not only in the expansion of the Sodom plant, but also in a new road. The latter problem was especially hard, because the terrain the road had to span is a very difficult one.

In November 1948, the government appointed a commission whose task was defined as "investigating the problems associated with the exploitation of the Dead Sea and its region." It was headed by Eliezer Hoofien (1881–1957), the chief executive of the APB. Significantly, two of the commission's members were known to be hostile to Novomeysky. One was the secretary of the union representing the company's employees.

Even today it is difficult to avoid outrage on reading the commission's report, which was submitted in August 1949. The report is full of fallacies and just plain nonsense, all of it designed to justify what under the circumstances must be judged as the forgone conclusion, which recommended that the government take over the company either through negotiations or, if necessary, through unilateral action. So hostile was the commission to Palestine's most glorious triumph of private enterprise that it alleged that the company had used outmoded techniques for extracting potash. In point of fact, the same technique is used to this day. The report distorted the financial record of the company, painting it as an enterprise in trouble. This despite the fact that the 1947 balance sheet shows an accumulated cash reserve of almost £500,000, and over £1 million in total current assets, as against only £561,000 in liabilities.[41] Paraded as a professional and impartial analysis, the report played exactly the role it was supposed to play.

In 1947, total potash output was about 100,000 tons, of which about 57,000 came from the south. Novomeysky prepared a plan to expand the southern plant to a capacity of 130,000 tons, at a total cost of approximately $8 million, of which $1 million was to be a loan to the government for the purpose of footing half of the bill of constructing a new road.[42]

The considerations affecting the road were crucial. If the road's only purpose was to serve the company, then it could not be viewed as a public good. In that case the road had to be financed privately, and if the company could not be profitable under these circumstances, then it should have ceased to exist. But this is true regardless of ownership: nationalization would not have turned an unprofitable into a profitable proposition. If, in contrast, the road had other purposes, then it was a public good and it was the government's business to build it. The government's demand that the company pay for half the cost of the road was either too modest, or excessive, depending on which of the two cases applied. But because the government was apparently interested not in economic logic but in forcing the company into submission, the fine points did not matter.

The government also demanded that its representatives be included on the company's board. As a price for allowing the company to borrow from the Export-Import Bank, the company was required to raise a loan of $2.5 million for the government. The government also demanded that the company agree to be taken over by the state on one year's notice. All this occurred while the company was trying to secure loans abroad.[43]

While this war of attrition was going on the company conducted itself as though it was about to resume operations. Hence, it continued to incur considerable costs, which it paid out of the accumulated reserves. But even though the reserves were substantial, they were finally exhausted, upon which the company gave up the concession. In 1952 the Dead Sea Works, a government corporation, replaced Palestine Potash. Then, in 1953, the 78-kilometer road from Be'er Sheva to Sodom was constructed, thus affording access to the southern plant.[44]

The 1930s brought another important development: in 1935, a stock-exchange-like institution began operations in Tel-Aviv. Representatives from a dozen banks would meet every weekday noon and trade in twelve to fifteen securities. The main securities traded were those of the APB and its subsidiary, the General Mortgage Bank of Palestine, which had been founded in 1921; Migdal Insurance Company; Palestine Electric Corporation; Palestine

Potash; Portland Cement Company; and Palestine Brewery. Except for the two banks and Palestine Electric, part of whose shares were owned by the Foundation Fund, all the others were purely private enterprises. Even Palestine Electric had been pioneered by a private entrepreneur, Pinhas Rutenberg, albeit with considerable financial help from the Zionist Organization. Although private capital was busy constructing industry, it did not neglect other spheres of activity. A lot was invested in citrus plantations, and almost all housing construction was financed by private capital.

Rhetoric vs. Facts

Despite these extraordinary accomplishments of private enterprise—the official estimate put private imports of capital in 1933 at £6 million, and in 1934 at £10 million, as compared with a mere £750,000 raised over this two-year period by the two national funds (the Foundation Fund and the JNF)[45]—the economic leadership of the Zionist Organization reiterated its belief that only national capital could bring about the circumstances required to fulfill the destiny of the Jewish homeland:[46]

> Enormous amounts of private capital were invested in the Jewish plantations economy, whose area comprises 140,000 dunams [35,000 acres—Y.P.], and is going to grow this year by another 30,000 dunams. And the plantations sector constitutes, as is well known, the most important item in our economy, in agriculture and in exports. But all this flourishing acquires a different shade when examined from the point of view of Zionism. From that standpoint, every Jewish farm is valuable only if the capital invested in it augments the capability of absorbing more Jews from abroad. And this is the only standpoint from which we ought to deliberate the national value of a farm and fix its place in the hierarchy of our building efforts.

The importance of this declaration cannot be overestimated, for it replaces profit as a criterion for economic viability with the capacity to employ. The first thing to note about this criterion is that it is insufficient for making a choice. Let us suppose that one is given a set of investment projects from which to choose, a capital expenditure budget from which the chosen projects must be financed, and the technical data concerning the production processes under each of the projects (the production functions). Then, if the only criterion for selecting the preferred projects is the amount of employment provided by each, a selection cannot be made. Other criteria must be provided or the selection must be otherwise constrained. In this case, output levels of each of the products must be predetermined; that is, a system rather like the Soviet central planning system must be devised.[47]

The framers of the criterion were, of course, unaware of its logical flaw, but they probably did realize that it had to mean the creation of an atmosphere not exactly conducive to business investment. What they were proposing amounted to a belief that even private investment could be motivated by noneconomic considerations, which in the long run proved sheer folly.

The turning point in the prolonged boom of the early 1930s came in 1936, brought about partly by the "Arab Revolt," otherwise known as "The Disturbances," against the British Mandate and the Jewish community in Palestine. It was also caused by the decline in immigration, brought about by the restrictions imposed by the British government, as a step to placate the Arab population of Palestine. Over the next few years economic activity slowed down considerably, including, in particular, capital imports. Whereas 1935 saw a record £10.1 million of private capital imports, the 1936 figure was down to £6.6 million, and in 1937 only £5.1 million was brought in—half the 1935 rate.[48]

The decline in immigration caused a severe recession in the construction industry, affecting adversely the newly built construction-materials industries at a very crucial point, as they were just trying to get operations under way. The decline in private capital imports lent new vigor to the advocates of national capital. Whereas during the Great Depression the most important economies of the West adopted the Keynesian view—namely, that governments must increase activity during the down phase of the trade cycle—the onset of a slowdown in economic activity in Palestine was perceived as justifying the conclusion that national capital was essential in the process of development.[49] In other words, recession was interpreted as an indication of failure of the capitalist system.

World War II had two conflicting effects on Palestine's economy. On the one hand, citrus exports were severely curtailed due to both loss of markets and shortage of shipping capacity, which was needed for the war effort. On the other hand, industry flourished as it shifted to supplying the armed forces of the Allies in the region. This included in particular the construction-related industries. When the war was over, industrial enterprises had accumulated considerable cash reserves, and the atmosphere was favorable for renewed investment on strict business considerations. British and U.S. business concerns were showing interest in cooperating with Jewish industry in Palestine.[50]

Utterances by top officials of the Zionist executive committee following the war indicated that there was no change in attitudes toward the role of national capital:[51]

In the first stages of development a country is not an attractive field for private investors. The private investor is interested in safe returns and will hesitate to engage in enterprises which, although of cardinal importance to the economy as a whole, involve a somewhat larger element of risk. Whole branches of the economy, such as mixed farming . . . are of fundamental importance to the reconstruction of the National Home and development of Jewish economy in Palestine. They, however, can hardly be considered as a lucrative investment from the point of view of the private businessman.

All the themes are here: the peculiar view of the entrepreneur as unwilling to assume risk; a confusion of what is necessary for national survival with what is essential for a healthy economic system; a failure to understand that enterprises which are not profitable cannot survive in the long run; and the complete oblivion to questions of moral hazard.

Early Statehood

The ideological makeup of the leadership of Labor, which was the dominant political power in the first government of the new state of Israel and which was to remain in that position for almost a generation, was clearly articulated on several occasions after independence. It viewed private capital as relatively useless to the national effort. Yet, owing to the lack of national capital, it was necessary to invite private capital to participate, albeit reluctantly. But this was to be done only insofar as private capital would prove helpful in the national effort, and such capital was to be subjected to state guidance and supervision, as well as to a hefty rate of taxation.[52] Needless to say, under these circumstances foreign capital did not stream into Israel.

These attitudes were indeed translated into policy, as evidenced by the description of the criteria that the newly created Investment Center proposed to employ. Its objective was described as not only to encourage and direct investment that was deemed desirable for the Israeli economy, but also to prevent investment that was not desirable. Desirability was to be judged by the prospective capacity to earn foreign exchange and to create a lot of employment.[53]

Then came the highly inflationary years 1951–53, with an average annual inflation rate of over 33 percent. The worst of the three years was 1952, with an inflation rate in excess of 66 percent. Yet even while inflation was raging, the government prevented the interest rates, on which the law imposed a ceiling, from rising. Consequently, real interest rates were so negative (the above average annual rate of inflation implies an average annual real rate of interest of minus 18 percent) that private savings could hardly be expected to provide the wherewithal for investment finance. But the very negative real rates of interest also meant that money extended from the development budget was extremely attractive, as it was hugely subsidized. It was therefore much more profitable to obtain government money than to try and raise equity on the capital market.

Consequently, in the entire six-year period 1953–58, there were only three share offerings to the public. The capital market was dead.[54] Against that background, the government embarked on issuing indexed bonds, a process that ultimately led to the de facto nationalization of the capital market.

Appendix

The objective of this appendix is to demonstrate that the employment criterion is not sufficient for selecting investment projects, also showing what additional specifications are required.

Let L_i represent the amount of labor employed in the production of good i, $i = 1, 2, \ldots, n$. If all production functions are well behaved, then we can write

(1) $L_i = g_i (K_i, y_i)$,

where y_i represents the amount of the ith good produced, and K_i represents the amount of capital employed. The labor maximization problem can now be stated as finding, for $i = 1, 2, \ldots, n$, the quantities y_i, L_i, and K_i, which maximize

(2) $\sum_i L_i$

subject to

(3) $L_i - g_i (K_i, y_i) = 0, \quad i = 1, 2, \ldots, n,$

(4) $\sum_i K_i - K = 0,$

where K represents the capital budget.

Let μ_i and η denote the Lagrangean multipliers associated with (3) and (4). Then the necessary conditions for a maximum are

(5) $1 - \mu_i = 0.$

(6) $\mu_i - \dfrac{\partial g_i}{\partial K_i} - \eta = 0.$

(7) $\mu_i \dfrac{\partial g_i}{\partial y_i} = 0.$

From (5) and (7) it follows that $\partial g_i / \partial y_i = 0$, which is nonsense, because it says that for a given amount of capital, an increase in output will require no change in labor input. The algebraic reflection of the nonsense is that there are only $2n + 1$ equations to solve for the $3n + 1$ variables L_i, K_i, y_i and μ. The system is thus underdetermined, which establishes the claim in the book. It also follows that the output levels y_i must be predetermined, which invites a Soviet-type planning.

4

Obstacles to Growth: The Economic Culture

The Economic Culture

The term *economic culture* is designed to describe the complex of attitudes members of a society develop toward the economic environment in which they operate. Every society develops its own ways of viewing its economy and the problems that it presents. People are not born with established economic philosophies or with the information they need to make financial decisions and political choices. Rather, opinions and information are acquired through a learning process, which is very much determined by the economic environment in which people grow up, and on the experiences which they encounter. In this chapter, we shall deal with the economic culture as it concerns the individual, or the consumer. Treatment of the business sector is undertaken in Chapters 6 and 7.

Israelis grew up, and in many respects still operate, in a contrived economy. A contrived economy is defined for the present purpose as one in which there exists a substantial wedge, mostly driven by the government, between the productive sector and consumers. The wedge separates consumers from the productive sector in two ways. First, it causes signals observed by producers to be different from the ones observed by consumers. For example, although producers observe a low rate of interest, consumers observe a high one.[1] Second, signals transmitted by the producing sector to individuals are distorted, so that individuals observe signals that do not give them an honest picture of the producing sector. For example, there may be a shortage for nurses, but hospitals are not allowed to convey this information by offering higher wages. Nor are they allowed to charge higher prices in response to the increased demand for health services that caused the nurse shortage in the first place.

Wedges of this nature exist virtually in all free economies to one degree or another. For instance, there is a wedge between the prices received by milk producers in the EEC and the lower prices paid for milk by consumers. Every price support, subsidy, and price control produces a wedge. There is therefore nothing unique in this respect as far as Israel is concerned, and it boils down to a question of extent. An attempt will be made to show that the extent of the contrived economy in Israel is such that individuals operate mostly in response to rigged signals. They therefore have scant opportunity to come to grips with the real world.

Three major areas of the contrived economy will be described. The first deals with the most crucial component of the wedge: the separation of the productive effort from the reward. It will be shown that consumers in Israel enjoy a standard of living, both in terms of the rate of consumption and in terms of personal wealth, that can in no way be supported by what they produce.

The second major aspect of the contrived economy is the image the government has as the creator of the economy. Government policies over long periods of time have convinced at least some parts of the public that economies are created by governments.

Third, we shall examine the impact of the wedge on the willingness of people to assume responsibility for their actions. Here one confronts what might be viewed as a sort of moral hazard, where people act irresponsibly in the belief that there exists an implicit government insurance that will bail them out in case of trouble.

First, let us ask what is so bad about creating contrived economies. The answer is that it can be deemed bad only in relation to some criterion or objective. The Germans may be perfectly happy with the milk-subsidization arrangement, but when economic growth is as important as it is for Israel, obscuring the signals transmitted by the real world is bad. It is bad because it generates a misallocation of resources and is thus detrimental to growth. In the example of the milk producers, the subsidy keeps many more of them active in milk production than would have been the case without subsidies. These superfluous milk producers cannot be employed in alternative trades, where from the standpoint of the real economy they would have been more productive. Each of the aspects of the wedge causes, as we shall see, distortions that reduce the chances of successful entrepreneurship and therefore reduce the outlook for economic growth.

The Wedge Between Effort and Reward

Even a cursory review of Israel's national accounts suggests that something is amiss. In terms of income generated by its inhabitants, Israel is a middle-income country comparable, for example, to Singapore. Israel's domestic product amounted in 1986, using the official exchange rate, to $27.5 billion or, with a population of 4.3 million, about $6,400 per capita. This was an output rate very similar to Singapore, with its output of roughly $6,700 per capita. But in terms of living standards, Israel was closer to Italy, with its per-capita output rate of about $10,500. In accordance, once again, with official exchange rates, Israel consumed in 1986, privately and publicly, about $6,200 per capita, while the corresponding figure for Italy was about $8,200. Singapore, in contrast, consumed only about $4,000 per capita.[2]

To acquire a fuller picture of what is going on, let us consider the national accounts for 1988 from a broad perspective. Out of the total resources of which Israel disposed, 63.9 percent constituted domestic product and the rest, 36.1 percent, were imported. Out of these resources, 25.3 percent were exported, and domestic investment commanded 11.6 percent. The rest, 64 percent, were consumed either privately (41.8 percent) or publicly (21.3 percent).[3] Note that the weight of total consumption in disposable resources was only .8 percent less than the share of GDP in these resources; that is, in 1988 Israelis devoured almost all of their net output. Put differently, out of the 11.6 percent of resources devoted to domestic investment, savings out of domestically generated income financed only .8 percent.

This leads us to a major anomaly concerning the Israeli economy; namely, the very substantial unilateral transfers that the country enjoys. In 1988, Israel received $4.51 billion in unilateral transfers.[4] Translated into national accounting figures, this amounted to 7.9 percent of total resources.[5] Consequently, even though Israelis saved a very small proportion of their domestically generated income, they did not have to borrow a lot abroad to finance domestic investment, because the 7.9 percent of transfers came on top of the .8 percent saved out of domestic income.

Looked at in this manner, 1988 was by no means a bad year by comparison to some other years that belong to the era of stagnation, starting with 1974. Thus, we find that in five out of the fifteen years considered, national savings out of domestic income were actually negative (1974 to 1976, 1978 and 1987). In six more of these years such savings were below 1 percent of total resources. The data also reveal the worrisome fact that no trend of improvement can be discerned. In fact, the best year was 1977, with savings of 2.5 percent of total resources.[6]

The very unilateral transfers that allow Israel to finance investment out of excess imports without generating too much foreign indebtedness can also explain, in part, the high rate of private consumption relative to what is being produced, for some of the transfers are received by individuals, not by the public sector. This means that part of the income that individuals receive is unearned, not only in the sense of not being related to the productive effort, but also not derived from ownership of capital assets. Looking, once again, at the last fifteen years, we find that transfers from abroad to individuals constituted between 4 and 10 percent of net disposable income derived from domestic sources. In 1988 net unilateral transfers to individuals came to about $1.07

billion, of which over half was in the form of reparation payments by Germany to victims of the Nazi government.

The very low rate of national savings out of domestic income is somewhat puzzling given the fact that as individuals, Israelis are, at least some of the time, quite frugal. The data to support this observation is presented in Table 4.1. *Disposable income* is defined for the purpose of the table as including transfers from abroad. As is evident, saving ratios came close, at times, to one-quarter of disposable income—a very high ratio by international standards. For comparison, consider the fact that for the period 1974–86, the average saving rate in O.E.C.D. countries was 12.1 percent, with the highest rate, 14.2 percent, occurring in 1975. Over the same period Switzerland featured an average saving rate of 12.5 percent, and the average for the smaller European countries was 10.3 percent.[7]

If Israelis are such avid savers, how can the high rate of consumption be explained? And why do Israelis save so much? The answer rests to a very large extent with government policies. The sharp change in these policies since 1986 will also be seen to provide the explanation for the drastic decline in private saving since that year (see Table 4.1).

Consider first domestic government consumption—domestic, because Israel imports defense materiel financed by U.S. aid, which counts as public consumption—a kind of consumption that requires neither taxation nor domestic borrowing and has therefore no consequences for national saving. Over the past seventeen years, domestic public consumption ranged between a low of 22.1 percent of GDP in 1979 and a high of 30.9 percent of GDP in 1980. In contrast, the O.E.C.D. average public consumption in 1984 was 17.5 percent of GNP, and in Japan public consumption in 1984 was under 10 percent of GNP.[8]

TABLE 4.1

Saving Ratios out of Total Net Disposable Income

Year	Percent	Year	Percent	Year	Percent
1975	20.9	1980	21.5	1985	10.6
1976	21.8	1981	23.5	1986	4.5
1977	13.4	1982	14.6	1987	4.1
1978	15.5	1983	7.6	1988	7.9
1979	15.0	1984	18.9	1989	11.9
				1990	9.8

Source: Bank of Israel disposable income statistics, as published annually in the *Annual Report*.

The high Israeli rate of government consumption contributes one part of the explanation for the high rate of private saving coupled with a high rate of national consumption. First, some items that would have normally constituted private consumption appear as public consumption in Israel. For example, the government owns hospitals. All the expenditures incurred by these hospitals—salaries, purchase of equipment and medication, and so forth—constitute public consumption. Had the hospitals been privately owned, the cost to the government would have appeared as transfer payments, augmenting both private income and private consumption. The computed private saving rate would have declined as a result. The Conclusion is that the high private saving rate is partly explained by the fact that, from a national accounting standpoint, the government is doing part of the individuals' consumption for them.

But the more important explanation lies with the way in which the government has been financing the high rate of public consumption. Over the past seventeen years, domestic budget deficits ranged up to over 21 percent of the GNP, with the highest rates occurring in 1974–75 and again in 1984. These deficits were financed largely by the sale of indexed bonds to the public. Recall that these bonds played a key role in eliminating the free capital market. Consequently, these government instruments constituted the lion's share of the financial portfolio accumulated by individuals. By the end of 1985, governmental debt instruments constituted close to 83 percent of the financial assets held by the nonfinancial (i.e., excluding banks and other financial institutions) private sector. Of the public sector's debt, close to 96 percent was indexed, 56 percent of it to the CPI, the rest to the dollar, on which more later.[9]

On the basis of these numbers, we may conclude that Israelis accumulated financial assets almost all of which were not backed by any real assets. Rather, they were balanced by government IOUs. This, however, would be of no real consequence if we were talking about small sums. In other words, if Israelis were poor relative to their income, then it would not matter much that what little they hold in financial assets were government obligations. But this is not the case. As has already been pointed out in Chapter 2, at the end of 1985, domestic public debt constituted over 133 percent of the GNP. Israelis were thus very rich in financial assets relative to their income.[10]

How rich Israelis became relative to their income is also evident from a study that compared net financial wealth to the GNP, which represents income, in several countries. The comparison is revealing indeed: at the end of 1979, net individual financial wealth in Israel totalled 104 percent of the GNP, whereas the comparable ratios were 37 percent for the United Kingdom and 8 percent for the United States.[11] The reason for this astounding gap is unambiguous: although in the industrial countries included in the study the inflationary process of the late 1960s and 1970s eroded the real values of both financial assets and financial liabilities (and this is true for all developed countries), that is, affected both sides of the household's balance sheet, the erosion process applied in Israel to household liabilities alone, because assets had been protected by indexation. Israelis thus became relatively well to do in a manner totally unrelated to their productive effort or to the accumulation of real assets by the economy. So what is the source of all this wealth?

One way to get an answer is to consider the balance sheet of every sector of the economy (households, firms, etc.), except the one for the central bank. If one adds up all the balance statements, then after all the like terms cancel out, one is left with an equation that has on one side household equity and international debt and on the other the real assets of the private sector, both consumption and productive assets. One can thus state that the source of finance of real private wealth is equity and foreign loans. But how did private consumers come by assets financed by foreign loans? The average Israeli certainly did not go to Chase Manhattan to take out a loan with which to finance his or her apartment.

The answer lies with the asymmetry of indexation. The government borrowed abroad, and lent unindexed funds. Money so extended was used to purchase, say, an apartment. But whereas the apartment was there to stay on the asset side of the balance sheet of households, the liability disappeared quickly because of inflation. So households were left with the assets, and the government was left with the liability. The money that households did not use to amortize the real value of their mortgage loans could be used for consumption, supplied to a considerable degree by imports.

At the end of 1988, the private sector was estimated to have owned real wealth of about $85 billion, reckoned at the official exchange rate. The net foreign debt stood at about $19 billion. This means, that upward of a fifth of the wealth was financed by loans from abroad. This is, partly, what people in Israel allude to when they say that Israelis are rich, but Israel is poor.

The differential effect of inflation on financial assets and financial liabilities of the household sector created a particularly interesting situation in housing. The first important consequence was that, because of debt erosion, the portion out of their income that Israelis had to devote to mortgage payments dwindled, so that, although they were increasing the share of equity (or the share of foreign indebtedness) in their houses or apartments, they could devote increasing income shares to the acquisition of other assets. Second, the anticipated subsidy translated, in the eyes of people looking for housing, into low housing prices. This caused a vast increase in the quantity of housing demanded, putting a lot of pressure on supplies. The market prices of houses thus soared. From the beginning of 1970 to the end of 1975, the housing price index increased by 33.6 percent relative to the consumer price index, implying a real appreciation of the average apartment by that much.[12] The upshot was then, and still is, that many Israelis own housing they would be unable to afford at market prices, given their disposable income.

The facts are unmistakable: in a survey that covered the period alluded to earlier—1970–75—the ratio of housing prices to incomes was found to range as high as 7.4. The average urban ratio for the last quarter of 1975 was 5.1, and in Jerusalem it was 6.9.[13] This means, that a family needed almost seven years of income to buy its dwelling. By way of comparison, consider the fact that in 1988, it was considered a sign of considerable affluence that middle-aged households in Britain were becoming the owners of housing whose value was three times disposable income,[14] whereas the total value of their real assets came to 5.7 times their disposable income.[15]

To further illustrate what the ratio of housing values to income in Israel means, suppose that the anonymous Jerusalem family mentioned in the survey could obtain a twenty-five-year mortgage loan at 8 percent interest, to be repaid in equal installments. Then our family would have to use almost *two-thirds* of its income each month to discharge the monthly payment on the mortgage. The normal portion of income devoted to that task in the United States, for instance, is 20 to 30 percent.

As pointed out, it is not clear that the government ever intended to subsidize housing on such a grand scale, but once a population gets used to this sort of a handout, it is very difficult to wean it. Thus, in 1988 the government was still providing substantial subsidies to "eligible young couples," one of the many eligibility groups to which we return later. The least eligible of the young couples received from the government a mortgage loan that financed 28 percent of the cost of a three-room flat, and the interest charged implied a subsidy of 9 percent of the cost; the most eligible enjoyed a finance rate of 55 percent, with an estimated subsidy of 38 percent. The accent here is on *estimated,* since part of the government mortgage loan is unindexed; that is, it is designed to erode with inflation. Because inflation rates are not known in advance, the subsidization rate can be only guessed at. Moreover, subsidization rates have been increasing, as have financing rates.[16] With the advent of the massive immigration of Soviet Jews to Israel, a repetition of the housing story is already in the making.

It is clear, then, that the mechanism which allowed the government to capture the capital market, that is, borrowing indexed and lending unindexed funds, is also the mechanism that facilitated the high rate of personal saving and produced private fortunes. But starting with 1985, the government slashed its deficit to such an extent that in 1986 and 1987 the deficit shrank to 1.7 and .9 percent of the GNP, respectively.[17] With the government doing very little new borrowing, indexed bonds became scarce. But because the capital market hardly offered alternative avenues for saving, personal saving rates plunged to 4.5 percent and 4.1 percent of net disposable income from all sources (i.e., including income in the form of transfers from abroad) in 1986 and 1987, respectively.[18] In 1989 the government's deficit increased to 5.8 percent, and the saving rate to 11.9 percent of the GNP.[19]

Indexed bonds and saving accounts have not been the only financial device that has driven a wedge between the Israeli citizen and the real economy; *patam* accounts have been another such device, but they have provided insurance against changes in the exchange rate, rather than against inflation. This type of account became widely accessible to the public after the Reform of 1977, which is discussed in detail later on. Its particular form of indexation allowed individuals to open accounts indexed to the rate of exchange of a foreign currency of their choice. For instance, suppose an individual deposited IS1,000 on May 1, 1980, for 3 months, indexed to the U.S. dollar. On the day the deposit was made, IS1,000 was worth $231.91. So the individual is viewed as having deposited that amount in dollars, although the transaction involved no foreign exchange of any sort. On July 31, 1980, when the account was due, the rate of exchange was IS5.238 per dollar. Hence, our individual could withdraw IS1,214.74 plus the interest accrued on this amount, which at that time happened to be 13.1 percent in annual terms, or 3.1 percent per quarter. The individual thus withdrew in all IS1,252.40. Of course, because of inflation most of the profit of IS252.40 constituted paper profit and not purchasing-power profit.

The peculiarity of this arrangement stems from the differences between it and indexation in general. True, in terms of benefits to the depositors, there is no difference in principle between indexation to the CPI and indexation to the rate of exchange. However, with regard to the former, banks could also lend indexed to the CPI, whereas they were barred from using *patam* deposits for lending funds indexed to the exchange rate. Hence, foreign-exchange linked liabilities of the banking system could not be matched by foreign-exchange linked assets, except by making deposits at the Bank of Israel.

For example, at the end of 1980 virtually all the liabilities of the commercial banking system generated by *patam* accounts were offset by deposits with the Bank of Israel. This meant that the commercial banking system was in effect holding 100 percent reserves against *patam* accounts.[20] It could do so because the Bank of Israel was willing to assume foreign-exchange denominated obligations that exceeded by far its real foreign-exchange reserves; hence the artificiality of the arrangement.

Consider, for instance, the balance sheet of the Bank of Israel for December 31, 1984: although its foreign currency assets totalled IS2,085.6 billion, its foreign-currency denominated obligations came to IS4,287.8 billion.[21] Of course, whereas assets consisted of real foreign currency, mostly in the form of bank deposits abroad, most of the obligations were in the form of shekel bank reserves indexed to foreign exchange. Still, if a run on foreign-exchange indexed bank accounts had taken place (a run that need not be a run on banks in general), the Bank of Israel would not have the theoretical ability to finance its obligations to the commercial banking system by selling foreign exchange on the domestic market. It would have had to resort to printing money. Put differently, the Bank would not have been able to neutralize the infusion of money into the economy by soaking it up through the sale of foreign exchange. The individual citizen was, of course, unaware of all these intricacies and responded as though *patam* accounts were actually generated by the real economy. As part of the reform started in 1985, new deposits in *patam* accounts are no longer accepted as of August 1, 1988.

The adverse impact of unearned wealth on economic growth manifests itself in two ways. The first, which is the more specific, is the distortion of resource allocation occasioned by the excessive demand for housing. Not only did highly subsidized housing cause Israelis to live in more spacious abodes than they would have otherwise, but the fact that houses yield an attractive rate of return on investment causes many Israelis to own apartments in which they do not live. In many cases these apartments were occupied by no one,[22] so contributed nothing to the supply of housing. People hold them as pure investment. This not only attracts more productive resources into the housing sector than would be needed if demand for apartments had merely represented demand for living accommodations, but also fuses the functions of saving and investment. It is the saver who decides, in this instant, how the savings will be invested. This is not generally an efficient distribution of decision-making.

The other, more general, ill effect of the high ratio of wealth to income lies with the very fact that Israelis are much richer than their earning power would have allowed them to become. This cannot be conducive to growth. When people become more affluent they place more value on leisure than on extra income, and this means less work. It is also well known that when pay rates exceed certain levels, labor unions shift the emphasis of their demands from pay hikes to fringe benefits, including in particular more generous vacation terms. In Israel this rearranging of priorities has been attained at much lower levels of productivity than in other countries, precisely because high levels of wealth have been attained long before the production rates that could create them.

Evidence to support this analysis emerges from comparing weekly working hours in Israel and some of the industrial economies. In 1986, the average industrial worker in Israel worked 39.3 hours per week.[23] Some comparable rates in 1986 were 37.1 hours in Australia, 38.6 hours in France, 40.7 hours in the United States, 41.3 hours in Ireland, and 42.8 hours in Switzerland.[24] The numbers suggest that Israel's industrial workers allocate their time between work and leisure roughly on a par with their counterparts in the most highly developed economies. This is despite the fact that, during working hours, Israelis produce a lot less than what is common in the rich economies. Moreover, the gap is increasing. For example, the cumulative productivity gain per worker from 1980 to 1985 was 2 percent in Israel; whereas in the United States it was 4 percent; in Canada, 5.5 percent; in France, 7 percent; in the United Kingdom, 12.5 percent; and in Japan, 15.5 percent.[25]

The wedge driven between individual effort and reward is also manifest to a very considerable extent in the labor market. In this particular instance the wedge is consistent with the basic tenet of socialism: *from each according to his or her ability, to each according to his or her needs*. The trouble is that it is far easier to educate people to demand from the system what they perceive to be their needs than it is to educate them to contribute to society what other people regard as their ability.

Consider the typical pay slip in the United States, which contains, at most, five items, only one of which denotes the wage. The other four constitute deductions: federal, state, and local income taxes and social security contributions. Contrast this with an Israeli pay slip for May 1992 for a Hebrew University employee, which contains no fewer than *fourteen* wage items, in the following order: (1) the "wage," which corresponds to the sole wage item in the U.S. slip; (2) a seniority supplement, although the first item already contains a seniority component; (3) reimbursement for travel expenses; (4) reimbursement for phone expenses (neither of the last two items requires an itemized statement by the employee); (5) an "institutional supplement" of unclear intent and origin; (6) intercampus travel allowance (although the employee in question, as well as most other such employees who receive this allowance, never travels to other campuses as part of his or her job); (7) "production council supplement," another unclear item; (8) collective agreement 1991; (9) "effort and risk supplement," although the work involves no unusual risks; (10) collective agreement 1991–92; (11) overtime pay, which sounds like a legitimate pay item, but is not (the employee does not have to report overtime to receive it); (12) framework agreement 1987; (13) reimbursement for cost of using the private car (again, no itemized statement is required!, and the employe receives this supplement in addition to item 3!); (14) remuneration for supplementary education (employees are entitled to this if they prove that they have participated in courses for a certain number of hours).

To the uninitiated, the list of pay categories may not look particularly exceptional or bizarre. After all, reimbursement of travel expenses by employees is commonplace, and firms send their employees to courses and cover the costs. But these are bona fide arrangements. The pay slip described here is different in that the names of the items do not convey their real content. In some cases the expenditures which are purported to be reimbursed do not exist at all. In other cases they exist, but no monitoring or reporting of the amounts involved occurs, and so there is no relation between the expense and the reimbursement.

On the basis of this description, one may identify two fundamental characteristics of the wage structure. First, an employee's salary is definitely not viewed as a reward for work. Rather, the employee is rewarded for imaginary expenses and other travesties. This is exceedingly important, because these imaginary expenditures bear no specific relation to the type of job being performed and can be awarded without reference to actual performance. Viewed differently, one could describe wages in Israel, other than the first item (the wage component) as constituting compensation for the hardship incurred in the input process, not as a reward for the produced output. Thus, a divorcing mechanism between contribution and reward is established.

Second, the employee knows that all the rest are fictional items, sanctioned by the government, the labor unions, and the employers. It is hard to overestimate the impact of living in an officially sanctioned, make-believe world on economic behavior. When official organs knowingly participate in what everybody knows to be a charade, this lends legitimacy to cheating, such as unreported absenteeism.

When wages are not considered rewards for contribution, there is no reason to expect any particular link between wages and productivity. Thus, from 1973 to 1986, the real wage per unit of industrial product rose by 9 percent.[26] Considerably more dramatic is the rise in real labor costs per unit of business-sector product: from 1975 to 1988, this increased by over 33 percent in real terms.[27] A good deal of it resulted from expanded fringe benefits, such as the social insurance contribution by employers, and the imposition of various taxes.

An interesting facet of the story concerns the tax status of the various fictitious reimbursement items. Until 1976, many of them were tax exempt, or were taxed at a preferential rate, so the treatment of these pay items had at least been consistent: if they are reimbursements for expenditures, then they should not be taxed. In 1976 a tax reform (which was given the misnomer "wage reform") discontinued the preferential tax treatment, recognizing that the plethora of reimbursement items constituted regular wages. Unfortunately, the reform was not bold enough to abolish this bizarre wage structure altogether. The reasons for this will be explored as part of the discussion of the Histadrut's role in the economy.

The Government as the Economy's Creator

Ever since the establishment of the state, Israel's governments were determined to disperse the Jewish population over the entire area of the new country. It was an objective based on the belief that only physical settlement of every part of the country could guarantee Israel's sovereignty, and that unsettled areas might one day be reclaimed by Arab adversaries. This is still a widely held belief, and it governed settlement policies from early on, but especially since the settlement efforts in the 1930s, which were partly inspired by the Arab riots of 1936–39. In addition, it was feared that thick urban concentrations would present the Arab countries with a tempting target for air raids, because such urban concentrations are vulnerable to damage inflicted on their infrastructure. Because all of Israel's governments had assumed that the outlying areas, especially those designated "development areas" for purposes of the LECI, could not attract business without the provision of artificial incentives, they proceeded to promote population dispersal actively.[28]

Certainly the artificial population dispersal contributed to the formation of the artificial economy that generates the economic culture. But even if population dispersal could be effected without creating a wholly artificial economy, it might still constitute an obstacle to growth, in light of the fact that the most bustling economies are invariably found in heavy urban concentrations.[29]

Even if one rejects the assertion that population dispersal is detrimental to economic growth, there is still a question of means. People can be attracted to outlying regions by job prospects superior to those in the city or by a better quality of life: cleaner air, less congestion, and so on. The approach chosen by the Israeli government was to provide cheap, but not particularly superior, housing. It sought to attract people to the development areas through the construction of housing with public funds, housing that was then put at the disposal of newcomers at heavily subsidized prices.

The need to provide means of support to the dispersed population brought about all the inefficiencies and waste of resources discussed in Chapter 2 in connection with the LECI. What concerns us here is the impact the dispersal policies had on the attitudes of the population. People in the development areas clearly acquired a view of the government as responsible for their economic well-being. This became especially apparent as unemployment in the development towns increased and reached double digits during 1988 and 1989. The mayors of these towns demonstrated in front of the prime minister's office, demanding that the government see that new businesses be established in their towns. As a result of the manner in which the dispersal policy has been carried out, people in the development towns came to view themselves, at least in part, as performing a public service.

The Relief from Responsibilities

One of the more serious problems facing the economy results from the impression, gained over the years, that individuals are not going to be necessarily held to obligations they freely undertook. The problem here is that an individual who has any reason to expect to be bailed out in case of difficulties arising from his or her actions is likely to incur risks that would not be incurred otherwise. The protection of people from the consequences of excessive risk also constitutes another facet of the severance of the reward (in this case negative) from that contribution. As we shall see, the outcome for the economy as a whole can be very serious.

We have already touched on the retroactive annulment of loan indexation in several places. It is time to tell the complete story. This extraordinary episode began after the devaluation of 1962 and, as noted in Chapter 2, initially concerned home loans. The government allowed holders of these loans to either repay such loans in whole or in part within a short time without any indexation at all or to substitute indexation to the consumer price index for indexation to the rate of exchange. At the same time, a commission was appointed and charged with devising ways to deal with pressures brought to bear by farmers who were holding indexed farm loans. Under the circumstances, there could have been little doubt as to what the nature of the commission's recommendations would be, so it came as no surprise when the commission recommended, inter alia: that (1) payments on most loans be exempt from indexation for a period of three years; (2) at the end of three years, the outstanding part of the loan would be indexed to the consumer price index.[30]

Although not of direct relevance in the present context, the deindexation of farm loans was accompanied by blatant discrimination, for the deal applied only to "mixed farming" communities. This constituted a very convenient way to favor Histadrut-affiliated agriculture over fully private farming, as the latter was, more often than not, based on monoculture, primarily citrus fruit and wine grapes.

With respect to both mortgage and farm loans, when indexation payments on these loans grew faster than the borrowers' incomes, the debtors were not held to their contracts. The government allowed them to escape.

The episode that demonstrates most clearly the potential magnitude of the damage done to an economy when citizens are absolved of responsibility for their own misdeeds is the October 1983 collapse of the banking shares. The story has its origins in the early 1970s, when commercial banks started to prop up their stock by a variety of methods. Basically, the banks were buying their own stock anytime it looked as though its market value might decline. Consequently, banking shares came to be regarded as securities with a substantial element of insurance.

Normally, the safer an asset, the lower is the rate of return on it; that is, there is a tradeoff between security and return. Not so with the banking shares under consideration. Despite the high degree of security they offered, they also carried rates of return similar to other shares. From 1977–82 the cumulative rate of return on all shares traded on the Tel-Aviv Stock Exchange was 256 percent, or about 24 percent in real annual terms. Over the same period, banking shares commanded an average annual real rate of return of 22 percent.

In addition to yielding rates of return comparable to those borne by shares in general, banking shares were also far more liquid than nonbanking shares. For example, in 1979 all shares yielded a rate of return of -27 percent, whereas bank shares yielded -7 percent. During the first nine months of 1983, before the October collapse, all shares yielded about -30 percent, whereas bank shares yielded +9 percent. So, although over the long run yielding virtually as much as other shares, bank shares also fluctuated less than other shares, and most of the smoothing was done at the lower end. This made bank shares an extremely desirable portfolio component. No wonder then that, although bank shares constituted only about 8 percent of the public's financial portfolio in 1976, they constituted almost 34 percent of the portfolio in September 1983, just before their collapse. Their increased attractiveness tended, of course, to reinforce the upward spiral of their values.

The original impetus for the manipulation policy the four largest banks, and some smaller ones, adopted was the government's stranglehold on the capital and credit markets. Because most bank lending out of deposits was directed to one degree or another by the government, the banks were looking for ways to mobilize financial resources that would not be subject to government control. The solution was to raise equity finance. But to do so on a large scale, banking stock had to be made attractive enough to allow the banks to issue new stock at regular intervals. The way to secure attractiveness was price manipulation.

In the late 1970s and early 1980s, this operation degenerated into a system whereby the market value of banking stock was increasing at rates far beyond what could be justified on the basis of actual profitability. Just before the collapse, the market value of the banking shares was more than seven times the value of the accounting equity.

The critical part of the scheme from the banks' standpoint was that they were obliged, in cases of downturn in the market, to buy as much of their own stock as necessary to prevent the shares from declining too much. The risk involved in this policy was catastrophic, as we shall see presently, implying that the banks were behaving recklessly. To see why, consider a bank whose share prices begin to decline. To stop the trend, the bank starts buying some of its own shares. If the bank guessed the extent of excess supply of its shares correctly, then it would have bought enough of them to arrest their decline. In that case the operation would prove a success. But suppose the bank guessed wrong and bought too few shares. Then prices would have continued to decline despite the bank's intervention. This would have caused the bank to try harder the following day. However, the amount of shares a bank can buy is limited by its resources, and when these are exhausted, the bank has to cease intervention. The trouble is that at that point the bank has accumulated and is holding the largest possible inventory of its own shares. So if their value continues to decline, the bank sustains the heaviest losses it could possibly incur—and in a situation where it had run out of resources anyway. Not only was this danger constantly present, but it could have been aggravated by the failure to arrest price declines on the first try. The public, fully aware of the fact that banks manipulated their shares, was prone to interpret the failure as a signal that the bank possessed insufficient resources to deal with the problem. This could cause panic selling—a run on banking shares as it were—thus bringing about the very insufficiency of resources that had been feared.

The evidence is very clear: on the eve of their collapse, the market value of the combined holdings of bank shares at the disposal of the manipulating banks amounted to almost twice these banks' combined equity. A drop of 50 percent in the market value would have wiped out the banks' net worth.

The willingness of the banks to incur risk to such an extent was itself a manifestation of the fact that they felt themselves insured by the government. This, by the way, despite the fact that, contrary to the United States, deposits in Israel are not formally insured, and Israel has no body equivalent to the FDIC or FSLIC.

The risk, which was severe in any event, was made even larger by the fact that the banks used foreign currency borrowing to finance the acquisition of shares. Banks would borrow dollars through their subsidiaries abroad, convert the borrowed funds into Israeli currency, and use the proceeds to buy shares. This means that they were acquiring domestically denominated assets with dollar-denominated obligations, thus entering a very dangerous position. A large devaluation of the domestic currency could result in grave trouble, if banking shares prices were to fail to keep pace with the foreign-exchange rates.

In October 1983, the worst fears materialized: the banks ran out of financial means without having stemmed the decline of share values. The government entered with a plan that turned the banking shares into dollar-denominated bonds, fixing their value at about 70 percent of what it had been just before the crash.[31] For the majority of owners, that meant a complete rescue, because share values had been climbing up until a few days before the collapse. Thus, only stock that had been purchased within six months or so of the collapse did not get fully compensated by the generous government arrangement. Once again, the government made it possible for the public not to honor a contract when the results of the deal governed by the contract turned out to be less gratifying than had been expected. We shall return to the story in Chapter 10, where its relation to the inflationary process and exchange-rate policy will be examined.

The latest episodes of retroactive rescue occurred in 1989 and 1991. People who had undertaken mortgage loans at interest rates exceeding, in some cases, 12 percent in real terms, had the interest reduced, after a series of demonstrations and vigorous lobbying. They were also allowed to refinance their mortgage loans at lower interest rates, without paying the penalty for early repayment of the old loans.

The moral of these stories is crucial. Put simply, the conclusion is that Israel's governments have been educating the citizens not to assume responsibility for financial decisions, if such decisions turn out to have been the wrong ones. This is a devastating approach because of the universal moral hazard it creates. The public acquires the notion that the government is in a position to provide it with blanket insurance, regardless of the outcome. So the public turns to the government whenever things go wrong, regardless of the cause. And every time the government responds, it reinforces the feeling that no personal responsibility need be assumed.

5

THE ECONOMIC CULTURE: THE ORIGINS

The Basic Ideology

The artificial economy of Israel is rooted in the very ideology that governed the early settlement of Palestine, both social and national. As already noted, the socialist Zionists who immigrated to Palestine after the turn of the century held that the national redemption of the Jews was necessarily intertwined with their social salvation. But the very welding together of the socialist ideology and nationalism already involved a certain amount of artificiality. The combination of Zionism and socialism had been challenged vigorously by the leader of the Revisionist Zionists, Ze'ev Jabotinsky (1880–1940). He insisted that Zionism must be the sole occupier of the ideological front seat, and that all other concerns should be postponed until after the main objective of Zionism—the creation of a Jewish majority in Palestine—had been achieved.[1]

In principle, socialism and nationalism were contradictory. Socialism was supposed to change the order of the world so as to render national differences insignificant. The real battle, according to the socialists, was not between nations, but between the oppressed workers of the world and their oppressors everywhere. Nor was there any real reason for hatred on the basis of race or religion: it had all been the contrivance of the ruling classes, who sought to perpetuate their rule by pitting worker against worker. The implication was that the salvation of the Jews would come automatically with the triumph of the socialist revolution. Hence, a reconciliation of socialism and Zionism presented a difficult intellectual problem.

The first to try to resolve the apparent contradiction between socialism and Zionism was Moshe Syrkin (1868–1924). His reasoning was based on the belief that antisemitism grew out of the class structure that characterized the Jewish community in the diaspora of Eastern Europe. But Ber Borochov (1881–1919), considered the father of Zionist socialism, provided the definite framework for doing what Syrkin had suggested.[2] His basic argument was that the Jews could not be salvaged unless they acquired an employment structure similar to that which characterized their host nations. The reality had been that Jews in Eastern Europe, with whom Borochov was familiar, were concentrated in small-time commerce and finance. This occupational structure had been brought about by a combination of expulsions of Jews from certain areas and restrictions imposed on them. On the one hand, they were prohibited from owning land, so they were forced to live in urban areas and engage in urban trades. On the other hand, they were chased from time to time from their places of abode and so preferred to have their wealth invested in easily movable assets. That implied financial assets, and so Jews engaged a lot in banking and other forms of financial market activities. This, argued Borochov, constituted a very unhealthy occupational structure, which he dubbed *the upside-down pyramid.* Liberation of the Jews therefore could be accomplished only if they again became farmers and industrial workers, that is, if the pyramid were rectified, and that could not be attained in the Diaspora.

The conditions of the Jewish population that had existed in Palestine prior to the start of immigration in the 1870s lent reinforcement to the perceived need to change the occupational structure. Of the 20–25,000 Jews living in Palestine at the time, practically all were concentrated in Jerusalem, Tiberias, and Safed. Although there were small merchants and artisans among them, they survived mostly on donations collected abroad.

The advent of Zionist socialism actually caused the Jewish socialists to split. Some, who formed the non-Zionist Bund, adhered to the idea that Jews would be liberated by the socialist revolution in any event and therefore did not need to form a national movement. They were wrong, but they were consistent in the sense that they did not bend their socialist beliefs to fit what were in principle conflicting aspirations.

The argument that had been invented to make socialism compatible with nationalism gained enormous stature in the Zionist movement. The idea of returning to a healthier occupational structure became so powerful that even a nonsocialist like Arthur Ruppin stated with great conviction:[3]

> Outside Palestine the Jewish population is composed in such a way as to resemble a pyramid whose broad base consists of merchants, their employees and commercial middlemen. These are followed by industrialists, by professional men (doctors, lawyers, engineers, teachers, journalists, artists, etc.), and by artisans (especially tailors, bootmakers, tinkers, glaziers, and goldsmiths), and it is only when we reach the narrow apex of the structure that we find farmers and industrial laborers. The order of that pyramid must in Palestine be exactly reversed, if agriculture is to be the foundation of economic life.

How uncritically Ruppin accepted this ideological dogma can be inferred from the fact that the pyramid he described, based on his Central

European experience, looked nothing like the pyramid of Eastern Europe, where the ideology was born. There were no Jewish industrialists in Eastern Europe to speak of, and the highly educated proportion of the Jewish population there was much smaller than that of Central Europe, which for the present purpose is taken to include the Austro-Hungarian Empire. So the extensive reference around 1925 to professionals is a bit out of context as well. In fact, half the Jewish population in the east was made up of laborers, small artisans, hawkers, and small shopkeepers and lived in conditions of near poverty. Almost half the delegates to the 1903 congress of the Russian Social Democratic party were Jews.[4]

That the principles governing the fusion of Zionism and socialism molded the policy of the Jewish labor movement, which dominated the Zionist Organization, was made very clear by David Ben-Gurion (1886–1973):[5]

> The main aim of the Labor Federation is twofold: (a) As part of the World Zionist Movement, to achieve the territorial concentration of the Jewish people in its own homeland . . . thus providing a lasting solution to the Jewish problem: . . . minority status, and the abnormal economic structure of the Jewish masses . . . (b) As part of the Labor Movement, to achieve in Palestine a Socialist Commonwealth, taking part in the struggle of the world Labor Movement for the abolition of Capitalism and the establishment of a Labor Socialist society throughout the world.

Ben-Gurion goes on to say that "Jewish Labor in Palestine was confronted from the outset with a unique task. . . . It had to transform middle class townsfolk into a rural working community."

The Origins of the Contrived Economy

As the preceding description and quotes suggest, the ideology, as modified to suit national objectives, was a purely social one. Nowhere is there any evidence that the belief in the primacy of farming was based on an economic rationale. In other words, the question of what kinds of economic activities were the most likely to provide the soundest economic foundation for the emerging Jewish community in Palestine was never asked. As we shall see later on, the preference for farming also acquired in time a political significance. However, even then economics did not play a role. In fact, the Zionist Organization was largely disinterested in economics, to the extent that Ruppin remarked: "I doubt, however, whether in an atmosphere so heavily charged with political interest I shall be able to hold your attention; for I am regretfully forced to the conclusion that among us interest in economic questions still takes second place."[6]

The important role played by ideology thus resulted in an attitude that ignored the economic incentives that the actual reality of Palestine provided. The labor movement and, due to its influence, the Zionist movement tried instead to implement an economic structure based on false considerations, creating over time the artificial system within which the economic culture developed.

There were two fundamental manifestations of this attitude. The first was the disdain the leadership had for urban life; the second was the framework within which agricultural settlement proceeded under the auspices of the Zionist Organization.

In the minds of the leadership, the city was associated with rootlessness. "Real production" meant primarily farming. We have already considered the role played by the perception of rapidly rising land values as the workings of pointless speculation. Because this process took place primarily in urban areas, and most particularly in the only all-Jewish town, Tel-Aviv, the leadership tended to associate the evils of speculation with the city.

The attack on city life became very vociferous in the wake of the Fourth Aliya, which landed on the shores of Palestine primarily between 1924 and 1926. It was a wave that brought considerable prosperity and spawned, as we have seen, the beginnings of real industry. The immigrants who arrived during this period were not all destitute. In fact, quite a few of them came with means, however modest.

The vast majority of newcomers chose city life over farming. Thus, the population of Tel-Aviv grew from 21,500 in mid-1924 to about 40,000 at the end of 1925. This was a growth rate unprecedented in Palestine. The burgeoning caused, predictably, land prices to rise at a very fast pace. A quarter acre in central Tel-Aviv, which had commanded E£30–40[7] in May 1924 fetched E£150–175 only a few months later.[8] All this prompted a key figure like Arlosoroff to state:[9]

> Here are the attributes which characterize this Aliya in the past two years: (a) Its excessive concentration in cities. Between October 1922 and January 1926, some 80 percent of all immigration to the country concentrated in our few cities, especially in Tel-Aviv—this is the main receptor of the new stream; (b) Within the cities the immigrants confined themselves to small-time commerce and industry and to all manner of intermediation. These sorts of economic branches do not provide a sound economic foundation and possibilities for expanded labor.

Particularly lucid in this respect were the pronouncements by Eliezer Kaplan, the treasurer of the Jewish Agency, made about ten years later, while the Fifth Aliya was streaming into Palestine from Central Europe. Like its predecessor, this wave also brought with it considerable financial means and settled overwhelmingly in cities:

> We saw in Zionism a revolution in the life of the Jewish People and its economic structure, a transition from a nation of intermediaries to a nation of real workers. Agriculture and the conquering of labor are therefore a necessary condition for the fulfillment of our desires. . . . My guess is that only 10 percent of the community are engaged in farming proper, both in plantations and heavy farming. Yet the question of the fate of the village is the question of the fate of Zionism.[10]

The ability not to look reality in the eyes is already clearly evident from these pronouncements. There is absolutely no question that the bulk of the immigration could not have been absorbed by agriculture. First, not enough land was in Jewish hands. Second, there was not enough capital. By one account, the settlement of a family on the land required £3,000, inclusive of land and buildings. This implies that even the settlement of only a few thousand families would have involved sums far in excess of what the Zionist Organization had at its disposal.[11]

The second quote also highlights a theme that has pervaded the thinking of almost everybody in the leadership of the Zionist movement, was accepted by the majority of the public, and comes through in some of the other pronouncements quoted here and in Chapter 3; namely, the distinction between "productive" and "unproductive" occupations. As we have seen, however, as concerns virtually every important question, here, too, there were dissenting voices, and none was more succinct than Jabotinsky: "All this literature which classifies occupations into productive and unproductive ones is three quarters useless and empty."[12] He goes on to argue that it is sheer folly to view only the production of physical objects as productive.[13] He cites several examples that put the distinction in an absurd light, among them the movie industry in Hollywood.

If national funds were inadequate, could private capital be expected to expand farming rather than pour into construction, commerce, artisanship, and industry in the cities? Given that the sort of agricultural settlement in which the leadership was interested called for small-time farming whose profitability was highly questionable, one could hardly expect this to happen. So the fact that the immigrants found opportunities in the cities was an unmitigated blessing. Not only that, in the cities they were busy building a self-sustaining economy and managed to support themselves and did not require financial assistance from the meager coffers of the Zionist movement. All this did not deter the leadership from bad-mouthing the city and portraying its economy as inconsequential.

Farm Primacy

The purity of country life in the eyes of the leadership, as opposed to the evils of city life, had a very practical implication: the financial efforts of the Zionist Organization in the economic sphere were directed over a long period almost entirely toward agriculture. But even here, as we have seen, economic considerations played little or no part in the process of allocating the national means. Agricultural settlement both constituted a goal in its own right and served as a means to another goal. As a goal, it was the diamond in the crown of the occupational transformation of the Jews. As a means, widespread agricultural settlement was guided by the belief that in the end, the shape of the Jewish state, which constituted the ultimate objective of the return to Palestine, would be determined by the physical presence of Jews on their land. This is also why the resale of land to Arabs had been abhorred to the degree described in Chapter 3.

There is good reason to believe that the logic behind the settlement of the land was sound. The thirty years of British rule had to be used to lay the foundations of a viable independent state from a territorial standpoint. And the effort had to involve a certain disregard for economic considerations. Had national considerations been the only motive for the settlement effort, then after Israel came into being, policies would have changed and economic considerations would have occupied their proper place. This did not happen because the settlement effort had also been motivated by a social ideology whose validity in the eyes of its exponents had been completely independent of the existence of a state. Hence, the settlement policy continued unchanged after Israel was established, and economic considerations continued to be ignored.

Because the settlements had not been based on sound economic considerations, that is, they had not been designed to open up financial opportunities for the individual settler, the new settlers could not be regarded as people engaged in farming for the sake of profit. Instead, they were seen by everybody, including themselves, as rendering a national service, at the expense of their own financial welfare, and as such they were entitled to all kinds of things. Most of all, this absolved the settlers from assuming responsibility for the economic consequences of their actions.

Consider an individual who engages in an enterprise on the strength of the belief that it will prove profitable. If the belief proves correct, our entrepreneur will reap the fruits of his or her efforts. If not, the entrepreneur will go under financially, and this will be the end of the story. Note that it does not matter whether the individual failed because the project could not be made profitable in principle (the individual had engaged in it initially on the basis of wrong expectations), or because the individual under consideration was simply not good enough and failed even though the project could be made viable in principle.[14]

Alternatively, imagine an individual who was told that, by undertaking a certain economic venture, he or she would be doing a lot of good to society, even though the venture itself may prove unprofitable. Suppose that it turns out that the project is actually in the red. In contradistinction to the first story, it now matters a lot whether the failure is personal or unavoidable (or both). If the failure is purely unavoidable, then the outcome simply represents the economic price that must be paid for attaining the social goal that had prompted the project in the first place. But there could also be a personal component of the failure, and in this case it is important to discern how much of the deficit is unavoidable. Otherwise, society would be paying a higher price than necessary to attain the noneconomic objective.

To identify the personal component, two conditions must be met. First, it must be identifiable in principle; second, somebody must constantly monitor the economic performance. In the case of the *kibbutz* type of settlement (for a brief description of types of settlements see Chapter 3), the first condition is not met. There is no way to compare the performance of one *kibbutz* with another, because no two are subject to identical circumstances. There are differences in climate, soil types, initial investment, security (some settlements were more prone to attacks by Arabs than others), infrastructure such as roads, and so on. Under these circumstances, the only monitoring possible was of the auditing kind, which is not a very reliable methodology, as it relies on hypothetical alternatives.

In the *moshav*, on the other hand, the first condition (identifiability in principle) is met. Here, a given settlement is made up of many similar and individual farms that can be compared to one another. So the "bad apples" can be identified, unless the entire barrel consists of them. But the second condition has never been met. In the first place, the lease contract with the JNF could not, for all practical purposes, be revoked. So even if a particular settler were found to be particularly inefficient, the land could not be taken away from him or her.

The other obstacle to implementing effective monitoring was that the *moshav* had been founded on principles of mutual assurance. This implied that the debts of any settler had to be borne by the community as a whole. In practical terms, this meant that the credit cooperative, one of the centerpieces of the cooperative form of farming, had to continue to extend credit to individual members even if they incurred considerable losses. And the cooperative itself was shielded from default through the generosity of, first, the Foundation Fund and later the government of Israel (the financial rescue operations that have occurred periodically are discussed in the next two chapters). Hence, there was no pressure on the cooperative to get rid of the less industrious and able members.

Only in the past few years has the system begun to break down, because the vastness of the financial mess in which farm communities found themselves outstretched even the means at the disposal of the government. This does not mean, of course, that the entire agricultural effort was a failure. But if nonviable enterprises can survive long enough by receiving shots in the arm, they create difficulties even for those communities that are basically healthy. The reason is that, if a sound undertaking cannot win the competitive battle because the unsound opponent cannot be dislodged, then the sound may become unsound.

One cannot avoid the conclusion that the thrust of the Zionist effort to create agricultural communities on as wide a scale as possible contributed significantly to the creation of the artificial economy, especially as it had been accompanied by a constant verbal onslaught on city life.

The Housing Sector

The housing sector's contribution to the artificial economy began shortly after the outbreak of World War II. During the first thirty years of urban development in Palestine housing, like everything else in the towns, had been provided by private capital. Immigrants with means, sometimes quite modest ones, would finance the building of apartment houses and lease the individual apartments to tenants for the market rent. Of course, like in any country with a fast-growing population, demand quite often grew faster than supply, causing rents to increase. However, the increase in rents engendered a clear benefit: tenants, in an attempt to find sources for financing the increased rents, were willing to rent out rooms. In that way they, in effect, shared their living space with newcomers. Everyone was thus living in a smaller space, but there was space available for everyone.

The special sensitivity concerning shelter is common throughout the free world. Shelter is the most basic of essential needs, and when people seem to have problems obtaining housing, the response is usually quite sharp. Housing shortages, real or imaginary, are always viewed as a sinister byproduct of the heartless capitalist system. In Palestine, such complaints acquired a special significance, because of their ideological hue. Quite early on, housing shortages in Tel-Aviv were blamed on rampant land speculation—a subject that has already been discussed at length.[15]

The first attempts to study the housing problem in a systematic fashion seem to have been made in the 1930s. The analyses that make the most sense focused on the problem of interest rates charged on mortgages. One such analysis drew on a comparison between conditions in Palestine and those in Europe and Britain.[16] In Palestine, expenditures on rent typically commanded 30 to 50 percent of a family's income, whereas the comparable figure in most European countries was 15 percent. The importance of the rate of interest charged on mortgages was demonstrated by a numerical example. The cost of constructing a typical family dwelling came to £400. As an approximation, it was assumed that buildings have an infinite life span. Then, if the rate of interest was 4 percent, a rent of £16 per year had to be charged, while at 9 percent interest the rent would have to amount to £36 annually. Say this sum constituted 40 percent of a family's income. Then £16 constituted only about 17.5 percent of the same income. Thus, the interest-rate differential explained the entire difference between the income shares devoted to rent in Palestine and in Europe.

Of particular interest is an analysis by the director of Shikun, the Histadrut's housing company. He declared flatly that neither his company nor any other could solve the housing problem, given the high interest rates. He observed that a typical worker, who earned £7 to £9 per month, had to pay £2.5 to £3 for a one-room apartment , or between 30 and 40 percent of his or her income.[17]

But all this only moves the question a notch, because one must still explain why interest rates in Palestine were so much higher than in Europe in the latter part of the 1930s. The question is particularly interesting because by that time Palestine, too, had been plunged into a recession, which started much later than the Great Depression. Interest rates of 8 or 9 percent are clearly not typical of severe recessions, certainly not recessions of the sort that characterized the first half of the century.

One possible explanation lies with the extraordinarily conservative policies of the leading banking institution in Palestine, APB, which held the controlling interest in Palestine's only substantial mortgage institution, the General Mortgage Bank. The attitudes of the bank are clearly exemplified by the key financial ratios it habitually maintained. In the period 1933–39, it maintained a reserve ratio ranging from 48.7 to 64.9 percent. That is, from every £100 in deposits it lent only between £35.1 and £51.3. During the same period, the equity-loans ratio ranged from 14.6 percent to 36.7 percent.[18] The General Mortgage Bank similarly followed an extremely conservative strategy. In the period 1936–42 it maintained an equity-obligations ratio (i.e., the ratio of equity to borrowed means) of between 18.3 and 31.9 percent. Moreover, from 1937 onward it kept increasing the ratio, and in 1942 had an equity-loan ratio of 25.5 percent.[19]

The explanation usually given to the extra-careful policies of APB is that Palestine had no central bank and therefore lacked a lender of last resort. Under these circumstances, the dominant bank saw as its duty to be prepared to act as though it was a central bank, for which purpose it maintained a very liquid position. Indeed, when the precipitation of the Abyssinian War perpetrated a run on some of the smaller banks in Palestine, APB did act as a lender of last resort, and successfully so.

It is not very fruitful to argue now about whether or not the APB should or should not have taken upon itself to act as a central bank. But the cost of its policy was definitely severe, as can be surmised from comparing the reserve ratios mentioned above to the ones maintained by the U.S. banking system prior to the establishment of the Federal Reserve system. From 1867 to 1913, the ratio fluctuated between 11 percent and 37 percent, with the higher rates occurring early on. By the turn of the century the reserve ratio was under 16 percent.[20]

Also, given the very secure position of APB, it is hard to understand why it was necessary for the General Mortgage Bank to be so extremely cautious as well. The point is important because it seems that the mortgage market was being unnecessarily starved for funds.

The Advent of Rent Control

Then came World War II, which brought with it a development that was to shape first Palestine's, and then Israel's housing situation for a very long time: the British Mandate's Rent Restrictions (Dwelling Houses) Ordinance No. 44, of 1940. The ordinance was issued, according to one account, in the wake of rapidly rising rents in Jerusalem, a process caused by the influx of people fleeing the Axis air raids on Haifa and Tel-Aviv.[21] The ordinance froze the rents which existed on February 10, 1940, and prohibited the eviction of normal tenants as long as they paid the rent prescribed by the ordinance. The rents for premises that had not been rented on the deciding date were to be fixed by rent tribunals, set up for this purpose on a regional basis.

Administration of the ordinance was placed in the hands of the War Economic Advisory Council, which set up for this purpose the Housing Accommodation and Rents Committee, chaired by Golda Myerson (1898–1979), who was to become famous as Golda Meir, the fourth prime minister of Israel. The committee's job was to advise the War Economic Advisory Council and handle the details, including in particular the assessment of rents in newly constructed buildings.

The proceedings of the committee and the correspondence associated with them reveal the magnitude of the problem created by the ordinance and the committee's dedication to its enforcement. Normally, when a price ceiling that is below the equilibrium price (i.e., the market-clearing price) is imposed, a black market is bound to develop, sometimes in an unexpected fashion. Usually, it takes the form of "under the table" dealing: the seller and the buyer agree secretly on a price that exceeds the prescribed level. The seller is rewarded by higher profits, and the buyer benefits by having been able to increase consumption of the controlled good.

"Under the table dealing" is unlikely to occur with a rental contract: a person could offer to pay a rent exceeding the legal ceiling, but once he or she assumed occupancy, the contract did not have to be honored. There was nothing the landlord could do about it, because the ordinance stipulated explicitly that no rent payments in excess of what had been prescribed could be recovered from the tenant. Hence, a different sort of black market had to evolve.

It did, and it acquired two distinct forms. First to flourish was the black market in subtenancy. Tenants began to charge subtenants rents that exceeded the rents they themselves paid. By doing so they violated the ordinance, which included subtenants in the definition of tenants. According to various sources, rents paid by subtenants could range from two to five times the rent paid by the original tenants.[22]

The implication was that economic rents were being created by the very restriction imposed on rents, but they were enjoyed by tenants rather than by landlords. According to some testimonies, there were cases where the original tenants, those who rented from the landlord, never actually occupied the rented premises, proceeding instead to sublet them.[23] Although the allegation was made by an interested party, it must have been true at least to an extent, because later on a decision to cancel the lease of tenants who fail to occupy the rented premises was indeed adopted.[24] From the standpoint of the housing problem, the existence of a black market in rentals was, of course, fortunate, otherwise some people would have found themselves on the streets. That is, if tenants had been prohibited from overcharging, it would not have been worth the while of at least some of them to sublet at all.

The other method for circumventing the ceiling on rents became known as the *key money* arrangement. Under it, a new tenant had to pay a substantial lump sum to the landlord to obtain the key to the premises. The practice had been widely enough spread by 1944 for the treasurer of the Jewish Agency to demand that the government take strong action against the practice, to the point of making it a criminal offense. Interestingly enough, he also demanded that in court cases involving key money, oral evidence be admitted.[25] The reason for this request is obvious: key money changed hands without leaving recorded evidence of the transaction.

Soon after Israel was established, it undertook to reinforce rent control. This it did through the Tenants' Protection Law of 1954. The consequences were unmistakable: although private construction for rental property provided the bulk of living accommodations prior to World War II, it practically disappeared after the birth of Israel. What the government did in response embodies perhaps more than anything else the total lack of comprehension as to the nature of economic systems and the way incentives work. It enacted two laws that were supposed to partially offset the impact of the Tenants' Protection Law. The Tenants' Protection (New Buildings) Laws of 1953 and 1955 stipulated that newly constructed buildings be exempt from the provisions of the

Tenants' Protection Law for the first five years after their completion. This was gradually extended to fifteen years.[26]

In 1972 all the then-existing rent control laws were replaced by the Omnibus Tenant Protection Law. A very significant stipulation of the new law was that any premises to which no tenant had a right on August 20, 1968 or premises that had been vacated after that date were exempt from it unless their letting involved key money. However, like its predecessors, the new law did not seek to abolish rent control where premises used for business purposes were concerned. Consequently, there are still many shops in Israel whose owners pay ridiculously low rent because they are protected by the law. No wonder, then, that by 1963, fully 60 percent of Israelis already lived in owner-occupied apartments.[27] Almost thirty years later, the incidence of home ownership in France and West Germany, among others, was lower than that.[28]

The question of whether the changes made in the law could have brought about a revival of construction for rent is, though, somewhat academic. This can be seen by considering the following chain of events. First there was rent control, which was strict enough to annihilate or at least sharply reduce construction for rental purposes. This created a situation in which people had to buy their places of abode whether they liked it or not. But because the government had already abducted the capital market, it had to direct the flow of funds to the mortgage market. Moreover, the government dominance also blocked the access of would-be builders of rental housing to the capital market. In addition, the government not only controlled the mortgage market, but also used it to subsidize owner-occupied housing on a large scale. This, too, made rental construction impossible, unless it, too, was going to be subsidized. But this sort of subsidization makes no political sense because the intended recipients do not receive it directly. The only way out was for the government to become the builder of rental housing. This has in fact happened, but only to a limited extent, through the government corporation Amidar.

It is not even clear that the successive changes in the law had been actually motivated by a desire to rejuvenate rental construction. One bit of evidence that seems to indicate that the government had never been serious about resumption of construction for rent is associated with the key-money institution already mentioned. It is, of course, impossible to determine whether this arrangement could have ever neutralized rent control to such an extent that construction for rent could resume, but the government made sure that the arrangement would not become powerful enough. In 1958 it enacted the Key Money Law, which provided that a tenant leaving an apartment is entitled to a certain share of the key money paid by his or her successor. In other words, the exiting tenant has thus been made by law a partner of the landlord.[29] The provision has been retained in the 1972 law. In fact, the law stipulated that a vacating tenant was entitled to part of the key money paid by an entering tenant, even if that tenant had paid no key money on occupying the premises.

Unions and Wages

The Histadrut, the General Labor Federation, was founded in 1920. Its very creation at this early stage is quite remarkable, because it occurred before a single real industry existed in Palestine. The only employers who could be construed to fit the model of a capitalist exploiter had been farmers themselves. Not only that, it was those very farmers on whom the leadership depended for training the newcomers and turning them into a "nation of workers." In other words, the farmers who constituted the object of the budding class struggle in Palestine performed the service of the Indians at Plymouth Rock. So an element of hypocrisy had been built into the Histadrut right from the start. A lot more will be said on this subject in Chapter 7.

It is also noteworthy that a strong federation of unions rather than a loose association was intended. Membership in the Histadrut as such is more important and carries with it more privileges than membership in an individual union.

The story of the wage structure has similar characteristics. On the strength of its pronouncements, the Histadrut struggled to achieve equality. It even instituted what became known as the "family wage." Under this system, wage differentials were based only on the number of the members in the wage earner's family. This was, of course, the ultimate incarnation of "to all according to their needs."

With all the rhetoric concerning equality, however, studies show that wage differentials within professional categories were not much different in Palestine from what they had been in other countries. Thus, in 1928 a typesetter in the printing industry in Tel-Aviv earned 83 percent more than his unskilled colleague, while comparable differentials were 97 percent in Tullin, 71 percent in Vienna, 41 percent in Copenhagen and 22 percent in Stockholm. Only Warsaw, with a wage differential of 180 percent, had a clearly higher rate of inequality than Tel-Aviv. As for the construction industry, a professional mason earned in 1931 in Palestine 100 percent more than unskilled coworkers, almost exactly like the difference in the United States; in Canada the difference was 190 percent, in Ireland 56 percent, in Austria 37 percent, and in Norway 11 percent.[30] So it is quite clear that Palestine did not exhibit a particularly egalitarian wage structure, at least not along differences in skill, even though skilled and un-skilled workers in a particular profession belonged to the same labor union.

The last caveat is important, because further examination of the data reveals an astonishing degree of equality across professions. In 1937, the lowest pay for a grade-A metal worker in Tel-Aviv was 144 percent more than the pay received by an unskilled counterpart; in the printing industry, the comparable differential was 140 percent. In 1963 the highest grade construction worker earned 70 percent more than an unskilled one; the comparable differentials in the metal and printing industries were 69 and 76 percent, respectively.[31] Another indication of the relative equality across economic branches is inherent in the distribution of mean wages across industrial occupations. In 1937, the standard deviation (scatter) of this distribution was ten, whereas in ten of seventeen countries included in a study that addressed the question, the standard deviation exceeded fifteen. Out of twelve industries, the highest paying (the food industry) paid in 1937 Palestine an average wage that exceeded the average wage paid by the lowest paying industry (apparel) by only 53 percent.[32] To understand the reasons for this phenomenon and the bearing it has on the structure of the wage slip in modern Israel, we must turn to an examination of the causes and consequences of the existence of a strong association of different labor unions.

On the face of it, there is no reason for labor unions in different trades to belong to a federation. The outcome of a wage bargaining process depends on the labor market conditions peculiar to each trade, and strong gains by one union do not imply strong gains by another, whether or not they are affiliated with a federation.

There are, however, at least two exceptions to this rule. The first is exemplified by the British system. There, a union could mobilize the assistance of another in case of a strike. For example, truck drivers would refuse to deliver a newspaper against whom the members of the printers' union were on strike. In this way a union could magnify the pressure exerted on an employer, and so win bigger concessions. This provides a clear incentive for belonging to a federation, whose members help each other.

Second, there may be political reasons for belonging to a federation. For example, unions might want to pool their strength on a regular basis to achieve common goals, such as passage of legislation in their interest. The story of the Histadrut as a labor federation clearly belongs in this second category.

The first rationale for a federation can be ruled out on clear empirical grounds. In Palestine, and especially later on in Israel, unions have desisted from striking merely to support the strikes of other unions. On the other hand, the political rationale was unusually strong in Palestine, and later on in Israel, because the Histadrut has not been merely a federation of unions; it was a political organization whose ideology and general political agenda was shared by the membership of the unions. Moreover, the federation was perceived as a means to achieve political power, first in the Zionist Organization and then in the independent state, by the political Left. One might say that the Histadrut represented an amalgam of Western trade unionism with Bolshevik political strategy.

When Israel was established, it inherited from the British Mandate only the most basic of labor laws, which had been enacted in 1945. These included, among other provisions, the banning of employment of young children and severe restrictions on the employment of older ones; restrictions on the employment of women in postnatal periods; and restrictions on the number of weekly hours for which women in industry may be employed.[33]

But perhaps more important as far as the labor market was concerned, the Histadrut thrived because of the fierce competition offered by Arab workers. With the objective being the transformation of the Jews into manual workers, it was imperative that Jews not be displaced by cheaper Arab labor. This could be achieved, however, only by obstructing the access of Arab labor to the labor market, which could hardly be achieved by each union individually.

An important instrument in the effort to limit access to the labor market was the labor exchange. Labor exchanges have existed since the early 1930s in agricultural communities, but they were not unified. Each federation of workers had its own, to the extent that in some places five or more different exchanges existed.[34] As was to be expected, the various exchanges competed fiercely with one another, a competition that sometimes led to violence.[35]

Efforts to create central, unified labor exchanges failed repeatedly because the smaller labor organizations feared that a central exchange would lead to their absorption by the dominant organization, the Histadrut, which according to a 1939 census included 77 percent of all farm workers. Not that the smaller unions had been opposed to a closed-shop arrangement in principle: they simply strove to maintain their organizational identity. Hence, they proposed to agree to a central labor exchange provided that employment would not be distributed directly to the workers, but rather through the various organizations.[36]

The first agreement to establish a unified labor exchange was concluded in Tel-Aviv in May 1937,[37] but it did not include all sectors of the economy and, partly because of this, did not last. The first branches of the more durable General Labor Exchange were finally established, under the auspices of the Jewish Agency in the rural communities in 1939 and in the cities in 1942. The various workers' organizations, with the exception of the Federation of National Workers, an organization affiliated with the Revisionists (the followers of Jabotinsky, the forerunners of the latter-day, nonsocialist Likud party), joined.[38]

In the end, on January 1, 1948, shortly after the United Nations had resolved to establish a Jewish state, the National Workers Union joined the General Labor Exchange, a step that ultimately led it to near oblivion.[39]

In all probability, the establishment of the all-important urban General Exchange can be explained as a natural outcome of developments in the labor market. The outbreak of World War II began to improve labor opportunities as of the end of 1939. True, initially the war served only to aggravate an already bad situation. The Palestinian economy had been gripped by a recession since 1936, and the war meant the loss of markets for Palestine's citrus industry. But later on, as Jews joined the British armed forces, and as Palestine became an important supply depot for the British forces (for example, the port of Haifa became an important British naval base), demand for labor grew quickly. With unemployment disappearing, the Histadrut no longer feared competition from the smaller labor organizations, and the latter became more confident that they would not be discriminated against in a unified labor exchange. After Israel was established, the Histadrut continued to play an important role as a political power base for Labor. It also played an important role in the massive social legislation that took place during the first decade of Israel's existence. However, the strength of the Histadrut also made it difficult to enact laws designed to transfer powers from voluntary organizations, such as unions, to the state.[40]

A case in point is the labor exchange, which became a state agency only after a prolonged fight. Still, the Employment Services Law of 1959 bears the fingerprints of the Histadrut to a considerable degree. This is primarily evident in that the law establishes a state-run labor exchange, the Employment Service, which institutionalized to a great degree the closed shop: it prohibited employers from hiring workers other than through the Employment Service. Hence, even though the closed-shop institution had never existed in Israel in the sense that all employees at a particular plant were forced to belong to the union, the conditions created by the law resembled a closed-shop arrangement. This is also reflected in the Collective Agreements Law of 1957. It renders the collective agreement a binding contract, obliging in many cases individuals who are not a party to the agreement. Thus, a collective agreement reached between a union and an employer applies even to those employees who are not members of the union. Hence, workers cannot compete by offering their services at a lower wage than the one specified in the collective agreement. The law also gives the minister of labor the power to extend by decree the scope of a general collective agreement.[41]

One important example where this power has been used on a regular basis is the collective agreement concerning cost-of-living wage supplements. Once the Histadrut and the Coordinating Chamber of Employers' Organizations reach an agreement in the matter, the government extends the agreement by decree to all salaried workers in the country, whether or not they belong to a union. A further strengthening of the Histadrut's grip on the labor market came with the adoption of the law for the Settling of Labor Disputes (Amendment No. 2) of 1972, a law that pertains to labor disputes in the public sector.[42] To settle a dispute, one needs representatives of both sides to talk to. So the legislators elected to choose on labor's side the union whose membership is the largest (even if it does not constitute a majority). In 100 percent of the cases, this meant a Histadrut union.

A very important support for the view that the Histadrut has been motivated to a great extent by the quest for political power lies with the fact that its representatives in the legislature opposed some fairly important labor legislation. Cases in point are unemployment insurance and minimum wage. It goes without saying that the Histadrut had not been against such legislation per se. Rather, it wanted to retain the administration of these labor-market institutions for itself, rather than letting the state do it.[43]

Paradoxically, the Histadrut's success in its efforts to achieve its goals through the legislative process eroded the joints holding it together. With every success, the common cause unifying the different unions shrank in scope; and the weaker the political bonds, the lesser was the subordination of various unions to the federation as a whole. In 1967 the Engineers Organization became autonomous, twenty-six years after its founding. It was followed by the Organization of Workers in the Humanities and Social Sciences, which became autonomous in 1969, the tenth year of its existence. The Union of Social Workers became autonomous in 1975, and in 1977 the Histadrut ratified a new form of labor union, which clearly pointed to an awareness of a growing incidence of special interests. This relatively new form of organization is characterized by unionism on the basis of an employer, rather than on the basis of craft, industry or profession.[44] Examples are the Union of Employees of Israel Electric Corporation and the Union of State Employees.

That a common political cause may be important in determining the strength of the federation relative to its component unions is also suggested by a survey that identified the components of wage increases. The main results are provided in Table 5.1. There are three sources for nominal wage increases: the cost-of-living allowance, the formula for which is negotiated for labor by the Histadrut; the component of the wage agreement also negotiated by the Histadrut; and the component of the wage agreements struck at lower levels, such as professional and local unions (we shall return in more detail to the mechanics of wage agreements in the next chapter). The period covered consists of two subperiods when viewed from a political standpoint. During 1976 and the first half of 1977, the Labor party still dominated the government; from the second half of 1977, the Likud party took over (while the Labor party continued to rule the Histadrut).

As the table makes clear, the share of the federation as a whole grew significantly after Labor had been ousted from power. The only exception is 1979, where the Histadrut's share was slightly lower than it had been in 1977, but still above the 1976 share. One can therefore conclude that the federation became relatively more active when the government was no longer dominated by its friends.

TABLE 5.1

Components of Logarithms of Nominal Wage Increases[45]

Year	Percentage of Increase Due to			
	COLA	Agreements		Share of the Histadrut
		Histadrut	Unions	in Total Increment*
1976	49.0	16.2	34.8	65.2
1977	56.5	14.3	29.2	70.8
1978	63.1	28.7	8.2	91.8
1979	58.8	11.1	30.1	69.9
1980	78.7	9.8	11.5	88.5
1981	76.2	12.7	11.1	88.9
1982	78.4	10.0	11.6	88.4

*Sum of first two columns.

Source: BOI, *Annual Report 1982*, p. 76.

In 1958 the Teachers' Union split: the high school teachers bolted the union and created their own independent union. This was a particularly important event because it was caused by the very attribute required to hold the Histadrut together; namely, a relatively equal income distribution. That within such an organization income distribution must be relatively equitable has been stated as a theorem:[46] "Distributional coalitions, once big enough to succeed, are exclusive and seek to limit the diversity of incomes and values of their membership."

In determining the boundaries of the set of feasible income distributions, the Histadrut confronted two constraints. First, the degree of equality could not be such that the stronger unions would be led to believe that they could do much better outside the federation's framework. Second, the degree of inequality could not be such that the weaker unions would be led to believe that they do not gain much by belonging to the federation. That is, they had to be convinced that they are getting something in return for not opting for independence. The problem was, of course, that the two constraints were not necessarily compatible, in the sense that there need not have existed an income distribution that could satisfy both. So a way was sought to allow sufficient inequality while maintaining a semblance of equality.

The solution was found in the plethora of wage items. The idea is simple: to devise a way that will legitimize inequality in the eyes of the less fortunate. That way the better qualified will have their cake and the less qualified will not feel cheated. This was achieved by paying for *input*, rather than for *output.* For example, rather than paying an engineer a higher salary than a technician because the services of the engineer are more valuable, he or she receives a supplement to purchase professional literature needed for his or her work. Similarly, the risk supplement is associated with the process of input, rather than production. This eliminates the jealousy factor. The extra risk incurred by a certain employee, real or contrived, legitimizes the extra pay in the eyes of those who do not benefit from a similar supplement.

Like any such contrived system, however, this one too has undergone considerable degeneration or entropy. One joke has it that now even those who cannot read, receive a professional literature supplement. Consequently, it has become more and more difficult for the Histadrut to control the individual unions.

Recently, a commission appointed to examine the wage structure in the public sector submitted a report that recommends the abolition of the plethora of wage supplements and the institution of a much simpler and straightforward wage structure. Both the public employers and the Histadrut praised the report, but, so far, no steps have been taken to implement the report's recommendations, and nobody on the Histadrut's side appears eager to push implementation.

6

OBSTACLES TO GROWTH: THE WOULD-BE BUSINESS SECTOR

The Business Sector—A Tour

This and the next chapters are designed to portray the business sector as dependent on the government to such an extent as to render it a private-public hybrid. Reviewing the main facts, the business sector may be divided into three categories: government corporations, Histadrut-owned enterprises, and the semi-private sector.

In 1987 the share of the Histadrut and its many affiliates in the economy accounted for 18 percent of all employed persons and for 21 percent of the GNP. Taken together with public sector-owned business, the two nonprivate components of the business sector accounted for 31 percent of all employed persons.[1] The largest industrial concern, Koor, is controlled by the Histadrut and together with some other Histadrut-affiliated industries accounted in 1980–81 for 22 percent of industrial product and 18 percent of industrial employment. In combination with the portion of industry run by the public sector, the shares in 1980–81 were 46 percent of the product and 34 percent of employment.[2] Out of the fifty largest industrial companies in 1988, the Histadrut controlled twelve (and the government seven). Out of a total of 102,600 workers employed in these enterprises, those controlled by the Histadrut employed 24 percent, and the share of government corporations came to 32 percent. Hence, less than half of the workers in the fifty largest enterprises were genuine private- sector workers. This is also evident on considering the ownership structure. In 1984 the public sector's share of ownership came to 25 percent, the Histadrut had 27 percent, and the private sector only 48 percent.[3]

The insistence on treating the Histadrut economy as a separate component of the business sector stems from its impact on the sector as a whole. To examine this impact we must turn to the foundations of the Histadrut economy.

The socialist founders of the Histadrut intended to organize the entire economy under its auspices in the form of a collection of cooperatives. Workers would own the enterprises that employed them, and no hired labor would be employed. All this was to be managed within the framework of Hevrat Ovdim, the Workers' Corporation, which was created in 1923 and in which every member of the Histadrut was to have a share. This should not be confused with what one normally means by *shares,* as the holders are not entitled to dividends nor could they sell their holdings.

Two attributes of the Workers' Corporation are particularly relevant to our story. First, the profit motive did not play a role. The charter of the corporation explicitly eschews profits, so there are no dividends to begin with. Instead of profits, the main objective was the creation of employment so as to facilitate the absorption of more immigration. The elimination of profits as an incentive had tremendous implications, because as far as the individual worker-owner is concerned, no meaningful incentive can be derived from the objective of creating employment. It cannot be translated into targets with which individuals can be presented.

The second important attribute of the Workers' Corporation was the link between the affiliated entities, which were organized as a mutual insurance group. The survival of every entity would be guaranteed by all others.[4]

For the first twenty years, the corporation owned only wholesale and retail networks and enterprises in the construction industry, such as the construction contractor Solel Boneh and the quarrying corporation Even Vasid. But in the early 1940s, the industrial holding company, Koor, was founded.

By its very nature, then, the Workers' Corporation could not possibly play the economic game along free market rules, because to survive in the free market a tireless quest for profits is required. However, it did not have to be profitable to survive. It could afford to play by rules other than those of the free market, because the parent organization has always had access to funds unrelated to its business activities, such as union membership dues. In years past, the Histadrut had also drawn on contributions, mainly from the labor factions of the American Jewish community. As noted in Chapter 2, the Histadrut has also had access to capital accumulated by pension funds managed by itself. This made it possible to remedy the connection between failure in the marketplace and survival by subsidizing its failing enterprises, at least for a while. As we shall see, this has, in fact, happened more than once.

The rules that governed the behavior of the workers' economy had very serious ramifications concerning the business sector as a whole. This is so because, if a group of corporations who do not play by the usual rules exists in the market economy and the group's size is significant enough to affect the market outcome, then other players should be expected to change their market behavior as well. Such a change would be induced by the need to play the survival game under rules that are not quite those of free competition. One possible outcome could be that the truly privately owned corporations will also look for sources of subsidy to cushion them against failure. Any success in this respect leads unavoidably to the creation of moral hazard, with all the adverse consequences for growth. As we shall see, this is exactly what happened.

The Economy's Openness

Israel stands out in terms of the openness of its economy. This means that Israel's trade with the rest of the world constitutes a very high proportion of its national product, when compared to other countries. The easiest way to compare the degree of openness is to examine the value of imports and exports relative to total resources—the value of goods and services of which a country disposes in any given year. It consists of what the country produces in the course of the year, its national product, and what it imports from the rest of the world. The disposition of resources consists of domestic uses, such as private consumption, and what is sent abroad—exports. The higher the ratio of trade, that is, imports and exports to total resources, the more open is an economy.

Applying this criterion to Israel, we find that during the past decade it has imported between 35 and 40 percent and exported between 23 and 29 percent of its total resources. For the purpose of comparison, in 1985 such world-class traders as West Germany and Japan exported 27 percent and 15 percent of their respective total resources.[5]

One crucial element in the explanation of Israel's foreign trade is the fact that the country could not have possibly reached an advanced stage of development without a great deal of imports. This is because of the almost total absence of natural resources. Israel must therefore import all the raw materials except those that can be produced by agriculture, such as cotton, and some minerals, especially potash and phosphate. Likewise, all energy needs must be imported. Nor is Israel capable of supplying its grain consumption, since rainfall over much of the country is too scant for growing unirrigated crops.

As noted in Chapter 4, Israel's external imbalance has for a long time facilitated negligible, or even negative, national saving rates. Thus, $4–5 billion in deficits, constituting up to 8 percent of the GNP, is quite common in recent years.

How are the deficits financed? Take, for instance, 1988, with a deficit of $5.4 billion. Unilateral transfers came to $4.7 billion. Of this, $2.9 billion constituted a grant from the U.S.; about $560 million came in the form of German reparation payments (which are now paid exclusively to individuals, not to the Israeli government); more than $600 million were transferred by the United Jewish Appeal and institutions such as universities raising money abroad; and the rest constituted various private transfers, such as property brought by new immigrants. It follows that $700 million of the deficit had to be financed by increasing Israel's net international indebtedness.

As long as its debt position does not deteriorate appreciably, Israel should have no trouble in rolling over its debt. However, it needs to service its debt meticulously. Net interest payments in 1988 amounted to 11 percent of exports, after having reached a peak of 17 percent in 1984. These interest ratios are not considered dangerously high by the international financial community, which is why Israel can still borrow without difficulty.[6]

What does Israel export? Turning first to goods, the two largest export categories by far were, in 1988, metal and electronics products, with almost 30 percent of the total, and polished diamonds, with 27 percent of exports. The metal and electronics category includes, in particular, Israel's exports of defense materiel. Next are mining products and chemicals, with a combined 15 percent of exports. These two categories are closely related, because a good deal of the output of chemical products is based on the two deposits of natural resources that Israel can draw on: the Dead Sea minerals and phosphate deposits. The fourth major group of exports consists of fresh agricultural produce and the agriculturally based food industry. Their combined exports came to a bit less than 12 percent of the 1988 total. Again, the two categories are closely related, because Israel's food industry draws much of its raw material from the country's farm sector. This includes, in particular, citrus fruit and tomatoes for the canning industry and cottonseed for the edible oil industry. The last category worth mentioning is the textile industry, with close to 7 percent of overall 1988 exports.

As far as comparative advantage in foreign trade is concerned, Israel's economy offers a mix of exports. On the one hand, many technology-intensive products are exported, as evident from the impressive share of exports originating in the metal and electronics industries. On the other hand, exports still contain a high component of polished diamonds, a product both labor intensive and requiring only relatively low skill. This mixed picture makes it very difficult to point to clear areas of advantage.

As concerns trade in services, the only aspects that deserve special mention are shipping and tourism. Regarding the first, Israel operates a large marine cargo fleet and two airline companies, handling both passengers and cargo. Total revenues of these operations came to $1.7 billion in 1988. Tourism earned in 1988 over $1.3 billion, whereas Israelis touring the world spent almost $1.1 billion. In general, although foreign exchange earnings from tourism are important, Israelis regularly spend almost as much for their foreign escapades.

The preponderance of imports of goods is made up of industrial inputs and capital goods, primarily machinery and equipment. However, the components of this category have changed substantially over time. One obvious example is energy: whereas in 1983 almost 19 percent of total spending on the import of goods (exclusive of direct imports of defense materiel) was devoted to energy, its share in 1988 was less than 9 percent. With raw diamonds, it is exactly the other way around: in 1983 they made up only about 10 percent of imports, whereas in 1988 their share approached 20 percent. The decline in the share of energy is, of course, due to the plummeting of oil prices. As for diamonds, their exports underwent hard times in the early 1980s, due mostly to the recession in the United States during that period. Diamond cutters found themselves holding excess inventories of unpolished diamonds, causing them to curtail imports sharply.

Industry

The most interesting aspect of Israel's private sector is the industrial story of technological evolution, which is important if one is to understand the country's place in the economic world. Between 1965 and 1984, the share of industry in total product inched from 26 to 29 percent, but a glance at individual sectors reveals a very uneven growth pattern, clearly biased toward more technology-intensive industries. Thus, for example, manufacturing of electric and electronic products grew from 1965 to 1980 by an average of almost 11 percent per year, or an impressive 360 percent over the fifteen-year period. The same rate of growth applies to means of transportation. The manufacturing of rubber and plastic goods grew about 8 percent annually over that period, and the output of petroleum-based and chemical products grew by about 9 percent annually. On the other hand, the output of textiles and clothing grew by only a little over 6 percent annually. More significant, in the last eight years of the reviewed period the growth in output of textiles and clothing reached only about 3 percent per year, whereas in electric and electronic equipment it was 7 percent annually.[7] So there is no doubt that Israel has been moving toward those industries that characterize more highly developed economies.

There are two ways to look at the composition of industrial exports. The first concerns the share of total exports each of the main exported items occupies, as was done previously. The second concerns the shares of sectoral outputs destined for export. Here a very different picture emerges. In the first it was found that, by percentage, metal and electronics constituted the most important export category. But an examination of the destination of the output produced by the metal and electronics industry reveals that most of it is sold on the domestic market. Thus, in the period 1973–80, the electric and electronic equipment industry exported 28 percent of its output, with metal products and machinery exporting 31 and 38 percent of their respective outputs. The textile industry, on the other hand, exported in the same period an average of about 50 percent of its output.[8] It follows that the textile industry was more export oriented than the metal industry. This is easily explained by the fact that a very sizable share of domestic procurement for defense comes from the metal and electronics industry.

In Chapter 2, it was pointed out that government domination of the capital market is likely to favor large industrial concerns. Reviewing the situation, one finds that although individual industrial plants are mostly quite small
by international standards, industry is highly concentrated. Although some
concentration in the sense of dominance of a particular market by few large
corporations does exist to a certain extent, concentration in Israel comes
mainly in the form of ownership. The nongovernment Israeli industrial scene
is dominated by three very large holding companies: Koor, Discount Investment Company, and Clal. In 1984 Koor owned factories in the food, chemical,
metal, electronics, mineral and mechanical industries. For example, its food
subsidiary alone owned, wholly or partly, more than forty enterprises, among
them some of the most important food industries in Israel.

Discount Investment Company and P.E.C. (Palestine Economic Corporation, the counterpart in the United States) are subsidiaries of I.D.B., the
holding company which owns Discount Bank, the third largest commercial
bank in Israel. Discount Investment has interests in the metal, electronics, textile, chemical, and paper industries. Outside of manufacturing, it is involved
in insurance, oil, shipping and construction.

Clal is itself dominated by the Discount Bank group and by Bank
Ha'poalim (Workers' Bank), which is the main financial arm of the Histadrut. It
has an industrial holding subsidiary, which has interests in a wide variety of
manufacturing enterprises, including paper and cement. The three groups are
intertwined not only due to the fact that Clal is dominated by a subsidiary of the
Histadrut, which also controls Koor, and by the Discount group which also
owns Discount Investment, but also because of joint interests. For example, in
1984, American-Israel Paper Mills were 25 percent owned by Clal and 14.9 percent owned by Discount Investment, which also owned 31.7 percent of Clal.[9]

One area of extraordinary mingling of the giants is the energy sector.
There are basically three oil companies in Israel: Paz, Delek, and Sonol. The
first is owned by a foreign investor, but Delek is dominated by I.D.B. and Bank
Ha'poalim; and Sonol is dominated by the Workers' Corporation and Clal.[10]

The extent to which I.D.B. is involved in Israel's business sector can be
further highlighted by considering the interests of its founders, the Reccanati
family. A study by the Research Department of the Tel-Aviv Stock Exchange
found that the family controls or has interests, directly and indirectly, in forty-
four corporations traded on the exchange, constituting 17 percent of all traded
corporations. In March 1990, the combined stock exchange worth of the
forty-four corporations was $1.7 billion, or 23 percent of the total value of
traded corporations. Another indication of the degree of concentration is provided by the observation that between them, corporations owned by the government, by Discount Investments, and by Clal constituted 50 percent of the
worth of all traded corporations.[11]

This degree of concentration has important implications in a number of areas. First, in a small economy like that of Israel, it constitutes a definite impediment to competition. Second, the political clout such concentration of ownership can bring to bear is considerable. Even if the government had not been inclined to intervene heavily in the economy for ideological reasons, it would have found it difficult not to intervene in the face of the concentrated ownership structure. For example, it may be relatively easy for a government to let an individual corporation collapse, even if it were a large outfit. And, as the Chrysler case in the United States indicates, not even that is always possible. It would be much more difficult to desist from intervening if a threat emerged to a concern that controls a sizable portion of the economy.

A recent case in point is that of Koor. In recent years the infusions that the Histadrut could inject into its industrial holding company dwindled relative to its size. Therefore, Koor was no longer able to survive the losses it incurred in 1987–88, which prompted the government to pledge a rescue package worth $50 million.

The third possible area of significance involves the commonly held suspicion that in the emerging postindustrial era, bigness is detrimental to innovation. If this is true, then the concentration in Israel's economy does not bode well for the future.

Agriculture

Israel is famous both for its colossal achievement in developing a very productive farm sector in the face of adverse natural conditions and for its particular forms of organization. Focusing on economic growth, however, the success of agriculture has been mixed. Some of the less gratifying aspects of agriculture have been discussed in Chapters 2 and 4, with more to come.

Agriculture was in 1985–88 one of the two least important of the economy's main business subsectors, contributing only about 8 percent to the domestic business product. Even construction contributed more, at 9 percent. This compares with 15 percent for transportation and communication and about 32 percent each for industry and trade and services.[12]

Still, thanks to its farm sector, Israel produces all of its fresh fruit and vegetables as well as its entire consumption of milk and its derivatives, cotton, poultry, and eggs. The most important import item is grain for both human and animal consumption and seeds for the edible oil industry. In terms of composition of revenue, the most important items in 1988 were fruit and meat, consisting of poultry and beef. Fruit, including citrus, constituted 25 percent of the total, and the share of meat was 20 percent. The combined activities of animal husbandry produced 42 percent of total farm revenue.[13]

Agricultural exports, though once again not very important as a component of total exports, are still quite substantial. Citrus fruit, which used to be the single most important component of exports in general during the early years of statehood, is still the most important agricultural export item. In 1988, citrus accounted for a third of the value of agricultural exports, with flowers contributing a quarter of the value of exports.[14]

An important feature of farm exports is the fact that they have been carried out almost exclusively by cartels or monopolies mandated by the government. Thus, for example, all exported fruit must be sold through the Fruit Production and Marketing Board. Selling in any other way constitutes a criminal offense. Similarly, export of fresh vegetables may be accomplished only through Agrexco, a government corporation. Only recently has the Citrus Marketing Board, which used to be the sole exporter of citrus fruit, been broken up and some competition in citrus exports has emerged.

Farm exports are not the only heavily regulated aspect of the agricultural sector. In fact, Israel's farm sector is subject to a vast system of regulation. Besides being afflicted with rudimentary government controls involving subsidies, quotas and support prices, Israeli farmers are subject to regulation in virtually every aspect of their business activity. Most of the regulation is carried out by production and marketing boards, the most important of which are statutory bodies whose powers are specified by the laws on whose strength they exist. Such powers include crop licensing, production quotas, exclusivity of marketing channels, etc. Farmers are also subject to irrigation-water quotas fixed by the Water Commissioner, under the jurisdiction of the Ministry of Agriculture. Even the wholesale trade in farm products is regulated. One cannot deal in farm-products wholesale without a license.

Housing

About 77 percent of Israelis live in owner-occupied dwellings. We have already described and analyzed the most important aspects of the housing sector, in particular the unusual ratio of equity in housing to earning potential. Another important, and not unrelated, feature of the housing market concerns the fact that very often the clients of construction contractors double as the latter's financiers. People sign purchase contracts on the basis of the architect's blueprints and make a down payment. As construction progresses, the client makes additional payments. Not surprisingly, quite a few clients found themselves out in the cold when contractors for whom they had acted as banks went bankrupt before completing their part of the deal.

Individually owned apartments require that buildings be organized as condominiums. But unlike the situation in the United States, there is no management with coercive powers. Everything is decided democratically. Although such a system seems very advanced, it harbors potential for trouble. For example, the owners of apartments in a building may decide by majority vote to spend a certain amount of money on renovation, say weather proofing.

But if one or more of the owners is reluctant, it may be impossible, or very costly, to compel them to pay their share of the bill. There is, therefore, a real danger that in a generation or so many of Israel's apartment buildings will look run down, not to mention the cost to the economy that this could engender. So worried is the government about this possibility that it actually subsidizes exterior maintenance of buildings, if the dwellers conform to some prescribed standards.

It is not only the organizational structure that is likely to produce this result. As we have seen, many people live in apartments they would not have been able to afford had they been obliged to buy them without subsidies. This implies that in relation to the dwellers' incomes, maintenance costs are going to be high, and therefore difficult to afford.

Labor

Some of the more troubling symptoms concerning the state of Israel's economy are labor related, though labor should not be held at fault for all or even most of the maladies plaguing the economy. Starting with the rate of participation in the labor force, it must be pointed out first that any comparisons should be regarded with caution, because the definitions of labor force are not identical across countries. In particular, Israel uses only the narrow concept of civilian labor force, because it keeps the size of its armed forces confidential. Hence, there are no published data concerning the total labor force. Still, estimates of the size of the armed forces do exist, and so two measures of labor force participation rates will be used here. Relying first on the narrower definition, the participation rate (the portion of the population belonging to the civilian labor force) was about 34 percent in 1984. Some corresponding numbers for the same year were 40 percent for Italy, 47 percent for the United Kingdom, 48 percent for the United States and 53 percent for Denmark.[15]

The relatively low Israeli rate is attributable to several factors. First, the population is younger relative to the populations of the other countries mentioned, so that the proportion of working-age people out of the total population is smaller (the population aged 14 and up in Israel in 1984 made up only about 69 percent of the total, whereas the population aged 15 and up constituted between 78 and 82 percent of the populations of the countries mentioned). The second obvious reason is the size of the armed forces relative to the population, for in addition to compulsory service, which causes the economy to forego the labor services of between two and three cohorts on a constant basis, there is also a relatively large regular army.

To partially compensate for the bias introduced by the nonsymmetric military situation, one might use estimates of Israel's military personnel. One widely used source estimated it in 1984 at 141,000.[16] Adding this number to the civilian labor force and assuming that the sum constitutes the total labor force, the participation rate in 1984 was 38 percent. This compares with a total (not just civilian) labor force participation of over 41 percent for Italy, 48 percent for the United Kingdom, about 49 percent for the United States and 53 percent for Denmark. An alternative source estimates the size of Israel's armed forces at 170,000.[17] If this estimate is used, then the participation rate, in terms of the total labor force, comes close to 39 percent. This is still relatively low, even if corrected for the difference in the average age of the population. Out of the countries examined for comparison only Italy constitutes an exception to this finding, because after correction for age differentials it ranks behind Israel.

The last, and perhaps most decisive, factor determining Israel's relatively low participation rate is to be found with the rate of women's participation in the labor force. Out of working-age (14 and up) women, only 37.6 percent participated in 1984 in the labor force. This compares with 42 percent for the United Kingdom, close to 48 percent in the United States, and over 68 percent in Denmark. Only Italy's figure is lower, at about 28 percent, which helps to explain why Italy ranks behind Israel after correction for age.

The labor-productivity issue has already been addressed extensively in Chapter 4. An additional consideration is that the heavy reliance of the country's defense forces on reserve duty certainly does not help to promote productivity. People who are plucked from their work place for thirty days or more annually are bound to produce less, not only because they are away, but because of the anxieties preceding their tour of duty and the difficulty of adjusting back to normal life after their return. Furthermore, when the individual who is called up for duty happens to be a floor manager or an engineer with day-to-day responsibilities his absence is likely to have a disruptive effect throughout the plant. It is therefore fair to state that not all the delinquency that characterizes Israel's labor productivity is produced by the adverse economic culture.

It has already been noted that Israel cannot be considered a member of the club of the highly advanced economies. Nevertheless, in some respects its economy features characteristics typical of highly developed ones. A case in point is the composition of employment. In highly developed economies, the proportion of people employed in agriculture is usually very small, whereas employment in business and personal services is relatively high. Using the 1988 employment data, one finds that agriculture claimed just over 5 percent of total employment, whereas employment in business and personal services, including financial services, amounted to close to 30 percent of the total. This was true even though the data includes workers from Judea, Samaria and the Gaza Strip, 109,000 of whom constitute 7 percent of total employment within Israel proper and who are particularly concentrated in agriculture.[18] Industry's share of total employment came to over 21 percent, which is also typical of more highly developed economies. The one category of employment that suggests that Israel's economy is not quite the same as the richest ones is employment in the public sector, which amounted in 1988 to 27 percent of the total.[19] One should note, this does not include either the standing armed forces or labor input in the form of military reserve duty. If personnel engaged in military service were to be counted, public employment in Israel would exceed a third of the total. In fact, if one excludes the workers from the territories, then civilian public employment alone accounts for almost 30 percent of the total.

Israel's unemployment rates have been relatively low by Western standards. One factor that governs the attitudes of Israelis toward unemployment to a considerable degree is the close connection between unemployment and emigration. This relation is amply demonstrated by developments over the past decade, concisely described in Table 6.1. In 1979 the economy boomed, and unemployment was the lowest for the decade under consideration. Then, in 1980, a new minister of finance pursued a policy designed to curtail private consumption. His policies managed to erode the public's purchasing power to such an extent that private consumption declined, in real terms, by about 3 percent,[20] with a consequent increase in unemployment. The initial effect on emigration was immediate, and hence net immigration declined substantially. But the full impact of the increase in unemployment was felt only in 1981, when net immigration became negative; that is, more people left the country than entered it.

TABLE 6.1

Unemployment and Immigration

Year	Unemployment, %	Emigration[*]	Net Immigration
1979	2.9	9,700	29,900
1980	4.8	4,700	17,500
1981	5.1	25,900	-11,400
1982	5.0	11,300	4,800
1983	4.5	4,700	14,400
1984	5.9	11,300	10,400
1985	6.7	17,500	-5,300
1986	7.1	17,100	-4,800
1987	6.1	10,100	5,500

[*]Defined as the number of citizens who have been outside the country twelve consecutive months or more.

Sources: CBS, *Monthly Bulletin*, various years; BOI, *Annual Report 1984*, p. 76; *1986*, p. 75; *1987*, pp. 75–78; *1988*, p. 85.

In 1981 the policy was reversed away from austerity, resulting in an increase of private consumption. The rise was significant: 11.5 percent in real terms. Although it took a little longer for unemployment to decline, the effects of the relaxed policies were not late in coming. Unemployment began to recede toward the end of the year and continued to decline in the following two years.

As Table 6.1 indicates, the decline in unemployment was accompanied by a return to a net positive inflow of people. Then, at the end of 1983 the administration at the Ministry of Finance changed again, and a new episode of belt-tightening began. Unemployment increased once again, and net immigration dropped. Unemployment continued to increase in 1985 and 1986. As a result, both years saw a net emigration. Then, as unemployment dropped back in 1987, the trend was reversed once again. Thus, one might say that the rate of unemployment in Israel can never become very high, because as soon as it rises it spawns emigration.

The exception occurs when unemployment is caused by immigration, as has been happening since 1989, due to the influx of Jews from the former Soviet Union. By 1992 unemployment exceeded 11 percent.

One reason for the close link between unemployment and emigration is the relatively high mobility of Israel's labor force, owing to its level of education. Skilled workers such as engineers, physicians, and scientists are able to move relatively easily between countries. Israel is blessed with a high proportion of such skilled individuals: 30 percent of every cohort graduate from high school, and in 1983, 29 percent of persons employed in Israel had at least one year of college education,[21] compared to approximately 38 percent in the United States in 1982.[22]

Wage determination is a three-tier process and involves negotiations on both basic wages and wage indexation formulas. First, the Trade Union Department of the Histadrut negotiates a countrywide, biannual wage contract with the Coordinating Chamber of Employers' Organizations, which is made up of, inter alia, the Manufacturers' Association, the Chambers of Commerce Association, and the Farmers Federation. The wage contract negotiated on the first tier constitutes, in effect, a lower bound for wage increases. No unionized worker will get less than what is stipulated in the general contract. The implication is that no matter where employed, a worker will receive the wage increase stipulated in the general agreement, regardless of the employer's financial situation. This constitutes, of course, one more aspect of the wedge driven between the individual and the real world or the severance between contribution and reward.

In the second tier, national unions can negotiate for additional benefits. For example, the Union of Engineers may negotiate separate benefits for its members.

The third tier in which workers can press for wage increases is at the level of the individual employer. Every business has to deal with one or more unions representing the workers in its employ.

In addition to contracted wages, various degrees of wage indexation have existed since before World War II. That is, Israel's wage earners have always had the privilege of receiving wage supplements based on changes in the cost of living. Wage indexation over the years has played a very crucial role in the formation of economic policy and will therefore receive a lot of attention later on. But in the present context, we limit the discussion to observing that the rate of indexation and the frequency of indexation payments have changed periodically.

Although real wages have undergone considerable fluctuation over time, a trend of wage increases is clearly discernable. Consequently, ever since the economy began to stagnate in 1974, there has been a marked redistribution of the industrial product between labor and capital. The data, not including subsidies to producers, appear in Table 6.2. As is evident, capital's share in the product and the rate of return to capital has been, on the average, not only below that of the boom years 1968–72, but also below the slowdown years 1965–67. That despite all of this the business sector survives more or less intact owes a great deal, as we shall see, to the institutional arrangements that prevent it from becoming a truly private sector.

The Wedge

Just as with individuals, the Israeli government embarked on several methods of driving a wedge between the market and the business community. The means chosen, apart from arrangements concerning the capital market, are subsidization and central planning, the latter being particularly relevant to the farm sector. As with individuals, the wedge produced modes of behavior detrimental to growth, as will become evident from the following description.

TABLE 6.2

Capital's Share and the Return to Capital 1965 to 1988, Percent

Period	Share of Capital in Product	Rate of Return on Capital
1965–67	33	12
1968–72	41	18
1973–79	27	9
1980–85	21	8
1986–88	16	6

Source: BOI, *Annual Report 1988*, p. 189.

The Subsidization Machine

The dependence of the business sector on the government in conjunction with the government's domination of the capital market was summed up quite early on as follows:[23] "It follows from the above [discussion of government finance of private enterprise] that the rate of profit on equity is determined primarily by the investment policy of the government, and not by the economic market forces." The aspect of this dependence with which we are concerned here is the subsidy component of the government's involvement in the capital market. It is a particularly interesting aspect, because one could conceive of a government allocating capital, but without at the same time offering subsidies. That would still make the private sector dependent on the government, but in a more subtle way, as there would still be no alternative to business success in the quest for profits. The subsidy component makes it possible for the business community to be less diligent in business management.

How wide is the wedge? For an answer, we might consider the subsidy component from several angles. Let us turn first to a study in which all the subsidies were capitalized to calculate the subsidy relative to the amount invested. It was found that, for a ten-year project in Development Area A, the subsidy came to more than 52 percent of total investment. In other words, the investor needed to put up only 48 percent of the capital invested; the rest was provided by the government in the form of grants, subsidized loans, and tax breaks.[24] In another study, the effect of subsidization on the expected rate of return on equity was estimated. There, it was found that a ten-year project that would have yielded a rate of return of 20 percent without subsidies, would be expected to yield more than double that rate after subsidization.[25]

A third method of gauging the role of capital subsidization is to consider macroeconomic data. Unfortunately, data concerning subsidization in this area have not been published prior to 1979. This is significant, because by 1980 long-term loans became indexed. Although this brought about a rapid decline in recorded capital subsidies, the effective degree of subsidization remained largely unaffected, at least for corporations that showed profits. This was because indexation payments could be deducted for income tax purposes in exactly the same way as interest payments are. Nevertheless, the official data on subsidies, which do not take into account the tax-relief component, did reflect the change after 1980, and they are therefore not very useful for our purpose. But if we look at 1979, we find that during that year capital subsidies amounted to about 28 percent of total domestic fixed capital formation.[26] There is good reason to believe that this rate is fairly representative and should not be viewed as a one-year aberration.

Perhaps the most effective way of driving home the significance of the subsidies generated by unindexed loans is to consider an hypothetical example. Suppose, that at the beginning of 1970 a business was granted a loan of $1,000 at 10 percent annual interest, to be repaid over five years in equal end-of-year installments, beginning with the end of the first year. The amount of each installment is $263.80. During 1970, the inflation rate, as measured by the consumer price index, was 10.7 percent. Hence, the real value of the first installment, calculated in terms of the purchasing power of dollars on borrowing, was $238.30 ($263.80/1.107). In 1971, the inflation rate was 13.4 percent. Hence, the real value of the second installment came to $210.14. In 1972, inflation hit 12.3 percent. Hence, the third installment amounted to $187.13 (obtained by dividing the nominal installment by the product 1.107 X 1.134 X 1.123). In 1973, inflation reached 26.4 percent, so that the real value of the fourth payment was reduced to $148.04. And finally, in 1974 inflation climbed to 56.2 percent, so that the real value of the last payment came to a mere $94.78. To calculate the subsidy, we need to discount the stream of real payments back to the borrowing date, at the loan's rate of interest. When this is done, we find the discounted real value of the repayment stream to be $690.86. This means, that the borrower enjoyed a subsidy of $309.14. Put differently, almost 31 percent of the original loan was turned into a gift. The much higher inflation rates that befell Israel in later years, the longer terms of loans in many cases, and substantial grace periods (during which the borrower pays only interest, rather than both interest and principal repayment) produced subsidy rates that turned the better parts of loans into gifts.

The most important areas of subsidization outside of the capital market proper have been exports, certain staples known as *essential goods*, and certain productive inputs. Turning first to exports, their subsidization on a large scale began in 1966. At that time, export goods were classified into value-added (foreign exchange earned less foreign exchange spent on inputs required for the production process) categories. Subsidies were then calibrated on the value added category to which a good belonged: goods with a value-added content of less than 25 percent of their total foreign-exchange value received a subsidy of 1 percent of that value; at 25 to 45 percent the subsidy was 3.5 percent; at 46 to 65 percent value added the subsidy was 6 percent of the export value; and for goods whose value-added content exceeded 65 percent, the subsidy constituted 8.5 percent of the export value.[27]

The classification process itself was quite remarkable because there is, of course, no universally accepted, unique way for determining value added. A correct calculation must take into account the total import component in a good's makeup, and this is by no means clear cut. It is easy enough to figure out direct import components, such as imported raw materials. But there are indirect import components. For example, water used in the production process is pumped by power generated with imported energy. Packing cartons produced domestically are made from cardboard made from imported wood.

And so on. To arrive at an accurate tally is virtually impossible, which leaves room for haggling over the value-added component. Indeed, by 1968 there were already goods classified as having a bigger value added content than generally believed.[28]

As has already been pointed out, subsidization schemes have an adverse effect on growth. The reason is that subsidies shield firms from the relentless scrutiny of the market, and so allow less efficient producers to survive. This is especially true where the subsidy element makes the difference between profit and loss, and in many cases, this is precisely what export subsidies accomplished.

The export subsidization mechanism Israel developed was even more detrimental to growth, because of its discriminatory nature. In fact, it favored exports with relatively low value-added content over exports with a relatively high value-added component. To see why, consider for example the 46–65-percent value-added category, which received a subsidy of 6 percent of the export value. For a good whose value-added component is 46 percent, a subsidy of 6 percent on total value translates into a subsidy of 13.3 percent on value added. And if labor's share of the value added is 60 percent, probably an underestimation, then the subsidy further works out to constitute one-third of capital's share. On the other hand, for goods with 65 percent value added, the 6-percent subsidy constitutes only 9.2 percent of the value added and only 23 percent of the share of capital. The implication is that the classification system generated a powerful incentive for exporters to have themselves reclassified from the upper reaches of one category to the lower reaches of the succeeding one, something that obviously many of them managed to effect.

The methods and rates of export subsidization have changed over the years. In general, they increased over time, although interim declines did take place occasionally. In any event, subsidies over the five-year period 1980–84 totalled 7.8 percent of the unsubsidized value of exports.[29] To realize how large such a rate of subsidization really is, assume that the value added in exports amounted to 60 percent of the exported value—probably an overestimation. Then subsidies during 1980–84 constituted 13 percent of the value added. If we continue to assume that labor's share of the value added was 60 percent, then the subsidies constituted 32.5 percent of the share of capital, a very respectable rate of subsidization from the recipient's point of view. In fact, as suggested earlier, at that rate subsidies could easily make the difference between profit and loss; that is, they could turn unprofitable exports into profitable ones.

The most noticeable subsidies for staples existed in the animal husbandry branches. For example, in the period 1971–77, subsidies for milk, eggs, poultry, and so on made up 16 percent of farm revenues in these categories. For milk, the subsidization rate during this period stood at a third of revenues.[30] One of the few aspects of reform that the government has carried out consistently in recent years is the almost total elimination of direct farm subsidies

But there are also indirect subsidies, mainly for productive inputs. One very important example concerns water for irrigation. Data are hard to come by, because a substantial component of the subsidy comes in the form of capital depreciation, for which farmers do not pay. This is a large item, as considerable investment is embodied in the network that provides irrigation water, particularly in the National Water Carrier. Other large investments were made in artificial reservoirs and deep groundwater recovery. There can be little doubt that without such subsidization agriculture would disappear from some areas, and assume a different nature in others.

The Veil of Agricultural Planning

A certain degree of separation of farmers from the markets exists wherever governments subsidize farm products, which is everywhere in the developed world. As a recent study shows, subsidization is especially pervasive in Japan and Canada, but is not insubstantial in the European Community and the United States.[31] Such subsidies allow farmers to receive prices for their produce which exceed those paid by consumers. The higher prices move farmers to produce more, thereby driving market prices further down, necessitating increased subsidies. Governments, in efforts to curb expenditures, either impose production quotas or bribe the farmers into abstaining from production by paying them for land left fallow. The former method is common in Western Europe, the latter in the United States. Because these are universal phenomena, which paradoxically are more frequent in economies otherwise based on free markets (in the less developed world, where economies are less free, farmers are often taxed rather than subsidized), there is little point in concentrating on the Israeli version of rudimentary farm subsidies. Rather, we shall concentrate on those aspects of government intervention in the farm sector peculiar to Israel and not already mentioned in conjunction with government intervention in the capital and credit markets.

The turning point for government intervention in agriculture was probably in 1960 when the government implemented several crucial measures that made the farm sector far more dependent on the government than it had been. First, the government issued a decree that prohibited planting fruit orchards without a license. The motivation was apprehension concerning the market's capacity to absorb the increasing quantities of fruit, such as apples and plums, at profitable prices. The implication was that further planting could be undertaken only where the government believed that profitability prospects were reasonable.

The second extraordinary step was a government ban on the planting of all varieties of tomatoes except one, the Moneymaker variety. The reason for this bizarre business-by-fiat measure was that the government had been spending a lot of money to subsidize surplus production, but the Moneymaker incurred the government's favor because of its physical sturdiness, which meant that any domestic surpluses could be exported without incurring excessive transportation costs. Unfortunately, that particular tomato was also characterized by a relatively stale taste, and Israeli consumers simply refused to buy it. The episode turned into a colossal fiasco, but the lesson had surely not been lost on farmers. The government making business decisions and therefore taking on responsibilities that belong more appropriately in the domain of the business sector.

The egg production industry was a third area in which the government attempted to deal with an economic problem by decree. The motivation, once again, had been surpluses produced by price supports. Here, the government sought to control the situation by restricting the use of inputs. First, because the government had been the sole importer of grains, including feed grains, it rationed the supply of feed grains on the basis of production quotas. Second, it slapped quotas on incubators to limit the production of laying hens.[32]

These steps set the tone for the farm sector for the following twenty years. During that period the government determined by advice, control and financing the new areas of farm activity. On the one hand, it made expansion of certain production activities very difficult; on the other hand, it provided cheap financing for the expansion of those farm activities it considered desirable. Consequently, farm activity assumed the form of what one might call fashions. Now it was fashionable to plant cotton, so everybody was planting cotton. Now it was fashionable to plant avocado, so everybody did that. Then came the turn of flowers. In every one of these cases, some mishap befell the farm sector at some point, and the government, understandably, was always held responsible.

The cultivation of flowers provides an excellent example in this respect, as Table 6.3 demonstrates. As late as in 1975, flowers had not been an important enough crop to merit a report on its cultivated area. Yet by 1978–79 the area was more than double what it had been in 1975–76, and over the same interval the value of exports tripled. The unhappy consequences of this rapid expansion caused a decline in both production and export from which the flower industry took several years to emerge.

It is not difficult to explain this course of events. At first, a lot of farmers entered floriculture because the government was handing out cheap investment finance. Investment in this case is substantial, because flowers are grown in winter in greenhouses that are artificially heated. In the absence of subsidized capital, entrance into the trade would have been gradual because of the

TABLE 6.3

Cultivation and Exports of Flowers

Year	Area Cultivated Thousands of Acres	Exports, Millions of Dollars
1970–71*	1.2**	7.3
1971–72	—	8.8
1972–73	—	10.9
1973–74	—	10.6
1974–75	—	15.8
1975–76	2.3	25.0
1976–77	3.1	34.9
1977–78	4.3	75.1
1978–79	4.9	77.6
1979–80	4.3	84.3
1980–81	3.8	81.6

*Agricultural statistics are reported on the basis of the agricultural year, which runs from October 1 to September 30.
**The availability of the figure for 1970–71 is due to the agricultural census that took place during that year.

Source: CBS, *Statistical Abstract of Israel 1986*, Table XIII–1.

risks involved. This would have left enough time for a marketing system to develop and get gradually acquainted with the expanding market. With the rapid entry caused by the flood of investment, the support systems developed under pressure, bringing about superfluous investment in grading and packing facilities and causing a lot of damage in the prospective markets.

The Moral Hazard

Unenforced Contracts

In Chapter 4, the retroactive annulment of contracts was described and illustrated with experiences that pertained primarily to the population as a whole, although some reference was made to the farm sector. It is time to elaborate. The most damaging is probably the agricultural debt story, which has acquired the nature of a cyclical phenomenon.

The details are simple: the farm sector would borrow short-term to finance long-term projects, thereby getting into severe liquidity shortages, or would borrow at interest rates that could not be justified by the return from the projects so financed. In either case, financial difficulties brought many farm communities to the brink of bankruptcy. On each of the occasions on which the farm sector found itself in a financial mess, the government simply bailed it out. This became known as *debt conversion*: the short-term, high-interest debt was converted to long-term, low-interest debt, with the government assuming the cost differential.

For example, during the years 1957–59 the government paid out I£20 million for debt conversion, an amount that constituted one-sixth of all outstanding short-term credit to agriculture at the end of 1959.[33] Yet, relief was very slow in coming. The Bank of Israel observed on the occasion that one reason for the inadequacy of debt conversion as a solution to the problem was the failure to deal with the causes that had brought about the financial mess in the first place.[34] But the government kept on pouring in money until in 1961 the conversion was credited with successfully driving down the market rate of interest paid by the farm sector and with easing the financial strain.[35] Not surprisingly, the farm sector went right ahead borrowing on the strength of having been rescued, and it was not long before a new rescue package had to be put together.

There is no point in chronicling all the conversion stories, but the one that occurred in 1979 is particularly instructive. Already in 1978, a credit fund of the sort discussed in Chapter 4 had been established, with the purpose of aiding farm settlements that found themselves in liquidity straits. But although by the end of that year the fund had dispensed a substantial sum of money,[36] this proved to be inadequate, and a special commission was appointed with the objective of investigating the farm credit situation. The commission found that, whereas the farm sector had suffered no shortage of short-term credit, it did use some of it to finance long-term investment. The financial "gap" thus created was estimated by the commission at about I£1.25 billion.[37] One way to grasp the immensity of this gap is to note that it constituted almost 10 percent of the gross domestic product of the farm sector.[38]

No less important than the actual willingness of the government to rescue the farm sector from financial difficulties is the fact that it understood that these very difficulties had been brought about by the farm sector itself. This is crucial, because rescuing somebody who had been hit by an earthquake, something beyond one's control, cannot be deemed harmful, as the individual in question would not be able to do anything about future earthquakes either, regardless of whether a rescue is expected. Not so with the problem at hand. It was clearly understood that incentives had been misplaced and that the problem had been created by deliberate actions. Furthermore, it was understood that the problem is of a recurring nature and that every rescue prepares the ground for another one.[39] Still, in 1980 the rescue operation went into gear.

Repeated rescues instilled in the agricultural community a sense of total protection, and it ran wild with irresponsible finances. Take as an example the largest *kibbutz* movement, Takam. Throughout the 1980s it invested large amounts in consumption assets even though net savings were negative throughout. In other words, indulgence was being financed on a grand scale with borrowed funds, some of them at outlandish interest rates (see Chapter 2). Similar behavior was common among many of the *moshav* communities and particularly characterized regional cooperatives, which plunged into investments that could in no way be justified by expected returns. By 1986, the financial roof again caved in, and this time on such a scale that there was no chance of another bailout of the form implemented before. The consequences are certain to have a lasting impact on the structure of the farm community. In particular, the rules of the game in both the *kibbutz* and the *moshav* are being changed to impose more personal responsibility. Socialism is going to be much weakened in the farming community from here on.

The Labor Market Conundrum

Labor markets in free societies range from the very centralized, such as in Sweden and Austria, to the very decentralized, such as in the United States and Canada. The middle ground is occupied by, for example, France and Australia.[40] In very centralized markets, wages are negotiated predominantly on the national level, between federations of labor unions and associations of employers. In very decentralized environments, wages are negotiated by individual unions with individual employers or, as in the American case, where union membership makes up a relatively low percentage of workers, by individuals with their employers.

Those who advocate centralized wage determination argue that, when unions negotiate economywide agreements, they are aware of the macroeconomic impact their demands have and will therefore act responsibly, so as to avoid unemployment. Thus, for example, when an economy's terms of trade deteriorate for some external reason, unions in a centralized environment will exercise restraint to prevent a recession. Unions acting in a very decentralized environment need not be concerned with the economy as a whole, but they usually have an interest in the survival of the employers concerned.

That self-interest would prompt unions in a decentralized environment to behave prudently can hardly be questioned, but the optimism concerning centralized dealing is much less natural. The reason is that, as we have seen in Chapter 5, a federation of unions needs to achieve two, possibly conflicting objectives. Not only does it have to negotiate wages for the membership, it also has to observe possibly rigid limits to the distribution of wages within its ranks. Indeed, the Swedish wage structure has been the most equitable in the free world. Suppose, however, that the structure of the economy is changing in such a way that in some industries labor productivity is growing much faster than in others. If the labor federation takes its cue from the less resilient industries, it risks alienating the unions whose membership belongs to the first group and could have obtained a much better deal if they had not been constrained by the federation. Hence, the federation will tend to demand wage increases that may be excessive as far as employers who belong to the slower growing group are concerned. The alternative—negotiating different wage increases in different industries—engenders a threat to the relative equality within the federation and so might endanger its existence.

But this is not all. The very fact that centrally set wages have macroeconomic ramifications implies that the government has to be interested in the outcome, because economic policy options may be affected. But this implies the danger that the government might be drawn into the process. This is indeed what has happened occasionally in various places, most recently in Sweden. But once the government is sucked in, moral hazard becomes a real danger.

The description of the labor market provided earlier in this chapter indicates that the wage-setting process in Israel belongs in the semi-centralized category. There seems to be some casual evidence indicating that this mixed model is the worst of the three possibilities.[41] Here, however, we are concerned with the centralized component of the system and, more specifically, government involvement prompted by centralized wage agreements. Such involvement usually comes in the shape of what is known as *social contracts.* Deals of this nature involve concessions by all parties concerned, including the government. And at times they include interference with the price mechanism.

Israel has had a string of these deals, known as *package deals,* the first of which was concluded in 1970. It was officially called "A Comprehensive Agreement Between the Government, the Histadrut, and the Coordinating Chamber of Employers on Wage, Price, and Tax Policies for 1970–71." The circumstances surrounding the agreement were novel in several respects. First, and most important, the previous wage settlement had been signed four years earlier, in 1966. In the wake of the slow-down of 1966–67, it was agreed in 1968 to extend the 1966 agreement for two more years. No wonder, the high rate of unemployment rendered the Histadrut in no position to bargain for new concessions on the part of employers. But unemployment vanished rapidly in 1969 (the numbers are quite impressive: although the average rate of unemployment in 1967 was 10.4 percent, it declined to 5.7 percent in the second half of 1968 and to only 3.7 percent in the first half of 1970[42]), and so the workers had high expectations concerning wages and other benefits. The agreement also represented the first occasion on which all employers got together for the bargaining process.[43]

The agreement contained the following main clauses:

1. Basic wages were to increase by 4 percent, only half of what the Histadrut had demanded at the outset. The increase was to be regarded as compensation for price increases and was to be tax exempt.
2. The workers were to receive a further 4 percent wage increase, to be paid in the form of government bonds, which the employers were to purchase.
3. The employers pledged not to increase prices in response to the increased wage costs.
4. The government undertook not to raise taxes beyond what had been agreed upon and also not to reduce subsidies for staples.[44]

The most interesting aspect of the agreement consists of the two items dealing with the employers' part of the contract. First, payment of part of the increase in wages in the form of government bonds meant that although labor costs were going to reflect the full increase in wages, wage income was not. This clearly implies a disregard for what we now call supply-side economics. Put simply, the government was willing to curtail the income of workers at the expense of increased production costs. This is accentuated by the fact that the bonds were nonnegotiable, so that they constituted a compulsory loan.

Second, the government must have thought that it could tax producers' expenditures without affecting either output or prices. As we shall see, disregard for production costs was to recur for fifteen years, taking various forms, before the government became aware of the foolishness of such attitudes.

There can be little doubt that governmental involvement must have contributed in a big way to the moral hazard with which the private sector had already been infected. The corrupting aspect of the agreement consists in educating the participants to expect to be rescued by the government in case of trouble. If the government is a party to a deal that ignores economic considerations such as production costs, then the bill can be submitted to the government. And once this is allowed, how can one delineate the cases where turning to the government for help is inadmissible? Thus, a deal of this nature signals to the parties involved that they can be more casual about business considerations, that is, create a moral hazard on an enormous scale, because it afflicts all business and all labor.

In November 1984 the first of a series of package deals was struck, culminating with the one that accompanied the stabilization program of July 1985. These deals featured the same attitude toward production costs reflected in the 1970 agreement. Employers undertook not to increase prices for a period of three months, but no similar freeze was imposed on costs. This time, though, it was not labor costs that were not being kept at bay. Instead, the costs of imported raw materials and other inputs kept increasing, as devaluations of the currency proceeded apace, at the average rate of 7.5 percent per month (138 percent on an annual basis).[45] The lack of synchronization between the rates of increases of production costs and product prices was so severe that the agreements collapsed, though they were never pronounced dead.

That the agreements could not survive should have been clear to everyone at the outset. Suppose that the import component in industrial output was 40 percent, and that labor's original share of value added (i.e., what is left after the cost of imported inputs has been accounted for) was 60 percent. Then it is easy to show that if wages do not decline, a monthly 7.5-percent increase in the cost of imported inputs due to devaluation translates into a monthly decline of 12.5 percent in capital's share of value added. Clearly, such a rate of decline cannot be sustained by employers for even a short period.

One of the symptoms of a tightly run business establishment is the occasional outbreak of strikes. The process that leads to strikes can be described as a game situation. There is a cake to be divided between the two sides to the wage negotiations. Each side would like to obtain as much as it can, without risking too high a price. The cake can be visualized as consisting of three parts, two of them relatively large and one relatively small. One large part represents what labor regards as the absolute minimum acceptable to it. The other large part is similarly viewed by the employer, and the small part represents what is subject to negotiation. An agreement constitutes a division of the small part between the two parties. The part the union regards as nonnegotiable is determined by the marginal tradeoff between giving up an additional piece of the cake and the loss incurred by striking. Similarly, the part regarded by the employer as nonnegotiable is determined by the tradeoff between giving up an additional piece of the cake and the loss, in the form of foregone profits, incurred by shutting down operations. The line set by the employer constitutes a check on union demands, because if the employer shuts down, the members lose income and perhaps even their jobs. The line set by the union constitutes a check on the employer's recalcitrance, because management risks a strike and thus the loss of profits and perhaps a decline in the firm's share of the market.

Negotiation can thus be viewed as a game of brinkmanship: each side tries to get the entire negotiable cut, but without overstepping the other's line of demarcation. This is easier said than done, however, because the demarcation line is fuzzy. Negotiations do not start off with each side announcing what it considers its own line of no retreat. In fact, the line may change in the course of the negotiations, as more is revealed about the adversary's willingness to take risks. Uncertainty is also produced by the fact that threats of strikes or shutdowns are not always believed by the other side. Hence, in the normal course of things, one side or the other will err occasionally, by misidentifying the location of the demarcation line, thus overstepping it. When the employer commits the mistake, a strike will break out.

It follows from this schematic description that, if we happen to observe an industry or an economy in which strikes rarely occur, chances are that we are looking at evidence indicating that employers do not negotiate very aggressively and hence yield a relatively large cut of the negotiable piece to the unions on a regular basis. This implication will allow us to understand one of the most important aspects of the excessive private-sector dependence on the government in Israel's economy, a dependence that has created the most pervasive and most damaging moral hazard of all.

Quite early on, it became evident that strikes in Israel are of a peculiar character: they were concentrated in the public, rather than in the private sector. Therefore, in 1965 almost 63 percent of all workdays lost in strikes were in the public sector. Even more impressive, over 71 percent of all strikers were in the public sector, although its share in employment was only less than 23 percent. In contrast, industry suffered only slightly over 17 percent of workdays lost and 10 percent of all strikers, although its employment share exceeded 25 percent.[46] This was not an aberration: the public sector and sectors tightly controlled by it went on suffering the lion's share of strikes. The peculiarity lies with the fact that in free economies in general, strikes are concentrated in the private sector and especially in industry.

The slow-down of 1966–67 put a damper on strikes in general, as there was no point in striking in the face of growing unemployment. Thus, although 156,000 workdays were lost to strikes in 1966, that number dwindled to only 58,000 in 1967. In 1968, strike activity, though showing some increase over 1967, remained low. But in 1969 it took off again, climbing to 102,000 lost days. Significantly, the public sector's share was again 63 percent. Then, in the agreement year 1970, an explosion of strikes hit the country, causing a loss of 390,000 workdays. The public sector accounted for 74 percent of the loss.

It had not always been like this. For example, in 1945–46 there were several bitter and prolonged strikes in the private sector. At both Nesher, the cement factory, and Okava, a manufacturer of razor blades, there were strikes that lasted for two months each, and in other cases strikes lasted for almost six months.[47]

The calm that settled on labor relations in the private sector in later years definitely did not come about as a consequence of meek labor unions. Rather, it indicates a yielding stance on the part of private employers. In fact, the strikes that broke out after World War II were themselves a result of changing attitudes on the part of employers. During the war, they refrained from fighting the unions, because in the inflationary conditions that prevailed then it was easy to burden the customers with the cost increases occasioned by higher wage settlements. After the war, when this option was no longer available, employers had to stand their ground, and so strikes broke out.

But at some point later on, employers again became more accommodating toward union demands. Yet corporations were not being driven out of business, nor did unemployment result. The resolution of this apparent paradox is what created the circumstances that produced the inflationary process that nearly ruined the economy.

The consequences of a business environment in which the private sector feels protected by global insurance due to government policies, were highlighted dramatically by the interest-rate episode of 1984–86. In the description that follows, real interest rates are reckoned for a borrower taking out a loan on the first of the year and repaying it, principal and interest, at the end of the same year. Inflation rates refer to the consumer price index.

During 1983, annual interest on working capital (line of credit) accounts was 181.6 percent, whereas the rate of inflation reached 190.7 percent. Thus, the annual real rate of interest was minus 3.1 percent. This means that the lender recovered only 96.9 percent of the principal and received no interest. Then, in 1984, inflation jumped to 444.9 percent, but interest rates shot up to 773.9 percent, implying the fantastic real rate of interest of 60.4 percent. Yet at the end of 1984, the real amount of outstanding credit was practically unchanged from the end of 1983.

In 1985 the rate of interest climbed to 93.8 percent. In any normal economy, this would have caused a business calamity, but not in Israel: business went right on borrowing as though nothing out of the ordinary had happened. In fact, by the end of 1985, the real amount of outstanding credit was 36.6 percent higher than it had been at the end of 1984. A good deal of the increased debt position was the result of interest payments that came due, were not discharged, and were simply added to the original principal. Put differently, debtors borrowed to pay interest on the outstanding debt. Although interest declined in 1986 to a real rate of "only" 33.6 percent, the real amount of credit virtually exploded, so that by the end of 1986 it was 72 percent higher than it had been at the end of 1985. During 1987, the real rate of interest inched up again, to 38.6 percent, which did not prevent borrowing from growing at about the same pace as in 1986.[48]

Of course, no business is profitable enough to be able to borrow at such incredible rates. This means that no firm would borrow at such rates if it had based its decisions on business considerations alone. Israel's business community, or at least that part of it which kept borrowing under these circumstances, must have had other considerations in mind. The only possible alternative is that it expected the government not to allow it to collapse. History provided a wealth of examples on which to base such expectations.

Perhaps even more significant is the fact that banks were willing to keep on lending under these circumstances. They were certainly aware of the fact that by charging these outlandish interest rates they were putting the borrowers in jeopardy and were therefore unlikely to recover the debt. So they must have assumed that the government would come to the rescue. The damage caused by these developments is going to take years to repair, and some of it is probably irreparable. More on this in Chapter 11.

A Market in Chains

One of the distinguishing characteristics of a capitalist society whose markets are competitive is that the economic system is designed to enhance the welfare of the ultimate user: the consumer. It is the consumer who reigns supreme, while the businessperson runs scared. This creates the interesting result that, although the potential producer favors obstacle-free access to the market, as this is best for the exploitation of potential opportunities, the established producer favors restricted entry, as this mitigates the threat from potential competition. As in the bus parable, which is famous in Israel: people trying to enter the bus plead with the passengers already inside to move closer together to make more room; but once in, they complain that it is already too crowded. Established firms are therefore often receptive to all sorts of government regulation and protection. In fact, as is well known, it is quite common for the regulated businesses themselves to be the most vehement opposers of deregulation.

The moral of all this is that the typical businessperson will compete fiercely in the market, if this is the only way open to make profits. But if someone should offer alternative ways to the same goal, ways that are less taxing, most entrepreneurs would be happy to switch to the alternative. As we have seen in the foregoing sections, one of the fundamental attributes of government involvement in Israel's economy is the degree to which the business sector has been offered alternatives to good business. Consequently, private business has become much more skilled at extracting more subsidies from the government than in learning how to run lean business enterprises. As far as growth is concerned, however, the results are devastating.

The legal framework for government-imposed regulation—indeed, management—of the Israeli marketplace is embodied in both ad-hoc laws and general legislation. The most important law in the arsenal that enables the government to interfere in the economy is the Commodities and Services (Control) Law of 1957. It virtually empowers the government to take over the marketplace and rule production, prices and distribution by decree.[49] Although the law has never been used to its full capacity, parts of it have been applied quite frequently. In particular, it has been used often to impose price controls. For instance, in 1962–64 the government both used price controls and coerced producers into not raising prices by threatening to lower import duties on competing products.[50] Particularly aggravating are the auxiliary arrangements that usually accompany the institution of price controls: a commission is set up empowered to grant "justified" price increases, when producers can prove that these are required because of increases in "legitimate" costs. Because costs can be calculated in different ways, there is considerable room for negotiation—one more reason for business corporations to devote more attention to dealing with the government than to running what would be, in the absence of all this governmental involvement, a good business.

A good example is provided by the price commission set up to monitor the price controls imposed in connection with the 1970 agreement and to handle applications for exemptions. The most recent episode of price controls started in November 1984 and reached a climax in July 1985, when 90 percent of the goods and services included in the consumer price index were brought under control. The length of the period during which controls applied this time was also extraordinary: by January 1987, 46 percent of consumer goods and services were still under control,[51] and in 1991, 20 percent were still under control.

An excellent example of ad hoc legislation is provided by the law for the Extension of Emergency Regulations (Arrangements in the Wake of Change of the Exchange Rate), 1971. Emergency regulations, which can be imposed by the government for up to ninety days, constitute an extremely powerful governing device, because they allow the government to institute regulations concerning virtually every aspect of life. The power to impose such regulations was granted by the temporary legislature set up on independence. It decreed on May 21, 1948, that a state of emergency had come into existence. At the end of ninety days, the government must turn to the legislature if it wants to extend the emergency regulations. That is, the regulations must be transformed into law.

On August 22, 1971, a devaluation took place that changed the value of the dollar in Israel from I£3.50 to I£4.20. Using its emergency powers, the government decreed a set of regulations designed to govern prices of imported goods. The law that extended the regulations contained, among other provisions, the following:

1. A levy imposed on producers holding foreign-exchange balances, constituting the difference between the old and the new exchange rates;
2. A levy imposed on anyone holding in stock imported goods earmarked for domestic disposal;
3. A restriction against any producer, importer, or merchant to charge a price higher than the price that had existed on August 15;
4. A government official empowered to exempt a good or service from the price freeze, for which purpose the official could require the applicant for the exemption to submit a full cost accounting of the good in question.

In free economies, governments usually bar businesses from colluding in the marketplace. This is done with the help of a legal framework that prohibits restrictive business practices. The law that has governed such practices in Israel for thirty years was the Restrictive Trade Practices Law of 1959, which dealt with cartels and monopolies. Remarkably, rather than obliging the government to intercede against cartels and monopolies, the law actually allowed it to approve virtually all manner of restrictive practices.

Turning first to cartels, the law appears to have been comprehensive, as the definition of what constitutes a cartel was very broad indeed. Any arrangement between business enterprises that imposed on any of them a limiting provision of any sort came under the definition of a cartel. So, on the face of it, the law provided a total protection from restrictive practices. In reality, however, it left so much room for discretion that it could be rendered totally ineffective.

The administrative machinery that facilitated discretion consisted of a controller of restrictive trade practices and the Restrictive Trade Practices Board. The controller had to keep a Register of Cartels. Any party to a restrictive practice had to register with the controller within fifteen days after joining the association that imposed the restriction. The parties to a restrictive practice agreement then had to apply to the board for approval of their restrictive arrangement.

The latitude given to the board blunted the seemingly sharp teeth of the law, for the board was empowered to approve a cartel if it was deemed to be "in the public interest." The public interest, for this purpose, has many facets. A cartel was regarded as being in the public interest if it:

1. Secured for the public a particular advantage that could not be obtained otherwise;
2. Protected the continued existence of an entire economic branch, considered to be advantageous to Israel's economy;
3. Enhanced the efficiency of production or marketing or reduced the price of a good or service;
4. Brought about an improvement in the country's balance of payments, through reduced imports or increased exports.

One interesting feature of these items of public interest is that at least one of them, the third, was based on ignorance. Basic economic theory clearly implies that no cartel of any kind could promote efficiency in the normal economic sense. Nor will a cartel ever result in price reduction, because its whole purpose is to restrict output. As is obvious from the wording of these provisions, particularly the first one (what is an "advantage"?), a justification for virtually any sort of restrictive practice could be established.

The government's true attitude was further revealed by the fact that the language of the law itself excluded certain businesses from its application altogether. Thus, if the restrictive arrangement was struck between corporations controlled by the government, it was exempt from the law, as was a restrictive arrangement between a corporation and its subsidiaries.

The government's application of the statute provides additional insight into its real intentions. In the very same year in which the law was approved, the government actually helped to form industrial cartels with the aim of reducing competition. The reason was that firms had been competing by extending customer credit, and the government believed this to be at odds with its monetary goals.[52] When the edible oil industry applied for approval of restrictive practices, the key witness *for* approval was the director-general of the Ministry of Trade and Industry.[53] Out of the 103 applications for approved restricted practices submitted in the first year of the law's existence, only 36 were rejected outright, and by the end of 1960, fully 48 of the applications were approved temporarily or indefinitely.[54]

But the most bountiful section of the law, as far as partners to restrictive practices are concerned, was the exemption its sanctions accorded to arrangements that could be construed as helping Israel's balance of payments. After the devaluation of 1962, in which the exchange rate was changed from I£1.80 to I£3 to the U.S. dollar, the government actively encouraged the formation of cartels in exporting industries. The context in which this was done is particularly interesting. One of the objectives of the devaluation of 1962 had been increased trade liberalization. The devaluation was supposed to replace, to a certain extent, administrative rationing of imports as well as import duties. But liberalization was not to be carried as far as endangering the existence of domestic producers. In other words, there was no intention of permitting imports to replace domestically produced goods, except on a limited basis. A commission charged with implementing the new policies was set up. Among other duties, its mandate included reviewing requests for continued high tariff protection. In thirty-one such cases, the commission was actually prepared to approve continued high protection, provided that the applying parties form a cartel.[55] That is, the applicants were promised protection from outside competition if they undertook not to compete with one another.

Even prior to that episode, the government had already sanctioned cartels in the domestic market to promote exports. Here, the story is an example of a classic textbook case in the economics of imperfect competition. Firms form a cartel in the domestic market, which allows them to exercise monopolistic power and thus generate monopolistic profits. But the reduction in domestic sales called for by the monopolistic practice is effected through exports, not reduction in output. That way, the cartel can choose the amount produced on the basis of cost considerations, without having to sell all of it on the domestic market. The excessive domestic profits allow the cartel to export at world prices that, had there been competition in the domestic market, would have been unprofitable. In effect, cartels had been formed to allow exporters to force the domestic consumers of their product into subsidizing exports, and the scheme won governmental blessing.[56]

Monopolies were treated in a similar manner. In fact, the language of the law in this respect did not even pretend to provide effective prevention of monopoly power. This is evident from the fact that a monopoly was defined as existing in cases where the provision or acquisition of any good or service was controlled by one agent to an extent that *exceeds the extent designated by the minister of trade and industry as monopolistic*. It is not merely that the law provided no definition of a monopoly, it also allowed for perfect discrimination, because the minister of trade and industry could declare for each commodity a different market share to constitute a monopoly. The law provided no criterion whatsoever. Beyond that, even if a monopolistic situation was declared, the law did not compel the government to do anything about it, whether or not action was taken was up to the restrictive trade practices controller.

In 1988 the old law was scrapped and a new one adopted in its stead. A brief review of the differences between the two laws demonstrates the degree to which attitudes have begun to change in recent years. The first important difference is that the new law requires court approval for restrictive practices, where in the old law approval was a purely administrative prerogative. But the court must consider a list of purported benefits of a restrictive practice that is very similar to the list in the old law. The new law also provides a list of restrictive practices that cannot be declared as such. The more interesting among them are restrictive practices in agriculture and international transportation. As concerns monopolies, the new law is much more specific. It stipulates that a monopoly exists whenever more than half of the provision of a good or service is controlled by a single agent. The new law also empowers the commissioner of restrictive practices to impose an administrative control on prices, quality, and regularity of supply where a monopoly exists. If the court finds such controls to be incapable of eliminating the harm caused by a monopoly, it may break it up.

Evidently, the new law constitutes an improvement over the old one, but in a country in which restrictive practices abound, it probably is not strict enough. In fact, a year after the new law had been adopted nineteen approved cartels existed, ranging from pasta to pharmaceuticals, and included, among others, an agreement between I.B.M. and the distributors of its products and a cartel of auto sales outlets.[57]

Perhaps the most farreaching example of government-sanctioned cartels is provided by Israel's energy sector, which might be regarded as a microcosm of all that is wrong with the Israeli economy. Government regulation starts with the import of oil. Although worldwide some 60 percent of the trade is in the spot market, Israel imports about two-thirds of its crude under long-term contracts, chiefly with Egypt, Mexico, and Norway. Until recently, imports were the exclusive prerogative of the three oil companies that operate in Israel, with each having a prescribed share of the total: Paz controlled 45 percent of the total, Delek had 30 percent, and Sonol 25 percent. No one else was allowed to import oil in any shape or form.

The ownership of the three oil companies is itself part of the problem. Paz was controlled until recently by the government, which sold its controlling stake to an Australian firm. The ownership of Delek is divided between Bank Ha'poalim (40 percent), Discount Bank (30 percent), and Bank Leumi (16 percent), with the remaining 14 percent of the shares in the hands of the public. The ownership of Sonol is divided between Ampal, a subsidiary of Bank Ha'poalim (25 percent), a subsidiary of Koor and Clal (37 percent), and a private firm.[58] So the same two conglomerates that control much of industry are also very prominent in the energy sector.

The right to ship the crude to Israel is given exclusively to Tanker Services, a company owned by the three oil companies and by Oil Refineries, a government-controlled monopoly. Shipping the oil is carried out under a cost-plus-fixed-fee arrangement. Once in Israel, the crude is consigned to Oil Refineries for refining according to specifications provided by the oil companies. Here, too, the operation is carried out on a cost-plus-fee arrangement. In fact, the dividends the company pays the Israel Corporation, which owns a 26-percent stake, are included in the cost structure. The fact that coverage of costs is guaranteed implies that no matter how far world prices of refined products fall, this will have no impact on the profits of Oil Refineries or on the prices of refined products in Israel.

The refined products are shipped to loading points through a network that is also owned by a combination of government, Oil Refineries, and the oil companies. The sharing of imports between the three oil companies is also applied to domestic marketing. This has been true until recently in the wholesale market and in the provision of energy to large customers like Israel Electric Corporation, and it still holds in the retail market. Paz owns 42 percent of the filling stations, with Delek owning 32 percent and Sonol 26 percent. In 1983–84, 45.6 percent of retail sales were made by Paz, 29.1 percent by Delek, and 25.3 percent by Sonol.[59]

Prices at the pump are determined by the government. Because the entire chain of marketing down to that point is based on a cost-plus-fee arrangement, the government in effect sets the profit margin enjoyed by the operators of the individual gas stations. One spectacular outcome of this situation was the gas station strike of 1987, which, owing to the completeness of government control, had the characteristics of a labor strike, even though the owners of gas stations are nominally business people.

In 1989, the first stage of what is supposed to constitute a farreaching reform of the energy sector was implemented. The first step consists of two main changes. First, imports of the one-third of the oil purchased in the spot market are open to competition. That is, the fixed allocation of shares among the three oil companies is restricted to the two-thirds of oil bought on long-term contracts. Oil Refineries is now permitted to import on its own up to a third of the oil, but it must market the refined products thereof through the three oil companies or sell them directly to the so-designated large consumers. These large consumers may now import oil for their own use, but for every ton so imported, they must buy two tons from the oil companies. The oil companies, in turn, are permitted to import refined products within the competitive segment. The problem here is that Oil Refineries operates the only available refined-products terminal in the country and is therefore in a position to make it costly to the oil companies to import refined products.

As bad as cartels are in general, they are particularly harmful when they occur in part of an economy's infrastructure, in this case in the energy sector. For then the inefficiency typical of the cartel shows up in the form of higher production costs throughout the economy.

Whatever the reasoning, the picture that emerges demonstrates a network of restrictive practices, partly instituted through collaboration between the government and the private business sector and partly secured by coercion. Economic theory tells us that such arrangements are harmful to the economy for several reasons. First, they deter entrepreneurs, because they involve obstacles to entering the market. Hence, they cause a likely loss of both talent and information. Second, they involve a loss of efficiency on the production side, because cartels are notorious for employing inefficient combinations of production factors. In particular, they are often associated with excess capacity, of which the citrus products and edible oil industries are two prominent examples. Third, such practices harm consumers, who are compelled to pay prices in excess of what they would have paid under competitive circumstances.

7

THE WOULD-BE PRIVATE SECTOR: THE ORIGINS

Early Farming Days

The history of the emasculation of the private sector is almost as long as the history of the renewed Jewish settlement of Palestine. The first settlement endeavors, we recall, were undertaken by courageous individuals who formed the first *moshavot* or farming communities based on individual property and effort. Many of these first beginnings encountered grave difficulties, however, as might have been expected under the circumstances. It is common in similar situations that many failures occur before a secure bridgehead is established, and so it was to be expected that some of the early enterprises might fail. Indeed, quite a few of the new settlements found themselves after a while in dire financial straits.

Enter Baron Edmond de Rothschild, who became known in later years as the "famous philanthropist" and undertook to save the early settlers from financial demise. This would have been a blessing had the baron based the extension of financial facilities on economic considerations. For example, he could have extended credit commensurable with the enterprising qualities of the recipients, but this is not what happened. Rather, the baron viewed the whole undertaking as a philanthropic enterprise and never expected it to lead to financial self-sufficiency.

The consequences were horrendous. In most of the colonies that enjoyed the baron's largess, the settlers were driven to a status of welfare recipients, losing their enterprising spirit. Fortunately, not all colonies subscribed to the baron's handouts, among them chiefly Rehovot and Gedera, both of which had been established just as the baron's operations were about to get under way. The settlers of both these colonies led the fight against the baron's welfare system.[1] Eventually, the baron pulled out quite disappointed, but continued to channel money through J.C.A., a foundation whose extension of credit was based a bit more on business considerations.

The baron's involvement in the settlement effort has been traditionally viewed as having saved the then-existing communities from ruin. This is, of course, impossible to prove, as is any similar assertion. Although the baron's intentions were, of course, beyond reproach, the legacy his operation left behind was certainly not conducive to the creation of a financially sound agricultural sector.

The baron's episode is important because it affected a significant part of the fledgling farm sector and constituted a harbinger for things to come.

The Ideological Background

In general, it is impossible to delineate a clear boundary between the attitudes toward private capital, already discussed in Chapter 3, and attitudes toward the private sector. Because private business enterprises must be based on nonnational capital, and in any event must have free access to capital, any ideologies which are hostile to private capital are per force hostile to private enterprise. Nevertheless, the two need not be identical, because capital mobilized by the public sector can be put at the disposal of private enterprises, as has been the case in Israel. Furthermore, in the prestate days the leadership did not have the power to confiscate private capital, and so the route to cowing the private sector through restrictions on access to capital was closed. The alternative methods chosen and the ideological foundations that guided them justify an inquiry independent of the analysis in Chapter 3.

The objection to private enterprise was twofold. Private enterprise was considered both *incompatible* with the objectives of the Zionist effort and *incapable* of accomplishing those objectives. In other words, the objections were both ideological and practical. Private enterprise was also very often identified with industry and trade or, more generally, nonagricultural occupations. Because agriculture retained an ideological supremacy over all other occupations, private enterprise was viewed unfavorably because of its concentration in nonfarm enterprises.

One of the clearest pronouncements reflecting the attitudes of the day toward free enterprise was made by Arthur Ruppin, who, having been more highly educated than most other leaders, possessed the gift of being able to state the prevailing positions with clarity. He proceeded from the assertion, as a matter of fact, that the Zionist Organization, with its anticapitalistic bias, deliberately discouraged private enterprise. He then proceeded to defend the bias.

In the first place, argued Ruppin, agriculture was more capable of absorbing mass immigration than industry. His reasoning was that agriculture required a smaller investment per new worker than industry. This was a fallacious observation that had been based on Ruppin's investigation of four industrial concerns. The ones he chose, like the Nesher cement factory, happened to be capital intensive. Ruppin found that the average investment per worker in these enterprises came to about £1,350, which exceeded the £1,100 he reckoned to be the needed investment per farm family.[2]

That Ruppin's conclusion on the subject was wrong can be verified from figures published in the wake of a 1930 industrial census taken by the Jewish Agency. Based on a survey of 2,276 industrial enterprises, to which figures from the large, capital-intensive industries were added, an average investment of £306 per worker was computed. This was considerably less than the investment required for the settlement of a farm family.[3]

Immigration absorption figures leave no doubt as to the invalidity of Ruppin's reasoning. By the end of 1923, 80 percent of the Jews of Palestine lived in its few cities; and after the wave of immigration in 1924–25, the percentage increased to 83.[4]

Ruppin's second justification of the objection to free enterprise was based on his misconception of the benefits of trade and on what he perceived to be the injurious consequences of competition:[5]

> Outside Palestine the Jewish community benefits by the commercial gains of individual Jews, because they are obtained from trade with non-Jews. Conditions in Palestine are totally different. Trade with non-Jews is . . . small and limited; as a whole, the Jews form a more or less self-contained economic entity; thus the gain by trade of an individual of the entity would usually not be a gain for the whole body; it would merely be a shifting of wealth inside the community, representing individual profit. Individual profit, however, is only desirable from the Zionist point of view, if it is also a collective profit of the whole Jewish community.

And "If yet another hundred little shops or miniature cafes are opened by Jews in Palestine, the only result would be that two families would now be forced to live or starve on an income which formerly barely sufficed for one, or that the consumer will have to pay higher prices in order to support yet another middleman." The first quoted paragraph represents a fundamental misunderstanding of the gains from trade. In Ruppin's view, trade is nothing but a redistribution of wealth.

The second paragraph contains two misconceptions. First, Ruppin ignores the value of competition as a catalyst to both efficiency and innovation. This leads him to the second misconception, which views the volume of economic activity as given, implying that greater competition merely leads to a thinner distribution of the fixed amount of material goods. That competition could lead to greater efficiency, and hence to a more economic use of the means of production, escapes him.

At about the time that Ruppin explained the reasons for the official disdain for free enterprise, David Ben-Gurion proclaimed one of the ideological cornerstones on which the objection to private enterprise had been based. He argued that public and cooperative enterprise should take precedence over private enterprise, because the latter was simply incompatible with the objectives of the Zionist movement. The reasoning was simple: private enterprise is motivated by private profits. Hence, it pursues a business course that is most conducive to generating profits. In Palestine, this meant the employment of indigenous Arabs instead of Jewish newcomers, because the former both were more productive as farm laborers and required lower wages. This implied that private enterprise was detrimental to the economic absorption of new immigrants and thus inimical to the main purpose of the Zionist Organization.[6]

Quite obviously, Ben-Gurion had been thinking strictly in terms of farming. Indeed, the individual Jewish farmers in the early colonies did employ a great many Arab workers, even when there was no shortage of Jewish ones. But by 1925, when Ben-Gurion and Ruppin articulated their positions, the Fourth Aliya had been already under way, having begun in 1924. It brought about a grudging change of attitude, for it was the first wave of immigrants to consist overwhelmingly of middle-class people from Central Europe. These were immigrants who had experienced a life very different from the one in Eastern Europe. They usually possessed modest means, many had been owners of small-scale industry, and they were much more skilled than their predecessors. They were also much less ideologically doctrinaire and saw no fault with city life and city occupations. Consequently, as we have noted elsewhere, they flocked overwhelmingly to the cities, engaging in industry, trade, and construction. Indeed, in these fields, the prospect for employing non-Jewish labor had been meager as the Arab workers simply did not possess the necessary skills. In fact, Jewish industry very rarely employed Arabs, even though the pressure not to employ them, which was being exerted by the labor movement, had been confined entirely to the farm sector. But Ben-Gurion had been so used to thinking in terms of the overwhelming importance of agriculture that the distinction simply did not occur to him.

The views expressed by Ben-Gurion and Ruppin were not just the opinions of a few ideologues or eccentrics. This can be easily seen from the fact that the press of the day described industry, with its attendant city life, as not even an afterthought in the public's mind. The evolution of Palestine's economy had been tied to farming, and farming had been tied to public, rather than private, enterprise.[7] Furthermore, nonfarm occupations had come to be regarded as somehow inferior, less honorable. Those who expounded the value of industry and trade were seen as heretics.[8]

Still, some nonfarm enterprises were regarded as essential and therefore not scorned. First, the job of supplying farmers with inputs needed for agricultural production and the marketing of farm produce were high on the list of honorable occupations; but there are other examples, such as construction, transportation of both people and cargo, and the provision of medical services. That all of these occupations were viewed favorably is evident from the fact that they were largely in the hands of cooperatives formed under the auspices of the Histadrut.

Special reference must be made to banking, which had been one of the most typical and therefore one of the least warranted occupations of Jews in the diaspora. Still, even though the Zionist Organization already owned a bank, A.P.B., in 1921 it initiated Bank Ha'poalim. Its express aim was to provide credit to the workers' economy; that is, to cooperatives in agriculture and elsewhere. Although the bank was to be controlled by the Histadrut, the Zionist Organization invested £40,000 in it.[9]

The events of the Fourth Aliya (wave of immigration), when thousands of immigrants were being absorbed relatively effortlessly and with no expenditure of public funds and when private investment boomed, signalled an end to the vision of a societywide socialist economy and signified the loss of agriculture's exclusive standing. Not that the leadership abandoned its regard for the supremacy of agriculture or disdain for private enterprise, which was still seen as striving to achieve goals in conflict with the national aspirations, but it could no longer pretend that agriculture was the only way to absorb mass immigration. However, the facts of life were recognized only reluctantly.

Reluctant acceptance meant that private enterprise was going to be tolerated but, unlike cooperative and communal enterprise, it would not be eligible for financial support. Public funds would be channeled almost exclusively to agriculture, where only very few new settlements had been the result of private initiative. The figures are very clear in this respect: in the post-World War I period, up to 1937, the two official Zionist funds, the Jewish National Fund and the Foundation Fund, together spent 51 percent of their total outlays on agriculture, whereas trade, industry, urban settlement, and direct investment between them commanded less than 9 percent of the total.[10] The remainder of the budget was allocated to education, health, security, and administration.

Acceptance of private enterprise required a new ideological framework in both social and national forms. Socially, the abandoned socialist yearning for an economy wholly based on public capital was replaced by a demand that private capital undertake national goals. In other words, private enterprise was going to be tolerated provided that it did not behave as private enterprise. There was no recognition of the profit motive as a useful guide to economic activity. One way by which private enterprise would be forced to ignore its interests would be the class struggle. This clearly constituted a retreat: in place of the classless, workers' society, there was now going to be a recognized bourgeois class, which had to be fought and compelled to behave along noncapitalist lines.[11] This was the new form that the identity between social and national goals assumed.

The translation of this ideology into practice took three distinct forms, one in agriculture and two in industry. In agriculture, a campaign known as the *Conquest of Labor* got under way. The aim was to force private farmers to replace Arab labor with Jewish labor.

In industry, the ideology manifested itself first as a distinction between "beneficial" and "nonbeneficial" undertakings. For a private enterprise to be regarded as beneficial, it had to be judged as having a national value. To have national value a new outfit had to provide, first of all, a lot of employment opportunities. This, however, was not necessarily sufficient if the output was destined for the domestic market. In that case the product had to be an item not previously produced, and it had to be deemed needed. If the new product was exportable, its nature did not matter: exports had been regarded with high priority since very early on.

The second line of action spawned by the new ideology and pertaining especially to industry consisted of a particularly nasty attitude by the Histadrut toward private employers.[12]

The Conquest of Labor

The drive to "conquer labor" was directed at replacing Arab farm hands, employed by the private Jewish colonists who had settled in the *moshavot* during the last quarter of the nineteenth century, with newly arrived Jewish workers. The necessity for an organized drive arose because the new Jewish immigrants were mostly unable to compete with the local Arab workers in a free labor market. This inability sprang from two sources. First, the newcomers had not been trained for this kind of work, and so their productivity was inferior to that of the Arabs, at least initially. Second, the Arab workers were receiving wages that the Jewish newcomers regarded as wholly inadequate, because they could not support a standard of living resembling what the newcomers had been used to in their countries of origin. Ruppin, again, succinctly stated the problem:[13] "But the fact that in Palestine the Jews will have to compete with a people of a much lower standard of life is even more serious [than the difficulty of changing the Jews' occupational structure]. The whole Orient is characterized by a frightful exploitation of human labor." And "To put it shortly: Even in Palestine the Jew wishes to remain a product of the twentieth century. . . . This fact, that the Jews wish to maintain in Palestine a European standard of civilization and must yet compete economically with a majority not accustomed to such a standard, contains the root of all the difficulties with which our agricultural colonization has to struggle." Ben-Gurion, too, stated that[14] "In Palestine there is another negative factor which renders

Jewish labor virtually impossible: the availability of abundant cheap, unorganized labor, bereft of class consciousness, with meager needs and permeated with a belief in enslavement and subordination, and unlimited exploitation."

The colonists who refused to replace Arab with Jewish labor were portrayed as a bunch of misers who were insensitive to the needs of the Jewish workers and pinched pennies rather than subscribe to the larger task of building a Jewish nation.[15]

To support this ideological rhetoric with hard facts, Ben-Gurion set out to refute the colonists' protestations that they simply could not afford to pay the relatively high wages demanded by Jewish workers and that the conquest of labor meant also the destruction of profits.

The details of Ben-Gurion's calculations are presented in the appendix to this chapter and reveal some fundamental errors. Basically, he simply did not know how to construct a profit-and-loss statement. In particular, he was completely unaware of the need to charge interest on both investment and working capital. Consequently, his figures do not even contain a quote for the rate of interest. This had to be obtained from a different source[16] to carry out the correct calculations, which are also presented in the appendix.

The difference in the conclusions could hardly be more striking. Ben-Gurion concluded from his erroneous calculations that the profit per box of oranges under Jewish labor was only 3 mills (the mill was one-thousandth of a pound) less than the profit under Arab labor. So, despite the fact that even this erroneous difference constituted 15 percent of the profit under Arab labor, Ben-Gurion inferred that[17] "The struggle against Jewish labor is based more on social considerations—class hatred toward the conscious Jewish laborer—than on economic ones. The 'national' employer needs the Arab worker as a whip against the 'impertinent' Jewish worker."

In fact, as the correct calculations that use Ben-Gurion's own data reveal, profits under Jewish labor were 36 percent less than profits under Arab labor. What is more, a drop of 20 percent in the price of oranges was sufficient to wipe out profits under Jewish labor altogether. Such a price decline was entirely possible, because the price of oranges underlying the calculations was high—the citrus industry did very well during the 1920s and early 1930s. But soon after Ben-Gurion arrived at his conclusions, citrus prices began to drop. By 1937 the price was a third lower than what it had been on the average between 1922 and 1931.[18]

But the hostility toward the colonists had not been based merely on ignorance in financial matters. The socialists also knowingly required the colonists to behave in an uneconomic fashion:[19] "For years we have presented the Jewish colonist in Palestine with a very difficult demand. We required him to do day in and day out something which is contrary to his immediate interest, and is against the main interest of ordinary people in their everyday life—

to ignore financial considerations, which requires not only a great financial effort but a great mental effort as well."

One of the more dramatic aspects of the struggle to conquer labor was the relationship between veteran farm workers and newcomers, which aggravated the financial demands placed on the colonists who employed them. Newcomers were, of course, less skilled than veterans, so it stood to reason that the newcomers would get paid less than the experienced workers. But because the latter feared the competition offered by the cheaper labor, efforts were made to secure equal pay for all.[20] The colonists actually complained about this practice, pointing out that the unexperienced workers were in need of a training period, during which they were still earning the same wage as experienced workers.[21]

The relevance of the drama of the conquest of labor to the evolving emasculation of the private sector lies with the fact that the Zionist leadership displayed hostility toward the colonists merely because they had been interested in what should have interested them if their aim was to survive financially in an ordinary business world. What is more, the leadership succeeded in getting public opinion overwhelmingly on its side.[22]

Thus, even though the campaign largely failed, it sent the clear message that, in Palestine, economic considerations take a back seat. Therefore, it is best to base financial survival on other than pure business considerations.

Quite naturally, many of the colonists who did succumb to the pressure and employed Jewish workers came to view themselves as rendering a national service at the cost of foregoing some of the profits. Hence, they thought themselves entitled to public help when their fortunes took a turn for the worse. Beginning with the mid-1930s, citrus prices abroad began to tumble as the Great Depression intensified. In 1937 the National Farmers Organization turned to the Jewish Agency for help.[23]

The application for help was entitled "Suggestions for the Alleviation of the Plight of the Citrus Economy." One suggestion was to expand the operations of the "Jewish Work Fund" established to subsidize Jewish labor, but there was also a specific reference to those growers whose financial circumstances could best be characterized as bankruptcy. Here, the applicants warned against the possibility that these desperate growers might sell their groves to "foreigners." However, the closing sentence of the application manifested the effects of the attempt to subordinate the colonists to noneconomic objectives: it expressed confidence that "The Jewish Agency will act with all the means at its disposal to rescue the agricultural branch which provides livelihood to thousands of families and constitutes a means of absorbing continuous immigration." This clearly constituted an adaptation to the rhetoric of the Histadrut.

On their knees, the colonists became eligible for cooperation from the

Histadrut. It came in the form of an application by the Agricultural Workers' Organization, the farm workers' union, to the Jewish Agency, requesting assistance for the citrus growers, among them the private ones. Specifically, the agency was asked to intervene with APB to reduce the rate of interest by 1 percentage point. There was also a request for the extension of more credit. The request was supported by[24] "The urgent need to extend help to this important sector of the economy, which employs thousands of Jewish workers. . . . The dangers are increased Arab labor, diminished cultivation expenditures and a pressure to reduce the Jewish workers' wage."

The quotations from the two letters crystalize admirably what became a recurrent theme and the epitome of the dependence of the private sector on the public sector, first in Palestine and then in Israel. When one cannot make it in the ordinary business world, because of obstacles imposed by the public sector or otherwise, enter instead what might be called the *business of selling Zionism*. This was by no means confined to requests for help on a sectoral basis. One finds pleas for help on behalf of individual producers as well. For instance, the Workers' Council of Petach Tikva asked the Jewish Agency to help a particular citrus grower because[25] "He was one of the few who obeyed the Jewish Labor commandment throughout the years. . . . His grove served as the training site for hundreds of immigrants." This, then, is the story of the emasculation of the private agricultural sector.

The First Failures of the Histadrut Economy

Failures of business enterprises are commonplace and in a capitalist economy often play the role of deadwood in the forest: make room for new, innovative, and more energetic enterprises. Hence, the failures of some Histadrut enterprises would be of no particular interest as such. But what is of interest is the reaction of the leadership to these failures.

In 1923 the construction cooperative Solel Boneh (literally, paver builder) was founded under the auspices of the Workers' Corporation. It replaced a predecessor, the Office for Public Works, and began operations in 1924. Already at its founding, its balance sheet looked peculiar indeed. Total assets amounted to about E£25,000,[26] all financed by debt—the company had no equity whatsoever.[27]

No less interesting are the comments made by the executive of the company on the loss incurred by its predecessor during the three years of its operation. It was deemed unavoidable and natural, owing to the "all-out charge to conquer the profession, and the extraordinary financial straits." Exegesis, the loss had been incurred as a price for a national service rendered. The company had not just been a business enterprise; it represented part of a national effort that cannot be assessed on ordinary business considerations. Hence, concluded the executive, "there can be no doubting the duty of the Zionist executive committee of coming to our aid in order to alleviate the excess burden."[28] The demand for assistance from the Zionist executive committee fell on fertile grounds, as aid had been flowing all along. It is estimated that in the period 1921–27, the Zionist executive committee provided E£54,000, more than twice what the Histadrut provided, and this excludes the emergency aid granted just before the collapse of Solel Boneh in 1927, an episode that merits special attention.

It may well be that Solel Boneh would have gone under even with impeccable management, but the record clearly indicates that the management had not been up to standard. The company became progressively less efficient: although business increased by almost 75 percent from 1924 to 1926, overhead expenditures grew from 13 to 15 percent of the total over the same period. This exceeded the normal standard for private construction contractors.[29] And even though it had become clear during 1926 that economic conditions were on the decline (leading in the end to the most severe economic depression in the modern history of Palestine; so bad was the depression, that for the first time since the renewal of Jewish settlement in Palestine, emigration of Jews exceeded immigration), the company kept increasing wages.[30] Administrative expenses kept rising; in 1927 they exceeded the 1926 level by E£5,000.[31]

As the situation worsened, the Jewish executive committee formed a consortium with the three major Jewish banks in an attempt to bail the company out. The consortium lent E£20,000, all of which turned into a grant when the company ceased operations at the end of 1927. There are conflicting data concerning the amounts given to the company by the Zionist executive committee, and the sums range all the way to E£100,000.[32]

The collapse of Solel Boneh exposed another feature of the workers' economy that allowed unprofitable outfits to survive: mutual assistance arrangements among enterprises. A particular form of this arrangement, which has existed for decades between the various Histadrut enterprises, allowed Solel Boneh to pay its workers in "funny money." During the months preceding its collapse, the company resorted to paying its workers with coupons that were redeemable against groceries at Hamashbir, the cooperative that distributed farm supplies, marketed farm products, and ran retail outlets throughout Palestine. It, too, required financial help from the Zionist executive committee, and when the construction contractor went under, the retailer was left holding the bag. The latter-day request by the faltering Koor for government assistance on a significant scale is nothing but the logical conclusion of a long history of reliance on public funds when business goes sour.

The comment made by the Solel Boneh executives constitutes the most succinct, and probably the earliest statement of what lies in the heart of the affliction that besets Israel's private sector. Even if one accepts the principle that business enterprises should be charged with nonbusiness duties, such a system is simply not workable. Once a company loses, it is impossible to tell which part of the loss is due to bad business and which part is the consequence of national undertakings. Hence, the profitability of such a company can no longer be used to assess the performance of its management, which creates an enormous moral hazard. Patriotism can be turned into a haven for the delinquent manager.

The idea that business enterprises should serve as instruments for the attainment of national economic objectives, and that these objectives conflicted with normal business objectives, continued to be widely held, both in Palestine and then in Israel. This can be verified by considering some very recent pronouncements. In 1987, speaking about the financial difficulties that beset Koor, the Histadrut's industrial holding company, its chief executive declared that[33] "This system is an uncommon creation. It has both national and social objectives, and it presents more difficulties than other systems."

In 1983 an entire issue of the *Economic Quarterly* was devoted to the Workers' Corporation and its subsidiaries. The collection of papers published therein, many of them by top people in the corporation's hierarchy, are impregnated with similar pronouncements. The secretary general of the corporation stated flatly that there is good reason to continue to view the corporation as having national and social goals, in addition to economic ones. The chief executive of Hasneh, Israel's largest insurance company, found that this requires particularly high capabilities of the corporation's management. The chairman of the Bank Ha'poalim observed that his bank is not like any other, in that it is not necessarily interested in returns to the shareholders, but endeavors to secure lasting economic well-being for the working public in general.[34]

Solel Boneh was revived in 1935 and immediately enjoyed financial assistance from the Histadrut.[35] The money used to subsidize the enterprises of the Workers' Corporation came from two sources. First, the Histadrut ran its own fund-raising campaign in the United States. Second, there was no clear distinction between what members of the Histadrut paid as union dues and what they paid as medical insurance premiums to Kupat Holim, the Histadrut's sick fund. The latter arrangement was deliberate: one cannot belong to the sick fund without being a member of the Trade Unions Federation. The sums granted to the various enterprises were quite substantial. For example, during the seven-year period 1952–58, I£8.3 million were used for this purpose.[36] In 1952 the total value of output of all the affiliates of the Workers' Corporation came to I£58.5 million.[37] If we assume that the subsidies were distributed evenly over the period, then the annual subsidy amounted to about 2 percent of the turnover. But to gauge its real impact, we must relate it to profits, not to turnover. Thus, even if the workers' enterprises realized a profit of 10 percent on turnover, which constitutes a healthy proportion, the subsidies would still make up 20 percent of profits—not a negligible contribution.

The Class Struggle—Unions and Wages

It was already noted that one of the methods employed by the Histadrut, after it had been necessary to abandon the vision of a totally socialized economy, was a fierce class struggle. This was based on the perception of similar attitudes in the well-developed capitalist economies, except that in Palestine it was clearly uncalled for: the capitalistic component of the economy was far too small and weak to constitute a target for socialist hostility.[38] Levontine, whose critique of the Zionist economic policy embraced every aspect of economic life, pointed out that[39] "Strikes are multiplying and expanding in a more aggressive fashion and the struggle of Labor against Capital [is taking place] even before the latter has arrived in our land."

The Histadrut's union activity involved two avenues of operation. First, there was the endeavor to monopolize the labor market to make sure that employers would have no option but to cooperate with the Histadrut. The drive to establish labor exchanges, described in Chapter 5, must be seen as part of this effort. Second, the Histadrut strove to institute a collective wage agreement that would oblige all the industrial employers.[40] With collective bargaining taking place between the Histadrut and a representative body of employers, the former would secure a centralized, firm grip on the labor market as a whole.

In its drive to monopolize the labor market, the Histadrut could rely on the fact that the great majority of workers belonged to it. It could therefore threaten individual employers as well as employers in general with industrial action unless they complied with its demands. For example, in February 1937 the Manufacturers' Association sent its members the following circular:[41]

Lately, there have been more complaints to the effect that producers employ only members of the Histadrut, while workers who belong to other federations, such as [here comes a list] are left out and cannot obtain work in the Jewish industry in our land. . . . We would like to remind you that at our last plenary session . . . it was resolved as follows: "Every Jew who comes here, regardless of his views and his party or his organizational affiliation—is eligible to obtain work."

The circular elicited the following reaction from the executive committee of the Histadrut:[42] "We protest in the strongest of terms the fact that your Association, whose duty it is to organize its members the industrialists, takes

the liberty of giving instructions concerning the organization of workers."
The response concludes with a threat of action in case there is an attempt to
act on the circular.

So adamant was the Histadrut in its effort that it even went as far as to
employ violence against an employer who happened to be a cooperative. On
December 7, 1938, Histadrut operatives forcibly expelled non-Histadrut
workers from a construction site operated by the Yetzira cooperative. The
next day they beat up a worker on the same site who belonged to a different
union.[43]

Where union activity ran into a very awkward situation was in the Histadrut's own enterprises. Recall that every member of the Histadrut was, at
least nominally, the owner of shares in the Workers' Corporation. Union
members who worked in Histadrut factories were therefore both employees
and owners. If a strike were to break out, such workers would nominally be
striking against themselves. The workers did not perceive it in this way, of
course, because their actual influence over how the Histadrut's economy was
being run was nil, nor did they enjoy any dividends.

In March 1946, a strike broke out in the Vulcan foundries (on which
more later), owned by Koor. The workers struck for higher wages, which the
management said were unjustified by productivity. The leaders of the strike
belonged to the local workers' council, whereas the Histadrut's central bodies,
having been put on the spot, ducked the issue. The workers won, but the concept of the workers' economy clearly lost.[44]

In its drive to institute collective wage agreements, the Histadrut used
its muscle to prevent the Manufacturers' Association from being represented
on the labor exchange even after the exchange became a Jewish Agency
organ.[45] The Manufacturers' Association argued that the structure of the labor
exchange and a collective agreement were two separate issues. Among other
things it feared, correctly, that a collective agreement might compel even
those employers who happen to be doing badly, to raise their workers' pay.
The association therefore required that a collective agreement include a mechanism for exempting such employers temporarily from certain stipulations of
the agreement.[46]

The Jewish Agency's position, as expressed by its treasurer, favored
collective bargaining. It went as far as stating that the financial arguments
raised by the Manufacturers' Association constituted a front behind which the
real, political arguments were hidden.[47]

The Credit Crunch

No private enterprise can exist in a modern economy without some
form of credit, unless it is so liquid that it can finance even its needs for work-

ing capital out of equity. Not only is this mostly impossible, but it is usually not good business. As is well known, financial leverage enhances, within certain limits, the rate of return on equity. Even in developing countries, there are agricultural credit arrangements centered on the relations between farmer and distributer-supplier.

Perhaps the single most important feature of industrial development in Palestine was the lack of anything resembling adequate credit facilities, and much of the character of private enterprise has been shaped by this. The lack of credit has been observed as early as 1924. Bank credit could be obtained for only up to three months, at 9 percent interest, which was very high by normal standards.[48] For example, in the United States in 1925 (1924 was a recession year, and so interest rates were even lower) the yield on commercial paper was 4 percent and on customer loans 4.5 percent.[49] Even at the high rates that existed in Palestine, the banks required collateral in the form of customers' notes. That is, the borrower had to extend credit to customers to obtain credit from banks.[50]

Industrial mortgage credit had not been forthcoming either, despite the fact that in 1922 two mortgage banks were founded, one of them as an affiliate of APB, and hence under the auspices of the Zionist Organization.[51]

Why did Palestine's economy suffer from lack of industrial credit? Was there a way to overcome this deficiency?

The answers are rooted partially in the ideological attitudes to industry in general and private industry in particular. As we have seen, given the conditions that existed at the time, credit for agriculture was plentiful. However, it was credit largely financed from national means and so cannot be viewed as normal business credit (not to mention that a good deal of it was never repaid). This fact had not been overlooked by Arlosoroff: "If you ask the advocates of private enterprise: what is it that must be done in order to promote private initiative—be sure, that 99–100 percent will reply: extension of credit."[52] The analysis that followed the observation concluded that, even if there were a lack of credit, this could not serve as an excuse, because the next logical question is, Why has private enterprise failed to generate credit facilities? The failure on the part of private business to establish credit facilities left national means as the sole source for credit, from which the author concluded that private enterprise could not really become viable to begin with.[53]

This is a chain of reasoning that, given the basic rules of the game as they existed, is immune to refutation. Ordinary commercial banks are not usually in the business of providing long-term or high-risk credit. They normally dispense short-term or medium-term credit. But even this observation does not really counter Arlosoroff's argument, because private enterprise had not yet managed to establish even short-term credit facilities. Even as late as 1939, industry commanded only 11.3 percent of all Palestinian credit, whereas agriculture's share was 23 percent, and that of trade 17.2 percent.[54] Even APB allocated only 16 percent of its total credit portfolio to industry in 1935. This compares to 31 percent of credit allocated to trade.[55] Toward the end of 1935 the bank had extended P£25,000 of medium-term credit (three to four years).[56] As a percentage of total loans as of the end of 1935, this came to a negligible less than 1 percent. This was true even though the equity-loan ratio stood at almost 24 percent,[57] which means that the bank was solidly solvent and thus was in a position to incur some risk. As for longer term credit, it could be supplied only by investment and mortgage banks, and banks of this type could not develop on a substantial scale because of the ground rules.

An investment bank was unlikely to emerge following the defeat of the Brandeis approach (see Chapter 3). Once the effort of building the Jewish community in Palestine was presented to the Jews of the world as a philanthropic enterprise, no room was left for long-term investment from abroad. And funds from abroad had been the only ones that could possibly provide resources for an investment bank.

Industrial mortgage, on the other hand, was largely excluded by the policy of national ownership of land. Those who provided the intellectual foundations for national ownership had not been oblivious to the mortgage question. They professed to believe, however, that the leasehold granted for forty-nine years could be mortgaged virtually like owned land:[58] "The hereditary lease as a real property right, can also be mortgaged. The lessee is as free as a landlord to borrow, not indeed upon the land, but upon his leasehold right. Here his borrowing capacity is about equal to that of the landlord." It seems that this assessment was based on the logical fallacy of confusing borrowing against an asset, and borrowing against earning capacity:[59] "The rating of a farm for borrowing purposes is determined by its market-value. The market-value, again, depends on the paying capacity of the farm, the yield of the soil, and the value of the buildings and other fixtures. The decisive factor, however, is the yearly net profit which the right of utilizing the soil and the buildings erected on the property can, with ordinary good management, yield to the proprietor." In an effort to substantiate this analysis, the author observes that residents in houses that were built on JNF land were able to secure loans against home mortgages.

The confusion seems to have stemmed from an inability to differentiate the market value of an asset from the ability to borrow against its earning capacity under a particular owner. The housing example helps to enforce this diagnosis. The value of a house does not depend on its occupant, because the flow of housing services generated by a home is a constant independent of occupancy or ownership. The capacity of an asset to generate income, in contrast, does depend on its owner, and may therefore differ from its market value. Hence, in the first case the bank does not face the sort of uncertainty that confronts it in the second case.

The assertion that a leasehold could be mortgaged just like the asset itself was wrong in principle. But even if it had not been, the scheme could not have worked because of a clause in the lease contract that stipulated that the JNF had veto power concerning the transfer of the lease. Thus, consider a farmer who borrowed against the leasehold and defaulted. A decision to foreclose meant the bank had to look for a new owner. Naturally, it would look for a farmer who was likely to produce a high income from the land. But the bank faced the risk that the JNF, which had in mind considerations other than profitability, might veto the deal. So its ability to recover at least part of the loss was at the mercy of the JNF. What bank would lend, under these circumstances, against the leasehold?

There is plenty of evidence concerning the impracticality of obtaining mortgage loans on nationally owned land. Consider, for example, the situation in the Haifa Bay area, which is to this day one of Israel's industrial centers:[60] "Industrialists whose plants are situated on JNF land complain bitterly. When these plants were founded, the land there was still relatively cheap and the owners of the plants could have bought it. Instead, they were given JNF land. So now, when the industrialist finds himself in financial straits, and wishes to obtain a mortgage loan, this is, as you obviously know, virtually impossible to obtain on JNF land."

A particularly vivid description of the situation has H. Margulies, a top executive of APB, confront an industrialist who asked for a mortgage loan and whose plant was situated on national land, by asking "what collateral can you provide?" The industrialist replied "you know that I have machinery, raw materials, and even a warehouse with finished goods." To this Margulies retorted: "Today you have a warehouse with finished goods. But when the time comes for us to liquidate, it will no longer be there. The machines naturally cannot be converted to cash, and the buildings, who knows if anyone will want to buy them?"[61]

Fortunately, the suggestion that industrial mortgages in Palestine were possible is not only a theory. In 1928, the Palestine Mortgage and Credit Bank began operating. It was wholly owned by the Palestine Economic Corporation (P.E.C.), which had been founded in 1921 by the Brandeis-Mack group in New York. The story of P.E.C. is interesting in itself, because in a way the company served as an incarnation of the ideas of Brandeis, rejected by the Zionist Organization. The corporation's objective, as stated in its charter, was "to afford an instrument through which American Jews and others who may be interested may give material aid *strictly on a business basis* to productive Palestinian enterprises and thereby further the economic development of the Holy Land and the resettlement there of an increasing number of Jews" (italics mine—Y.P.).[62]

For a period of about three years, the P.E.C.'s bank conducted an exper-

iment in the extension of mortgage and other industrial credit, with funds supplied by the parent company. During that period, the bank extended ninety-
one loans totalling almost P£18,500. Of those, sixteen loans were given
against mortgages on land alone or on land and other assets.[63] The term of
almost half of the sum was from thirty-one to thirty-six months and over 6
percent was extended for periods exceeding three years, terms that until that
time had been unheard of. Interest was at 8 percent, which was the going rate
at the time; that is, the bank did not charge extra for the added risk involved in
the longer terms.

The experiment proved a success. Out of the P£18,500 extended,
P£10,800 was repaid by the end of May 1931 and only P£697 were in arrears,
partly because of the 1929 disturbances.[64] But the operation faded after a
while, for reasons that are not entirely clear. One explanation for the decline
was reduced demand for loans, because the Mortgage and Credit Bank did not
offer the whole range of banking services. In particular, it did not offer check-
ing facilities. For its part, APB began to offer medium-term credit to industry
only in 1934. And by 1937 there had still been no sign of long-term credit.[65]

The difficulties Palestinian industry had to endure because of the credit
problem were many and varied, but two particularly vivid examples deserve
special mention. These are the stories of Phoenicia, Palestine's first glass
manufacturer, and Vulcan, the first foundry.

Phoenicia was founded in April 1934 by the Buchsbaum brothers, who
invested in it their own means and raised equity capital. According to the balance sheet of November 11, 1936, the company had paid-up capital of
£36,300, and debts of £25,400. That would seem like a comfortably leveraged
balance sheet, except that the debt was mostly to the Industrial and Financial
Corporation (IFICO), which was constantly breathing down the company's
neck. In particular, Phoenicia did not own its land, and so could not secure a
reasonable mortgage loan. Instead, it borrowed a negligible amount against a
mortgage on the leasehold, living proof of the folly underlying the assumption
that national ownership of land could be instituted without ill ramifications for
the economy.

Because of the disturbances that started in 1936, the construction
industry, whose demand for plate glass had been the object of the company,
was badly disrupted. IFICO, worried about its loans, forced Phoenicia into
receivership before the company ever started normal operations. The balance
sheet for December 1, 1939 shows equity capital of £40,000 and virtually no
debt. In this condition it was bought by Solel Boneh in 1940, to become the
Histadrut's first genuine industrial plant. By December 31, 1941, the balance
sheet showed the same amount of equity, but also £34,000 of debt, of which
more than a third was granted by APB, with almost another half coming
from the new parent company.[66] By the end of 1942, debt made up 65 per-

cent of the company's liabilities, but the lion's share of it was owed to the parent company.

The story of Vulcan, which was founded in 1934 by Mr. Kremner, runs along similar lines. As in Phoenicia's case, Solel Boneh bought Vulcan in 1941, paid off the creditors and refinanced the company out of its own sources. After Koor was established in June 1944, it purchased most of the shares of both Phoenicia and Vulcan.[67]

The problem of industrial credit had not been ignored by the Zionist leadership and received at least nominal attention. Since the early 1920s there had been talk of establishing an industrial bank, and from the deliberations it appears as though it had been conceived as a full-fledged investment bank.[68] The Palestine Industrial Bank, which at long last began operating in 1933, was a far cry from the concept of an investment bank. Moreover, it was partially owned by the Jewish Agency and APB[69] and was therefore unlikely to chart radically new avenues in industrial credit extension. It is interesting to observe that official assistance to the new bank came partly in the form of Jewish Agency deposits, from which certain funds, to be discussed shortly, were financed. One could view the arrangement as the earliest forerunner of "government deposits for credit extension," or earmarked deposits, which much later became an important instrument for government domination of the credit market (see Chapter 2).

The Adaptation of the Private Sector

How did the private sector respond to the hostile environment to which it was subjected partly by circumstance and partly by design? The environment with which private enterprise had been confronted required a strategy for survival other than managing sound businesses. The incentives were cast in a different way, and the business community responded to them just as one would have expected.

The organizational instrument for carrying out the transformation was formed in 1923 by a small group of entrepreneurs. The Manufacturers' Association (henceforth M.A.) initially comprised twelve members. By 1935 the M.A. claimed to represent 95 percent of all industrial capital.[70] At first, there was not much to be done, as industry was still in its infancy, but after the Fourth Aliya, and especially after the Fifth, which was spurred by Hitler's ascent in Germany, the scope for activity expanded considerably.

In the context of the present discussion, two areas of M.A. activity are relevant. First, it adopted the rhetoric favored by the socialist leadership. That entailed projecting an image of industrialists who are engaged in business not for the sake of profit, but rather to participate in the building of Palestine's Jewish community. Second, it was active in promoting cartels.

The Zionist-rhetoric offensive of the M.A. began in 1935, after the association had asserted itself as the representative organ of the industrial establishments. First, the M.A. cast itself in the role of immigration absorber and fighter against unemployment. For example, at a meeting of its representatives with the Jewish Agency in 1936, the chairman of the M.A. proposed to discuss urgent measures for dealing with unemployment, which had been on the increase.[71] This concern with employment was also hinted at when A. Shenkar, the president of the M.A., stated that[72] "Not a few industrialists are thinking about idling their plants in order to minimize the losses, and our Association is doing its utmost to convince its members not to traverse that road, in the hope that the Zionist Congress will find a solution to this searing problem and will thereby avoid serious complications." On another occasion, a representative of the M.A. stated that, from a financial standpoint, many employers should have closed down their operations, which would have created alarmingly high unemployment, but they did not do so because this would have been at odds with their "nationalist-political views."[73] Similarly,[74] "The political state of the Zionist Movement at this juncture intensifies the Zionist value of industry, which achieved in recent years a level enabling it to absorb most of the immigrants for the purpose of arranging for them productive employment, and it thus behooves the Congress to resolve to provide full national support to industry and to the industrial movement."

The second theme was the issue of Jewish labor. Here, the strategy was to emphasize the fact that there had been almost no Arab labor in industry. Thus,[75] "Palestinian industry, which employs only Jewish workers and which insists, despite competition, dumping, etc. on the principle of Pure Jewish Labor, constitutes today a first-class stronghold in the life of the community." And again, as part of recounting the virtues of industry,[76] it expressed its "Complete loyalty to Jewish labor and to the interests of the national economy."

The fact that industry employed almost no Arabs is indisputable, but the attempt to portray this practice as the consequence of devotion to national values was a charade. In fact, hardly any Arabs were qualified enough to work in industry. Moreover, the Arab workers that had been employed by private farmers came mostly from the countryside. It would have been too expensive and cumbersome to transport them to the major industrial areas, as this would have to be done on a daily basis, given the lack of facilities to stay overnight.

The third theme in the Zionist symphony played by the M.A. was exports. Here, as in the provision-of-employment chapter, the M.A. was catering to what the leadership had defined as "nationally useful" enterprises. In contrast to the former themes, the exports argument lent itself to quantification, and so could be used for requesting specific assistance:[77] "Export development should not be left exclusively to the producers. This is a problem of national importance of the first order. The entire [Zionist] Movement must shoulder the efforts and the expenses which are required to pave the way for Palestinian produce in foreign markets. Our fledgling industry will not be able to promote the cause of exports without assistance from the nation and from the Movement."

In addition to these major themes, the M.A. also promoted the industrialists as a collection of devotees to the welfare of the community. This could take the form of general declarations of patriotism, such as[78] "We came to this land by right and not by anyone's charity; we brought to our people a lot of devotion, love, economic and technical experience, and have invested all of these in the sands and rocks of this barren land." Or, it could be stated as the furtherance of a particularly important cause, such as[79] "The M.A. never viewed itself only as a guild, whose duty it is to protect its members. The M.A. considers its task as being mainly the development of industry, and it gears its effort according to this fundamental principle." Other such causes included mobilizing foreign investment capital, for which purpose the M.A. established an office in New York. This was described as constituting part of the effort for securing the future of industry.[80] The M.A. also portrayed itself as fighting price increases of domestically produced goods. The reason given is quite interesting: price rises were bad because they could attract foreign competition, which would destroy Palestinian industry.[81]

Export promotion was not the only component of the M.A.'s Zionist drive that could be used directly to obtain financial benefits. The other was the campaign to Buy Locally Made (the *Totzeret Ha'aretz*, literally, "produce of the country" campaign).

To promote domestically produced goods, the "Union for Domestic Produce" (henceforth the Union) was established and described as[82] "An autonomous organization that is in constant contact with economic bodies, which by their nature are interested in buttressing the community's economic strength."

The Union became relatively effective because of the recession that started in 1936. For example, the joint committee of the Jewish Agency and the M.A. resolved to recommend that the former intercede with mortgage banks to get them to extend credit only to those construction firms that used domestically produced building materials.[83]

As the campaign to promote domestically produced goods gathered momentum, the rhetoric became evermore fantastic. Thus,[84] "Total loyalty to domestic produce is a fundamental Zionist and communal obligation. . . . All means should be used to intensify the activity of the Union." And a few years later, the executive committee of the M.A. declared that[85]

The securing of the domestic market's loyalty to domestic produce is not intended to further the welfare of industrialists alone; it is in the entire community's interest, the entire Zionist structure depends on it. . . . The Executive Committee demands of the community and its institutions to set and implement a regime of loyalty to domestic produce. The regime, based on national subordination . . . will compel every producer, worker, merchant and consumer—the entire community, with no exception, to total loyalty to domestic produce.

Under these circumstances it should come as no surprise that after Israel came into being, the industrialists willingly cooperated with the government in the imposition of import restrictions and a licensing system, in the belief that they could navigate such a system to their own advantage. Towards the end of 1948, while Israel was still fighting the war for survival, the M.A. called on the government to guide imports in a manner conducive to exports—whatever that meant.[86] Next, the Union proposed that a consulting body be established and charged with advising the officials dealing with imports. It observed that this was necessary because[87] "The decision concerning each application for an import license requires professional consideration and profound knowledge of the economic and technical aspects of domestic production—a task beyond the competence of the governmental apparatus." There followed a list of criteria for import licensing. The first was whether the requested import competed with domestic goods. The second was whether the good in question was produced domestically in quantities that "satisfied the population's consumption needs."

Turning to cartels, the conceptual foundation for cartelization was provided by both the M.A. and people outside it, especially from the banking community. Various pieces of the ideological foundation were provided at different times. One rationale was of the type used throughout the world as a justification for restrictive practices: stability or prevention of cutthroat competition,[88] which was also viewed as "hindering advance." The remedy was for each branch of industry to "organize its existing market and then proceed to concentrate on the extension of its outlets both at home and abroad."[89]

Another rationale for restricted competition was based on the recession that started in 1936. Cartelization was needed, so went the argument, to protect the producers from the hardships of the recession, for cartelization could arrest the price declines and so prevent bankruptcies.[90]

Setting up the joint committee of the M.A. and the Jewish Agency, some of whose deliberations had already been mentioned, provided a convenient forum for mobilizing official support for cartelization. Here we find another line of reasoning in support of cartelization; namely, that in its absence firms will collapse, thus creating "catastrophic" unemployment. This is, of course, false reasoning. The aim of cartelization is reduced output, which implies reduced employment.[91] Another such fallacy is inherent in the argument that internal competition served only to enhance imports.[92] This line of reasoning was carried even further when domestic competition was termed *internal dumping*.[93]

The bankers' point of view was that cartelization was needed if industrialists were to harbor realistic expectations concerning credit. The core of the argument here was that cartelization provided a guarantee in the sense of diminution of the risk incurred by the lending bank. The industrialists were exhorted to "put their house in order" before presenting more demands for credit.[94] The existing state of competition was termed *sick*.

The task of organizing branch-by-branch cartels fell to the M.A.'s Sections Department, which operated with official blessing.[95] Its objectives were described as[96] "The creation of fair business relations among producers. . . . Sometimes the Department manages to accomplish this in the area of marketing by implementing agreements, designed to eliminate or limit unfair or ruinous competition." Later on the M.A. established, in addition to the Sections Department, a Cartels Department, which endeavored to assist producers in the creation of associations designed to facilitate a "reorganization of marketing channels," a euphemism for carving up the market among them. By the end of 1940 the Cartels Department had managed to assist in the establishment of thirteen associations, comprising fifty enterprises.[97]

We have already seen that the Histadrut, for reasons of its own, pressed for collective wage bargaining between itself and the M.A. But why did the latter agree to collective agreements? One can think of three reasons for the M.A.'s acceptance of the principle of collective bargaining, leading to a wage agreement between the Histadrut and industry as a whole. First, it feared that individual employers would be virtually powerless if they were to negotiate with the Histadrut (rather than with a particular union) on their own.[98] The second reason belongs in the cartelization category: a fear of competition among employers in the labor market. Here the idea was to reach a labor accord that would bind all employers, and therefore hinder everyone from offering higher wages in an attempt to recruit more workers.[99] Third, the M.A. must have hoped that collective agreements would prevent the Histadrut enterprises from exploiting their special relations with the trade unions in competing with private business.

From a purely economic standpoint, collective wage agreements, at least in the form adopted in Palestine, were very bad, for they ignored sectoral profitability differentials, and there is little doubt that this had been understood by the M.A.[100]

The price requested by the M.A. for its coyness and for the adoption of the official rhetoric was considerable. Only a partial chronicle is possible here. The M.A. asked the Jewish Agency to provide P£50,000 to the Palestine Industrial Bank. In fact, for a while the M.A. expected the Jewish Agency to agree to an arrangement whereby the latter would provide most of the capital for the bank, whereas the former would control the board.[101] Another credit-related request was that the Jewish Agency provide credit guarantees to facilitate bank lending. The aggressiveness of the M.A. in this respect was remarkable:[102] "In principle, the task of the industrialists is to produce. The [Jewish] Agency should have taken the initiative and present the M.A. with practical proposals. Instead, it shirks its responsibility and thinks that it can placate the industrialists with pennies."

In its attempt to hook up with the Jewish Agency's lifeline, the M.A. also proposed two institutional arrangements. First, it requested that an advisory board, made up largely of M.A. members, be set up to "guide" the activities of the Department of Trade and Industry of the Jewish Agency.[103] Second, it fought hard for the institution of compulsory arbitration in wage disputes. If successful, this would have been a marvelous achievement, as it would place the responsibility for the wage structure squarely in the lap of the Jewish Agency.

Later on, the M.A. went as far as demanding that the political parties that made up the Zionist Organization incorporate pro-industry planks in their political platforms and include industrialists among their representatives. These representatives would then work with the M.A. to promote the case of industry in the central bodies of the Zionist Organization.[104]

The kowtowing of the M.A. was not in vain: it yielded tangible results. In 1937 the Jewish Agency established the Fund for Industrial Recuperation and Encouragement (henceforth the Fund). One of its directors (who was to become the first governor of the Bank of Israel) observed that the Fund was needed because of the "high interest rates on debt capital, and the short-term nature of obligations, which compelled borrowers to follow unhealthy financial policies." Although roundabout, the statement clearly describes an environment suffering from insufficient credit facilities.[105]

The principles that guided the Fund in its decisions as to who was eligible for its credit, constitute a clear manifestation of the reshaped ideology concerning the place of private enterprise in general, and industry in particular, in the construction of the Jewish entity in Palestine. According to these principles, credit was going to be extended only in cases where the recipient had reasonable chances of becoming profitable and where the risk involved would be minimal. But in addition, the recipient had to have "national value." To be eligible for this status, the firm had to possess at least one of the following characteristics: (1) be the only one of its kind; (2) produce mainly for export; (3) produce a good most of whose consumption is supplied by imports.

Once the barrier had been breached and the Jewish Agency became involved in industrial finance the involvement of the official organs of the

Zionist Organization in industrial finance expanded and spawned instruments that served as a model for independent Israel later on. By 1942, in addition to the Fund, the Jewish Agency was involved in the Joint Fund for Small Loans A, Joint Fund B, Medium-Term Industrial Credit Fund, Fund for Letters of Credit, and Fund for the Execution of Government and Military Procurement, the last having been a consequence of British procurement in connection with the war.[106]

The Jewish Agency also actively helped in organizing cartels. Not only did it provide continuous verbal support, it actually used its good offices for the cause. For example, although it could not accept the demand to forbid new immigrants from transferring their wealth to Palestine (mainly under the "Transfer," an agreement reached with the German government under which Jews leaving Germany could take with them part of their assets, provided they did it by purchasing German goods) in the form of machinery, it could mitigate the effect of such imports. Thus, sometime between 1937 and 1940, the Department of Labor of the Jewish Agency arranged that a newly constructed bakery, using modern equipment, limit its output to allow the older, less modern bakeries to stay in business.[107]

Early Statehood

After Israel came into existence, and the Jewish Agency's executive committee of yesteryear became a government with powers of legislation and taxation, new vistas for intervention opened up. The government announced early on that it would assist industry in a planned manner, assistance seen as both necessary for attainment of the long-run goals of the country and deserved by the pioneers who had toiled at establishing the industrial economy.[108]

The leaders of the M.A. not only acquiesced in the government's increasing interference in the economy, but actually demanded more "planning" by the government.[109] Planning meant, first of all, controlling imports in a manner commensurate with the "needs" of industrial development. Second, it meant government intervention in labor relations to the extent that industry could carry on its "obligations" unhampered by strikes and other industrial action. Third, the government was to assist in the housing of industrial workers. Fourth, the government had to play a central role in the allocation of credit and in direct investment.[110] It is hard to believe that all this was put forth by the president of the M.A., rather than by a socialist ideologue. Later on, the M.A. proposed that many of these items be included in a law for the encouragement of industry.

The government, both driven by its own ideology and prodded by the M.A., was swift to assume control. Two areas in which the government aggressively intervened right away were foreign trade, including foreign exchange and exchange rates, and the domestic pricing and rationing of an array of "essential" goods.

The intervention in foreign trade proceeded along two lines. First, and most irksome, was the institution of import licenses. But licensing was not based on announced rules, applied equally to everybody. Rather, applications were examined and approved, or rejected, on a case-by-case basis. Thus, for example, a producer could be granted permission to import new machinery, but then denied permission to import spare parts, without which the machinery could not be operated.[111] The second method of intervention employed by the government was a system of multiple exchange rates. In February 1952 there were three official exchange rates. The first, I£0.357/$1, was the rate at which a tourist could exchange dollars for Israeli currency. It was also the rate applied to the export of polished diamonds. The second rate, I£0.714/$1, was applied to citrus exports (which at that time constituted the lion's share of all exports). The two rates were also applied to the imports of certain "essential" goods, such as staples. But for most import transactions, the rate of I£1/$1 was applied.[112]

But in addition to the official exchange rates were also unofficial ones. First, there existed an arrangement known as *imports without payment.* Under it individuals, say American Jews coming to visit their relatives in Israel, could bring with them certain kinds of goods that they had purchased abroad and sell them on the domestic market. The implied exchange rate ranged in 1952 up to I£1.5/$1. Then there was the black-market cash exchange rate, which ranged up to I£2.8/$1.[113]

Intervention in the distribution of consumer products in the domestic markets was governed by the Austerity Plan. Accordingly, the government placed some 600 items under price control. Included in the controlled category were consumer goods, such as staples, clothing, footwear, and furniture. Chief among producer goods under control was cement. Services such as transportation, hotels, and restaurants were also price controlled. Rationing of foodstuffs was implemented by linking each consumer to a particular retailer, mostly the neighborhood grocer, and by providing the consumer with a ration card.[114]

The peculiar twist here is that the plan had not been dictated by any real shortage of supplies. Rather, it constituted a weapon in the fight against inflation.[115] It was a doomed fight, because the government kept printing money to finance its deficit, on the one hand, but maintained a set of artificially low exchange rates, on the other. Consequently, real incomes were incompatible with the amount of goods coming onto the market, and so domestic prices were bound to rise. But because many prices were controlled, black markets developed in many goods.

The industrialists discovered early on that once government management of the economy is unleashed, it may not be controllable by those who sought to benefit from it. Thus, the M.A. complained bitterly as early as 1949 that the allocation of import licenses, whose institution it had supported, was not "working properly."[116] Still, it never questioned the principle of government involvement. Its only goal was to steer such involvement toward its own gain.

The most serious consequence of the way in which the nominally private economy had evolved is that Israel has never developed and is still bereft of a political constituency based on the liberal (in the European sense) philosophy. The General Zionists, a party widely viewed as wearing that mantle, was in reality just another interest group, no more liberal than the present-day Likud. Its leader, who by then was a member of the legislature and was to become the minister of trade and industry, supported the government's intervention in the capital market, and his only qualm was that it had not been done right and that his constituents, meaning the members of the M.A., had been discriminated against.[117] So the political road was wide open for the socialist and interventionist policies described in this and in the preceding chapters. The one place on earth that the Jews sought to call their home is the place where the "natural capitalists"[118] had no place.

Appendix:
The Profitability of an Acre of Citrus
Under Arab and Jewish Labor

Ben-Gurion's Version

Ben-Gurion's crucial error in his calculations was his disregard for the alternative cost of funds, the rate of interest. That meant that he neglected both to charge interest on working capital and to include capital recovery charges in the costs. Concerning the latter category, he committed the additional error of reckoning the cost differential between Arab and Jewish labor as a percentage of costs, instead of as a percentage of profits.

Start with the easiest part: interest on the annual expenditures in a mature grove, which must be considered working capital. If we apply an interest charge of 8 percent to the total cost figures in Table 7.1, then Ben-Gurion simply omitted an item worth P£1.24 in the case of Arab labor, and P£1.86 in the case of Jewish labor, which adds another P£0.62 to the cost differential.

Next, consider expenditures during the first five years, the investment period. Basing himself on the total costs figures under Jewish labor, excluding the costs of land and the well, in Table 7.2, he takes the arithmetic sum of these figures and concludes that costs during the first five years come to P£57.50. This constitutes an error, because one cannot add sums of money over time without using a proper capitalization factor. Doing the same thing for Arab labor, and assuming that fifteen out of the seventy-five workdays

TABLE 7.1

Expenditures (in £) per Quarter Acre of a Mature Fruit-Bearing Grove
Yielding 120 Boxes

Workdays Exclusive of Picking	30
Labor Costs:	
Arab Labor	3.60
Jewish Labor	6.00
Picking, Grading, and Packing:	
Arab Labor, .047/box	5.64
Jewish Labor, .060/box	7.20
Other Expenses	10.00
Total Costs:	
Arab Labor	19.24
Jewish Labor	23.20

required over the period would be supplied by Jews in any event (because
skilled labor is involved on these fifteen days), his figure for total costs under
Arab labor comes to P£52.70. Thus, he figures costs under Jewish labor to
exceed those under Arab labor over the entire five-year span by only 9 percent. And if the cost of land and the well are added, then the cost differential
shrinks to only less than 7 percent.

All this, however, plays no role in the computation of the profit differential, because no capital recovery is charged. For the profit differential, Ben-

TABLE 7.2

Expenditures (in £) per Quarter Acre of Oranges by Age (in years) of Grove
Prior to Fruit Bearing

	1	2	3	4	5
Workdays	20	15	12	13	15
Labor Costs:					
Arab	2.40	1.80	1.44	1.56	1.80
Jewish	4.00	3.00	2.40	2.60	3.00
Other Costs	36.00*	7.00	6.60	6.40	6.50
Total Costs:					
Arab Labor	38.40	8.80	8.04	7.96	8.30
Jewish Labor	40.00	10.00	9.00	9.00	9.50

*Including £20.00 for the cost of land and a grower-owned well.

The Poltical Economy of Israel

Gurion bases himself solely on his erroneous version of the current expenditures in a mature grove. He quotes a figure of revenue of P£0.30 per box "on the tree"; that is, before picking, grading, and packing costs are incurred. If we assume, as would be most advantageous for Ben-Gurion's point of view, that the figure is based on picking, grading, and packing costs under Jewish labor, then the proceeds from sale at the grove's gate are P£43.20 (consisting of P£0.30 x 120 plus picking, grading, and packing charges of P£7.20—see Table 7.1).

From the sum of P£43.20, one subtracts the Ben-Gurion version of total costs: P£19.24 and P£23.20 under Arab labor and Jewish labor, respectively. The resulting profits are P£0.20 and P£0.17 per box, respectively.

The Correct Calculation

In the correct calculation, the rate of interest is taken to be 8 percent for both working and investment capital (see Table 7.3). The reason is that at the time, that is, the 1920s and 1930s, private farmers had no access to long-term capital facilities; they used revolving credit to finance both long-term and short-term capital needs.

TABLE 7.3

Profit Statement (in £) per Quarter Acre of Oranges

Proceeds from Sales at Grove Gate	43.20
Total Current Expenditures, including interest at 8%:	
Arab Labor	20.78
Jewish Labor	25.06
Capital Recovery, 30 Years at 8%:	
Arab Labor	8.60
Jewish Labor	9.28
Total Costs:	
Arab Labor	29.38
Jewish Labor	34.34
Profit:	
Arab Labor	13.82
Jewish Labor	8.86

8

OBSTACLES TO GROWTH:
THE ALMIGHTY WEAKLING

A Summary of Government Activities

In the six preceding chapters attention has been focused on the damage to the economy inflicted by excessive government involvement. In this chapter, we shall concentrate on the impact of the interventionist policies on the government itself and on its ability to function as a government. Let us first consider the role played by government relative to the GNP. In what follows, all financial magnitudes will thus be stated as percentages of the GNP.

Total expenditures comprise public consumption, transfer payments, public sector investment, interest paid on the domestic debt, and net interest on foreign debt. So defined, total public expenditures exceeded 70 percent in each of the years 1980 to 1985, with the 1980 share constituting the peak at 76 percent. In the latter part of the 1980s the share has been declining steadily, standing at 55.6 percent in 1991.

Taxation alone cannot finance such a rate of expenditures, but due to U.S. aid and other foreign non-debt sources, this is not really necessary. In the Lebanon War year 1982, enough foreign resources were mobilized to allow the government to facilitate the 71.5 percent of the GNP in expenditures (Table 8.1), with only 56.6 percent in domestic finance. The main source of domestic finance was a heavy tax burden, the rest came from borrowing and income generated by government corporations and other property (e.g., revenues of the Port Authority).

Although 1982 saw a huge tax burden (45.5 percent), in 1986 the tax burden was even higher, 48 percent of the GNP. Perhaps even more important are the high marginal income-tax rates. For example, in 1987 the rate for the top income bracket was 52.8 percent.[1] How do Israelis cope with these heavy average and marginal tax rates? Part of the answer is provided on considering the vast transfer payments, to which we now turn.

TABLE 8.1

Government Finances, Percent of GNP, 1982

Total Expenditures:	71.5
Of which Financed by:	
Transfers from Abroad	9.1
Foreign Borrowing	5.8
Domestic Taxes	45.5
Domestic Borrowing	7.7
Other	3.4
Composition of Expenditures:	
Public Consumption	39.7
Direct Transfers	11.5
Subsidies	9.7
Debt Service	10.6

Source: BOI, *Annual Report 1984*, pp.88, 100; *1986*, p91; *1987*, p. 90; *1990*, p. 164

From Table 8.1 it emerges that the government spent 31.8 percent of the GNP on transfer payments and debt service. Direct transfers formed 11.5 percent, including income maintenance, social security payments, unemployment benefits, and so forth; a further 5.8 percent was spent on direct subsidies, chiefly for staples and basic services (bread, milk, public transportation, etc.) and for exports; and another 3.9 percent was spent in the form of credit subsidies for industry, housing, and the like. Altogether, then, the government engaged in direct and indirect transfer payments totaling 21.2 percent. So, although the gross tax burden in 1982 was enormous, the net burden was only 24.3 percent, certainly not excessive when compared to most Western economies.

The distorting effects of the gross tax rate and the high marginal rates are not alleviated, of course, by transfer payments. But the transfers do resolve the apparent contradiction between the tax burden and the relatively high rate of private consumption.

Table 8.1 also reveals a high rate of domestic borrowing. The consequences in terms of the capital and credit markets have been discussed at length. In addition, the heavy borrowing created a huge domestic national debt. In 1985 the debt burden reached a peak of 127 percent of the GNP. Things have improved a bit since then: in 1990 domestic debt was down to about 102 percent of the GNP.[2]

One of the chief tasks of any government is the provision of public goods. In Israel, defense occupies the lion's share of this category, so let us consider it first. Table 8.2 contains the essential information concerning the recorded defense burden. There are two sets of figures in the table: those concerning total consumption for defense, and those containing the domestic component thereof. The distinction is important because of the way in which defense imports are financed. Beginning with the 1973 Yom Kippur War, the U.S. government has been providing Israel with grants to finance defense procurement in the United States. This means that such imports have constituted, and still do, a gift, and therefore do not generate claims on domestic resources. Earlier, beginning in 1967, the U.S. government extended defense loans to finance procurement. These loans, too, have been regarded as neutral insofar as claims on domestic resources were concerned. From a policy standpoint, this was a questionable attitude. True, the loans did not generate claims on resources at the time, but deferred claims have a capitalized value that should have been taken into account. Now the future is here, and Israel is in the process of repaying those loans.[3]

Two features stand out clearly in Table 8.2. First, total consumption for defense fluctuates considerably, almost to the exclusion of any clear pattern. Domestic consumption for defense, on the other hand, features very distinct trends. The fluctuations in total consumption are caused, at least in part, by the bulkiness of imports. This is true especially as concerns combat aircraft. When a new generation of aircraft comes aboard, there is usually a wave of procurement, which peters out until the next novelties arrive. For example, the jump from 1968 to 1970 is associated with the arrival of the F-4 Phantoms.

The total consumption figures also delineate very clearly the aftermath of the 1973 war. The share of the GDP devoted to consumption for defense reached a zenith in 1975, due mainly to a hefty increase in imported materiel.

TABLE 8.2

Defense Consumption, Percent of the GDP

Year	Total	Domestic	Year	Total	Domestic
1966	10.4	6.6	1978	23.0	13.2
1967	18.2	9.8	1979	18.9	12.8
1968	17.9	11.9	1980	22.4	13.8
1969	19.6	12.5	1981	23.5	13.5
1970	25.2	13.6	1982	20.5	14.1
1971	22.6	14.1	1983	18.3	13.8
1972	19.0	12.1	1984	19.6	13.4
1973	29.9	14.8	1985	20.2	12.5
1974	29.3	17.1	1986	16.1	11.4
1975	31.7	15.9	1987	19.5	10.5
1976	27.4	14.5	1988	17.9	10.6
1977	21.7	13.6	1989	13.5	10.1

Source: CBS, *National Accounts*, various years.

As for domestic consumption for defense, there was first a quantum jump in the burden following the Six Day War, and it kept increasing steadily until 1971. What could have become a declining trend thereafter turned into another upward leap in the wake of the Yom Kippur War. A declining trend then set in and continued until 1979. It increased slightly thereafter, reaching a local peak in 1982, the year of the Lebanon War. Ever since then, the burden has been declining, reaching in 1989 and 1990 rates that have not been seen since the Six Day War of 1967.

The declining trend since 1982 reveals an interesting aspect of Israel's policies; namely, under economic duress, the defense budget becomes one of the easier targets. This is somewhat surprising in light of the fact that physical security has been the country's overwhelming concern since the announcement of its birth on November 29, 1947. There was certainly room for cutting defense expenditures after the cessation of large-scale hostilities in Lebanon. But in all other respects, defense problems have not eased, as the Gulf War has clearly indicated. Yet consumption for defense alone has been absorbing the cuts in public consumption. From 1982 to 1988, domestic consumption for defense declined in absolute terms by 3.3 percent, whereas civilian consumption increased by 8.5 percent. Consumption for defense declined even in 1988, despite the advent of the *intifada* (the Palestinian uprising), which since the end of 1987 has required the commitment of nonnegligible military resources.

Comparison with other countries reveals that even reduced, Israel shoulders a very heavy defense burden, a fact that has had important consequences for the country's economy. The latest year for which figures are more or less complete is 1985. Enlisting once again the comparison to Singapore and Italy, one finds that, although Israel spent 20 percent of its GNP on defense in Fiscal 1985, Singapore devoted 6 percent and Italy 2 percent of their respective GNPs to that purpose. Such a low defense spending rate is not uncommon: the Netherlands and Sweden spent 3 percent of their respective GNPs on defense in 1985 and the United States's relative defense spending was the same as Singapore's, despite its worldwide defense commitments.

Factoring out defense expenditures allows one to address the question of the standard of living relative to the productive effort in a more precise way. This can be done by looking at the share of the GNP spent on private and *civilian*, rather than total, public consumption. The results put Israel in a much better perspective when compared to some other countries. Private and public expenditures on nondefense consumption in Fiscal 1985 came to 79 percent of the GNP, as compared to 92 percent in Italy, 72 percent in Holland, and 77.5 percent in Sweden. The odd man out in terms of living standards is Singapore: in 1985 it spent on nondefense consumption only 52 percent of its GNP. So, although the standard of living in Israel relative to the population's productive effort is still very high by international standards, it is not as high as the raw consumption figures might lead one to think.[4]

These figures do not tell the whole defense story because several important items are not reflected at all, or at least not adequately, in defense consumption data. To begin with, soldiers in compulsory service, to which men are subject for three years and women for two years, are not paid their alternative cost to the economy. That means that their pay does not reflect the income they could have produced had they been a part of the civilian labor force. Hence, the true cost to the economy of compulsory service is not reflected in the national accounts.

Second, citizens on reserve duty get paid by the National Insurance System (Israel's equivalent of the U.S.'s Social Security Administration), payments that are not counted as public consumption. Such payments are classified as transfers from the government to the employers, who keep paying wages to employees doing their reserve duty. Third, Israel has to repay past U.S. loans for defense. As has been pointed out, this constitutes a deferred defense burden, but appears nowhere in domestic defense consumption figures. The loan repayments are buried in the government's capital account, which makes no reference to the origin of the various payments. When one takes all this into account, then the defense burden must be reckoned to exceed 30 percent of the GNP. But this is the gross burden. If one assumes that the transfers from abroad which Israel enjoys, especially U.S. aid, are motivated by the desire to alleviate part of the defense burden, then these transfers must be viewed as constituting that part of the burden borne by non-Israelis. The remaining part of the burden, that which Israel shoulders, is still two times higher than the American defense burden and six times higher than that borne by most other democracies.

Let us evaluate public expenditures in the key civil areas by considering the picture in 1984. Regarding education, Israel spent 5.8 percent of the GDP, compared to 5.3 percent for Singapore, 5.4 percent for the United Kingdom, and 7.7 percent for Denmark. One should remember, though, that Israel's population is very heterogeneous and diverse in its cultural and educational background. In particular, there is a sizable component of relatively recent immigrants from Third World countries, who understandably had had none of the education that the citizens of a country aspiring to be an industrial power should have. It therefore behooves Israel to concentrate on investment in education. Judging from the preceding numbers, this has clearly not been the case.

In expenditures for health, Israel's weakness is more apparent: in 1984 Israel's public-sector health outlays claimed but 2.3 percent of GDP, compared to 4.1 percent for the United States, 5.3 percent for Denmark and the United Kingdom, and 5.9 percent for Switzerland, a country in which the government is relatively invisible.[5]

The central government in Israel is heavily involved in local government, as is reflected in the increase of its share in the income of municipalities. Central government contributions grew from between one-fifth and one-third in the 1950s to over 50 percent by 1981.[6] In part, this large transfer is simply an administrative device by which the government finances, for example, the educational system. Even though education is organized in the administrative sense on a local basis, most of the finance (e.g., to pay teachers' salaries) comes from the central government. The municipality administers the schools within its jurisdiction only in a bureaucratic sense. But part of the transfer of funds from the central government finances genuinely local activities. The municipalities are obliged, in turn, to obtain the approval of the minister of the interior for their budgets. Nor can they raise certain taxes without such approval. As we shall see, the moral hazard this symbiosis generates has caused the central government ample headaches over the years.

Another area of vast government activity that finds no expression in the size or composition of public expenditures concerns government ownership of means of production. The 1985–86 report of the Government Corporations Authority lists 189 government-owned companies, of which 111 were pure business enterprises. Of these, the wholly owned ones employed 68,000 workers—5 percent of the labor force. This does not include property owned through entities not classified as government corporations, such as the Israel Land Authority.

Some of the most important government corporations are in the defense industry. Included are Israel Aircraft Industries, the largest single employer in the country; the Military Industries; and Elta Electronics. The government owns another large chunk of the defense industry in the form of two enterprises that do not even have the status of a corporation: the Maintenance and Restoration Centers, which maintain the military's mechanized equipment, also assemble Israel's main battle tank, the Merkava, and are run by the army's Quartermaster General; and Rephael, the big defense R&D organization.

Outside of the defense sector, the government owns some of Israel's most important corporations. In terms of financial significance, the most important of these are, not necessarily in order, Israel Electric Company, the monopoly supplying the country's electricity; Israel Chemicals, a holding company that either wholly owns or has a majority interest in such subsidiaries as the Dead Sea Works, Israel Phosphates, Fertilizers and Chemicals, and a host of other companies at home and abroad that between them own all of Israel's mineral deposits. The government also owns Mekoroth, the monopoly which supplies Israel's water; Bezek, the telephone monopoly; and the country's sole railway. It also owns El-Al, Israel's airline, and has substantial interests in the country's refineries. In the financial sector the government owns an insurance company and has substantial interests in the Industrial Development Bank of Israel. It also owns, through various authorities, both of Israel's television stations, both radio networks and all the ports and airports. It also owns and runs a network of hospitals. It even owns the Shekem chain of department stores, which sprang out of the military PX.[7]

Besides involving the government in a tangle of commitments, a subject discussed in detail later, this heavy involvement in the economy creates vast opportunities for patronage and favoritism. From an economic standpoint, the main damage lies with the widespread appointment of directors whose only qualification is their closeness to the appointing ministers. The result is boards of directors inhabited by people who are incompetent to carry out their jobs. Moreover, sometimes the result is no boards of directors at all. For example, as these lines are written, Israel Chemicals has no board because the ministers of finance and of industry and trade are on such bad terms that neither will approve the appointments of the other.

To administer its vast economic activities, the government maintains no fewer than thirteen ministries with substantial economic roles. In addition to the Ministry of Finance and the Ministry of Defense, there are ministries for Industry and Trade, Economics and Planning, Agriculture, Transportation, Communication, Tourism, Energy and Infrastructure, Environment, Labor and Welfare, Housing and Construction, and Science and Development.

The Illusion of Strong Government

Big government constitutes an obstacle to growth not because of its strength, but rather because of its weakness. Big government in a democratic society spells weakness but a strong government is conducive to growth. The definition of a strong government here is definitely not one that is heavily involved in the economy.

To define more precisely the common concept of a strong government—not the concept adopted here—let us conceive of the economy at any given moment of time as being described by a list of what are generally called *state variables*. Each such variable describes the quantity or the price of a good or a service, or the income of a productive factor, such as labor and capital, or the value of any other relevant variable. A complete list of these state variables constitutes a comprehensive description of the economy at a point in time; and the evolution of these variables constitutes a description of where the economy is going.

Next, think of the government as trying to bring about a particular set of values or a particular time path for these variables, and assume that in its drive to intervene, it is powered by noble intentions; that is, it believes that it truly acts in the interest of the public's welfare. To realize its objectives, the government operates a set of levers called *control variables*, or *instruments*. These include taxation, regulation, laws, allocation of government expenditures, monetary policy, and any other democratically available policy instrument. Then a government's power may be measured by the extent to which it can move the state variables toward the target values, through the use of the various instruments. The definition takes into account that the use of certain instruments may be costly. For example, excessive taxation may cause a retardation of economic activity, thus providing fewer resources with which to achieve the desired allocation. But this cost is reflected in the ultimate allocation and is therefore an integral part of the definition of power.

It should be emphasized that the definition hinges on the values of the individual state variables. Individuality is important, because it implies that the government can change the allocation of resources in the economy as well as the income distribution, not just the overall level of activity; and *power* is defined here as the ability to affect the allocation of resources. For example, a government may use a restrictive monetary policy, causing a slowdown of general economic activity. But this does not necessarily bring about a shift of resources from one sector to another or from a specific activity to another. Under this definition of *power*, we are interested in the control over the allocation of resources and income distribution.

Has Israel's government been powerful? On the face of it, using the preceding definition, it has. It has controlled the capital market and the banking system; that is, the financial lifeline of the economy. It owns a set of very important business enterprises. Through taxation and borrowing, it commands the allocation of half or more of the income generated in the economy. It administers a plethora of transfer payments, including social security, unemployment benefits, income maintenance, and subsidies. It runs an administrative machinery designed to dictate farm production and can affect the allocation of resources between production for the domestic market and production for exports. It controls the imports of key items, such as energy, and affects the housing sector to a large degree. In short, it is prominent in virtually every aspect of the economy except parts of domestic commerce. But is it really as powerful as the description suggests?

The answer given here, one for which considerable evidence will be provided, is in the negative. The test to be applied is how close the government comes to realizing its objectives. The evidence suggests that the extent of failure is too great to call Israel's government powerful. But before reviewing that evidence, let us try to argue the case on logical grounds.

The argument rests on the observation that, to move the state variables in the desired direction, the government needs to exercise discretion when pulling those power levers. That is, the government needs to be able to stick to its original objectives conceived, as we have assumed, in the public interest. Specifically, the arms pulling the levers may not be guided by bodies whose interests do not coincide with the public's welfare.

Given this notion of power, I contend that a powerful government in the present sense is an impossibility; that the loss of discretion is an integral part of the very attempt to exert influence on a lot of state variables. The reason is that as soon as a government starts to intervene in any particular area of the economy, it creates an incentive for the parties most affected by its intervention to band together and form a lobby or pressure group with the purpose of influencing the direction intervention will take, for intervention creates a common cause where none may have existed before. For example, if the government stays out of the textile industry, there is little reason for textile manufacturers to believe that much can be accomplished by forming an association for lobbying purposes. But as soon as the government decides, say, to subsidize investment in textile plants in depressed areas to generate employment, it creates an incentive for the textile manufacturers to get together. In fact, just as the marketplace generates by its very existence an incentive for firms to form cartels, the political system, once the government intervenes, creates an incentive to band together to acquire political power.

The idea that there is a causal relationship between government activity and the formation of pressure groups is not new. It was suggested by James Buchanan and Gordon Tullock, in their path-breaking book.[8] However, they lay less emphasis on the role of government as the triggering mechanism for the formation of pressure groups. They also equate government intervention in a particular sphere with the desire to deliver benefits to a particular group, rather than being motivated by the "public interest." The present argument both explains the formation of pressure groups by government intervention and does not depend on the assertion that the government is trying to favor particular groups.

For example, the government may subsidize agriculture because it believes that the public as a whole benefits from the existence of a group of people firmly rooted in the land, from food security, from limits to urbanization, and so on. Yet intervention turns the farmers into a pressure group, which will then try to secure truly special favors.

The more numerous the spheres of government intervention, the more numerous are the lobbies. Each lobby brings pressure to bear, and in a democracy this takes very tangible forms, such as providing financial support for campaigns or withholding it. Lobbies can be particularly effective in a political environment in which party machines are prominent, which is in fact the case in Israel. They are also particularly effective in a proportional representation democracy, where every minority group is represented.

As pressure groups become numerous, the need to respond to them inevitably causes the loss of discretion. Moreover, the range of options from which the government can choose narrows, because the various lobbies are likely to have conflicting objectives. For example, if the government imposes high tariffs to protect the local textile industry, it will have prompted the formation of two lobbies diametrically opposed to each other. The textile lobby will strive to prevent any tariff reductions, and the chamber of commerce, representing the outlets whose business is hurt by the high tariffs, will try to achieve the exact opposite. If such conflicting pressures abound, the government may find itself virtually paralyzed, because whatever it does is bound to offend somebody.

There is another way to describe the combined negative effect of pressure groups, associated with the fact that such groups are primarily concerned with income distribution questions. Pressure groups are concerned about how the cake should be divided, not about how it should be baked. Once the government is bogged down with problems of income distribution, it can no longer act on behalf of the "public interest," even if this had been the original intention. Moreover, the obsession with income distribution actually hurts growth, because it distorts incentives. Mancur Olson goes even further, ascribing to pressure groups a pivotal role in the decline of industrial powers.[9]

My personal observations—based on my experience as adviser to the minister of finance in 1982–83, during which I attended sessions of the Israeli cabinet—is that Israel's government has had virtually no room for discretion. Its choices were in effect predetermined by the many and conflicting pressures exerted on it and invariably had to do with income distribution problems.

If a powerful government according to the usual perception is an impossibility, what *is* a powerful government? The view taken here is that a strong government is one that shuns discretion and opts instead for enforcing the rules of the game without budging in the face of special interest groups. It is powerful in the same sense that referees in a football game are considered powerful. Such a government would, on the whole, interfere to represent the interests of the community, in those areas in which a market mechanism does not exist. The powerful government would thus respond to precisely those interests that are incapable of producing pressure groups.

In particular, a strong government would represent the voters not yet born: the future generations, who might have to pay for the mismanagement of natural resources, the environment, and the like. This is probably what people vaguely think about when they lament the absence of leadership. Leadership is the willingness on the part of government to undertake the unpopular measures; that is, those that incur the wrath of this or the other interest group, but are known to be beneficial to the population as a whole, present and future.

The Emasculation of Israel's Government

Let us now review the evidence that the attempt by Israel's government to be powerful in the traditional sense has rendered it weak. We begin by considering the government priority of dispersal of population, already discussed in Chapters 2 and 4. It constitutes a very clear example of policies designed to affect the allocation of resources rather than the overall level of economic activity. There is also no doubt that the motivation was laudable: the government thought that population dispersal was essential for the well-being of Israel. First, was the policy a success? The most obvious criteria for evaluation are population and employment. Between 1967 and 1973, years of exceptionally high growth, development towns suffered a net population loss of 24,000 people. During that period the government constructed 620 dwelling units in Beit Sha'an, while the population declined by 400.[10]

Even so, in many a development town local government is the largest employer by far, and unemployment rates regularly exceed the average. In 1988 the overall unemployment rate was 6.4 percent of the labor force. In the South, the rate was 8.5 percent; in the North, 6.6 percent; and in Jerusalem, another important development zone, 7.3 percent. By contrast, the unemployment rate in the Central Region was 5.6 percent.[11] These figures should not be regarded as aberrations: unemployment rates in the South and in the North have been consistently higher than in Israel's center and around Tel-Aviv.

Even though the policy has proved to be far from successful, the government cannot change direction, because it is prevented from doing so by the lobbies its very intervention had created. First, the LECI, which has constituted the main vehicle for developing peripheral zones, provided a perfect incentive for the business community to band together to pressure the government to extend more benefits under the law. One excellent example of this sort of pressure is the extension of the benefits of the law to areas hitherto not eligible for its largess.

Second, the people who have settled in the development areas as a result of the dispersal policy by now constitute a powerful pressure group, represented by the mayors of the development towns and the members of the Knesset and the government who come from the development zones. Thus, for instance, the mayors of Be'er Sheva and Arad, the two main urban communities in the Negev, the desert region that constitutes 62 percent of Israel's land area but houses only 7 percent of the population, stated that the government has not invested enough in the Negev and that no private entrepreneur will go there if not given an incentive to do so. Hence, they concluded that businesspersons going to the Negev should receive much more help than elsewhere in the country, and the inhabitants of the region should enjoy drastic tax breaks.[12] That we are dealing here with a pressure group is clearly evident from the fact that the two mayors could hardly be more explicit in expressing their belief that no profitable business is possible in the Negev. Yet they still think that the government should invest there, the inescapable logical implication being that the population of the Negev ought to be forever subsidized.

The government obliged the southern mayors:[13] in June 1986, the Knesset found it necessary to adopt a special Negev Law. It established a special council whose job it is to advise the government on ways to develop the Negev. The government thus became a hostage to its own policies. And more recently a comparable Galilee Law was adopted.

Some of the more important evidence concerns the impact of government intervention on the business sector. In some cases, as the following examples reveal, intervention caused segments of the business community to behave as though they were hired hands, with the government as their employer. In each of these cases the government gave in, producing outcomes that had certainly not been intended.

The first example concerns the strike of the bus cooperatives in 1956. To realize the depth of involvement in public bus transportation, consider that the government approves each route separately, sets the location of bus stops and the frequency of service, and fixes the fare. The strike broke out because the government refused to approve rate increases. In the wake of the two-week strike, an average rate increase of 8.5 percent was granted. Also, the government undertook to cover any future deficits arising from increased costs of inputs, save wage costs, to avoid further rate increases.[14]

Until 1971, the amount of subsidies paid to the bus companies was determined through negotiations that had not been based on any formula. The bus companies had thus been given, in effect, a blank check, a result the government could not possibly have intended. Only after 1971 did a public commission define a "basket of inputs" on the basis of which costs would be computed in a normative manner. This was supposed to eliminate the disincentive inherent in the former arrangement. But the agreement lapsed in 1974 and for years, in the absence of any clear rules, the government kept footing the bill.[15]

As later agreements have proved, the existence of an objective subsidization criterion has not achieved its purpose. The bus cooperatives, cognizant of the fact that under the existing institutional setup nobody else could provide public transportation and that the government lacked the resolve needed to change the situation, kept incurring expenditures over and above the prescribed formula. By January 1989 the larger of the two cooperatives, Egged, was in arrears of over NIS368 million (around $200 million). In March 1989, a new agreement between Egged and the government was signed, awarding the company up to NIS750 million annually, in return for which the cooperative pledged to put its house in order.[16] There is no reason to believe that the situation will change in any important way until the government gets out of the public transportation system and allows competition.

Not in every case is it possible to quantify failure or even assess its degree. For example, it is impossible to say how exports would have developed without government subsidies, and hence it is impossible to determine the extent to which the subsidies worked. However, it will be possible to identify the sorts of pressures on the government that its intervention provoked and the degree of discretion the government managed to retain in the face of these pressures.

In some cases, the government achieved virtually the opposite of its professed objective, as in export subsidization, designed to promote exports in an effort to improve the country's foreign balance. In the last quarter of 1980, export subsidies ranged from $.115 to $.288 to a dollar of value added. Yet the highest rate of subsidization was enjoyed by exports of jewelry, where the value-added component is one of the lowest of any exports. Also, exports of paper and paper products enjoyed a subsidy of $.202 on the value-added dollar. The point here is that the value added in these products hardly exists, because inputs consist of imported wood and the services of imported machinery and the imported energy implicit in the water used in the process of paper production.

In 1982, a commission was set up to monitor export profitability. It consisted of representatives of the government and the M.A. That is to say, the people who stood to benefit from the commission's findings participated in its deliberations not as witnesses, but as members. Under these circumstances, it is not surprising that the commission submitted a report that concluded that export profitability had declined from 1980 to 1982.

An independent analysis of the commission's own data suggests otherwise. True, by the last quarter of 1982 export prices were 6.1 percent lower than they had been on the average in 1980. However, the costs of imported inputs declined by much more, 12.4 percent. Although the cost of domestic inputs grew over the same period by 8.9 percent per unit of output, all employers had to do to preserve, and even improve, profitability was to let wages rise only in line with productivity gains. In fact, wages per unit of output rose 10.5 percent, constituting the decisive factor in the decline of profitability.[17] And why not? After all, the government could be counted on to foot the bill.

It did indeed. The extent to which it was pushed by external forces can be concluded from the fact that, throughout 1982 and beyond, the government applied as much pressure to the M.A. as it could muster, in an effort to avert excessive wage increases; that is, to limit wage increases to what could be justified by increases in labor productivity. The effort met with total failure. Wages in the private sector rose during 1982 and the beginning of 1983 in a manner that could be explained only by the laxity of employers, who knew that the government would not be able to avoid rescuing them.

An area of government involvement that does not come readily to mind in the present context is government itself. But in fact, the excessive involvement of Israel's central government in the affairs of local government has created a situation much like the conditions created by government interference in the private sector. Municipalities kept hiring new workers even after a freeze on public employment had been announced. They also regularly borrowed from banks in order to finance current expenditures. All this, of course, was done under the assumption that the central government would have to rescue any municipality that became insolvent. The situation became so bad that in 1985 the law of the Foundations of the Budget, imposing (among other provisions) severe restrictions on local government, had to be adopted. Thus, a municipality may not borrow without the approval of the minister of the interior, who also sets the ceiling for employment by local government. A municipality that breaks the rule is liable to sanctions imposed by the central government. Of course, as in all other instances, the original motivation for the intervention of the central government in the affairs of local government was the public interest. For example, the government wanted to permit all children to acquire a good education, regardless of the resource base a particular community had at its disposal.

As has been argued earlier, one sign of a strong government is its preoccupation with aspects of the economy with which the unmitigated market mechanism cannot adequately deal. As an example take the environment. The market mechanism cannot deal with the various forms of pollution, because there is no market in which pollution rights can be traded. So the government must create the institution that will allow such a market to come about. Maintenance of environmental quality is definitely in the public interest, but it does affect certain groups in a differential manner. Namely, it hurts polluting industries. There will therefore be an incentive for polluting manufacturers and their employees to form a pressure group to block the adoption of more severe pollution standards or at least mitigate their severity.

But if government intervention to create a substitute for absent markets has the same effect as the preceding sorts of intervention, what is the difference between the two kinds? The answer is that there is no difference in principle. And the conclusion is that, if intervention is unavoidable, discretion must be avoided as far as possible. For example, the government could create marketlike mechanisms, such as tradable fishing licenses, and so immunize itself against pressure groups. But in any event, successful intervention to supply public goods and eliminate harmful externalities is a clear indication of a strong government.

On these tests, the Israeli government must be judged to be very weak. And no wonder, its preoccupation with pressure groups created by years of dabbling in matters that should have been none of its business has caused a severe neglect of precisely those areas in which the government cannot be supplanted by the market mechanism. The government has neither provided public goods in a manner befitting a modern society, nor has it paid attention to the damage inflicted by externalities. In fact, it helped aggravate some of them.

One of the areas in which government neglect is felt the most is transportation. The conditions on Israel's roads have come to resemble, in recent years, the situation one encounters in many developing countries: a road system creaking under the weight of traffic too heavy to be accommodated by the existing network. Nor have the existing roads been maintained at anywhere near the rate at which they should have. A survey conducted in 1990 by the Public Works Department, the government unit responsible for building and maintaining roads, found that on a scale of 0 to 100, the condition of Israel's roads today merits a 37, compared to 69 in 1981 and 75 in 1975.[18] More concretely, the director general of the department observed that half of all the roads were being maintained at substandard levels and 35 percent were substandardly paved and not fit for modern-day trucks.[19] It is therefore no surprise that driving is becoming ever more hazardous, with highway fatalities reaching proportions of a national catastrophe. In recent years, Israel has sustained between 400 and 500 fatalities annually. With all of its wars, many more of its citizens have been killed on the highways than have died in combat and all other forms of hostile activity combined.

As an example of environmental neglect, consider the fact that out of sixteen streams that flow from east to west into the Mediterranean, fifteen are biologically dead. That is to say, they are so polluted that no form of life can survive in their waters.[20] The pollution of streams and, in some places, even ground water is the consequence of unregulated disposal of sewage and industrial waste.

Not surprisingly, very little is being done concerning air quality. Air pollution standards are broken routinely. Atmospheric inversion (cold air locating above hot air) is not uncommon in Israel. And yet there are never any restrictions on vehicle traffic.

But the most glaring neglect concerns the state of the country's most precious natural resource: water. Israel is a country with relatively scarce water resources. They are scarce enough so that an externality is associated with their utilization, just as with other scarce resources. The externality is generated when water resources are overdrawn; that is, when the long-run average use of water exceeds the average rate of replenishment through precipitation. Then the use of an additional gallon of water in the present implies a reduced availability of water in the future by at least the same amount. The *at least* emanates from the possibility that excessive use of water not only means more severe constraints on future use, but also the possibility of pollution of water not currently used. Because Israel has indeed overdrawn its water resources on a fairly regular basis, Israelis are consuming water at the expense of their offspring. They are also polluting parts of the water reservoirs.

This is a classic case for government intervention. The free market is incapable of generating a price that will reflect the externality because the future generations are not present in the market, and so their demand for water plays no role in determining the price. So it behooves the government to set a water price that will exceed the price that a free market would have generated. Instead, the government has succumbed to pressure from the powerful farm lobby, whose existence and range of activities have been created over many years of heavy public involvement in all aspects of farm settlement. So, instead of actions to mitigate the externalities associated with water consumption, the government may have exacerbated the very damage that it was supposed to avert. Instead of pricing water stiffly, it has been subsidizing it.

The excessive use of water in hot regions, where evaporation is considerable, has had another damaging effect; namely, it has caused progressively higher salinity of both groundwater and soil. In some cases, farming had to be abandoned because the land became too saline.[21]

The loss of governmental discretion in connection with the pricing of water may be documented in a manner much more salient than normal. In a recent attempt to refute the calculations of the Office of the Budget in the Ministry of Finance concerning the true cost of water,[22] the Agricultural Center, the Histadrut's farm organ, made its interests plain. The most significant demand advanced by the center was that amortization on irrigation capital (pumps, water mains, etc.) be calculated at the subsidized rate of interest of 2 percent. This alone would have pared 20 percent off the price calculated by the Office of the Budget. One of the main rationales for the stance adopted by the center was that most of the water was being used for growing export products (mainly citrus fruit, avocadoes and cotton). In other words, the center was demanding subsidies so it could export a scarce resource. Nor did it hide the fact that it was perfectly aware of the scarcity problem. Yet economic pricing as a means of coping with scarcity was rejected out of hand.[23]

In sum, the Israeli government finds itself, after decades of intervening in areas best left alone, in the weakest possible situation: where it has unwittingly intervened, it is incapable of achieving its purposes because of the enormous pressures exerted on it; and the areas to which it should have turned most of its attention suffer from gross neglect.

But however indicative of the government's basic weakness these examples are, the most dramatic manifestation of all is the inflation that plagued Israel for over a decade. However, the inflationary process involves other very fundamental aspects of the Israeli economy and therefore deserves separate treatment.

9

THE INFLATIONARY PRESCRIPTION: INSTITUTIONS AND POLICIES

In Chapters 2 through 8, an attempt has been made to link the economy's failure to grow since 1973 to a host of structural problems, all of which emanate in one way or another from a systematic distortion of incentives by excessive government involvement. It was also pointed out that despite the stagnation that gripped the productive side of the economy, consumption kept on growing because of the illusion of wealth, created by the government-induced proliferation of real assets and financial assets not backed by real ones. The consequence was a steady deterioration of the balance of payments, with the attendant increase of foreign debt. The government, fearful that Israel might one day find itself insolvent, embarked on policies designed to reduce the deficit in the balance of payments. But instead of dealing with the fundamentals, it has used stopgap measures that only aggravated the situation. The visible component of the aggravation was the inflation that raged for a decade, until mid-1985, and has continued since at an excessive, but much more moderate pace. This chapter and the next are devoted to telling the story of inflation, how it came about and why it can be interpreted as the most serious consequence of the obstacles to growth.

This chapter is devoted to describing the gathering of the inflationary forces. In particular, attention will be focused on the institutional arrangements and policies that concern the labor market, the monetary system, and the foreign-exchange market. It is mostly in these areas that excessive government involvement created the conditions that proved conducive to the inflationary process. The next chapter is devoted to the inflationary process itself.

The Cost-of-Living Allowance

The institution of the cost-of-living allowance (COLA) cannot be regarded as an isolated development. It was tied, of course, to the overall attitude toward labor and wages as manifested, for example, by the battle to "conquer labor" and the general disregard for profits. This tie will emerge clearly as the story of wage indexation unfolds.

The first COLA payments were made as early as 1935, and perhaps earlier, but they were confined to public institutions such as the Jewish Agency and the Hebrew University. In July 1936 the Jewish National Fund, the Hebrew University, and the Hadassah Medical Organization wrote a joint letter to Eliezer Kaplan, then the treasurer of the Jewish Agency, complaining that despite the disturbances, otherwise known as the Arab Revolt of 1936–39, the Jewish Agency had decided to keep up the COLA payments. The arguments advanced by the writers, which do not appear in the letter but can be inferred from Kaplan's reply, are exceedingly important.

In an oral discussion of the COLA problem that had evidently taken place, the writers pointed out that the rise in the cost of living was occasioned by the disturbances. These were exogenous to the economy and hurt it in general, so that both employer and employee suffered. Hence, they argued, there was no justification for continued compensation. Even though Kaplan acknowledged the facts, he rejected the conclusion, insisting on continued COLA payments.[1] This implies that the leadership's view was that salaried workers have the right to be compensated regardless of the costs to the employers.

In October 1939, the first COLA agreement was signed between the M.A. and the Tel-Aviv branch of the Histadrut, the Tel-Aviv Workers Council.[2] It did not establish an automatic compensation mechanism. Rather, it was perceived as a temporary measure occasioned by the unforeseen developments brought about by World War II. In fact, it applied only to those employers who "enjoyed a prosperity in the wake of the war."[3] Furthermore, a commission on which the M.A. and the Histadrut had equal representation was set up to investigate those cases in which employers claimed that their circumstances did not justify the payment. The head of the Jewish Agency's Labor Department played a mediating role in the commission's deliberations.[4]

In December 1940, a similar agreement was signed with the Histadrut and applied on a countrywide basis. It called for a 20-percent wage increase, a rate that constituted two-thirds of the increase in the cost of living.[5] Once again, employers who had not shared in the prosperity caused by the war were allowed to pay a reduced 15-percent supplement and in some cases were exempted altogether.[6]

All these details are important because they point to the fact that the participants in the agreement were at least partially sensitive to profitability constraints. True, the institution of COLA as such was still motivated by exogenous events, so that compensation was to be given for developments beyond the control of employers. But at least the signatories on labor's side did not think that workers should be compensated regardless of the financial circumstances of the firms that employed them.

In one respect, the COLA agreements could be viewed as a clever way of changing existing wage agreements so as to take account of events that had not been foreseen when the agreements were negotiated. The COLA agreements represented a relatively cheap method for renegotiating wage agreements on a limited basis. Rather than reopen for negotiation the whole panoply of subjects that make up a labor contract, a costly process indeed, renegotiation was concerned with a narrow and well-defined component of the contract.

The tempered attitude on the part of the unions did not persist, and consequently the agreements did not prove durable. By 1941 a protracted dispute over indexation was in progress, aggravated by demands on the part of the Histadrut for general wage increases.[7] It was not until 1943 that a new agreement was concluded with the help of the Mandate government, which had set up a special commission for this purpose, chaired by the chief justice. From an economic policy standpoint, the new agreement represented a significant deterioration in attitudes. It no longer provided for exceptions: all employers had to pay. In fact, the agreement was extended to include workers who did not belong to the Histadrut.

The one earlier feature that was retained in the new agreement was the partiality of the compensation. COLAs were paid on wages up to a certain maximum. Thus, compensation on the first £8.5 of monthly income constituted 80 percent of the rise in the cost of living;[8] the next £2.0 of income were compensated for only 40 percent of the actual increase in the cost of living; and no compensation at all applied to additional income.[9] This implied a considerable erosion of wages for workers with higher incomes. For example, a worker who earned a nominal wage of £13.5 at the start of the war, lost 27.5 percent of the real purchasing power, because the cost of living rose 75 percent by the end of 1942.

The rationale behind partial rather than full compensation for inflation seems to have been the desire of labor unions to retain more room for bargaining. But the use of indexation payments as a wage equalizer must have been motivated by ideological considerations.

After the establishment of the state, the principles of COLA were kept intact. In July 1957 a new agreement was signed. Among other changes, the notion the COLAs were a temporary feature of the wage structure was abandoned. The new agreement also instituted a reduction in the frequency of payments, from quarterly to annually. This could be done, because inflation rates at that point were very low compared to what they had been: whereas in the period 1951–53 the average annual rate of inflation was 33.5 percent, by 1956 it was a mere 4.6 percent.

Of particular interest are two adjustments made in the price index prior to its use as a basis for computing COLA. First, the price-index component representing the cost of fruits and vegetables did not enter the calculation in its raw form. Rather, the CPI was modified to include only the average annual change in the prices of fruits and vegetables. Second, the price index of housing was excluded from the CPI.

The justification for the special treatment of fruits and vegetables was their tendency to display a pattern of seasonal price fluctuation.To smooth them out, only annual averages were considered.

To see why such smoothing is important, consider the actual events that took place between September 1982 and March 1983. Table 9.1 provides data concerning price inflation in the consumer price index and some of its components, selected to demonstrate the vast differences among various rates of price changes, particularly due to seasonal fluctuations peculiar to the farm sector.

Our story begins with the very harsh winter of 1982–83, which caused the supplies of farm produce to decline sharply. Consequently, their prices soared. As Table 9.1 indicates, fruits and vegetables contributed almost 1.5 extra percentage points of inflation to the consumer price index in the fall and 3 extra percentage points in the winter.

Consider a producer of fixtures used in maintaining apartments. Given that the COLA rate at the time was 80 percent of the rate of inflation, the firm had to increase employees' pay in the winter by 17.4 percent, instead of by 16.3 percent, which would have applied had the prices of fruits and vegetables increased in line with the average rate of inflation. Then, in the spring of 1983, the producer had to pay another 17.3 percent in wage increases, instead of paying 14.9 percent. Over the two periods, then, our producer had to pay wage supplements totaling 37.7 percent, instead of 33.6 percent, the rate that would have applied had the CPI excluding fruits and vegetables been used. And our producer had to make these payments despite the fact that the prices of its own products rose by only 34.6 percent.

This was clearly an unsustainable situation, so in the spring the prices of housing fixtures took off, exceeding the CPI by quite a bit. The spurious increase in the prices of fruits and vegetables has thus been transmitted to the rest of the economy through the COLA system.

TABLE 9.1

Selected Quarterly Rates of Inflation, Percent

	1982.4	1983.1	1983.2
Consumer Price Index	21.8	21.6	23.8
Fruits and Vegetables	45.6	61.2	-6.8
CPI, Excluding Fruits and Vegetables	20.4	18.6	26.9
Apartment Maintenance	15.0	17.1	36.4

But there is more to this story. As can be seen from Table 9.1, supplies of farm products increased with the arrival of spring to such an extent that their prices actually declined. However, by then the CPI could not fully respond to this decline, because the accelerated pace of inflation in the rest of the economy, caused by the original surge of farm prices, was offsetting part of the benefits from increased farm supplies. This can be deduced from the fact that in the spring the rise in the CPI excluding fruits and vegetables was almost half as much again as its rise in the winter. This, in turn, was fed back into the economy through the next round of COLA payments, and so on. It follows that the spurious rise of the prices of fruits and vegetables was being transmitted to the entire economy through the COLA system, thus being transformed into systematic inflation.[10]

It is impossible to calculate by how much inflation would have been mitigated had smoothing taken place, for the actual data already contain the effect of the tremendous inflation in farm prices. Still, some indication can be obtained by contemplating annual figures. If only the average annual price increase for fruits and vegetables were taken into account, the resulting COLA would have been smaller: the average price of fruits and vegetables in 1983 was 174 percent higher than it had been on the average in 1982. This is a far cry from the 466-percent (annual terms) rate by which the prices of fruits and vegetables increased between September 1982 and March 1983.

As for housing prices, most Israelis live in owner-occupied apartments or houses. For these people, any increase in the cost of housing is at the same time an increase in real estate values and so an increase in income. Hence, COLA should include compensation for increases in housing prices only for those who rent their places of abode; that is, those for whom such increases imply increased out-of-pocket expenses. The distinction would be redundant had housing prices moved in perfect unison with the other components of the consumer price index. In that case they would not have a distinguishable effect on the index and therefore would not have affected COLA computations differentially. However, as is well known, housing prices fluctuate more than the overall price level because of the distinct cyclical nature of the housing industry. And, as in the case of fruits and vegetables, once housing prices are fed into the system through COLA during housing booms, they cannot be completely expunged from the system during housing recessions.

As an example consider that during 1972, housing prices increased by 31 percent, whereas the consumer price index rose by only 12.5 percent.[11] And during 1979, housing prices increased by 159 percent, whereas the consumer price index rose by 111 percent. And this, despite the fact that by then the exclusion of housing prices from COLA calculations had already been abandoned. This means that the figure for the consumer price index already contains the effect of the much more rapid inflation of housing prices.[12]

The institution of various adjustments to the price index prior to using it for calculating COLA payments clearly indicates that the designers of indexation were aware of the dangers of mindless application of wage indexation. This is not to say that the scheme was not fraught with danger. Although the adjustments described did prevent certain specific supply-side shocks from being transformed into systematic inflation, nothing was to prevent economy-wide supply shocks from such transformation. This flaw became critically crucial in 1973 and 1974.

In both 1973 and 1974, the prices of imports rose more rapidly than the prices of domestic products. Thus, average import prices in dollars, not including changes in the exchange rate or duties, rose by 27.6 percent from 1972 to 1973. At the same time, domestic-product prices rose by only 18.3 percent. The quicker pace of increase in import prices caused the consumer price index to increase by 19.9 percent. This extra increase was then being fed back into the system through COLA payments. The story repeated itself in 1974, when the average price of imports rose by 37.8 percent over the 1973 average, whereas domestic-product prices rose by only 26 percent. In contrast to 1973, this time the shock of imported inflation, caused primarily by the Oil Crisis and the general rise of commodities' prices, was aggravated by the devaluation of November 1974 and import-duty increases. Consequently, the consumer price index increased by 38 percent, which was again recycled back into the system through the COLA payments.

This pumping of cost-push inflationary pressure into the economy produced adverse effects in 1975 and 1976. In 1975, the world slumped into a brief, but sharp recession. Consequently, the price of imports increased in 1975 by only 3.9 percent and declined in 1976 by 1.9 percent. Exogenous circumstances had thus been ideal for reducing inflation. However, because of the earlier increases in costs, the domestic economy could not take advantage of the situation: domestic-product prices rose by 41 percent in 1975 and by another 30.6 percent in 1976.[13]

A shock of the type suffered in the wake of the Oil Crisis constitutes a reduction in product, because after the shock more exports are needed to finance a unit of imports. This means a decline in income. Hence, individual incomes must decline, whether in the form of wages or profits. This can be viewed from the production side as well: the dearer imports push up the cost of production. Hence, domestic prices must increase, causing a reduction in the purchasing power of incomes. A typical example is a massive crop failure. Food prices increase and so consumers can no longer buy with their income the quantities they used to purchase. Crop failure has made everybody poorer.

But if workers are compensated for the higher food prices, then producers will face higher wage costs, thus aggravating their plight. If they have no other recourse, unemployment will follow. The alternative is to pump demand into the economy through monetary expansion. When this is done, then prices will climb not only because of decreased supply, but also because of increased demand. Unemployment will thus be averted at the cost of inflation. What the monetary authorities do in these circumstances will determine which way the economy will go—which brings us to monetary policy.

The Impossibility of Monetary Policy

The law that established the Bank of Israel charged it with the conduct of monetary policy, but restricted it from making free use of monetary policy instruments. For example, government approval was needed for changes in reserve requirements imposed on the commercial banking system. And the government reserved the right to set reserve ratios on savings accounts as part of its control of the capital market. Under these circumstances, it was not to be expected that the central bank could follow an independent monetary policy.

Whether or not the central bank should have exclusive control of the monetary scene is a subject for legitimate debate. In many of the most developed economies central banks are constrained to one degree or another by government regulation. Only in West Germany and the United States are the central banks considered to be virtually autonomous. But the Israeli case does not fall within the band of legitimate debate. Here the degree of government involvement produced circumstances under which no monetary policy was possible at all, independent or otherwise.

Some Basics of Monetary Policy

Why is monetary policy needed at all, and what is it supposed to accomplish? The simplest answer rests with the fact that money not only serves as a medium of exchange, but also as an accounting unit, or the measuring rod of the economy. As the basic unit of measurement, it is important to keep it stable. If it were not, it would be like an architect having to work with a changing meter. In particular, if the purchasing power of a dollar were to differ a lot over time, then it would become very hard to make investment decisions, or any other decisions involving amounts of money at different points in time.

Basically three nominal magnitudes can be targeted by the monetary authority: some monetary amount, such as the amount of loanable funds; the interest rate; and the exchange rate. Because of the interdependence of these magnitudes, the authority can target at most two of these magnitudes independently. If the economy is open to international capital movement, then only one of the three magnitudes can be targeted. If the economy is closed to capital movement, then two of the magnitudes can be targeted. Being closed means running a strictly balanced goods-and-services account. Armed with these basic observations, let us consider the evolution of the monetary story in Israel.

The Hijacked Targets

The seeds of what we shall call, for lack of a better term, *monetary policy* were planted by the government prior to the establishment of a central bank. In March 1951, the government instructed banks to maintain a reserve ratio of 50 percent on all existing deposits and a ratio of 75 percent on all new ones, this in an attempt to slow down credit expansion. In 1952, the reserve ratio on new deposits was raised to 90 percent, which, in effect, meant an almost complete freeze on the expansion of credit.[14] But already in 1951, the government began granting exemptions from reserve requirements for those loans made according to government priorities.[15] That is, a bank could lend in excess of what the required reserve ratio permitted, provided the excess loans were given to borrowers designated by the government. Thus the way for directed credit was opened.

The importance of this practice cannot be overestimated. It meant that the government was confusing monetary policy with credit allocation policy. Consequently, a monetary policy instrument was being crippled, reducing its effectiveness. Put differently, the government hampered its own use of a macroeconomic policy tool, by imposing on itself constraints of a microeconomic nature—in this case catering to the credit requirements of a particular sector of the economy.

Since 1954, monetary policy has been the domain of the Bank of Israel; and any systematic discussion of the role played by the Bank's policy in the economy must begin with its decision, mentioned in Chapter 2, to refrain from exempting the commercial banking system from the interest-rate ceiling in existence since Ottoman times.

The decision to retain below-equilibrium interest rates had serious consequences in more than one respect. But the most serious by far was that the Bank of Israel was left without a monetary policy target. To see why, recall that a central bank can select at most two of the three candidates for monetary targets. The Bank of Israel was confronted with a rate of exchange that had been fixed by the government at a level thought to be propitious for achieving balance-of-payments objectives. Although this had, of course, implications for the monetary system, setting the rate had not been guided by monetary considerations. The Bank had thus been deprived of one of the three potential monetary targets. By deciding to retain the legal rate of interest, the Bank was forsaking another monetary target whose setting, once again, did have monetary consequences, but was determined without having monetary goals in mind. The government had thus disempowered the Bank, leaving it stranded without a target for the execution of any monetary policy at all.

Credit Allocation and Monetary Policy

Under these circumstances, the Bank chose to pretend to manage the monetary system. Pretense took the form of continuing to do exactly what the government had been doing before.[16] In fact, not only did the Bank carry on the former policy, but it was actually engaged in developing the philosophy behind government allocation of credit, under the euphemism *qualitative direction.*

The need for centrally controlled credit was justified by the first governor of the Bank (who governed for seventeen years) on the grounds that Israel was a small country, poor in natural resources and facing extraordinary security burdens on top of the imperative of rapid economic development. Under these circumstances, it was argued, no productive factors could be wasted, and hence there was a need for qualitative direction of credit. The governor also supplied the reasoning as to why the government was as efficient as the commercial banks in carrying out the prescribed policy. He claimed that the central bank was better suited to allocate credit on a sectoral basis because, unlike the commercial banking system, it had a broader view of the needs of the economy. Hence, it was better positioned to direct credit according to national priorities, which might be in conflict with commercial ones.[17]

The governor was David Horowitz, who had managed the main industrial credit facility of the Jewish Agency. The criteria for credit allocation developed then were carried over intact to the central bank. The approach was also consistent with the ideology that produced the view that private profitability did not correlate well with national priorities.[18]

The fact that the Bank refrained from abolishing the interest-rate ceiling, and so was totally deprived of monetary targets, should not be interpreted as implying that if it had behaved differently it could have instituted a monetary policy. This is because monetary policy objectives would still be in conflict with credit allocation objectives, over which the Bank had no real jurisdiction in the first place. Indeed, the Bank's attempt to control credit expansion would have failed for this reason alone. The evidence for this observation can be found in the Bank's own words, when policies in 1955 were described as "careful expansion of credit toward high-priority objectives, such as production for exports." The word *careful* represents the monetary policy component.[19] In 1956 the conflict became even more evident, as a result of the wage increases mentioned earlier in connection with COLA payments. The Bank found itself accommodating the pressures for credit expansion, which were occasioned by the wage hikes.[20]

Over the next few years the Bank kept manipulating, on the one hand, required reserve ratios; but on the other hand, it kept granting more exemptions from reserve requirements. The outcome was that the de facto reserve ratio changed very little over time: from 1955 to 1960, it fluctuated in the narrow band of 37.2 percent to 40.6 percent. Even more to the point are the events of 1961, when the Bank attempted to further tighten credit. In the event, the reserve ratio actually dropped to 30.4 percent.[21]

Even before the Bank attempted to arrest credit expansion more rigorously, a process of financial disintermediation had been taking place. That is, ultimate borrowers were going directly to the original lenders, the public, instead of borrowing through the financial intermediaries, the banks. The credit market outside the banking system was referred to by the public and by the authorities as a *black credit market,* as though there was something sinister about it. In fact, it was a market much like the commercial paper market in the United States. This similarity holds especially with regard to commercial paper backed by stand-by letters of credit issued by commercial banks. The "notes intermediation market," as it came to be known professionally, was actually made by banks outside the banking system. In this system, corporations were borrowing using customers' promissory notes as collateral. Interest rates on such loans exceeded, of course, the legal ceiling. The banks both intermediated the deals and, later on, also guaranteed them.

In its first years, however, this so-called black market was relatively small, indicating, perhaps, that the interest-rate ceiling had been close to the equilibrium rate. But attempts by the Bank of Israel to impose tighter credit conditions prompted the intermediation of notes to grow from 25 percent of outstanding credit in 1962 to 40 percent by 1966.[22] Interest rates ranged up to 19 percent, while the legal rate was 11 percent (it had been raised to that level from the previous 9 percent in 1957), indicating a huge gap between the equilibrium and the legal rates of interest. When the interest-rate ceiling was removed in 1970, the market in intermediated notes disappeared within a few months.[23]

Tailoring Philosophy to Reality

Instead of stating clearly that under the government-imposed rules it was impossible to implement any monetary policy at all, the Bank of Israel chose to invent a philosophy that created the impression that monetary policy was possible, albeit difficult. This produced in time the Bank's central theme or conceptual framework: in essence, it was that the Bank alone could not possibly offset the expansionary fiscal policies of the government. This line of reasoning was well articulated in a comprehensive review of the Bank's monetary policy, one of the writers of which was the then-governor of the Bank.[24] It merits close scrutiny because, as will become evident, it provides a considerable part of the underpinnings that made possible inflation in later years.

But first some preliminaries are required concerning the rules governing the creation of base money in the Israeli economy. In principle, money can be created in four ways. The first two constitute the normal instruments of monetary expansion that any central bank uses. They are the purchase of government securities on the open market and loans extended to commercial banks through the rediscount of financial instruments. The third way could be dubbed *money printing* by the government: here, the government borrows directly from the central bank by, in effect, an overdraft on its account there. This third mechanism is not common and, as we shall see, has been practically abolished in Israel too since 1985. In the United States, for instance, the government can borrow only from the public by selling bills or bonds. The Federal Reserve then determines how much of this debt to monetize, by deciding what portion of the debt issued by the government it purchases on the open market. In Israel, in contrast, the government had been virtually free to print money at will.

The fourth avenue for money creation is associated with foreign-exchange transactions. Suppose an Israeli individual or corporation receives foreign exchange for either goods or services exported or as a unilateral transfer; for example, German reparation payments. The recipient of the money will deposit it with a commercial bank. If the bank has no current need for the foreign exchange, such as transferring it abroad as payment for imported goods, it will sell it to the central bank. This is how foreign-exchange reserves are accumulated. But the central bank buys the foreign exchange for domestic currency, which it prints. Hence, the accumulation of foreign exchange creates domestic currency. The government, too, can sell foreign exchange to the central bank in return for domestic currency. This, for example, is done with that portion of U.S. military aid which Israel is allowed to spend at home rather than in the United States.

We may now examine the philosophy behind the Bank of Israel's policies from its creation until 1972, as described by its own governor. Curiously, the governor did not think it necessary to discuss the period after 1970 separately. He should have done this, because the abolition of the interest-rate ceiling in that year created a new situation. The basic observation that guided the Bank's policy all along was that the Israeli economy was under a constant threat of actual or potential inflationary pressures. These were attributed to the creation of money, mainly through loans to the government and the accumulation of foreign exchange. The Bank therefore perceived its main macroeconomic duty as counteracting the inflationary pressures. Yet it concluded that the job was so Herculean as to be beyond its ability to handle. How was this conclusion arrived at?

First, so the argument went, even if a reserve ratio of 100 percent were imposed on the banking system, monetary expansion through money printing by the government could still be large enough to cause inflation. The argument is false: if the central bank has no room for monetary policy, then it can do nothing by definition. But if monetary policy is possible, then if the central bank has at its disposal a sufficiently large stock of government securities, the money pumped into the system by the government's deficit finance can be soaked up by the central bank by offering these securities on the open market. Of course, the central bank must be willing to sell these securities at a discount rate attractive enough for people to part with their money. When this happens, the outcome is as though the government had borrowed from the public in the first place instead of borrowing from the central bank (printing money). The latter can also neutralize the creation of money by the government through the sale of foreign exchange. Of course, this could result in an appreciation of the domestic currency, thus making its exports less profitable and imports cheaper. Therein lies the antiinflationary thrust of the policy, because it would lead to an increased supply of goods and services on the domestic market. The government's excess demand would thus be met by increased supplies of goods and services, which would eliminate or mitigate the inflationary pressures.

The second argument advanced by the Bank of Israel was that, even if very high reserve ratios had been sufficient to counterbalance governmental profusion, they could not be implemented. High reserve ratios would have meant lower interest rates for savers, thus driving away deposits from banks. With deposits chased away from banks as they had been during the heyday of the market for intermediated notes, the argument continued, the Bank would have lost what little control it had, because credit extension outside the commercial banking system is not subject to central-bank regulations.

Once again, we know that even if the Bank had pursued a policy of increased reserve ratios, it would have been to no avail, as exemptions from the increased ratios would most likely keep pace. But as it stands, the argument is false, for the very simple reason that, outside the banking system, the reserve ratio is always exactly 100 percent. When Mr. Doe lends Ms. Bee $1,000, Mr. Doe forgoes the opportunity of using any of the borrowed sum until it is returned. So the lending in this case constitutes a mere transfer of purchasing power between two people. Although Ms. Bee uses the money, Mr. Doe has no access to it, which is unlike the situation with commercial banks, even with very high reserve requirements. There, the original depositor has continuous access to the deposit, even if some of the money has been lent to someone else. It is as if two individuals could use a given amount of money simultaneously. Thus, chasing money away from banks constitutes the imposition of a 100-percent reserve requirement, and if the objective is to limit the creation of money by banks, nothing can be more effective. Of course, in the process banks as we know them would be wiped out.[25]

The reason why under very high reserve ratios lenders can realize higher interest rates outside the banking system than they can earn on their bank deposits is that the commercial bank must hold so much of its assets in a barren or nonperforming state, and out of the very high interest rates it charges on loans it can pay only a fraction on deposits. That is, high reserve ratios generate big interest-rate spreads. When the spread gets big enough, it pays even lenders to incur the additional risk inherent in lending to specific borrowers (i.e., forego the insurance implicit in lending through a bank). The reward comes in the form of splitting the interest-rate spread with the borrower.

Even if the Bank of Israel could have stepped on the monetary brakes, it would probably have chosen not to do so, because the danger of unemployment was so abhorred. This is why whenever reserve requirements were raised, the proportion of loans exempted from reserve requirements was raised as well. Thus, for instance, in March 1961, reserve requirements were increased to 62 percent, but at the same time 22 percent of deposits were exempted from the requirements altogether. A series of further increases of reserve requirements followed that brought the required reserve ratio to 65 percent by 1966, but the proportion of exempted deposits grew as well, to 25 percent. The extent to which the Bank was chasing its own tail can be demonstrated by the fact that a 62-percent reserve requirement on 78 percent of deposits (the other 22 percent were exempt) amounts to an overall reserve requirement of 48.36 percent. When a 65-percent reserve requirement is applied to 75 percent of deposits (the other 25 percent being exempt), the overall reserve requirement amounts to 48.75 percent. From the monetary standpoint, the two ratios are indistinguishable. It must be concluded that the Bank was feigning a tight monetary policy, while in fact it did not pursue such a policy at all.

It is quite clear that deep down the Bank knew that it did not really attempt to tighten the monetary grip:[26]

The ability to affect directly interest rates poses a difficulty in connection with the carrying out of [the sale of Bank of Israel bills], because of opposition by certain parties to any steps that cause rates of interest to rise. One should remember that many fail to understand that rising interest rates help to restrain demand, and the opposition of the mentioned parties limits the discretion of the monetary authorities in the use of classic instruments to combat inflation.

And[27]

It is obvious from the list of steps taken by the Bank of Israel in 1972 that the intention was to limit the ability of banks to expand credit and to prevent excessive expansion of directed credit, without creating direct pressure on the interest rates. . . . The intensive use of measures to set the amount of credit and not its price reflects, on the one hand, the strong public opposition to increased interest rates and, on the other hand, the difficulty of explaining to the public the antiinflationary effect that such raised rates have.

It is hard to surpass this sort of doubletalk. Only once did the Bank hint that the restrictions placed by the government ruled out effective monetary policy. It stated that, under the government policy of stabilizing the real rate of return on indexed bonds, the Bank's ability to conduct open market operations had been effectively preempted.[28]

The Oil Crisis and the New Economic Policy

The New Ideas

The developments in world markets toward the end of 1973 had a profound impact on Israel's position vis-à-vis these markets. Although the price index of imported goods in the last quarter of 1973 exceeded the average for that year by 52 percent, the concomitant increase in the price index of exported goods came to only 31 percent. This spelled a 13.5-percent decline in Israel's terms of trade in one quarter, a substantial supply shock.[29] As in the crop-failure example used in conjunction with the discussion of wage indexation, the deterioration of the terms of trade is also the sort of event that should have brought about a decline in real income, including real wages.[30]

The balance of payments reflected the shock clearly: whereas in 1972 excess imports had reached $1.1 billion, they were $3.3 billion in 1974. This caused considerable concern and put the balance-of-payments problem, once again, at the top of the economic policy agenda; so much so that the Bank of Israel could declare[31] "The central objective of the economic policy that has been followed since mid-1974 is the reduction of the deficit in the goods and services account, which had reached unsustainable proportions. A necessary condition for the attainment of this goal is moderated demand" and[32] "The main criterion for evaluating developments must be the extent of the balance-of-payments problem facing Israel's economy and the progress made during the past year toward solving that problem."

The fact that the Bank advocated reduced demand as a remedy is extremely interesting, because this indicates that it was recommending once again the use of unemployment. Even without reduced demand, some unemployment was to be expected, because the dearer imported productive inputs, particularly energy, were eating into business profits. This, in turn, was bound to cause production to shrink, thereby creating some unemployment. If, on top of this, demand were to fall as well, even more unemployment would result. This, the Bank hoped, would cause wages to fall. Exporters would thus be able to offset at least some of the increased costs of materials with a reduced wage bill, which would restore some of their lost competitiveness. At the same time, reduced demand would put a damper on imports of both consumer goods and inputs used in production for the domestic market. Between the two effects, the current-account deficit could be kept to an acceptable rate.

But in the wake of the 1966–67 experience, there was little chance that the government would follow the Bank's recommendations. A possible course of action was to use the political process to cajole the Histadrut into accepting wage reductions. But under the circumstances, the government lacked a credible threat in the event of labor unions' refusal to cooperate: it could not tell the unions to either cooperate or face unemployment.

This brings us back to wage indexation, for the precipitous increase in import prices was now being transmitted through the COLA to wages. Exporters thus faced double jeopardy: not only did they have to pay more dearly for imported inputs, but in terms of foreign exchange they also had to face higher wages, which increased precisely because imported inputs became more expensive. In the first nine months of 1974, the average real wage was down by only 1.4 percent compared to the 1973 average. This means that nominal wage increases virtually kept pace with price increases. With the rate of exchange fixed, that meant a considerable increase of wages in terms of foreign exchange.[33] The supply shock had evidently no impact on real wages.

Under these circumstances, the government elected to try to reduce excess imports by causing real wages to decline, but without resorting to the unemployment weapon. To this end two courses of action were chosen. First, consumer prices were given a boost through a substantial increase in the prices of subsidized staples and by the imposition of higher taxes, mainly import duties.[34] Second, to restore some of the lost export profitability, the currency was devalued against the dollar in November 1974, from I£4.2 to I£6, almost 43 percent in one swoop. This, after the exchange rate had been fixed since August 1971, when a devaluation of 20 percent took place.

The measures did not prove adequate. The goods-and-services-account situation continued to deteriorate during 1975, when the deficit topped $4 billion. So in its determination to cause wages to erode without resorting to unemployment, the government undertook to change the rules of the game in two important areas: wage indexation and exchange-rate adjustments. As concerns wages, a reform of the COLA formula was adopted. As regards the exchange rate, the fixed rate was replaced in June 1975 by a crawling peg, which amounted to small devaluations, up to 2 percent per month, on a continuing basis. The combination of the two reforms was to provide the engine that powered Israel's inflation later on. Hence, it merits careful description and examination.

The acceleration of inflation in 1973 brought about a demand for increased frequency of COLA payments from once a year, which had been in place since the 1966–67 slowdown, to twice a year. Consequently, an extra COLA payment was awarded in July 1973. The new arrangement persisted on an ad hoc basis until 1975, at which time the twice-yearly COLA payments were institutionalized as part of the COLA reform. From then on COLA payments were made in April and October of each year, until the frequency increased to four times annually five years later.

The COLA reform was agreed upon in July 1975. Its two important provisions were, first, the elimination of all CPI adjustments for the purpose of COLA calculations and, second, the reduction of the rate of compensation to 70 percent of inflation.[35] The second of the two provisions constituted the main objective of the COLA reform. It was prompted partly by the desire to remedy the transformation of import-price increases into systematic inflation through the COLA mechanism. The policy makers also realized that the COLA formula severely limited the government's policy options.[36] For example, whenever the government increased import duties, thus raising the domestic price of imported goods, this fed into the consumer price index and through it to the COLA. The government thus found itself compensating wage earners for completely legitimate economic-policy measures.

Particularly sticky was the question of the prices of subsidized staples, which are characterized by a high import component. In the case of bread, milk, and eggs, the imported component is grain; in the case of public transportation, it is the capital equipment (buses) and fuel. When world prices of these components go up, the government has to either increase expenditures for subsidies or raise the prices of the subsidized items in line with the increase in their dollar prices. The same holds in the event of a devaluation. What makes this problem a particularly difficult one in respect of the COLA is the fact that price increases of subsidized goods occasioned by dearer imports, but perceived as "inflation," do not benefit domestic producers. These are price increases that do not augment domestic profitability; they merely reflect cost increases. Yet, producers have to pay the COLA in the wake of such increases, imposing on them even higher production costs.[37]

The commission that adopted the COLA reform agreed, on the basis of these considerations, that there is no economic rationale for unconditional prevention of the decline of real wages. It correctly stated that if this were done, the only choice would be between unemployment and inflation. But the operational conclusions drawn were utterly wrong. Logically, the commission should have recommended that full (i.e., at 100 percent of the rate of inflation)

COLA payments be made only to compensate for those price increases that did not result from clearly identifiable supply shocks, such as increased import costs or bad farm crops, or from tax measures. Instead, it opted for the 70-percent clause. The reasoning advanced is puzzling: if the price index were adjusted for price increases originating in exogenous factors, real wages might decline too sharply, causing labor unrest.

The resolution was bad both ways. By granting a 70-percent compensation for price increases regardless of cause, the commission saddled employers with the burden of compensating their employees for price increases with which they have nothing to do and from which they do not benefit. The idea that the producer of pencils should compensate employees for 70 percent of the increase in the price they pay for imported gasoline is preposterous. On the other hand, by adopting the 70-percent clause, the commission signaled employees that they were not going to get fully compensated even if inflation was of the sort that does benefit their employers. Under these circumstances, it should have been expected that labor would seek redress through the bargaining process. Not to expect this was to believe that workers, of their own accord, were willing to accept only partial compensation on faith, assuming that the 30 percent of price increases for which they were not going to be compensated were indeed attributable to external developments or to supply shocks in general.

The biggest policy mistake in conjunction with the COLA commission was its very creation, for the commission's resolutions lacked the full force of an agreement between employers and employees. Neither side could be expected to view itself as being fully responsible for the new formula that, in a sense, was imposed on both. The consequences were not long in coming.

The second piece of the structure designed to cause wage erosion without the consent of labor was the exchange-rate reform. Believing that it gained a breathing space generated by the pegging of wage indexation at only 70 percent of the rate of inflation, the government sought to cut the purchasing power of wages by instituting exchange-rate inspired price increases. That is, inflation was chosen over unemployment as a mechanism for reducing wages. It is very important to stress that one is dealing here not with inflation engineered to benefit the government's budget; that is, we are not talking about inflationary taxation. Rather, this brand of inflation was designed to benefit employers, particularly the exporters among them. It thus constitutes a prime example of the government undertaking responsibilities that belong elsewhere. As we shall see, the moral hazard this generated was to have farreaching consequences. The planned inflation was dubbed *functional inflation*.[38]

To understand how functional inflation was supposed to bring about a reduction in excess imports, it is important to remember that Israel possesses hardly any natural resources and so has to import almost all its raw materials and energy. In addition, only a relatively small proportion of capital goods used in farming and manufacturing is produced domestically. It follows that Israel's ability to compete in the international markets depends crucially on the cost of labor. This is what prompted the Bank of Israel to say, in contradiction to its call for reduced demand:[39] "It seems, that in order to bring about a significant increase in export-oriented employment, a substantial decline of real wages is required. Various studies indicate that an increase in unemployment helps to tame wage increases. It is not clear, however, that the balance-of-payments situation justifies such drastic measures, and it is doubtful that unemployment can be sustained long enough to achieve the goal." The alternative was wage erosion brought about by functional inflation.

The Efficacy of the New Policy

The evaluation of any economic policy must rest on two tests. The obvious one is whether the policy is effective in attaining the desired goals. Second, even if effective, it also entails costs. Therefore, an assessment must be made as to whether the costs are in an acceptable proportion to the benefits. But there is a third aspect, which does not bear directly on the specific policy implemented but rather on the manner of implementation. Namely, the use of any particular policy instrument must be accompanied by a consistent setting of all other policy means. Otherwise, policy makers might defeat the purpose of the policy even if, on its own merits, as adjudicated by the two tests, it is a good one. On the strength of all of these evaluations the new policies of the mid-1970s must be judged not only a failure, but actually a total disaster. We turn first to the effectiveness question.

At first, the new policies looked as though they were moving the economy in the right direction. The most frequently mentioned justification for this assessment is the substantial narrowing of the deficit in the goods-and-services account, as this constituted the top economic-policy priority. Indeed, the deficit declined by $816 million from 1975 to 1976 and by another $636 million in the following year. This brought the deficit from a peak of about $4 billion in 1975 down to a little over $2.5 billion in 1977. However, a closer look at what really happened casts serious doubts as to whether a real improvement was taking place, for it looks as though the deficit reduction was of a very short-run nature, and no improvements in principle were occurring. What is more, even those improvements that had a more lasting effect could hardly be ascribed to the new policy. So let us turn to the components of the decline in the deficit, starting with imports.

The first thing to note is that imports did not decline at all: they were down marginally in 1976 (by $95 million), but then shot up by close to half a billion dollars in 1977. No less significant is that even these import numbers were made possible only by substantially reduced military imports. These declined by $303 million in 1976 and by another $462 million in 1977. The short-run nature of the cuts in defense imports can be inferred from the fact that they had not been occasioned by any change in Israel's defense doctrine. In other words, no fundamental changes in the military force structure had been planned. Therefore, any significant reduction in defense imports could be achieved only temporarily, by postponing purchases. Moreover, some of the reduction was simply the result of diminished U.S. aid in the aftermath of the 1973 war: gross U.S. aid declined from about $2.1 billion in 1976 to $1.6 billion in 1977. In 1978 it recovered to $2.2 billion, and defense imports were up as well, by $525 million as compared to 1977.[40]

As for nondefense imports, it is important to note that imports of consumer goods did not decline. On the other hand, imports of investment goods stagnated. The failure of imports to decline cannot be blamed on energy imports either, as they increased by only $100 million over the two-year period under consideration.

The longer-term contribution to the reduction in the current-account deficit came from exports, which grew at an average 13.5 percent per year in real terms over the period 1975–77. Moreover, a structural change took place in the sense that the share of value added in exports out of total value added (or, equivalently, the share of exports out of total resources) increased from 19.4 percent in 1975 to 26.5 percent in 1977.

The very rapid rate of growth of exports could not be expected to continue. Furthermore, it had been achieved at least partially through artificial means. First, the very structural change that caused so substantial an increase in the share of exports out of total resources meant that significant future export growth could be attained only through economic growth and not by shifting resources from other uses. Precisely this sort of shift facilitated most of the growth in exports during 1976 and 1977.

Second, there was no reason to believe that exports could continue to grow at that buoyant rate even if a continued shift of resources could be effected. The reason behind the assertion is that the fifteen-month period which started at the beginning of 1974 saw one of the most severe recessionary processes to hit the United States since the Great Depression. When the United States is undergoing a severe recession, the world economy slows down. This is always reflected in reduced trade. When the United States climbs out of a recession, as it did in 1976 and 1977, it pulls the world economy with it. There is therefore no doubt that part of the lively export performance during these two years was facilitated by the U.S. recovery, and the attendant increase in world trade. Therefore, world trade in 1976 expanded by over 12 percent, a development unlikely to be repeated, because it came on the heels of a 5-percent decline in 1975.[41]

Third, the increase in exports had been facilitated at least partially by a

significant augmentation of export subsidies, a good deal of which came in
the form of a tremendous increase in credit subsidization. Whereas export
subsidies constituted 15.6 percent of the market value of exports (national-
accounting terms) in 1975, the subsidization rates were 18.5 and 18.9 percent
in 1976 and 1977, respectively.[42]

But even if the impact of world developments and subsidization on the
performance of exports is discounted, the bright picture still had its worrisome
shades. First, a very significant proportion of the increase in exports came from
defense-related industries.[43] The problem with such exports is that they do not
reflect secular economic developments to the extent that is normal in other sectors. This is because defense materiel is procured by governments, and the
motivation for choosing a particular supplier is quite often political rather than
economic. Governments that are in the market for, say, tanks refrain from buying the Israeli tank not because it is inferior. In fact, it is one of the best tanks
made and not too expensive. Even the very timing of military procurement may
be the result of political developments and not economic ones.

In addition, it is by no means clear that any fundamental changes in
export profitability were taking place. The only improvement that could be
identified was in the alternative costs of exporting; that is, the domestic prices
that could be obtained for export goods declined relative to the foreign prices.
But in accounting terms, profitability actually declined in 1976; that is, the
profit margin over costs shrank.[44]

An examination of the national accounts confirms the conclusion that
the improvements were bound to be short lived. Because of the inflationary
erosion of wages in 1975 and 1976, private consumption per capita grew by
only 2.5 percent in each of the years 1976 and 1977. That was an improvement (in light of the primary objective, reducing the current-account deficit)
because the 1974 increase had been 4.5 percent.

That these achievements were bound to be only temporary and that
therefore the policy goals had not really been attained can be also deduced on
closer examination of the magnitude of real wages, which was supposed to
carry a substantial share of the burden. The average real wage declined by less
than 1 percent in 1975 in comparison with 1974, and by 1976 it not only
regained all of the lost ground, but exceeded the average for the first nine
months of 1974. The dismal results prompted the Bank of Israel to declare
that[45] "It should be emphasized, that the data do not indicate a decline in real
wages, as is implied by the policy aimed at improving the goods-and-services
account. . . . The attempt to use only partial wage indexation did not prove
successful." and[46] "The crawling-peg method . . . can hardly keep up, in the
face of rapid inflation, with the rise in prices and domestic costs."

The conclusion has to be that workers managed to maintain the real
value of their wages by means other than formal indexation. In fact, they were

able to do so partly with the help of increased industrial militancy.[47] So in 1978 private consumption increased by 5.7 percent per capita.

Given that the main goal was the reduction of the external imbalance, the Bank of Israel was also candid when it stated that the reduction in the rate of excess imports came about mainly as the consequences of the price shocks administered by the government's policies,[48] instead of the sort of structural change required if a long-run solution to the problem was to be attainable.

The Cost of the New Policy

Let us turn now to the question of costs: suppose, contrary to the preceding analysis, that the new policies were effective. Did their effectiveness justify the costs? Costs can occur in two areas. First, the attainment of certain objectives may entail forgoing other objectives. Second, costs can come in the form of limitations on policy instruments; that is, fewer policy degrees of freedom.

Let us begin the list of costs with the decline in investment, reflected also by the sharp reduction in capital-goods imports. Over the two-year period 1976–77, investment declined by 18.6 percent in real terms, a decline from which it has never fully recovered (i.e., until 1988 it had never returned to the 1975 rate). Thus, although gross domestic investment made up, on the average, close to 32 percent of the GNP in the years 1970–72, it declined to 24 percent of the GNP in 1977. No less significant is the fact that gross domestic capital formation exclusive of residential housing declined from 19 percent of the GNP on the average in 1970 to 1972 to 15 percent in 1977. One cost of the new policies, then, was the damage caused to long-run growth prospects.

Some may argue that, in view of the excess capacity that already existed in Israel's economy, particularly in industry, at least a temporary decline of investment was called for in any event. But excess capacity in, say, the apparel industry does not offset potential shortages of capacity in those industries toward which the economy is developing. The Bank of Israel, for one, was perfectly aware of the danger posed to future growth when it pointed out that, although private consumption grew by 14 percent from 1973 to 1977, investment declined by 16 percent. It concluded that the reduction of the current-account deficit had been made possible largely by, as the Bank put it, the creation of a large deficit in investment.[49]

The decline in investment was accompanied by a marked decline in private saving. We recall that part of the attempt to shift resources into exports consisted of measures aimed at reducing consumption. But the public elected to fight back by maintaining consumption at the expense of saving. Thus, although real private disposable income originating domestically (some of the income originates abroad, e.g., German reparation payments) declined by 2.6 percent from 1974 to 1976, real private saving declined over the same period by almost 20 percent.[50] It seems that the public did not believe that the government would persevere in its stern measures. The decline in income was thus regarded as a transitory circumstance. Consequently, saving could be reduced without too much long-run risk. The same sort of response was to recur time and again over the following decade.

Another important cost element was inherent in the very COLA reform that was to provide one of the major vehicles to improvement. First, as experience has clearly demonstrated, there are ways other than indexation arrangements for wage protection. The notion that indexation is responsible for wage rigidity may have been inspired by economists' preoccupation with its alleged destabilizing effects.[51] What really counts is basic attitudes: if the economic culture holds, as it has in Israel, that workers are entitled to have their wages protected regardless of the causes of cost-of-living increases, then wages will be protected whether or not this is accomplished by formal indexation.

But this does not mean that no harm was done when the rate of compensation was reduced to 70 percent of inflation. Because the representatives of labor had not been persuaded of the imperative of reduced real wages, the diminished protection from inflation with which they had to make do because of the new formula merely led them to look for alternative ways to protect the purchasing power of wages. This meant that discretionary wage increases would replace formal indexation.

The great advantage of formal indexation is that it vitiates guessing. Wage-indexation payments are always made after the fact; that is, after the rate of inflation for which compensation is awarded becomes known. Hence, indexation payments can be tailored precisely to the rate of inflation, and there is no danger that they will cause real wages to increase. In contrast, inflationary protection of wages without formal indexation involves guessing, because the protection component must be built into the wage contract which is signed before the rate of inflation is known. Such a protection clause has the characteristics of an insurance policy, granting a fixed sum of money. And like with any fixed-sum insurance contract, there is always the risk that the sum will turn out to be insufficient for the purpose for which it had been conceived. In the case of protection against inflation, the risk is that inflation will exceed the anticipated rate, in which case wages will decline in real terms. It is therefore natural on the part of labor to try to avoid underestimates of future inflation, which means that it will usually push for a more generous insurance policy. But the more generous the policy is, the higher will be the wage increases granted, and therefore the higher is the cost-push component of the inflationary process. In other words, high inflationary expectations incorporated into wage contracts have a tendency to justify themselves. Hence, protection from inflation agreed to before the fact may itself become an inflationary factor. The Bank of Israel, for one, became fully aware of this fact[52] and advocated an increase in the rate of wage indexation.[53] In effect, it recommended the repeal of the COLA reform, although it refrained from formulating its recommendation in these terms. The Bank was clearly right: if a decline of real wages is considered impossible to engineer, the method of full indexation, which the COLA reform abandoned, is preferable.

This brings us to the most serious cost associated with the new policies: inflation. During 1975 prices rose by 23.5 percent, and during 1976 the pace accelerated to 38 percent. That the inflationary process had been the direct consequence of the new policies was clear even at the time, as is evident from the fact that the Bank of Israel declared:[54] "The inflation in 1976, like in the two preceding years, resulted mainly from the government's policy aimed at improving the balance of payments and reducing the private sector's demand."

The historian Paul Johnson has pointed out that what he calls *Cathedocracy*, meaning the people who because of their high level of education have attained leadership positions, has shaped Jewish history for most of the time since the destruction of the Second Temple.[55] Perhaps this legacy is the reason why in Israel, too, academics enjoy considerable public respect and can therefore exercise influence over the course of events. Hence, it is important to observe that the wisdom of abandoning the fixed exchange-rate regime was hardly questioned by academic economists. The desirability of devaluation in general was undisputed. The only subject for debate was how best to go about it and what the precise goal should be. The debate centered on whether devaluations should be used merely to prevent a real appreciation of the domestic currency or aim at real depreciation.[56] The question of whether real depreciation was an attainable goal in the first place had never been raised, even though the possibility of inflationary effects of devaluation under full employment was recognized.

Economists who had the government's ear at the time also argued as to whether a crawling peg or a complete float was preferable.[57] Although the COLA reform was to provide inflationary fuel in the longer run, the immediate power behind inflation was the exchange-rate policy. But it also had some important implications for the monetary system. We have already established that the rate of exchange had never been considered a target for monetary policy. Yet there can be no disputing that, as long as the exchange rate was fixed, it at least provided a nominal anchor for the monetary system. That is, this particular target assumed some definite value, even if not motivated by monetary considerations. But once it became a crawling peg, it no longer provided an anchor. The loss of the monetary anchor was particularly crucial because, as has been made clear, the Bank of Israel had not been managing any of the other potential targets. The conditions under which the measuring rod itself becomes a function of developments in the economy had thus been brought about.

The new exchange-rate policy also engendered ramifications concerning labor relations. The devaluation policy could not but reinforce the impression that the government would go to any length to prevent labor-market developments from creating unemployment. Aware of this, labor unions could press their demands, because the removal of the threat of unemployment removed the main risk normally associated with aggressive wage demands. Employers, too, could now give in to those demands, because they knew that the government would not permit them to go under, lest there be unemployment.

The very fact that the government was deeply concerned about the balance-of-payments difficulties—the concern that prompted the new policy to begin with—could not but reinforce the sense of security on the part of manufacturers, for if the government was so worried about exports, then it could be expected to do all that was necessary to guarantee that exporting remained worthwhile. The Bank of Israel actually implored the government to take measures designed to ensure proper export profitability.[58] It became therefore unavoidable that the government would find itself more and more just reacting to developments on the wage front and less and less able to follow a deliberate macroeconomic policy. It would not be an exaggeration to say that the degree to which the government found itself handicapped in this context exceeded in scope all the examples discussed in Chapter 8.

It was also the most salient feature of the dependence of the private sector on the government. The new policy can be described as having constituted an invitation to the private sector, especially the Manufacturers' Association, to lay all its problems at the government's door. Astute business became even less important than it had been. A trip to the office of the prime minister (if the minister of finance did not capitulate first), who would be lectured on the declining profitability of exports and the imminent calamity this would precipitate in terms of the balance of payments and employment, was much more profitable. The remedy was always the same: more devaluations; that is, more "functional inflation," and more export subsidies.

In 1978, labor contracts were up for renewal. The negotiating process was very drawn out, especially in the public sector, where talks stretched over the entire year. The tough stance on the part of the government was designed to achieve two objectives: to keep wage increases to what was considered an acceptable rate and create an incentive for labor to move from the public to the private sector. This particular methodology was totally consistent with the government's decision to refrain absolutely from using labor-market softness as an economic policy instrument. The government was not going to reduce the public sector's work force, thereby creating the labor-market slack that would discipline the unions.

The government failed to attain either objective. First, private employers accepted labor's demands without a real fight. The Bank of Israel observed:[59] "Wage increases in the private sector in 1978 were brought about by stiff wage demands. . . . In fact, employers acceded to these demands without much opposition. The number of strikes was lower this year than in 1977 and the private sector hastened to conclude a wage agreement that exceeded the government's guidelines." But the obstinacy of the government concerning public-sector wages did not bear any fruit either:

> In the public sector the government attempted to pursue a policy designed to create a wage differential in favor of workers in the productive sectors; but after a long negotiating process, which was accompanied by labor disputes, sanctions, and strikes at a rate far in excess of that experienced in recent years, the newly signed labor contracts were concluded at the end of the year. The rate of wage increases according to these contracts does not lag behind the private sector's.

What the description lacks, however, is an association of the failure with the philosophy underlying the government's policies since 1970 and with the general weakening of the government along the lines discussed in Chapter 8.

The Inconsistent Implementation of the New Policy

We next turn to the question of whether the government took care to harmonize its various policies with the new regime. The general consensus even at the time was that a crucial area in this respect was government finance. And it was widely agreed that fiscal restraint should be practiced.[60]

What happened was the exact opposite. On the face of it, developments looked promising: public consumption declined in real terms by 9.7 percent in 1976 and by a further 13.4 percent in 1977. However, a closer scrutiny of the components of the decline reveals that, just as all the import reduction came from reduced military purchases, so all the decline in public consumption came from reduced defense expenditures. These declined by 14.4 percent in 1976 and by a further 19.4 percent in 1977. In fact, nondefense public expenditures increased in both years. And, as already pointed out, the decline in defense expenditures was bound to be short lived, especially because most of it came in the form of reduced procurement.

Perhaps more counterproductive still was the ballooning of the welfare state. To grasp the magnitude of this development, some key data are provided in Table 9.2. The figures concerning transfer payments constitute both genuine transfers, such as social insurance payments, and subsidies, including credit subsidization. Not only is the increase of transfers awesome in real terms, especially in 1975 (the first year of the new policies), but so is their ascent in terms of shares of the GNP. The last measure is especially impressive: over the three-year period 1974–77, the share of transfer payments in the

GNP rose by fully 60 percent. Whereas in 1974 it would take five years of transfers to exhaust one year's GNP, by 1977 it would take only a little more than three years to do the same.[61]

Both kinds of transfers were indicative of the government's inability to give its own policies a chance. A major factor in the surge of subsidies was the failure to raise interest rates in line with inflation, thus creating a large credit subsidy. The expansion of credit subsidization has already been mentioned in connection with exports, but it was by no means restricted to them. Credit for nonexported output was also subsidized at increased rates. Particularly the latter kind of subsidy suggests that the government was actually unwilling to let the ax fall where it should have.

The tremendous increase in transfer payments was financed, in part, by a no less important increase in taxation, as Table 9.2 partially reveals. Although in the early 1960s taxes constituted less than a quarter of the GNP, they increased to over a third at the beginning of the 1970s and approached one-half of the GNP as the decade of the 1980s drew near.[62]

Although increases in indirect subsidization could be construed as a temporary measure, to be discontinued on short notice, new direct transfers and the increase in taxes were embedded in legislation not easily repealed. In 1973 the Parallel Tax Law was adopted, compelling employers to pay 2.7 percent of employees' wages to the sick funds to which the employees belonged.

TABLE 9.2

Transfers and Taxes

Item	IS million				% Change, Real		
	1974	1975	1976	1977	1975	1976	1977
Transfers:							
Subsidies	348.4	1121.9	1556.6	2384.9	131.2	5.7	13.8
Direct	712.6	1073.2	1408.0	2079.3	7.8	0.0	9.7
Total	1061.0	2195.1	2964.6	4464.2	48.5	2.9	11.9
Taxes:							
Direct	1176.6	1684.3	2484.4	3506.1	2.8	12.3	4.0
Indirect	1128.4	1563.3	2356.9	3207.3	-0.8	14.8	1.1
Total	2305.0	3247.6	4841.3	6713.4	1.1	13.5	3.0
	Share in GNP, Percent						
Transfers	20.1	29.3	30.7	32.0			
Taxes	43.6	43.3	50.2	48.1			

*Deflated by the average annual CPI.

Source: BOI, *Annual Report 1978*, pp. 170–71, 174, 178; *1979*, pp. 181, 183, 188–89.

The percentage was increased in 1974 to 3.4. In March 1975, the Employers' Tax Law was adopted, which required employers to pay a tax amounting to 4 percent of their wage bill. All these taxes created a widening gap between the cost of labor to employers and the gain from labor to employees.

In July of the same year the personal income-tax law was reformed. One of its most important features was the abolition of personal exemption for children and the adoption instead of a system of child allowances. These are very much like a tax credit system, except that the latter benefits only taxpayers, whereas the former is universal. Each family with children receives a monthly check from the National Insurance Institute in an amount reflecting the number of children. The reformers chose to adopt the change even though the replacement of exemptions with allowances meant an increase in marginal tax rates, a definite disincentive to work. Furthermore, to finance the allowances the national insurance tax was increased, thereby causing a further increase in the marginal tax rate.[63]

In December of the same year, the law imposing a value-added tax was adopted.

The fortification of the welfare state is also evident from figures concerning expenditures associated with various welfare programs. Thus, total expenditures on such programs increased from 12.8 percent of the GNP in 1975 to 17 percent in 1977, an increase of a third over only two years.[64]

No less significant is the fact that the public sector was the only one besides the financial sector in which employment rose in 1976. Thus, employment in the public sector increased by over 3 percent, whereas total employment increased by only 1.2 percent.[65] This means that the public sector was robbing the private sector of the very labor that was needed if export-oriented growth, or any growth at all, was to take place.

The 1977 *Mahapach*—Economic Reform

The word *switch,* perhaps, better conveys the meaning of *mahapach* than "reform." In Hebrew it means something halfway between evolution and revolution. In 1977, two events won that title. The first was a political switch: in the elections of May 1977 Labor failed, for the first time in Israel's history, to emerge as the dominant political party. Consequently, the Likud, which had been doomed for a generation to sit in opposition, got to form the new coalition government.

The relevance of the political switch to the present discussion concerns the social and economic outlook of the new regime. The Likud had been formed as an alliance of two political parties: Herut and the Liberals. The first regards Jabotinsky, the founder of the Revisionist faction in the Zionist movement and the organization's most articulate liberal (in the European sense, conservative in the U.S. terminology), as its ideological father. The second constituted a transformation of the erstwhile General Zionists, whose main support had been among the independent farmers in the *moshavot* and in the business community especially. Indeed, if one were to go by the platform of the Likud, one would conclude that its philosophy was dominated by liberal, market-oriented values. The platform advocated, and still does, a much larger role for markets and a much smaller one for the government. But an analysis of the vote that powered the Likud into dominance suggests that its attraction had not been generated by liberal principles. Indeed, the Liberals, who through the years have emphasized their economic ideas in election campaigns, found it politically astute to join Herut, whose salient feature in the eyes of the electorate was its political stance (more hawkish) rather than its economic philosophy. If the Liberals had thought that liberal ideas were very popular, they would have opted for running an independent election campaign.

Perhaps more to the point, it is generally agreed that the swing from Labor to Likud consisted of citizens who regarded themselves as left out of the mainstream. These were mostly Jews of Afro-Asian origin who came to Israel in the 1950s and 1960s and who were immersed in the prevalent economic culture ever since their arrival. Indeed, after a generation of Labor's policies, the majority of voters probably found it impossible to even imagine a market economy, much less to support it. Yet, they perceived Labor as not granting them equitable access to the table of government largess. Political prudence was thus on the side of the opponents of any great move toward a market economy, and the Likud depended on some of them for a parliamentary majority.

Still, the Likud was bound to at least change appearances, which brought about the second switch in October 1977. It was consistent with liberal principles not only outwardly, but also in substance, as far as it went, for it abolished a regulatory system that had been in place since Israel's early days. But it was very limited and failed completely in driving home the message of free markets, with the all-important notion of responsibility for one's decisions that goes with it. The switch is usually regarded by Israel's public opinion as the event triggering the inflation that was to break out in full force soon thereafter. One possible reason for this misconception might be that the Likud unwittingly paraded the switch as a true break with past economic policies. Talks held with Professor Milton Friedman, who is known throughout the world as a staunch champion of market economies, prior to the announcement of the reform, undoubtedly helped to reinforce that impression. In fact, as we shall see, the switch did not constitute a break with old policies.

The switch consisted of the following main measures. First, the exchange-rate regime was altered from the former crawling peg to a free float. Second, this was accompanied by a devaluation from I£10.78 to I£15.96 to a unit of the currency basket[66]. At 48 percent, this was the second largest devaluation in Israel's history. Its size was dictated largely by the government's desire to get rid of the direct exchange-rate subsidies, which had still existed in spite of the crawling peg system. Thus, on the day before the devaluation, an export good considered to embody at least 66 percent value added, was receiving a I£3.27 subsidy per unit of currency basket exported, on top of the official exchange rate.[67] Hence, the abolition of direct subsidies meant, from the standpoint of the exporter of such a good, that the devaluation amounted to a mere 13.6 percent.

The third component of the switch consisted of the removal of some restrictions on foreign-exchange transactions. Viewed from the perspective of subsequent developments, the most important changes were, first, the removal of restrictions on short-term capital movements into and out of Israel and, second, that the foreign-exchange indexed bank accounts known as *patam* became commonly accessible (whereas up to that point only exporters and recipients of German reparations could maintain such accounts). The only difference between these foreign-exchange accounts and ordinary accounts was that no checks could be written on them; withdrawal had to be made at the bank.

The one clear explanation for why this particular set of steps had been chosen for the switch is to be found with the fact that the new government, like its predecessor, considered the balance-of-payments problem to be of paramount importance. This was despite the fact that the data available to the economic chieftains indicated an intensifying inflationary process. Thus, although inflation during the twelve months ending in September 1977 reached 33.7 percent, down from the 37.6 percent of the preceding twelve months, it rose to annual rates of 38 percent during the six months ending in September and 43.6 percent during the three months ending in September 1977. Inflation had thus been obviously on the increase even before the switch was announced, and the rate of acceleration was considerable. Evidently, this had not been enough to cause a change in priorities, as indexation protected the public from the ravages of inflation, especially where the value of accumulated savings is concerned. And because many groups actually benefitted from the process, as it eroded the real value of their debts, there was no political constituency for fighting inflation.

The switch was designed, for the main part, to achieve unification of the different effective exchange rates and to "liberalize" the foreign-exchange market. In fact, it is quite clear from looking at the stated rationale that nobody had a very clear idea as to what liberalization meant and what it was supposed to accomplish. This includes, in particular, the Bank of Israel. As in the case of the crawling peg, a close look at the interpretations given by the Bank to the liberalization will provide some essential points of departure when we try, later on, to make sense of the inflationary process.

First, the Bank offered no clear ideas as to why a floating exchange rate was better than a crawling peg. It simply accepted the new government's political agenda.[68] The reason for the institution of a float, as articulated later on by the Bank's governor from 1976 to 1981, was that a free float made it possible for the exchange rate to respond more smoothly and quickly to changing exogenous conditions. Among other things it was to provide, according to the governor, a better check on the flight of capital.[69] On the other hand, the Bank feared that a free float would hinder the desirable evolution of the exchange rate, thereby causing the current-account deficit to increase. All of these arguments may have been valid under the circumstances, but they had nothing to do with monetary considerations, although the institution of a free float had a profound impact on the nominal system, as did the institution of universal foreign-exchange indexed bank accounts.

These are not just theoretical fine points. By the time the switch had been contemplated, the evidence pointed to a monetary system increasingly out of control. The commercial banks were incurring chronic and substantial liquidity deficits, which constituted the equivalent of an expansion of 11 percent in the supply of high-powered money (monetary base) in 1975 and 8.7 percent in 1976.[70] Although deficits in the first ten months of 1977 were more moderate, they still ranged up to 7.8 percent of reserve requirements.[71] They constituted a clear indication that the Bank of Israel was having serious difficulties in controlling the monetary system to begin with. The institution of a free float was bound to weaken the Bank's capabilities even further.

The removal of restrictions on capital movements implied that domestic rates of interest would be determined by world rates. An attempt to keep them above world rates would attract an inflow of debt capital, creating pressure both on the domestic interest rate to decline and on domestic currency to appreciate. The latter alternative would have clearly gone against the grain of official intentions, because it would have tended to cause an increase in the current-account deficit. Hence, it was to be expected that steps would be taken to prevent domestic interest rates from exceeding international ones. With rates of interest thus determined and the exchange rate a clean float, there was again no room for monetary policy, regardless of governmental restrictions.

The results were quick in coming: by 1978 the monetary system was roaring out of control.[72] First, immediately following the switch, liquidity deficits in the commercial banking system increased substantially. Whereas during the first ten months of 1977 they averaged 4.9 percent of the reserve requirements, they jumped to 13.2 and 11.6 percent of requirements in November and December of 1977, respectively.[73] That this was no aberration is clear from the fact that average liquidity deficits for 1978 stood at 14.8 percent of requirements.[74]

The second ominous development, to which we shall return with more analysis in the next chapter, was that the Bank of Israel became the major source of infusions to the monetary base. In 1977, the government created about I£8.9 billion of base money by borrowing from the Bank, and the latter added I£6.9 billion of its own. But in 1978, the government created I£10.9 billion, and the Bank created an additional I£14.4 billion. There could be no doubt that this flood of money emanating from the Bank was not the result of planned monetary actions. Rather, it represented a deepening loss of control.

A good deal of the increased monetary infusion by the Bank had to do with directed credit and foreign-exchange credit for domestic uses. When the switch that reduced foreign-exchange controls was implemented, the office of comptroller of foreign exchange at the Ministry of Finance was abolished and a watered-down version of it created at the Bank. Its chief remaining responsibility was the dispensation of directed credit. This constituted an institutional blunder, because it created a conflict of purposes inside the Bank. On the one hand, the Bank was now saddled with the responsibility for financing a particular and, in the eyes of the government and the public, very important sector of the economy. On the other hand, it was expected to carry out restraining monetary policies, which could hurt the very same sector.

The loser in this conflict was monetary policy, although not all the deterioration should be necessarily ascribed to administrative blunder. Whereas in 1976 directed credit to the public constituted 62 percent of total credit, that percentage increased to 72 percent in 1977 and 75 percent in 1978.[75] In other words, the scope for monetary policy narrowed severely.

A very important conclusion that emerges from the discussion of the switch is that the new government did not really deviate in any important way from the policies of the mid-1970s. Floating the exchange rate merely carried the crawling peg to its logical conclusion. Monetary policy, if anything, became even less evident than it had been. Furthermore, it was clear that the new government was not going to change the institutional setup of the Israeli economy. Hence, labor relations were untouched by the change, and the dependence of the private sector on the government remained as fundamental as ever.

The only real change was the liberalization of the foreign-exchange market. From an ideological standpoint, liberalizing the domestic markets for goods, credit, and capital was, and still is, much more important. From an economic standpoint, the order of liberalization of markets matters, and liberalizing the foreign-exchange market first is like putting the cart before the horse.[76] Thus, all the ingredients for the terrible inflation that was about to begin were left intact. The switch was a nonswitch.[77]

Appendix

Consider the representative utility function

$$u(y_1, y_2) = a_1 ln y_1 + a_2 ln y_2$$

where y_i denotes the amount consumed of good i, and a_i are positive constants. When maximized under a budget constraint, this utility function produces the demand functions

$$y_{id} = \frac{a_i}{\sum a_i} \cdot \frac{I}{p_i}, \quad i = 1, 2$$

where p_i denotes the price of goods i and I denotes income.

Next, assume production proceeds according to the function

$$y_i = \alpha_i L_i^{\lambda_i}, \quad i = 1, 2$$

where α_i and $\lambda_i < 1$ are positive constants and L denotes labor input. Let

$$\frac{1}{1-\lambda_i} \equiv \mu_i, \quad \frac{\lambda_i}{1-\lambda_i} \equiv \sigma_i, \quad i = 1, 2$$

Also, let w denote the wage rate. Then the demand for labor is given by

$$L_i = (\alpha_i \lambda_i)^{\mu_i} \left[\frac{p_i}{w} \right]^{\mu_i}, \quad i = 1, 2$$

and the supply of goods is described by

$$y_{is} = \alpha_i^{\mu_i} \lambda_i^{\sigma_i} \left[\frac{p_i}{w} \right]^{\sigma_i}, \quad i = 1, 2$$

Assume labor supply is inelastic at L_0. Then market equilibrium requires

$$y_{id} = y_{is}, \text{ and } \sum_i L_i = L_0$$

Let us denote the amounts of labor in equilibrium by L_{ie}. Consider next a supply shock represented by a decline in α_1, and assume the government mobilizes all the means at its disposal, specifically an accommodating monetary policy, to keep employment frozen at the same rates and allocation as in the pre-supply shock equilibrium. That is, if the new equilibrium rates of labor are denoted by L_{ig}, then $L_{ig} = L_{ie}$.

The supply shock causes, in the first period following the initial equilibrium, a rise in the price of the first good. This requires, in the second period, wage indexation payments. It is assumed that indexation is calculated on the basis of the Lespeyres index and that labor is fully compensated. Thus, the consumption bundle that serves as a basis for calculating inflation is that which prevails under the initial equilibrium.

Because the objective is to show that once a spurious supply shock is transmitted to the price system through indexation it can no longer be expunged from the system, assume that in the period following the supply shock, the constant α_1 returns to its initial value.

The system was simulated for the following numerical values:

$$\frac{a_1}{\sum a_i} = .6; L_0 = 300; \alpha_1 = 60; \alpha_2 = 40; \lambda_1 = .5; \lambda_2 = .4$$

The supply shock was represented by a reduction of α_1 to 75 percent of its initial level.

Under the rigid conditions imposed on the system, particularly the condition that labor allocation remain unchanged, the system returns in the third period to the original equilibrium as far as real values are concerned. The equilibrium values for all three periods are displayed in Table 9.3.

The evolution of the story behind the numbers is as follows. The supply shock causes a decline in the supply of the first good by 25 percent. This causes its price to increase from 1 (arbitrarily chosen for the initial equilibrium solution) in period 1 to 1.33 in period 2. Hence, the price index for the second period is 1.2. For the third period, α_1 is restored to its initial value but the wage rate increases by 20 percent due to indexation payments. The combined effect of these changes is a decline in the price of the first good, to 1.2, and an increase in the price of the second good, to 2.62, due to the increased production costs. And although the real wage is back to its initial value, the whole price level in the third period exceeds the initial price level by 20 percent. It follows that if this were an open economy, the result would have been

TABLE 9.3

Simulation Results

Variable	Period 1	Period 2	Period 3
Labor in Good 1	195.65	195.65	195.65
Labor in Good 2	104.35	104.35	104.35
Output of Good 1	839.25	629.44	839.25
Output of Good 2	256.72	256.72	256.72
Price of Good 1	1.00	1.33	1.20
Price of Good 2	2.18	2.18	2.62
Wage Rate	2.14	2.18	2.57
Real Wage	2.14	1.82	2.14

an appreciation of the domestic currency. Put differently, in terms of foreign exchange, the wage rate in period 3 exceeds the initial wage rate by 20 percent. This implies diminished competitiveness of the exporting sector of the economy, which would have produced pressures to devalue and so create more inflation.

10

Inflation! The Obstacles Gang Up

Inflation, it is said, brought down the Roman Empire. But the hyperinflations that shook Germany, Poland, Austria, and Hungary, to name a few examples, prompted modern economic research into the causes and consequences of sustained inflation. Common to all these episodes was the suffering inflicted on the population. Therefore, whether inflation had been of the ordinary sort or hyperinflation, the average citizen had an interest in putting an end to it. In those cases where inflation was allowed to get out of hand, it happened not because the population did not mind, but because the government was too weak to cope, as in pre-1991 Argentina, or was dealing with impossible circumstances, as in the case of post-World War I Germany.

Against this background, Israel's near-hyperinflation stands out as a process regarded with indifference, if not welcomed, by the citizenry. This is where the artificial economy created over decades by successive governments produced its most important consequences: although inflation was, as we shall describe, wrecking the economy, the ordinary citizen was sheltered from its ravages. In general terms, the Israeli variety of inflation did not entail declining standards of living. Savings were not being wiped out. The frequency of wage payments did not increase. In the German hyperinflation of the early 1920s, in contrast, wage earners ultimately got paid every morning, so they could rush to buy before the daily price hike took place. So immune was the ordinary citizen to the inflationary disease that for a long time it was virtually impossible to convince anyone that inflation presented a serious threat to the economy. With no political constituency for halting inflation, politicians were in no hurry to undertake the task of ending it, which is why it was allowed to go on for over a decade.

When, at long last, the first attempts at halting the process were made, it turned out that some of the major attributes of the economy which were detrimental to growth also proved to be formidable obstacles to stabilization. In the end, it took an unusual combination of near economic disaster and political alliance to implement the stabilization plan of July 1985.

Phase 1: The Early Stages

Double-digit inflation appeared for the first time after the 1966–67 slow-down in 1970. It has never dropped below double digits until 1992. But in the early stages, inflation rates had not been outrageously out of line with what was happening in quite a few other countries, among them especially some members of the industrialized world. Even in the United States rates were creeping up, and President Nixon tried his hand at wage-price guide posts.

The relevant numbers are provided in Table 10.1, which is partitioned into two periods: 1970–74 and 1975–77. The first period is characterized by rising rates of inflation in all five countries. Although Israel seems to diverge from the general pattern in 1973 and 1974, it must be remembered that a good deal of this extra inflation was brought about by the Yom Kippur War. In the second period, Israel's pattern clearly differs, as its inflation rates increase steadily, whereas those of the other countries fluctuate with a downward trend. The year 1975, it should be recalled, brought world recession, which helped to check inflation at rates below those of 1974.

The inflationary process in these early stages was predominantly inter-preted in Keynesian terms: excess demand causing the economy to heat up.[1] But there was an added concern that emanated from the evolution of wages.

The government's solution to the excess-demand problem was also typ-ically Keynesian: it imposed a variety of taxes. These included increases in income-taxe rates imposed on both individuals and businesses and an increase in social insurance payments imposed on employers. This particular step con-stituted a self-defeating measure, because it increased the labor costs incurred by the employers, a development that should have been expected to generate

TABLE 10.1

Rate of Inflation of the Average Quarterly CPI Between Successive Fourth Quarters

Year	Israel	France	Italy	United States	United Kingdom
1970	10.2	1.6	5.3	7.1	8.3
1971	12.4	5.6	4.7	3.5	9.2
1972	12.1	6.9	7.2	3.4	7.7
1973	24.3	8.3	11.6	8.4	10.3
1974	48.0	15.0	24.7	12.1	18.2
1975	32.5	9.9	11.6	7.3	25.3
1976	35.8	9.9	21.2	5.0	15.0
1977	40.2	9.2	15.1	6.6	13.1

Sources: For Israel, the CPI as published by CBS; for other countries: IMF, *International Financial Statistics*, various years.

price increases. In fact, 1970 marked a turning point in this respect.[2] There-after, the wedge between total labor costs and the part enjoyed by employees widened steadily. A number of indirect tax rates were also increased, notably a levy of 20 percent on most imports. Sales tax on many domestically pro-duced items rose by 10 to 15 percent, and subsidies for public transportation, milk and its derivatives, eggs, and meat were slashed, forcing a rise in prices.[3]

Whatever else one thinks of taxation as a means of dealing with excess demand, there can be no doubt that, if it is to work at all, the government must refrain from using the additional revenues to expand its own demand. Yet in fact, domestic public consumption grew, in real terms, by 11 percent in 1970 and by another 10.6 percent in 1971. That is, over the two years public con-sumption rose by almost 23 percent in real terms while the GDP grew over the same period by 20 percent. To be fair, one must take into account that during 1970 Israel was engaged in the War of Attrition, and that the bulk of the increase in public expenditures came from increased consumption for defense. Still, in 1971 civilian public consumption increased at a rate exceeding popu-lation growth; that is, did more than keep up.

What prevented an outright aggravation of the excess-demand situation was that private consumption rose at a rate much lower than the GDP growth rates. Hence, total private and domestic public consumption grew, over the two-year period, by only 12.2 percent. In fact, in 1970 per-capita private con-sumption did not grow at all.[4]

During 1968 and 1969, wage demands were moderate, as workers were still under the grim impact of the 1966–67 slowdown. But by 1970 the econ-omy was buoyant enough to generate considerable pressure for increased wage benefits. To avert possibly adverse effects of what was viewed as exces-sive wage settlements, the government engineered the Package Deal dis-cussed in Chapter 6. The concern was probably premature at that point, because wage-costs per unit of industrial output were actually declining. Over the period 1968–72 they declined at an average of 4 percent:[5] although real wages did rise, labor productivity rose even faster.

If inflation was the government's prime concern, the measures which it initiated certainly failed to achieve the objective. In fact, they probably aggra-vated the situation. This is evident from the fact that until August 1970, prices rose at a pace not much different from the 1969 rate. Only after the imposition of the new taxes did inflation accelerate. Between the second quarter of 1969 and the second quarter of 1970 prices rose only by 4.3 percent, which con-trasts sharply with the 10.2-percent rate of Table 10.1.[6] Nor were the new taxes negligible in terms of the overall tax burden: although total tax and com-pulsory loan receipts in 1970 constituted 35.6 percent of the GNP, the 1971 burden came to 40.8 percent.

Between December 1970 and June 1971, prices rose at an annual rate of

9.3 percent, which was very close to the 1970 pace. But in August 1971, the Israeli pound was devalued by 20 percent against the dollar, and the effect was immediate: inflation from June to December 1971 soared to 17.6 percent on an annual basis.

The devaluation must be seen in the same context as the earlier taxes. The objectives were the same, but this time the government opted for devaluation because, in addition to inflation, the civil component of the deficit in the goods-and-services account was deteriorating: it grew by almost 16 percent from 1969 to 1970 and by another 8 percent the following year. Like the new taxes, however, the devaluation was implemented when the economy was at full employment and demand pressures were deemed excessive. To devalue under these circumstances meant that demand pressures would become even worse, unless steps were taken to ensure the smooth release of production factors, especially labor, from the non-traded-goods sector to the traded-goods sector.

On the basis of the various short-term indicators the devaluation was a success, even though the government used the opportunity to reduce direct export subsidies. They declined from the predevaluation range of 24 to 32 percent of the exchange rate to the range of 20 to 21 percent after devaluation. Consequently, exporters enjoyed a de facto rate of devaluation of between 10 and 16.6 percent, with the highest devaluation going to the goods belonging to the lowest value-added class. Although not immediately relevant to the subject of inflation, it should be noted that the upside-down incentive structure induced by the devaluation is an unavoidable result of trying to eliminate or diminish a graduated subsidization scheme.

But the fact that exports did not enjoy the full benefit of devaluation did not matter so much, because wages did not keep up: real wages rose by only 2.4 percent in 1971 and by 1.1 percent in 1972, far less than productivity gains. Consequently, the civilian component of the deficit in the balance of payments shrank in 1972 by 9 percent, putting it just below the 1970 deficit. The Bank of Israel concluded that the economic policy measures had been largely a success.[7]

But as Table 10.1 indicates, things began to look a bit different in 1973, when Israel experienced an inflation rate of close to 25 percent, which did not yet reflect the impact of the Yom Kippur War and the oil crisis. In fact, during the first 9 months of 1973, prior to the outbreak of the war, inflation reached 21.6 percent, as against the 8.6 percent of the comparable period a year earlier. This was not the only bad news. The civilian goods-and-services-account deficit increased by 122 percent in the first nine months of 1973 as compared to the same period a year earlier. Industrial exports, which grew by an average annual rate of 20 percent between 1967 and 1971, increased by only 9 percent in 1972 and by 4 percent in prewar 1973.

The failure of exports to grow as vigorously as they had was attributed to lack of profitability, about which there was a lot of concern. The 1974 report of the Bank of Israel is full of references to the inadequacy of export profitability.[8] In particular, it was seen as suffering from too rapid an increase in wage costs. There had also been concern with the evolution of private consumption. In the first three quarters of 1973 it exceeded on the average the year-earlier rate by 12.4 percent in real terms, although the GDP increased by only 8.4 percent. The evidence clearly pointed to the short-lived nature of the measures of 1970 and 1971, and it particularly cast doubt on the wisdom of devaluations.

However, by the time these statistics became known, the 1973 war had already occurred and the Oil Crisis pushed many countries, including all the ones surveyed in Table 10.1, into double-digit inflation. This might explain why the lessons of early 1973 were lost on both policy makers and economists. So in 1974 the government served another portion of the policies discussed in Chapter 9. It has already been concluded that these policies did not lead to the desired improvements. Table 10.2 recapitulates this conclusion in a more concise and comprehensive manner.

TABLE 10.2

Policy-Oriented Economic Indicators

	1974	1975	1976	1977
Millions of Dollars:				
Excess Imports	3319	4016	3200	2380
Direct Defense Imports	1225	1846	1555	1084
Civilian Deficit*	2094	2170	1645	1296
Share in Total Uses, Percent:**				
Civilian Deficit*	12.1	9.5	7.6	5.3
Gross Domestic Investment	19.5	18.9	16.2	14.9
Private Consumption	36.8	35.5	37.1	37.2
Total Consumption[†]	61.4	61.7	61.2	58.6
Percent:				
National Savings[††]	-3.3	-4.7	-3.6	4.1
Private Consumption Growth	7.7	.3	4.8	4.8

* In the goods and services account, exclusive of direct defense imports.

** In national accounts terms.

† Private and public consumption.

†† Share of GNP left after disposal for total consumption.

Phase 2: 1978

By 1978 it was becoming increasingly clear that the economy was settling into a pattern of inflation and stagnation from which it could not be easily extricated. After several rounds of tax increases, two changes in the
exchange rate regime and numerous devaluations, the problems these measures were supposed to solve persisted.

As seen in Chapter 9, developments in 1978 prompted the Bank of
Israel to have serious second thoughts concerning the wisdom of the COLA
reform. It was also taking a second look at the problem of subsidization of staples. There was no disagreement as to the desirability of at least a reduction of
the rate of subsidization. But there was a question as to the wisdom of cutting
subsidies under the circumstances that characterized Israel's inflation. Said
the Bank:[9]

Reducing the rise in basic commodity prices has a moderating effect on
the consumer price index, though its strength is not sufficiently clear.
An estimate of its impact from the expenditure side indicates that a 25
percent increase in the prices of basic commodities should push up the
index by 3.7 percent. . . . This includes the direct effect of the price rise
of basic commodities, an indirect effect on the cost of products for
which basic commodities serve as inputs, and the effect of the COLA.

The issue was to become the subject of an extremely heated debate between
the government and academic economists in 1981.

Another important development in 1978 was the full indexation of tax
brackets. As is well known, inflation creates a fiscal drag: nominal incomes
grow, pushing people into higher tax brackets. However, real income usually
does not grow or grows at a much slower pace than nominal income. Consequently, people find themselves paying taxes at rates that exceed what they
would have paid given their real income, if there were no inflation. This drag
was partially averted by applying to tax brackets the same formula that
applied to wages: indexation of 70 percent of the rate of inflation. But at the
rate of inflation that existed by 1978, even this left ample room for fiscal drag.
Hence, 100-percent indexation was introduced.

Tax-bracket indexation was one of the elements that helped ensure that
no political constituency formed for fighting inflation. The process is an interesting one: first there is inflation, with the attendant suffering on the part of
consumers. This generates political discontent. The right response is to eliminate inflation. But Israel chose instead to make it possible for consumers to
live with inflation. Once this is done, the political incentive for fighting inflation vanishes.

In addition to the failure to achieve the objectives for which they had been implemented, the continued application of the policies devised in 1975 generated ever-accelerating rates of inflation. The Bank of Israel summed it up very well when it said:[10]

The numerous devaluations during 1974–77 (from November 1974 to the eve of the foreign-exchange switch in October 1977, the foreign-exchange value of the lira was slashed 2.5-fold), which were intended to alter relative prices, together with increasing taxes, intended to reduce the public's disposable income, the mounting pressures for wage hikes . . . —all these caused prices to shoot up. . . . An accommodating monetary policy was followed throughout most of the period, permitting the extra costs to be passed on to prices, thereby avoiding the generation of unemployment.[11]

In the fourth quarter of 1978, the CPI rose by 49 percent, up by 9 percent from the 1977 rate. But this annual statistic hides an even more interesting fact; namely, inflation during the first half of 1978 was actually much lower than it had been during the second half of 1977: 39 percent as against 67 percent. The fact that the rate of devaluation during that first half was also only 34 percent and that no new taxes were imposed[12] suggest that the Bank's observations were accurate.

In 1978 the task of stopping inflation would be extremely difficult politically, as the public was actually benefiting from the process. It was estimated that the public enjoyed a capital subsidy of about I£25 billion. The immensity of this transfer can be grasped by noting that the subsidy exceeded 10 percent of the GNP. This huge transfer was made possible by the failure of interest rates on government-controlled credit to keep up with inflation. For example, directed credit for exports extended in domestic currency carried an interest rate of 12 percent.[13] As inflation during 1978 was 48 percent, the real rate of interest on such credit was minus 24 percent. That meant that, out of every I£1,000 in credit, I£240 constituted a gift or a transfer payment rather than a loan. In effect, the direct export subsidies abolished on October 29, 1977, were being lavishly replaced by indirect subsidies through the credit mechanism.

All this was not yet sufficient to cause the Bank of Israel to think that inflation was grave enough to rate as Israel's most pressing economic problem. The balance of payments was still at the top of the agenda:[14] "The balance of payments problem, which caused the turn of events in Israel's economic development since 1973 . . . still constitutes the core of the problem facing the economy." The Bank concluded that monetary restraint was called for—clearly a mistake when free capital movement is allowed. Consequently, the domestic interest rate on nondirected credit began to rise to a range of between 25 and 40 percent. With Eurodollar rates at around 10 percent, a powerful incentive for Israelis to borrow abroad and for foreigners to oblige was being created. Even at an annual rate of devaluation of 25 percent, it was profitable to borrow Eurodollars rather than pay 40 percent on domestic credit. And the rate of depreciation of the Israeli pound during the second half of 1978 did not reach 25 percent in annual terms.

The result was a flood of foreign credit inundating the country. Whereas during the first three quarters of 1978 the public bought from the Bank of Israel an average of $225 million per quarter, it sold to the Bank $328 million in the last quarter.[15] The flood of foreign exchange was so significant that the Israeli pound actually appreciated against the dollar in December 1978, which made it even more profitable to borrow abroad. To see why, let us suppose that the Eurodollar rate is 5 percent, whereas the Israeli rate is 10 percent, and assume the rate of exchange to be NIS1.5 per dollar. Then a bank could take out, say, a one-year, $1 million-loan on the Euromarket, convert it to NIS1.5 million in Israel and lend it there for a year. If the rate of exchange remains the same, then at the end of the year the bank will be repaid NIS1.65 million (principal and interest). At the above rate of exchange, this can be converted into $1.1 million. Of that amount the bank needs to repay on the Euromarket only $1.05 million, and so it makes a profit of $50,000. If, in addition, the new shekel appreciates to, say, NIS1.375 to the dollar, then by the time the loan is repaid in Israel, the lending bank can purchase for the proceeds $1.2 million. Its profits this time will therefore come to $150,000.

It was the first time Israel has experienced some of the effects of free capital movement, and what happened threatened to generate an even larger gap in the balance of payments. The appreciating Israeli pound made foreign goods cheaper and hence more attractive, and foreign lending provided the wherewithal for financing the increased imports. Hence, the first of what was to become a series of retreats from the foreign-currency switch took place: the Bank of Israel imposed a charge on foreign lending, thereby making it less attractive and ending the unrestricted movement of capital. The Bank also began intervening in the foreign-exchange market to accelerate the rate of depreciation of the pound, thereby abandoning the "clean" float for a "dirty" one. That is, the rate of exchange would still be determined in the foreign-exchange market rather than by decree, but the invisible hand would be the Bank of Israel's Foreign Exchange Department.

What Caused Israel's Inflation?

The main indicators of the inflationary process from 1978 to 1985 are portrayed in Figures 10.1 to 10.4. The quarterly rates of inflation are also provided in Table 10.3. Both the table and Figure 10.2 make it clear that the rate of inflation took a leap in the second quarter and another in the last quarter of 1979. Devaluation too took a leap in the second quarter. These events pushed the debate about the causes of inflation onto center stage.

As we have seen, the Bank of Israel described the inflationary process as belonging to the cost-push category quite consistently up to 1979. It is doubtful that many people, especially economists, ever paid much attention to these pronouncements. The Bank's reports are not usually read by politicians,

TABLE 10.3

Quarterly Rates of Inflation, Percent in Annual Terms

Quarter	1979	1980	1981	1982	1983	1984	1985
1	64.6	122.9	113.4	110.1	118.9	334.2	180.8
2	97.3	143.7	106.1	134.2	148.9	447.8	365.4
3	100.1	105.0	75.3	143.8	104.1	426.6	375.4
4	163.0	179.0	127.4	135.3	406.6	710.9	40.6

FIGURE 10.1

Inflation and the Real Wage

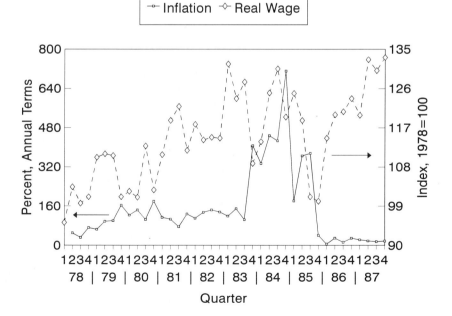

FIGURE 10.2

Inflation and Devaluation

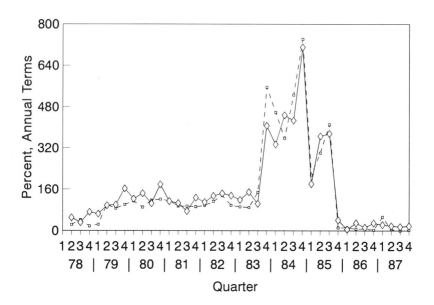

including in particular those in charge of economic policy, because they are very technical and written with an academic hue. As such, they are not read by the public or even by journalists and can thus be safely ignored. Yet, on the other hand, the academic community did not appear to be sharing the Bank's views. It viewed the process in traditional, excess-demand terms and therefore concentrated attention on government deficits, on the one hand, and demanded more rapid currency devaluations, on the other. The academic establishment also suffered a lack of awareness concerning the monetary system. One clear indication is the enthusiastic support the foreign-exchange switch enjoyed in academic circles.

Perhaps because of this the Bank began to change its attitude as well. Although the cost push resulting from excessive wage increases was still mentioned, its 1979 report is already ambivalent concerning the inflationary consequences of devaluations. For the first time inflation is described as resulting primarily from government excess demand; that is, budget deficits. Thus,[16]

FIGURE 10.3

Devaluation and Wage Inflation

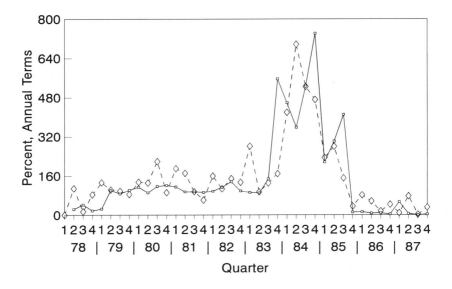

"Since the Yom Kippur War and the oil crisis an inflationary process has been taking place. It is a complex one, and can be understood only on the basis of its particular background: large excess demand and large-scale monetary infusion by the public sector." Also, "Because of the incompleteness of COLA and the uncertainty as to future inflation rates, the workers demanded a high nominal compensation in the biannual 1978–79 wage agreements. The high-wage agreements were signed against a full employment background that, in conjunction with COLA, caused a large increase in the rate of growth of nominal wages, constituting an important factor in the inflationary process."

    As for devaluations, the Bank stated, on the one hand, that[17] "In the past two years the nominal exchange rate fluctuated considerably, but it seems that this did not have a significant effect on the public's inflationary expectations or on the inflationary process in general." On the other hand,[18] it observed that "As for the foreign-exchange rate policy and its impact on the change in the relative price of imports and exports, it seems that especially in the last two years [1978–79], the effectiveness of nominal devaluations has declined, but their inflation-enhancing impact has increased."

FIGURE 10.4

Devaluation and Real Wage

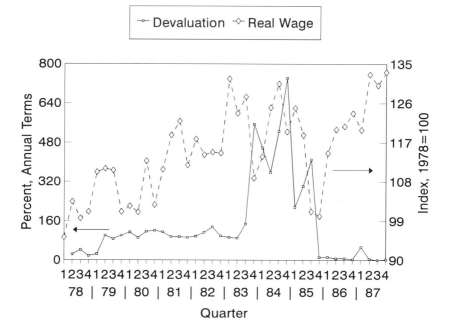

By 1980 the Bank was blaming the bulk of the inflationary process on self-fulfilling inflationary expectations,[19] what economists refer to as an *inflationary bubble*, on excess public demand, and on rapidly rising wages.[20] The rate of devaluation no longer played an important role.

At the end of 1979, a new minister of finance took office against the background of an increasing consensus blaming the inflationary process on excess demand in general and public deficits in particular. He therefore embarked right away on administering hefty doses of the old medicine. Subsidies to basic goods were sharply reduced. For instance, subsidies for farm products were cut from 9 percent to 3 percent of the value of farm output. Fuel prices also increased sharply, partly as a result of the second wave of OPEC oil-price increases. A deposit of 10 percent on imports was imposed. The institution of the deposit was a very unusual and highly interesting step. Because the deposit was unindexed, it represented the explicit imposition of an inflationary tax, in contrast to the normally implicit tax imposed by inflation. That meant that the government, instead of fighting inflation, was using it explicitly to its advantage.

The new minister also undertook to accelerate the rate of devaluation. Even though he took office only toward the end of 1979, the faster depreciation during the last quarter of 1979 (see Fig. 10.2) is largely the outcome of events which took place in December, during which month the pound was devalued at an annual rate of 157 percent. After a relative respite during the first two quarters of 1980, the rate of devaluation was again accelerated in the third and fourth quarters of 1980, reaching annual rates of 117 and 121 percent, respectively.

The attempt to prove any of the alternative assertions about the cause of Israel's inflation falls beyond the scope of this story. But a brief statement concerning the nature of the two types of inflation is required to follow the discussion. Briefly, a demand-pull inflation is characterized by excess demand, financed by printing money. The effects will be rising prices and increasing deficits in the foreign account. In a cost-push inflation, the problem originates with costs that rise faster than productivity. If the monetary authority does not respond by increasing the money supply, unemployment will result. But if it follows an accommodating monetary policy, then instead of unemployment, the consequences will be the same as in a demand-pull inflation.

How does one distinguish between the two cases? If the government runs a balanced budget and there is still inflation, then it must be of the cost-push kind. But the existence of a deficit does not necessarily imply demand pull. A cost-push process may exist on top of the deficit. What is more, under certain circumstances the budget deficit itself may be a consequence of cost-push inflation, rather than a cause of demand-pull. Which of the two scenarios best describes the Israeli experience?

The question is not just academic. If inflation is of the demand-pull variety, then it can be dealt with by reducing the budget deficit. But if inflation is primarily of the cost-push kind, then cutting the budget deficit will help reduce the trade deficit without having much of an impact on inflation. The cure for inflation in this case will be reduced wages either through the pressure of unemployment or by agreement. Distinguishing the two kinds of inflation has essential policy implications.

I believed then and still do that Israel's inflation was primarily of the cost-push sort. This means that the Bank of Israel was right about it in the first instance, before it changed its mind. In the absence of a formal proof, the evidence will come from a careful examination of the data.

Table 10.4 provides the data on the strength of which money creation by the government was seen as the chief villain in the inflationary story. There is no doubt that the government was creating a lot of money, in both absolute (purchasing power) and relative terms. However, the table also reveals that the monetary authority was creating a lot of money on its own, so much so that by 1978 its printing exceeded that of the government and in 1979 it

TABLE 10.4

Base Money, Flows, and Stocks

		Infusion of Money			
		In I£ million by		As Percent of GDP	
Year	Monetary Base on First of Year* I£ million	Government	Bank of Israel	Total	Government
1975	8,131	4,255	1,560	7.5	5.5
1976	10,088	6,009	2,157	8.1	6.0
1977	12,260	8,857	6,884	11.0	6.2
1978	17,967	10,684	14,350	10.8	4.6
1979	25,471	8,650	26,833	7.8	1.9

*Including reserve deficits in commercial banks.

Sources: Bank of Israel, *Annual Report 1976*, pp. 282, 289; *1977*, p. 294; *1978*, pp. 252, 257, 274; *1979*, pp. 289–90; *1980*, p. 73.

printed three times the amount issued by the government. The profusion of the Bank suggests a cost-push situation, because it indicates monetary accommodation, which is unnecessary with demand pull.

The instruments through which the Bank flooded the financial markets were, primarily, directed credit and open market operations. As concerns the latter, the Bank continued to commit itself to facilitate cheap borrowing by the government (see Chapter 9). Consequently, it had to prevent government-bond prices from falling. This it accomplished by buying bonds on the open market whenever their prices were threatened. Bond prices were therefore subject to only relatively minor fluctuations. This meant that people could buy bonds knowing that they could sell them at any time without risking capital losses. Government bonds thus became highly liquid assets. The Bank officially acknowledged this by starting to lump bonds with base money, terming the bundle *liquid assets base* in its reports.

Table 10.4 contains more evidence pointing in the direction of cost-push inflation. Monetary infusion as percent of GDP indicates the purchasing power of the money printed. From 1975 to 1977 the shares of the GDP that the government was able to grab through printing increased slightly. But just as inflation began to accelerate in 1978, and then really take off in 1979, the government's revenues declined dramatically. It is hard to believe that it could stimulate ever-higher inflation by issuing less purchasing power. Moreover, even with the Bank's infusion, printing relative to the GDP declined considerably between 1978 and 1979. This once again suggests monetary accommodation.

The first systematic attempts to use Israeli monetary and foreign-exchange data to verify this description were made in 1978 and 1981.[21] Then, in 1983, the Bank of Israel began publishing tables that provided the data in the form necessary to verify the story. An excerpt from these tables is displayed in Table 10.5. The table is constructed by identifying the various ways to finance the budget deficit. There were three ways to do it: borrow from the public, sell foreign exchange to the Bank of Israel, and print money. The alternative of selling foreign exchange arises because the government receives unilateral transfers from abroad and can also borrow on the international financial markets.

The second line of Table 10.5 reports how much of the government's excess demand was actually being supplied through increased imports. What it tells us is how much of the money printed by the government ended up buying foreign exchange rather than chasing domestically produced goods. In five out of the eight years covered, imports satisfied a greater share of the excess demand than money creation. The table affords another angle of looking at the government's revenue through money creation. It tells us that even while inflation was going from 48 percent to almost 450 percent per year, the part of the purchasing power created by the government that did not leak out through the balance of payments remained remarkably stable in relation to the GNP.

Most of the evidence mobilized so far is of the negative kind: it helps reject the demand-pull version, but does not directly verify cost push. Table 10.6 contains evidence of the second kind. If wages are the main engine that powers cost-push inflation, and devaluations are designed to prevent wages from rising too much, then we should expect to see rising wages followed by

TABLE 10.5

Budget Deficits and Their Finance, Percent of the GNP

	1978	1979	1980	1981	1982	1983	1984	1985
Domestic Deficit*	15.1	16.0	13.8	12.0	10.6	7.6	12.5	10.4
Purchase of Foreign Exchange	-1.3	5.5	5.2	1.9	2.6	6.3	8.6	4.8
Money Printing	1.7	1.0	2.1	2.0	1.7	2.3	3.0	6.5
Inflation Rate During Year, %	48	111	133	101	131	191	445	185

*Including interest paid by the Bank of Israel.

intensified devaluations, which reduce wages for a while. The data in Table 10.6 seems to conform to this description. After wages gained mightily in 1978 and 1979, increased devaluations toward the end of 1979 and during 1980 reduced labor's share of the product. In 1981 and 1982 devaluations slowed down, allowing labor to increase its share. In the latter part of 1983 devaluation accelerated considerably, taking away some of labor's gains. The sharp decline in 1985 and the subsequent rise in labor's share in 1986–87 must await the stabilization story of the next chapter.

To further buttress our findings, let us look at Figures 10.3 and 10.4. The first imparts a feel for the race that was raging between the rate of exchange and the wage rate. It is quite clear that until 1985.3, rates of devaluation and rates of wage increases proceeded hand in hand. Figure 10.4 reveals that, until 1983.2, wages had the upper hand. True, in terms of short-term intervals, real wages fluctuated violently, but the long-run trend is definitely an increasing one. It is also clear from Figure 10.4 that sharply increased rates of devaluation were invariably accompanied by declining real wages, as, for example, in 1983.4 and 1984.2. All this was achieved, just as the cost-push inflation story has it, at the cost of ever more intensive inflation, as Figure 10.2 clearly indicates.

As is also evident from Figure 10.4, whenever the rate of devaluation tapered off, real wages surged. The most clear episode in this respect occurred from 1980.4 until 1981.3, when the rate of devaluation declined from 121 to 94 percent in annual terms. Over the same period, real wages rose by over 18 percent.

Next, let us examine Figure 10.5, which focuses on industrial wages. The figure displays side by side the indexes of two definitions of the real industrial wage. The first is the conventional real wage, expressed in terms of purchasing power of the domestic currency. The second is the index of wages expressed as purchasing power in terms of foreign exchange. To calculate it, the wage in domestic currency was converted to foreign-exchange terms

TABLE 10.6

Labor's Share of Industrial Product at Current Factor Prices, Percent

Year	Share	Year	Share
1978	76.0	1983	88.4
1979	90.4	1984	84.8
1980	88.0	1985	79.9
1981	82.7	1986	91.4
1982	85.0	1987	92.6

Source: CBS, *Statistical Abstract of Israel 1985*, pp. 193, 196; *1989*, pp. 199–200.

FIGURE 10.5

Real Industrial Wages in Terms of CPI and Exchange Rate

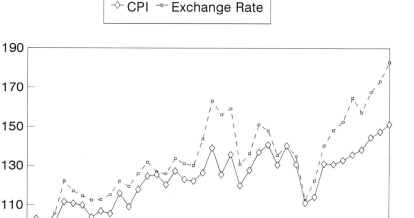

through the use of the official exchange rate of the basket of five currencies representing the country's foreign trade composition. The result was then deflated by a weighted average of the price indexes in the five countries represented in the basket.

The appendix to this chapter shows that, if the rates of change of the two real wages are identical, then the rate of devaluation would conform to the purchasing-power-parity prescription: it proceeds by the difference between the domestic and the foreign rates of inflation. Similarly, if the real wage in terms of foreign exchange increased faster or declined more slowly than the real wage in domestic terms, the rate of devaluation would fail to keep up with the difference between the domestic and foreign rates of inflation. The opposite holds true when the real wage in domestic terms grows faster or declines more slowly. Graphically, intervals over which the two graphs of Figure 10.5 come closer together indicate that the rate of devaluation more than covers the difference between the relevant rates of inflation. The opposite holds true whenever the graphs grow further apart.

With this added information, let us look once again at the period covering the quarters 1980.4 to 1981.3. With the exception of the first of these four quarters, the two graphs come progressively close together. This means that over the first three quarters of 1981 the rate of devaluation was more than enough to cover the difference between the domestic and the foreign rates of inflation. But the relentless increase in real wages according to either defini- tion meant progressively declining profits. Figure 10.4 tells a similar story concerning all, not just industrial, wages. During 1982, real wages in terms of domestic currency remained roughly stable: the average overall wage rate for 1982 was almost exactly like the 1981 rate, and the average industrial wage for 1982 exceeded the 1981 average by 2.2 percent. But in terms of foreign exchange, the real industrial wage in 1982 exceeded the average of 1981 by 5.5 percent, hence the growing gap between the two graphs of Figure 10.5 throughout 1982. The gap reached a maximum in the last quarter of 1982 and was also very large in the second quarter of 1983. During all that time, infla- tion remained more or less steady. Most important, the average for 1983.3 was only 104.1 percent, the lowest for two years.

The growing gap between the two values of real industrial wages gener- ated an ever more noisy clamor for intensified devaluation. It came about in October 1983, and the rate of inflation for 1983.4 jumped to 406.6 percent in annual terms—four times the rate in the preceding quarter. This episode pro- vides the most powerful indication that the inflationary process was by and large of the cost-push sort. The rapid devaluations of 1983.4 did draw the two graphs closer together and managed to erode real industrial wages—but all this for exactly one quarter. By 1984.1 wages were rising again and the two graphs were growing further apart. So in 1984.3 and 1984.4 the pace of deval- uations was accelerated; hence, the two graphs of Figure 10.5 come closer together during the second half of the year. But the cost in inflation was terri- ble—see Figure 10.2: the average rate of inflation for 1984.4 was 710.9 per- cent in annual terms, the highest quarterly rate Israel has ever known. And yet, the impact on average industrial wages was relatively small.[22]

As has been observed, the difficulty in identifying Israel's inflation as a cost-push process emanated from the continued budget deficits and govern- mental money creation. Fortunately, the existence in principle of a pure cost- push process can be verified by using data from the economy of Iceland. In the early 1980s, until mid-1983, Iceland experienced steadily accelerating rates of inflation, of up to an annual rate of 130 percent. Yet it never incurred budget deficits and in some years, including inflationary ones, there had been budget surpluses. The case was so clear-cut that the IMF, always quick to blame infla- tion on government deficits, had to conclude that[23] "Inflation . . . rose from 48 percent during 1981 to 60 percent during 1982. The acceleration reflected the resumption of a policy of sharply depreciating the exchange rate. . . . The depreciation, consisting of both step-wise adjustments and a downward crawl, fed the price-wage spiral . . . and the process was accommodated by an easy monetary policy."

In May 1983, Iceland froze the exchange rate as a key fixture of its effort to stop inflation. Later, however, when unions managed to secure a large wage increase, it resumed devaluations as a means of eroding the real wage increment. The policy was the exact duplicate of Israel's tactics in the mid-1970s.

In both the Israeli and the Icelandic cases the battle to reduce real wages was simply fought on the wrong battleground. The attempt to mitigate the outcome of the labor-market process by tampering with the rate of exchange not only failed to solve the wage problem, it also created inflation.

The Cost of Inflation

By the end of 1980, Yigal Hurwitz quit as minister of finance over his failure to bring about significant reductions in government spending, and in January 1981, Yoram Aridor assumed the post. The tale of Aridor's tenure at the Ministry of Finance is the story of how the various obstacles to growth combined to prevent him from carrying out what was to prove later on a very sensible and relatively painless program for stopping inflation. The story therefore merits detailed recording.

Aridor's assumption of the job marked a definite turning point, for he was the first minister of finance to put the fight against inflation at the top of the economic policy agenda. This was the first time in almost thirty years that a minister of finance sought to reshuffle policy priorities. His approach was based, on the one hand, on the conviction that inflation was devastating to the economy in the longer run and, on the other hand, that it could be stopped without dealing immediately with the entire scope of the budget deficit. Rather, he subscribed to the view that inflation was primarily the effect, not the cause, of devaluations and that it was therefore easy to stop without going through the wrenching political process of deep cuts in government spending. Moreover, it would be easier to deal with the underlying real imbalances in the economy once prices were relatively stable. To see why, a description of the cost of inflation is necessary.

The classic treatment of the subject focuses on the damage caused by the redistributive effects inflation has on income. Redistribution derives from the inflationary erosion of nominally fixed incomes, such as wages set by labor contracts in nominal terms, pensions, and the like. Inflation also erodes savings denominated in nominal terms—this is how the real debt of the government in many countries declined through inflationary erosion. On the other hand, people who hold real assets are not hurt by the process, and in some cases even gain, as the public seeks refuge from inflation in real assets. This causes demand for such assets to increase, benefiting those who already hold such assets.

Most of this description does not apply nowadays, especially not in the Israeli case. In the first place, wages have not been set in purely nominal terms, as they were at least partially indexed. Second, the bulk of savings was fully indexed, including the interest. With the indexation of tax brackets and pensions as well, inflation had no clear distributive effects. Under these circumstances, was there a case for calling inflation harmful?

Before dealing with this fundamental question, a word of warning is called for. Namely, the ill effects of inflation as described here apply to high rates of inflation, but perhaps not to low ones. The point is that economic theory has not yet been able to establish that low rates of inflation harm the economy, when savings, loans, and wages are adequately protected through indexation.

With this in mind, one can generalize by stating that inflation is harmful because it causes economic agents to engage in activities profitable to them personally, but not to the national economy. That is to say, inflation, if intensive enough, promotes an artificial economy, which bids resources away from the real economy and so hampers growth. Put differently, inflation drives a wedge between what is gainful to the individual and what promotes the economy as a whole.

We have already discussed and demonstrated the huge inflationary subsidies associated with nonindexed loans to the public. In 1979 an attempt was made to plug this hole, by indexing all loans to the CPI. The attempt proved a total fiasco, because its architects did not take into consideration the fact that, for income tax purposes, indexation payments were treated as interest payments and were therefore deductible. In fact, there were instances in which the inflationary subsidy increased due to the change.

This brings us to the interaction between inflation and the tax code. In Israel, as in many other countries, interest payments by corporations are tax deductible, but dividends are not. This creates a bias in favor of debt as opposed to equity financing. In the presence of inflation, interest charges increase as the rates go up. Hence, the bias is intensified. Consequently, there is a growing incentive to substitute debt for equity. As we have seen, loan indexation did not change this incentive, because indexation payments enjoyed a tax status comparable to interest payments. Hence, corporations were being systematically robbed of equity and financial leverage increased enormously. This generated a very risky financial environment, as companies became bereft of reserves needed to absorb losses.

Inflation at the rate it existed in Israel also created tremendous opportunities for quick profits in the financial markets. Such opportunities are generated by information lags, which become more likely as inflation intensifies.

As an example, consider the market for indexed government bonds. Being indexed, their market value depends to a large degree on people's beliefs concerning future rates of inflation. Each month, after the latest consumer price index was announced, bond prices adjusted to the newly updated rate of inflation perceived by the public. If the latest price index indicated intensified inflation, bond prices were bound to rise, as people expected higher rates of inflation.

To illustrate, let us focus on the months of June, July, and August 1980. Monthly inflation in both June and July was around 4.5 percent. Then, in August, it jumped to 8.2 percent. Anyone able to guess the jump before its announcement could buy a lot of indexed bonds and then unload them after the announcement, reaping the profits from the increased bond prices. Prospective profits became so lucrative that banks and other enterprises set up their own price-monitoring departments, whose job it was to forecast the price index. This was a clear example of employment with no payoff to the economy, but a potentially handsome payoff to the employer—a major wedge.

The national employment data indicate very clearly the growing attraction of the financial sector. Table 10.7 reports the most relevant of these figures. During the fifteen years covered by the table, the share of the financial sector in employment almost doubled, going from 5.2 to 9.5 percent of the total. And this probably constitutes a gross underestimation, because the statistics do not include people employed in financial departments of nonfinancial corporations. Yet such departments grew enormously over the inflationary years. Indeed, vice-presidents for finance were taking the corporate front seats, as financial profits became, in some cases, more important than manufacturing profits.

Inflation also imposed considerable costs on retail businesses. It was not uncommon to find products on supermarket shelves with three or four different price stickers applied on top of one another, reflecting the frequency with which stores had to adjust prices. Such adjustments are costly: they involve labor and they disrupt service. In the end, the situation became so bad that stores no longer displayed prices on the products. Instead, goods were identified by code numbers, and cash registers were programmed to translate these codes, punched in by the checkout attendants, into prices. However, this constituted a cost transfer to the consumer who from then on had to shop in the dark, not knowing the prices of products pulled off shelves. Under these circumstances, it became difficult to budget a shopping trip. Financial planning by the consumer was thus disrupted, reflecting the transfer of costs from the retailer to the consumer.

Although wages were not being set in nominal terms, the indexation rate of 70 percent, upgraded to 80 percent in 1980,[24] was far from providing adequate protection from inflation. But beyond that, it was becoming clear

TABLE 10.7

Evolution of Employment Structure

	1970	1974	1976	1978	1980	1982	1984
	Employment, Thousands						
Total	963.2	1,096.5	1,127.2	1,212.6	1,254.4	1,298.3	1,359.0
Industry	234.1	278.3	274.2	285.1	294.3	295.0	311.7
Finance*	50.1	68.5	76.2	91.1	102.5	116.5	129.5
	Percent of Total						
Industry	24.3	25.4	24.3	23.5	23.5	22.7	22.9
Finance	5.2	6.2	6.8	7.5	8.2	9.0	9.5
	Average Annual Rate of Growth, Percent						
Total		3.3	1.4	3.7	1.7	1.7	2.3
Industry		4.4	-.7	2.0	1.6	.1	2.8
Finance		8.1	5.4	9.4	6.1	6.6	5.5

*Including business services; finance accounts for the bulk of this category.

Source: Central Bureau of Statistics.

that, even if wages had been fully indexed and even if indexation payments had been made at a monthly, rather than at a quarterly frequency, wages would still not be fully protected against sufficiently high rates of inflation. To see why, consider the following example. Suppose that in conditions of stable prices, a wage earner is paid $1,500 per month on the morning of the first of the month. Let us also assume, for the sake of simplicity, that this money is spent at a steady rate: $50 per day of a thirty-day month. The spending takes place on the evening of each day. Suppose, also, that inflation proceeds at 10 percent per month (213.8 percent per year) and this too takes place at a steady daily rate (.318 percent per day). Under these circumstances, the wage earner loses almost 4.8 percent of his or her purchasing power, when reckoned at the price level that obtained on the first of the month.[25] If wages are fully indexed, then at the first of the following month the pay will be $1,650, and the process will repeat itself.

The story has two quite important implications. First, wage earners are bound to require autonomous wage increases to compensate them for the lost purchasing power. Suppose that they manage to increase their nominal pay to the point where their expenditures will actually be worth $1,500 in real terms. In that case they will get $1,575.13 on the first day of the first month. Similarly, on the strength of indexation, the pay on the first of the following month will be $1,732.65 instead of $1,650.[26] Note, however, that the increment is given in anticipation of inflation, rather than after the fact. That is, inflation need not happen first for workers to get this increment. Herein lies the problem, for suppose that as of the first of the second month inflation stops. Then our wage earner will get to spend during the month an amount whose real purchasing power is $1,575.13 rather than $1,500. The increment intended for protection against inflation thus becomes a real increase in the standard of living. This means also that employers will have to foot a wage bill they may not be able to afford. The example demonstrates why it is difficult to stop cost-push inflations: there is danger that declining inflation will be accompanied by rising unemployment, as employers who find themselves paying higher real wages reduce their labor force. The prospect of rising unemployment renders it politically more difficult to fight this kind of inflation.

The second implication of our story is that workers will try to escape the erosion of their purchasing power through financial manipulation. One common arrangement was to deposit the monthly pay check in a *patam* (foreign-exchange indexed) account, then withdraw the money little by little as the month progressed. But because checks could not be written on such accounts, withdrawals required a trip to the bank or at least a phone call. It also involved bank personnel in paperwork, as would be the case if a withdrawal from a savings account were sought. The effects were unmistakable: people constantly filled banks, many times during working hours. In addition to the lost labor, an enormous demand on bank services was created, which is clearly reflected in the figures of Table 10.7. Those people who could not or elected not to go to the bank used the phone. The Israeli phone system, not the best under ordinary circumstances, became even more clogged. And again, this was being done largely at the employers' expense in as far as both lost working hours and phone bills were concerned.

Although retailers face considerable costs when they have to adjust prices frequently, they can still do it or, as we have seen, find ways to avoid the costs. But there are areas in which virtually no amount of expenditure will overcome the problems created by the constantly changing value of the currency. Consider, for instance, the effect of inflation on the informational value of corporate financial statements. When a corporation prepares an annual profit-and-loss statement, it figures the difference between revenues and the cost of production. Suppose that the time lag between the purchase of raw materials and the sale of the output for which they are used is four months. This means that, by the time the output is sold, prices of raw materials may be, say, 50 percent higher than they had been at the time of their purchase. To fix ideas, suppose the cost of raw materials at the time of purchase was $1,000 and that the product sold for $2,000. If wages and other costs amounted to, say, $500, then the profit from this hypothetical batch was $500. But if the accounting were done in real terms rather than nominal ones, raw materials would have to be figured at their replacement cost, which by our assumption increased by 50 percent, to $1,500. That would mean no profits at all. Yet such cost accounting in real terms is virtually impossible, because no universal rules can be applied. It all depends on the timing of purchases and sales, and this varies from corporation to corporation. Hence, when inflation is serious enough, financial statements lose their informational value, with all that this entails for the people who run corporations, for investors, lenders, and people who monitor the economy. Furthermore, it creates the spectacle of corporations paying taxes on profits which do not really exist. In our numerical example, if the corporation cannot erode the $500 worth of computed profits, it will be liable for taxes. Under the correct, but impossible-to-implement accounting, this would mean an after-tax loss.

This sort of failure of the accounting system suggests, perhaps, where one should look for the damages inflicted by low rates of inflation as well. The problem arises because, even if everything has been indexed, the one thing that cannot be indexed is the unit of account; that is, money.

The interaction between inflation and corporate taxation has another facet, this time engendering advantages for the corporation. The fundamental institutional fact here is that corporations do not pay taxes in real time, when the profits are generated. Corporate taxes are paid with a considerable lag, after the financial statements for the year have been completed. This contrasts with the institutional arrangements for wage earners, where taxes are mostly withheld at their source and so paid when the income accrues.

In the absence of a tax-indexation scheme, the real value of the taxes at the time of remittance could be a fraction of what it should have been. At low rates of inflation this was obscured, to a large extent, because in Israel corporations pay advances on their tax bill, calculated on the basis of past taxes. Of course, in inflationary conditions these advances, based as they are on past figures at past price levels, no longer represent the real value the tax collector had intended to receive. However, when rates of inflation are low, the loss of real value is hard to discern. When inflation is galloping, however, the difference between the rates of inflation in two successive years can be quite considerable, and so the impact on the real value of tax payments is substantial. The most dramatic episode in this context occurred in 1984, when inflation leaped from about 191 percent to nearly 445 percent. We shall return to this story later on.

Another big problem for budget management in circumstances of high inflation is associated with the way the government contracts for procurement. When inflation in Israel became rapid enough, suppliers of the government demanded to index the agreed prices. On the face of it, it sounded as though this provided the guarantee suppliers sought for the real value of their earnings. Not so.

Suppose the government contracted on July 10, 1983, to purchase school equipment in the amount of IS1 million. On that day, the last known price index pertained to the month of May, published on June 15. It stood at 986.5. Assume that the May index served as the basis for indexing the contract. Suppose next that the equipment was delivered on October 10 and that the payment agreement called for a thirty-day term, so that the government paid on November 9. On that day the last known index was the September figure, published on October 15. It stood at 1268.3. So, the government paid an amount of IS1,285,656.36.[27] Six days later the October index was published, and turned out to be 1535.5. This means, that in terms of May purchasing power, the supplier received only 82.6 percent of the contracted sum.[28] Suppliers, who had grown used to expecting events of this nature, took care to build into the contract an insurance margin. They would initially quote a price high enough to take into consideration the inflationary component, which is unknown, on the day of payment. But as with workers not protected by wage indexation, the tendency was to overinsure. It therefore stands to reason that the government paid, on the average, more than it would have done in real terms if there had been no inflation. This implies that the deficit may have been partly the effect of inflation and not its cause, not only because of inflationary erosion of tax receipts, but also because of peculiarities created by inflation on the expenditure side.

The constantly changing value of the currency made budgetary deliberations incomprehensible to ministers. Shekel figures were meaningless without a date attached to them, so that one could know what size shekel, in terms of purchasing power, was being used. But it was practically impossible to present all the data on the same price-level basis. To circumvent the difficulty, the cabinet resorted to using the relatively stable dollar for accounting purposes. But although the cabinet was using dollar terms, the Office of Budgets and the accountant general were earthbound by domestic currency figures. This means that the language of the execution differed from the language of the plan. Little wonder, then, that communication between plan and deed became strained at best.

Inflation is also costly in a variety of areas of activity of the financial sector. Loan indexation can eliminate a great deal of the hardship imposed by inflation, but not all. The reason is that inflationary figures are available on a monthly basis only. Hence, for example, it is impossible to apply indexation to corporate lines of credit, where the amount changes daily. Although one could reduce the magnitude of the problem by indexing, say, the average monthly balance, the borrower or the lender is still likely to lose if rates of inflation are high enough. To illustrate, suppose inflation proceeds at 20 percent per month.

If the rate is steady throughout the month, this translates into approximately 61 basis points (six-tenths of 1 percent) per day. Suppose a corporation has $1,000 of credit on the first of the month, and that the credit grows by three-tenths of 1 percent daily. Thus, on the second day of the month credit outstanding will be $1,003, on the third day $1,006.01, and so on. The average credit outstanding for the month will thus be the total of the daily figures divided by 30, which in this case comes to $1,044.74. To find out how much the firm owes at the end of the month, this sum must be indexed to the monthly rate of inflation. The calculation yields a debt of $1,253.69 ($1,044.74 x 1.2).

Now consider the alternative, precise way of computing the debt. This involves indexing the initial $1,000 for the entire thirty days. The next increment of $3 is then indexed for twenty-nine days, the next increment for twenty-eight days, and so on. When all these indexed sums are tallied, the outstanding debt at the end of the month is $1299.42—3.6 percent more than with the averaging method. So the bank is penalized, and the corporation reaps a windfall. If, on the other hand, credit outstanding declines by three-tenths of 1 percent daily, the outcome is reversed: the averaging method yields an end-of-month debt of $1,149.23, whereas the precise method produces $1,108.36.

Implementing either of these methods is cumbersome and costly. The rate of inflation for the month becomes known only on the fifteenth of the following month. Moreover, inflation most likely does not proceed steadily, so that its daily rates fluctuate. But this never becomes known, because daily data are not available. In sum, short-term credit is virtually impossible to index and, even if it can be, either banks or firms stand to lose unknown amounts.

Inflation also creates considerable problems for another area of business activity: investment. Of the various difficulties involved the most obvious is the problem created by the need to assess the costs of investment projects. In the more narrow context, a cost estimation is needed especially if the project is to be financed by borrowed funds. The problem arises because costs change with inflation, and so one has to assess the rate of price increases of the various materials going into the project, as well as the rate of wage inflation. The problem is aggravated by the fact that price increases are not continuous and smooth; they occur in steps. The timing of expenditure is therefore crucial, which makes accurate planning more important than under conditions of price stability.

To illustrate, consider that, from 1982.3 to 1982.4, the average wage increased by 23.6 percent, whereas in the next quarter it soared by almost 40 percent. This occurred while the rate of inflation declined a little, from an annual rate of 135 percent to 118 percent. When a firm floats a bond issue or otherwise borrows to finance an investment project, the size of the loan is dictated by the estimate of the project's cost. If the estimate is too low, the investing firm will have to borrow more to complete the project. That such additional funds will be available when needed is not guaranteed. Even if they are, the rate of interest at which they will have to be borrowed cannot be secured ahead of time, unless the borrower undertakes hedging operations, which in themselves make the project costlier.

In other words, indexation makes sure that the lender will recover the loan, principal, and interest, in real terms, but it does not index the value of the principal to the cost of the project to be financed. The consequences are strewn across Israel in the form of uncompleted investment projects. The most obvious eyesores could be found in the agricultural sector where, for instance, many greenhouses for horticulture remained half constructed, with plastic sheets blowing aimlessly in the wind.

The inflation-induced flight of households into real estate welds saving and investment decisions. Normally, households decide on saving, and entrepreneurs decide on investment. That is, saving decisions are separate from investment decisions. When households decide to save via the acquisition of real estate, that separation no longer exists. This usually implies that investment is not efficiently allocated from the standpoint of the economy as a whole—another instance of the wedge driven by inflation between what is optimal for the individual and what is optimal for the economy. In Israel, the indexation of financial assets presumably ought to have been sufficient to stop this process. It did not. From 1977 to 1983, the real cost of apartments rose by over 27 percent. And there were periods, especially during the initial rapid inflationary acceleration of 1978 and 1979, when the real prices of apartments rose by 50 percent or more.

The First Attempts to Stem Inflation

One of the most perplexing aspects of inflation was the role of subsidies. Suppose the government, in response to economists' urging that it reduce its deficit to fight inflation, cuts the rate of subsidization of basic goods (one of the favorite recipes of the IMF). This will, of course, make them dearer for consumers. Because of indexation, the price increase swells public spending on wages and procurement. Private employers, having to pay higher wages without having enjoyed any of the price increase, will now hike their own prices. This precipitates another round of wage indexation payments, causing another increase in the government's wage bill. If exports are to be protected from the first-round wage increases, an accommodating devaluation must be effected. This causes all prices in the economy to rise, resulting in another round of wage hikes. More dramatic still, devaluation causes the prices of raw materials used in the production of basic goods to increase, as these materials are largely imported (grains, energy). Hence, the rate of subsidization rebounds by default, unless the government allows a second round of price increases for these goods. In the end, has the reduction in subsidies decreased or increased government expenditures?

Aridor concluded that under these circumstances it was not even clear that government deficit reduction in the short run was possible other than through tax increases.[29] Because he believed firmly, however, that inflation had not been caused primarily by the deficit, he decided to embark on an attempt to check inflation first, and deal with the deficit later. So on assuming the minister's post, he announced a reduction of duties on a selected number of imported consumer items and let the rate of subsidization of basic goods increase by refraining from adjusting the prices of these goods in the wake of currency depreciation.

The outcry prompted by these policies doomed them to failure and in the end proved fatal to Aridor politically. First, he was accused of populism, because elections were scheduled for mid-1981. His steps were widely interpreted as an attempt to bribe the electorate. Second, he was ridiculed by the academic establishment that shared, by and large, the philosophy on which economic policy since the mid-1970s had been based and so accused him of voodoo economics. When the Likud narrowly beat Labor in the elections, this was widely attributed to the perceived bribery tactics.

Yet the credit for victory was probably misplaced. Those who accused Aridor of bribing the electorate must have proceeded from the assumption that he did so out of cynicism, not out of conviction. Hence, they must have expected him to reverse his policies once the elections were over. But if those expectations were shared by the public, the so-called bribe could not have worked. Rational voters would have taken the "bribe" and then voted for whomever they wished.[30]

The statistics for 1981, published in May 1982, seemed to bear out the accusations. The domestic government deficit was computed as having increased from 14 percent of the GNP in 1980 to 20 percent of the GNP in 1981.[31] The huge increase was blamed on increased subsidies and decreased indirect taxes.[32]

But Aridor's detractors had to face a very important fact that did not conform to their theories: despite the huge recorded increase in the government's excess demand, the rate of inflation slowed from 133 percent in 1980 to 101 percent in 1981 (see Table 10.3). The confusion this created was clearly reflected by the Bank of Israel. Because the data of Table 10.5 had not yet been available, the attempt of the Bank to reconcile the seemingly conflicting facts led nowhere.[33] Nevertheless, it subscribed to the establishment views concerning the role played by the budget deficit as a key cause of inflation. It provided the following description:[34]

The contractionary policy of 1980 was fruitful concerning the balance-of-payments deficit, and the rate of growth of domestic consumption and investment slowed down. As concerns prices, the inflation did not abate, in absolute terms. Unemployment increased, immigration declined and emigration increased. For various reasons, the government did not persevere in the contractionary policy (a perseverance that, as noted, is essential in such a policy for arresting inflation).[35]

The statement observes, on the one hand, that the reduction in the deficit did not achieve its main purpose—reduced inflation. On the other hand, it did not want to imply that deficit reduction may not be all that important in the short run for curbing inflation. So the Bank suggested that austerity did not last long enough to have any impact. The phrase *various reasons* refers, of course, to the widely perceived political motivation behind Aridor's moves.

In fact, the data as published were totally misleading. The updated figures show that the domestic deficit actually increased only very slightly: from 12.7 percent of the GNP in 1980 to 13.2 percent in 1981.[36]

The mounting pressure exerted by the media and the academic establishment forced Aridor to return partially to more orthodox policies. Therefore, during the second half of 1981 the rate of subsidization was reduced. The inflationary effects were not long in coming: from an annual rate of 75 percent in the third quarter, inflation rebounded to a rate of 127 percent in the fourth quarter of 1981.

In 1982 the collective wage agreements were up for the usual biannual renewal. Aridor, who, as noted, had been keenly aware of the cost-push nature of the inflationary process, tried to attack the wage problem on two fronts. First, realizing that partial wage indexation prompted unions to seek alternative wage increases, which was sure to lead to difficulties in the fight against inflation, he advocated full indexation. Any wage increases beyond that were to be tied to productivity gains. Second, aware of the need to make employers more adamant in wage negotiations, he applied as much pressure as he could bring to bear on the Manufacturers' Association not to succumb to excessive wage demands.

A cursory look at Figure 10.1 creates the impression that these efforts proved partially successful, for the graph describing real wages remained flat throughout 1982, indicating real wage stability. In reality, however, the behavior of wages in 1982 was probably more the effect of the intensifying rate of inflation than the outcome of union moderation. As Figure 10.3 indicates, the average 1982 rate of change of nominal wages was roughly the same as that of 1981 (an average quarterly increase of 24 percent in 1982 vs. 22.3 percent in 1981). But because of the retreat Aridor had to make from his earlier policy of increased subsidies and reduced taxes, inflation rates grew steadily over 1982, and so the real wage rate could not rise.

Aridor's failure to break new ground was exemplified by the new wage agreement signed just as the Lebanon War broke out in June 1982. As data were to prove much later, the Manufacturers' Association assessed correctly that the government would prevent excessive wage concessions from creating unemployment and would do whatever it took to maintain business profitability. When the lavishness engendered in the new private-sector wage agreements became known, Aridor could no longer hold the line concerning the wages of public employees, and so real wages in the first quarter of 1983 were almost 15 percent higher than in 1982.4. This was the highest wages had ever been, and it would take more than four years before this level would be reached again; see Figure 10.1, 1983.1 and 1987.2. It is very instructive to note, however, that by 1984.3 the average real industrial wage already surpassed the rate in 1983.1. This sheds additional light on the role of the private sector in the evolution of wages.

As for full indexation, Aridor was portrayed as, and attacked for, trying to vitiate the role of the Histadrut as an economywide wage negotiator. So once again, his suggestions were painted as having been motivated by political considerations.

Although by July 1982 it was already clear that the private employers had granted excessive wage increases, the magnitude of the concessions was unknown and vastly underestimated by the Ministry of Finance. In addition, nobody imagined at that time that Israel would get bogged down in Lebanon for so long, with all that this implied for the economy. So, in October 1982, Aridor embarked on the plan that became known as *the five-five plan*. It was based on the logic which saw the bulk of the inflationary process as a race between wages and the rate of exchange. The assumption was that if all rates of increase—wages, rate of exchange, and prices of goods controlled by the government—could be slowed down in a synchronized fashion, inflation would wind down.

The initial inflationary target was to slow rates to 5 percent per month (79.6 percent per year), hence the plan's name. If successful, the plan would constitute a considerable improvement over October 1982, which saw a monthly rate of inflation of 8.3 percent (163 percent in annual terms).

The Manipulation of Bank Shares

The problems created by inflation were exacerbated by the bank shares' problem, who's basics were described in Chapter 3. Recall, that in 1979, the rate of return on an average share was about 70 percent, whereas the rate of return on the average bank share was 105 percent; and Bank Ha'Poalim shares yielded a rate of return of 117 percent.[37]

The authorities were aware of what was happening: the supervisor of banks at the Bank of Israel commented that it was possible that the banks were beefing up demand for their own stock by buying some of it to prevent its market price from declining too much relative to the overall price level. Shares bought in this fashion would then be released to the market when demand was strong enough. As the supervisor of banks also commented, the motivation for this activity was the desire on the part of the banks to make their shares attractive enough, thus enabling them to issue new stock from time to time. Whatever the reason, the manipulation of bank shares constituted a dangerous practice. And the fact that neither the government nor the Bank of Israel thought it necessary to curb such manipulation was to result in Israel's largest ever financial catastrophe.

In view of the bank shares situation and the generally frenzied activity on the Tel-Aviv Stock Exchange, the October 1982 plan was preceded by the imposition of a 2-percent tax on every sale of financial paper. With all of Israel's heavy taxation, there was no capital gains tax of any kind on financial assets, not even on very short-term gains. This had a devastating effect on the credit market. A corporation could borrow funds and use them to purchase common stock. The capital gains on the stock went untaxed, yet the interest on the loan was tax deductible. Not much risk was involved either because of the availability of manipulated bank shares. This, of course, created immense demand in the stock market, and the whole atmosphere on the stock exchange came to resemble a casino, in which the house could be easily beaten. Consequently, share prices were rising out of any proportion to the real value of the underlying corporations.

Table 10.8 provides an overview of this process. The data describe real rates of return, based on the appreciation of stock values. Of immediate relevance are the rates of return on all shares, which in 1980 and 1981 made no sense, considering the virtual absence of economic growth. Largely as a consequence, both the gross and net worth of the public grew by about 14 percent in real terms from 1980 to 1981. This made people feel richer, leading to accelerated growth in private consumption, which leaped by 12.6 percent from 1980 to 1981 (and was attributed to Aridor's "election bribery"). Something had to be done to ease the pressure.

The new tax was very well conceived under the circumstances. It clearly penalized frequent trading. For investors who entered the stock market for long periods of time, the tax was negligible; for frequent traders, it was quite hefty. The tax also took care not to deter new issues: the original sale of shares was exempted.

Another step taken in connection with the stock-market situation, but also because of the various adverse interactions between inflation and the tax code, was the submission to the legislature of the draft Law for Taxation Under Conditions of Inflation. Its main purposes were to tax corporations and the self-employed in real terms and to eliminate the fiction that allowed the deduction

TABLE 10.8

Real Annual Rates of Return on Shares, Percent

Type of Share	1978	1979	1980	1981
All Shares	3.4	-23.7	62.9	26.0
All Banking Shares	3.0	-3.0	40.6	33.2
Ordinary Shares:				
Bank Leumi	2.8	-3.0	37.7	39.2
Bank Ha'Poalim	2.1	-.9	41.7	36.7
Discount Bank	2.7	-3.7	28.5	36.1
Bank Ha'Mizrahi	-20.9	-2.4	47.1	33.8
Indexed Bonds	8.0	-5.7	10.4	-8.0
Interest Rate on Overdraft Credit*	2.5	-2.8	18.0	29.5

*Interest rate on ordinary revolving credit accounts, deflated by an estimate of the expected rate of inflation.

Sources: Rates of return: Bank of Israel, Examiner of Banks, *Israel's Banking System*, Annual Survey 1981, p. 163. Interest rates: Bank of Israel, *Annual Report 1980*, p. 205; *1981*, p. 220.

of indexation payments on loans for tax purposes. But the proposed law was also supposed to eliminate taxation on the sort of dummy profits just described. In short, it attempted to simulate taxation under conditions of price stability.

The law was adopted, but its implementation proved largely a failure. It was so complex (three commissions of experts tried their hands at drafting a simple version) that no two tax collectors could agree on how to compute taxes.[38] Vast new opportunities opened for tax consultants and the system became progressively bogged down. The failure provided another indication that, contrary to what many had argued, it is not possible to devise a system that would make inflation harmless.

A New Approach to Inflation—"Dollarization"

Despite adverse circumstances, the "five-five plan" did cause inflation to decline. As Figure 10.2 indicates, inflation was on a downward trend from 1982.3 to 1983.3, with a blip in 1983.2, which is attributable to the huge wage increases in 1983.1 and rapidly increasing fresh produce prices, due to an exceptionally harsh winter (the story was used in Chapter 9 as an example of the drawbacks of wage indexation). In fact, by 1983.3 inflation reached the lowest rate in two years.

The large wage settlement awarded by private employers meant, however, that the plan could not be sustained, as it depended critically on the synchronization of wages and prices. The new wage contracts defeated that purpose, as they produced the predictable, recurring pressure exerted by the M.A. to accelerate devaluations. The pressure, joined by the media and many in academe, bore fruit: the rate of devaluation was accelerated. Consequently, the average monthly rate of inflation for the year was 7 percent, far above the 5-percent target. The plan was doomed.

Even the tax imposed on the stock market did not achieve its purpose, although it generated considerable revenue. The real rate of return on all shares in 1982 reached an incredible 71 percent, most of it due to a boom in nonbanking shares, which recorded a real rate of return of 140 percent![39] Although the rate of growth of the population's wealth did slow down, it was still far in excess of what could be justified on the basis of real economic growth. From 1981 to 1982, the net financial wealth of the public grew by about 10 percent in real terms.

The postmortem performed on the "five-five plan" at the Ministry of Finance led to the conclusion that its failure had been largely the consequence of its gradualism. Because it had been designed as a stepwise program, it could not eradicate the beliefs widely held. In particular, there was no way to convince labor and industry that the government would hold the line on devaluations. It became obvious that as long as room was left for speculating against the government in this respect, there was no chance of success. Aridor, and the government of which he was a member, simply did not possess the political leverage needed to render a gradual plan successful.

The new plan for dealing with inflation became known as the *dollarization plan*. It was designed to achieve several objectives simultaneously and drew on the lessons of its predecessor. It is not usually helpful to describe a plan that never came to fruition. In this case, however, it is worthwhile to make an exception because of the similarities between it and the stabilization plan implemented in July 1985 (see Chapter 11). Also, what separates the two plans will go a long way toward explaining why in 1991 Israel was still experiencing a 20-percent inflation and why the Bank of Israel became progressively more adamant in its attempt to maintain a fixed exchange rate.

The program consisted of the following main components:

1. After an initial, sizable devaluation, the currency would be pegged to the dollar at a fixed rate. This would shut down one of the two main engines powering inflation.
2. Wages were to be fully indexed to the exchange rate. In effect, this amounted to quoting wages in dollars. The purpose here was to make it clear to the Histadrut and the M.A. that devaluations could no longer save them from the consequences of excessive wage settlements. The effectiveness of devaluations in the erosion of real wages would be neu-

tralized, which would rob the M.A. of its main instrument for exerting pressure on the government.

3. About $500 million dollars, the amount of government spending that was in fact financed by printing money, were to be lopped off the budget. The figure was arrived at as follows. The 1982 GNP had been estimated at about $25 billion. Money printing as a source of real government revenue was estimated at 2 percent of the GNP—the figure for 1982, as reported in Table 10.5, corresponds to 1.7 percent of the GNP. Therefore, the budget had to be reduced by 2 percent of $25 billion. A reduction of this size implied cutting domestic government spending by about 3.5 percent, not too difficult to achieve even with the fragile coalition government that existed at the time.

4. The government would be barred from printing money. The only recourse open to it other than taxation and domestic borrowing would be to sell foreign exchange to the Bank of Israel. This implied that the government would be forced to look abroad for the wherewithal for financing increased deficits. The logic was that, under a fixed exchange rate, an increase in the budget deficit would be quickly translated into an increase in the foreign-account deficit. The restriction was designed to compel the government to come up, in advance, with the foreign exchange needed to finance the additional excess imports generated by the budget deficit.

5. An optional clause called for the temporary introduction of the U.S. dollar as legal tender in Israel. The object was to achieve instant credibility. For if the dollar were actually used, it would be clear from the outset that both devaluation and governmental money printing simply cannot occur. The government of Israel can neither devalue the dollar nor print it.

6. After the initial phase, the domestic currency was to be indexed to a basket of currencies, rather than just the dollar, to mitigate the fluctuations the exchange rate vis-à-vis other currencies (especially the German mark) might be subject to if the shekel were linked to the dollar alone. The initial indexation to the dollar was essential because many prices in Israel by that time were being quoted in dollars, and an immediate indexation to the basket of currencies would have created a lot of confusion. The timing of the indexation to the basket depended on the speed and degree by which Israelis would return to the denomination of prices in terms of the domestic currency.

In January 1983, an event took place that led the plan's architects to have greater confidence in the possibility of success: the so-called free shares', that is, nonbank shares' (the latter, recall, were being manipulated by the banks) crash. This brought to a halt the frenzy that had characterized stock trading in the three preceding years. The combined market value of free shares declined from $8.8 billion at the end of 1982 to $5.9 billion by the end of June 1983 (and went on to sink to only $2 billion by the end of the year).[40] This represented a loss of 33 percent, a much steeper decline than the one that occurred on "Black Monday" of October 1987 on the New York Stock Exchange. It was hypothesized that the decline would dampen private consumption, thus easing demand pressure, which would improve the chances of reducing inflation.

The Bank Shares Debacle

While work on the plan was going on, the bank-shares' problem was becoming more ominous by the day. In view of what was going on in the rest of the stock market, this implied growing manipulation by the banks. This was financed chiefly by borrowing abroad, through their overseas subsidiaries.

The burden of preventing the prices of bank shares from falling became progressively more difficult, because of macroeconomic developments. The trade deficit had been mounting, exports had been declining in dollar terms (though not quantitatively), and the M.A. was constantly clamoring for accelerated devaluations to promote exports. Consequently, expectations of an imminent, large devaluation became palpable. The evolution of Israel's external debt also caused worry: from 1980 to 1983, net foreign debt grew from $11.6 billion to $18.3 billion. The most often watched debt-burden criterion, interest payments as a fraction of exports, was nearing what is usually considered the critical mark of 25 percent. There were even rumors (though unfounded) that Israel was having trouble raising credit on the world financial markets. In these circumstances, the public was shifting into foreign-exchange linked assets, expecting to make profit quickly from devaluation.

The problem for the banks was that the asset from which the public was shifting out was chiefly bank shares. Had the banks quit buying their shares at that point, share values would have collapsed, the public would have lost the incentive of moving out of the shares, and the whole course of events would have been different. But the banks continued to buy their shares. This encouraged the public to move out, as the shift from bank shares to the more promising foreign-exchange assets involved little loss. The plight of the banks added pressure to devalue, because this would have stopped the public's migration from bank shares to foreign-exchange assets. Devaluation would have satisfied expectations and allow the public to reap the expected profit and return to the shares.

On August 10 the government succumbed to the pressure and devalued by 7.2 percent. It was the first time that the Ministry of Finance had undertaken an action that demonstrably constituted a departure from the "five-five plan." It was also the first time that a devaluation was motivated by financial considerations, and it represented a very dangerous practice whereby the instruments of macroeconomic policy would be subordinated to a particular interest group. The devaluation had the expected consequences: the public began returning to bank shares.

But not for long. By September the public's expectations of accelerated devaluation grew again, and the stock market avalanche resumed. By the beginning of October the banks were holding close to $1 billion worth of their own stock. This was more than they could swallow, and they notified the Ministry of Finance that they could not go on buying. A discontinuation of purchases by banks meant a sharp decline in demand for the shares. With supply going strong, the upshot would have been a collapse of prices. This meant, in turn, that what the banks could get for the shares they already held would not have been nearly enough to cover the debt incurred for buying them. The banks would have thus faced a big loss—too big to be absorbed without rocking the banking industry. Such an event would have been particularly catastrophic, because the Israeli banking community had upwards of $6 billion in foreign deposits. Any whiff of a threat to the banks' stability would have caused the owners of these deposits to run on the banks, plunging the country into a foreign-exchange crisis that could amount to virtual bankruptcy.

The routine way out of the mess would have been a large devaluation, much larger than the one in August. But Aridor, realizing that the rate of exchange was being turned into a hostage to developments on the bank-shares' front, decided that the prospective damage a vastly accelerated inflation would cause was too threatening to risk. He therefore decided not to rescue the bank shares and let them fall. Getting rid of this time bomb was, moreover, essential for the success of the dollarization plan or any alternative plan to combat inflation. For as long as the bubble continued to exist, a policy of fixing the exchange rate could not be made credible. Hence, on October 6, 1983, the stock exchange was closed for two weeks, pending a government decision about what to do to alleviate the crisis.

Aridor's last action was a devaluation of the shekel by 23 percent. With the value of the bank shares fixed nominally, this meant a decline of almost 20 percent in their real value. As is evident from Table 10.9, at the end of October 1983 the shares were worth only about 57 percent of their value a month earlier.

The intention to let the public suffer the full consequences of the collapse was defeated. The government decided to bail out the public on generous terms. It pegged the shares to their dollar value on the eve of the decision to discontinue trading. Two major schemes were offered to the public. According to the first, holders of shares could deposit them with the government. Shares deposited for three years would be redeemed at the pegged value, plus an interest payment of about 2.8 percent annually in real terms. Those deposited for six years would enjoy annual interest at 5 percent.

TABLE 10.9

The Evolution of Bank-Shares' Value and Ownership, Millions of Dollars

Date	Owner	
	Public	Government
December 31, 1982	6,804.3	—
June 30, 1983	8,141.8	—
September 30, 1983	7,589.6	—
October 31, 1983	4,292.6	—
December 31, 1983	2,421.8	569.6
December 31, 1984	2,417.4	620.8
December 31, 1985	3,067.7	1,242.4
December 31, 1986	3,431.1	1,449.8
December 31, 1987	4,378.7	2,668.0
December 31, 1988	1,551.9	5,847.5

Source: The figures were obtained from BOI, *Annual Report*, various years. The bank reports each year the market value of the stocks in domestic currency terms at current prices. Theses were converted into dollar terms by applying the appropriate official exchange rates.

Alternatively, owners could treat their shares as though they were still shares and trade them on the stock exchange. At the end of five years, if it was worth their while, the owners could choose to sell the shares to a special corporation created by the government at the pegged value plus an annual interest of less than 1 percent.[41] The special corporation was necessitated by the fact that the scheme effectively turned the bank shares into government bonds. This, however, had to be accomplished without creating the impression that the banks were being nationalized.

Table 10.9 provides an idea concerning the magnitude of the problem created by the enormous obligation the government decided to undertake. The table also reveals the actual outcome of the decision. At the time, it looked as though the government was undertaking an obligation of about $7 billion. This constituted an additional public debt equal to roughly one-fifth to one-quarter of GNP, huge by any standard. As the table shows, most people opted for holding on to their shares, rather than depositing them. In October 1988, the five years were up and the government increased its holdings from about $2.7 billion at the end of 1987 to over $5.8 billion. These are market values. Hence, if the government could actually realize them, then the burden would have turned out to be not so terrible after all. But as of October 1991, the government has yet to sell a single share of the banks involved.

Old Habits Die Hard

The atmosphere surrounding Aridor's departure from the Ministry of Finance was something like what happens when a foreign occupier is chased out. The conventional wisdom was already referring to his tenure as *Aridor's Merry Days,* meaning that his policies facilitated an economywide party in which the nation's resources were wasted, but individuals became rich. The evidence was seemingly in the numbers presented in Table 10.10.

The table contains five years, of which the middle three constitute Aridor's tenure as minister of finance. The deficit in the goods and services account increased steadily during Aridor's years, declining a bit after he left. Similarly, both categories of private consumption, and the increases in imports of consumer durables, indicate a substantial increase in the standard of living. Exports stagnated, suggesting disregard for the productive sector.

The new minister of finance, Yigal Cohen-Orgad, therefore made a 180° turnaround and returned with renewed vigor to the old policies, whose most recent follower had been Hurwitz. As Figure 10.2 indicates, devaluations assumed an entirely new pace, ranging quarterly between 350 and 525 percent at annual rates. The figure also reveals a very interesting development taking shape: adjustment lags were disappearing. It was virtually no longer

TABLE 10.10

Economic Indicators

Indicator	1980	1981	1982	1983	1984
Deficit in Goods and Services Account, $ million:					
Total	3,785	4,249	4,566	4,821	4,767
Excluding Direct Defense Imports	2,082	2,182	3,155	3,778	3,331
Rate of Growth of Real Private Consumption, Percent:					
Total	-2.8	13.0	8.0	8.7	-7.0
Durable Goods	-8.4	43.6	13.3	20.9	-31.8
Imports of Durable Consumer Goods, $ million	188.5	305.1	359.1	456.4	256.4
Total Exports, $ billion	10.1	10.8	10.5	10.5	10.8
Domestic Budget Deficit Percent of the GNP	12.7	13.2	10.2	6.3	16.4

possible to effect surprise devaluations, thereby gaining what the advocates of the policy saw as a period of respite. Inflation rates were adjusting almost instantaneously, which is why it becomes difficult to tell the two graphs of Figure 10.2 apart. Figure 10.5 conveys the same story. After accelerated devaluations began in the last quarter of 1983, it took industrial wages only three quarters to fully recover, even though devaluation continued apace.

The reason was that the economy was becoming progressively dollarized in fact, if not by design. This took many forms. Some business deals were actually financed with greenbacks, particularly in the real estate sector, where large sums of money must be held in cash between two halves of a deal, such as selling the old apartment and buying the new one. In other sectors domestic money was used, but prices were denominated in dollars, so much so that many store windows displayed prices in dollars. Pricing in dollars was the sensible thing to do in very rapid inflation, because the price index is published only once a month, whereas the rate of exchange is known on a daily basis. The loss from inflation is minimized if prices are indexed to the rate of exchange.

With domestic prices being adjusted continuously to the rate of exchange, it was no longer true that devaluations caused first only a rise in import prices, with other prices adjusting after the appropriate lag. Now an everincreasing share of the economy, whether or not involved in foreign trade, was adjusting on a daily basis, taking its cue from the exchange rate. This is why the graphs in Figure 10.2 become almost identical. As Figure 10.3 indicates, wage rates kept up very smoothly as well.

The considerably higher rates of inflation exposed forms of damage not recognized at lower rates. Chiefly, inflation was eating away the real value of corporate taxes. Thus, in 1984 real corporate taxes fell by 55 percent (a loss of more than half!) compared to 1983. Largely as a result of this, total tax revenues declined by 13 percent in real terms.[42] This was a major factor in the considerable increase of the domestic budget deficit[43] from 1983 to 1984; see Table 10.10. The last line of Table 10.10 vindicates Aridor's priorities: inflation was impossible to live with. Moreover, the increased deficit in 1984 provided a clear indication that causality could run from inflation to deficit rather than the other way around. A glance at Figure 10.6 shows that the deficit in 1984 was the highest for almost a decade.

The main object of the 1984 return to the failed policies, was an improvement in the balance of payments. It did improve: the deficit excluding direct defense imports declined by about $450 million (see Table 10.10), or about 12 percent. Exports improved a little, too. But how much of it was due to accelerated devaluations and substantially higher export subsidies is unclear, for the rising exports coincided with the United States's emergence from the deepest recession since the Great Depression. The recession caused a

FIGURE 10.6

Domestic Government Deficit and Domestic Public Debt, Percent of the GNP

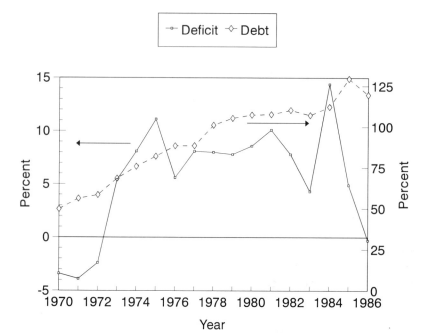

significant reduction in world trade. This explains in most likelihood the stagnation of exports in 1982–83 to a greater extent than do Aridor's policies.

The elections of 1984 produced the "national unity" government. The new Minister of Finance, Modai, continued the policies of his predecessor, only more vigorously; see Figure 10.2 for the rates of devaluation and inflation in the last quarter of 1984. Not surprisingly, inflation hit the highest quarterly rate until then or since: 711 percent on an annual basis. The situation became so obviously precarious that the government resolved to change its policies. But it had not yet accumulated sufficient political will (nor perhaps the necessary intellectual underpinnings) to embark on the only possible course of action, and so it resorted to a sequence of "package deals."

The first of these was concluded in November 1984 for a period of three months. It included the following main clauses: first, the Histadrut agreed to forego one-third of wage indexation payments; second, beginning with February 1985, workers were to enjoy a 5-percent reduction in income tax; third, a general price freeze was to be imposed; fourth, the government was to ensure export profitability and prepare an income-tax reform.

At first, it looked as though the deal was going to work. In the two months from November 1984 to January 1985, prices rose at an annual rate of only 69 percent. But the various components of the deal were incompatible with one another, and hence it was bound to fail. First, the promise to improve export profitability without resorting to a decline in nominal wages implied continued devaluations. Over the two-month period the shekel declined at an annual rate of 171 percent against the new basket of currencies. This was definitely incompatible with price stability. The government also strove to improve its finances and chose cutting subsidies as a means to this end. Hence, those prices most closely controlled by the government rose much faster than the overall price level. Thus, over the same two-month period, prices of transportation and communication rose at an annual rate of 113 percent. This, too, was incompatible with price stability.

As January 1985 drew to a close, the pressure to increase prices built to the point where the partners to the deal found it necessary to alter its terms. So "package deal b" was signed, to take effect as of February for a period of eight months. The objective of the deal this time was described as slowing inflation down to a rate of between 3 and 5 percent per month. The new agreement also contained a complicated formula for a COLA that was to replace part of the regular indexation payments. It also included sharp reductions in subsidies, again inconsistent with the deal's main objective.

This time around the deal proved a failure right from the start. Prices in February 1985 rose by 13.5 percent (358 percent in annual terms) and by another 12.1 percent in the following month. As in the first instance, here too the prices controlled by the government rose faster than other prices. For example, in February the price of food (excluding fruits and vegetables, whose prices are mostly uncontrolled) rose by 18 percent and those of transportation and communication by over 20 percent. In March the shekel was devalued by 13.5 percent.

In April "package deal c" was signed. This time, prices were to be frozen again, but to no avail: by June, the inflation rate climbed to 15 percent. Something much more drastic was clearly called for.

Appendix

Let p and π denote the domestic and foreign price levels, respectively, let W denote the domestic nominal wage rate, and let E stand for the exchange rate expressed in units of the home country's currency per unit of foreign exchange. Then we may define two measures of the real wage rate: $w = W/p$ is the wage rate in terms of domestic purchasing power, and $w_f = W/E\pi$ is the wage rate in terms of foreign purchasing power.

By taking time derivatives of the two real wage definitions, one shows that

$$\frac{dw_f/dt}{w_f} - \frac{dw/dt}{w} = (\frac{dp/dt}{p} - \frac{d\pi/dt}{\pi}) - \frac{dE/dt}{E}$$

Clearly, if the expression on the right vanishes, then the rate of devaluation equals exactly the difference between the domestic and the foreign price inflations: the PPP-policy of foreign exchange. It also follows that

$$\frac{dw_f/dt}{w_f} - \frac{dw/dt}{w} \left\{ \geqq 0 \Rightarrow \frac{dE/dt}{E} \left\{ \leqq \frac{dp/dt}{p} - \frac{d\pi/dt}{\pi} \right. \right.$$

This means that, if the real wage in terms of foreign prices increases at a faster percentage rate (or declines at a slower percentage rate) than the real wage in terms of domestic prices, then the rate of devaluation does not keep up with the difference between the domestic and foreign inflation rates. The opposite holds true as well.

11

STABILIZATION AND MISSED OPPORTUNITIES

Stabilization: The Program and Its Impact

In recent years, the economics literature has devoted considerable space to the question of how best to stop inflationary processes, so much so, that the debate exceeded the boundary of strict academe and spilled over to, for instance, *The Economist*. In particular, the debate centers on the question of whether orthodox or "heterodox" policies work better in stopping inflation. *Orthodox* means, in this context, tight fiscal and monetary policy. *Heterodox* means a policy that, in addition to employing traditional means, opts for some unconventional instruments, such as income policy, price controls, exchange-rate stabilization, and so forth.[1] Israel opted for the heterodox alternative.

In doing so, the architects of stabilization adopted to a considerable degree the reasoning that provided the conceptual underpinning of the dollarization plan.[2] Stabilization started on July 1, 1985, about ten months after the new government had come into office. In terms of design, the plan was based on two core parts. First, the shekel was devalued by about 19 percent relative to the dollar and COLA was suspended temporarily. The effect slashed real wages to their lowest level since 1978, see Figure 10.4. In fact, the average real wage in the last quarter of 1985 was equal to the 1978 average. When COLA came back later on, it had a different formula: from then on indexation payments at a rate of 80 percent of inflation were made either every three months or whenever the cumulative increase in the consumer price index reached 4 percent, whichever came first. With wages sharply reduced, it was no longer necessary to keep devaluing, and so the exchange rate was fixed at IS1,500 to the dollar.

The second part of the plan consisted of reducing an array of government expenditures. By far the most important was the reduction of two subsidy items: to exports and to basic goods and services. Both cuts were facilitated largely by the first part of the plan. The large devaluation, unaccompanied by wage increases, increased the profit margin on exports and import substitutes, to the point where part of the subsidization could be eliminated. The government could increase food and other prices without thereby generating several rounds of indexation payments. Price increases of staples and essential services averaged 45–75 percent and in some cases doubled.[3]

In addition to these main components, a price freeze was instituted, and a price control mechanism set in motion. It is widely recognized that artificial price controls, if they work at all, are effective only in the short term. If they do work for a while, then they can be very useful for a stabilization program of the sort under consideration, because the success of such a program depends on its credibility. And there is nothing like quick initial success to generate the needed credibility.

A new currency was also issued, the new shekel, a unit of which is equal to 1,000 units of the old currency, the shekel (which had been introduced in 1980 and denominated at 1 shekel = 10 Israeli pounds).

The program proved an instant success, which is plainly evident from Table 11.1, an extension of Table 10.3. In the third quarter of 1985 inflation still raged at an annual rate of 375 percent, but it tumbled in the fourth quarter to only 40.6 percent. In the first quarter of 1986, at 5.2 percent, it was getting close to a par with inflation rates in the developed economies.

In Chapter 10, we interpreted the tremendous increase in the budget deficit in 1984 as supporting the view that the deficit was more an effect of inflation than a cause thereof. This is further reinforced on inspection of the deficit developments after July 1985. The relevant comparison is between 1984, the last full year prior to stabilization, and 1986, the first year following it. The deficit declined dramatically: from 14.4 to minus 0.3 percent of the GNP between the two years.[4] But the really remarkable fact concerning the decline is that it was facilitated more by increased revenues than by reduced spending. Revenues increased by an amount equal to 9.4 percent of the GNP, whereas spending declined by 8.4 percent of the GNP. The two numbers together exceed the total improvement. This is because interest payments on the national debt took a leap, increasing by 3.2 percent of the GNP.

Revenues increased because inflation declined, just as they had decreased when inflation galloped. The spending decline consisted of a

TABLE 11.1

Quarterly Rates of Inflation Percent in Annual Terms

Quarter	1985	1986	1987	1988	1989
1	180.8	5.2	22.5	17.5	30.7
2	365.4	29.3	18.0	18.0	20.4
3	375.4	12.6	14.9	10.8	14.2
4	40.6	29.0	17.5	19.5	18.1

decline in public consumption worth 4.7 percent of the GNP, with 3.2 percent of the GNP coming from defense spending. The rest came from reduced transfer payments, mainly subsidies.

The plan's instant success, due largely to the unions' temporary cooperation, hid the fact that it contained no fundamental change as far as labor relations were concerned. It did not facilitate an extrication of the government from involvement in what should have been a bilateral relationship between employers and unions. The government retained its control over the rate of exchange to eliminate the damage caused by excessive wage settlements. Hence, the basic mechanism that ignited inflation in the first place was left intact.

This contrasts sharply with the full dollarization instituted by Argentina in 1991. There, the government committed itself unequivocally to a fixed exchange rate through the Convertibility Act. Accordingly, the central bank was turned into a currency board of the sort that has existed in Hong Kong since 1983. The board may issue new domestic money only by purchasing foreign exchange or gold. This means that the domestic monetary base is fully backed by foreign exchange and gold reserves. In addition, Argentine citizens are allowed to keep foreign exchange accounts both at home and abroad and may do business using foreign exchange.

In Argentina the government deficit was completely eliminated and, as in Israel, the bulk of the balancing came from increased taxes. To be precise, from a deficit of $6.1 billion in 1988, the budget swung over to a $200 million surplus in 1991. Of the $6.3 billion difference, $5.3 billion came from a real increase in the value of tax receipts.[5] The Argentine plan also eliminated by law all forms of indexation.

At this point it is still impossible to conclude that the Argentine plan is a success. Wages have been going up and threaten the competitiveness of the country's exports. But all the necessary mechanisms to deal with this situation are in place, and only political collapse could cause a derailment of the economic policy.

For evidence that Israel failed to implement the necessary mechanisms, look first at Figure 10.4. It indicates that after the initial decline in real wages, they rose again rather sharply, starting with the second quarter of 1986. The evolution of wages forced the government into a devaluation in January 1987—see the blip in the graph that represents devaluations in Figure 10.4— but to no avail. The real-wage graph reveals that employers still treated wage demands lightly, relying instead on government rescue. By the second quarter of 1987 the average real wage not only recovered all the lost ground, it topped the predevaluation level. Real wages kept their upward movement thereafter and by the last quarter of 1988 reached their highest level ever.

More significant, as Figure 10.5 indicates, real industrial wages increased relentlessly since 1985.4, an increase that even the devaluation of 1987 did not arrest. It managed to reduce the real wage only in terms of foreign prices and even that for only one quarter. Industrial wages, too, reached their all-time high in 1988.4, even though unemployment was rising steadily as of the second quarter of 1988. The number of requests for unemployment benefits in December 1988 exceeded the January rate by 50 percent.

The evolution of real wages brought with it the usual complaints from the Manufacturers' Association concerning the fate of exports, and the unavoidable frenzy in anticipation of devaluation set in. The attendant run on foreign-currency reserves began in mid-1988, and by the end of the year the public had caused the official reserves to decline by over $1.5 billion, close to a third of the prerun reserves. So at the end of December and beginning of January 1989, a devaluation of 13 percent took place. The public promptly reaped the speculative profits: within four months reserves were back to their former level.

After this episode, the Bank of Israel adopted the European exchange-rate mechanism (ERM). Under this system, all the currencies of the European Community were pegged to the deutsche mark. The last country to join the system was Britain toward the end of 1990. The peg consists of a central rate of exchange with a band about it within which the exchange rate is free to fluctuate. The band extends in most countries to 2.25 percent above and below the central rate. In Israel, a band of 5 percent was adopted.

The motive for adopting the ERM system was that it combines the discipline of a fixed exchange rate, without the rigidity of a complete peg. Its record in the fight against inflation is excellent, as events in Britain and Italy, for example, have proven. So successful has the system been, that even countries outside the European Community, such as Sweden, have recently joined it. The setback suffered by ERM in September, 1992, was caused by inconsistent policies, not by an inherent deficiency of the system.

But in Israel it proved unsustainable. Since the system was adopted, the central rate was devalued more than once, and at the end of 1991 the Bank of Israel abandoned the system altogether in favor of a graduated depreciation. According to the new system, the central rate was to depreciate by 9 percent over 1992, so that instead of a flat line it constitutes an upward-sloping one. Hence, the band also became an incline. The new exchange-rate policy amounts to a declaration that the government will not pay the price necessary to reduce Israel's inflation to the rates that prevail in the industrialized world.

What is really worrying is the fact that the reduced position of the fight against inflation on the national priorities ladder is not without its ideological underpinnings. In the face of rapid immigration from the former Soviet Union, it is argued that growth has become more important, and the final battle against inflation must therefore be postponed. This implies a view that holds the fight against inflation and growth as alternatives, whereas, in truth, low inflation is a necessary condition for growth.

In June 1992 Labor won the general elections after having languished for fifteen years in the opposition. The new government came under considerable pressure, from various directions, to start reviving the economy by devaluing. The proponents of devaluation have resorted to arguing that, when unemployment stands at around 11 percent, there is not much danger that devaluations will precipitate accelerated inflation, because the softness in the labor market will compel workers to accept the erosion of the real purchasing power of their salaries.

Fortunately, data are now available that cast a question mark over this premise. They are presented in Table 11.2. The fact that 1985 is the first year in the table is very convenient, because, as we have seen, wages declined dramatically due to stabilization. It is therefore safe to assume, that everybody will agree that the average 1985 wage rate was not excessive from the standpoint of employers. Given this point of departure, the data are interesting for several reasons. First, there is a sharp difference between the behavior of wages in the nontraded and traded sectors of the economy. Whereas real wages in the nontraded goods sector have declined since 1989 on both measures, wages in the traded goods sector declined much less in terms of the CPI and increased continuously in terms of producer prices. The difference between the effects of consumer and producer prices on wages is easy to explain: the price inflation in such items as housing and goods and services under price control was much faster than the average. And these items do not affect producer prices.

TABLE 11.2

Wage Developments in the Traded and Nontraded Sectors, Indexes, 1985 = 100

Year	Real Wage per Employee Post			
	In Terms of Consumer Prices		In Terms of Producer Prices	
	Nontraded	Traded	Nontraded	Traded
1986	113.2	109.0	110.7	116.2
1987	122.9	118.3	115.1	128.5
1988	130.4	123.0	118.3	135.8
1989	126.5	122.6	112.4	136.3
1990	123.8	121.7	108.2	143.3
1991	120.1	117.6	103.9	146.3

Source: BOI, *Annual Report 1991*, p. 148.

But the difference in behavior of wages in the traded and nontraded sectors is hard to explain, as one would expect the opposite sort of behavior. Due to immigration from the former Soviet Union, parts of the domestic economy were booming. On the other hand, the performance of exports was lackluster, due mainly to the decline in world trade, brought about by recession in some of the more important economies of the world (the United States, United Kingdom, and Canada, to name a few). One would therefore expect demand for labor to be stronger in the nontraded goods sector than in the traded goods sector.

Whatever the explanation, despite the rather steeply growing unemployment since 1989, real wages in the traded goods sector kept increasing in terms of producer prices. And in terms of CPI, they declined by only 4.3 percent as compared to 1988, whereas their counterparts in the nontraded goods sector declined by 12.2 percent.

The fact that wages can decline in terms of the CPI—the terms are the ones in which the wage earner is interested as a consumer—and increase in terms of producer prices—terms in which the employer is interested as a profit maker—reveal one of the major problems created by continued inflation. Labor costs to employers keep increasing, but the workers do not get to enjoy the added outlay.

The data can also be used to shed light on the fierce argument that underlies the fight over devaluation. Namely, has export profitability been declining? To look at this, the data of Table 11.2 are used to reconstruct the evolution of nominal wages in the traded goods sector. Table 11.3 reports the result together with data concerning production and sale of goods for exports. To use these data to carry out profitability computations, it is assumed that the gains in labor productivity in industry overall apply also to traded goods.[6] Over the period 1986–91, labor productivity has risen by 10 percent.

TABLE 11.3

Various Indices for the Calculation of Export Profitability (1985 = 100)

Index of	1985	1991
Exchange Rate, NIS per 5-Currency Basket	100	231.8
Price of Industrial Exports, Excluding Diamonds	100	131.1
Price of Imported Inputs, Excluding Diamonds*	100	111.3
Wages in the Traded Goods Sector	100	406.9
Industrial Labor Productivity	100	110.0

*Because energy prices have declined considerably since 1985, the index was computed as a weighted average of oil imports and other imports. Oil was taken to constitute 20 percent of input imports, which was its share in 1985. So the weighted price index is a Laspeyres index.

To carry out profitability calculations, assumptions must be made as to the composition of the output and of the product, or value added. Costs in 1985 are assumed to consist of 40 percent imported inputs and 60 percent value added.[7] It is further assumed that labor's share of the value added is 60 percent.

Revenues for exports have increased over the period by 203.9 percent. On the other hand, the prices of imported inputs have increased by only 158 percent. Hence, recalling the assumption about the shares of imported inputs and the value added in total output in 1985, the price index of the value added has gone from 100 to 334.5. We can now use the result in conjunction with the changes in nominal wages and productivity. These lead to the conclusion that the wage per unit of output has increased by 269.9 percent. It follows, that the share of labor in the product increased to about 66 percent, whereas capital's share dropped to 34 percent, losing 15 percent of its share. The detailed calculations are presented in the appendix.

These, then, are the developments that produce the demand to devalue. However, the recommendation of the medicine does not follow from the diagnosis of the disease. One must first show that the medicine is effective under the existing circumstances. Israel's own experience, and that of other countries as well, cast considerable doubt on the effectiveness of devaluation for the promotion of exports in the long run. Theory, too, does not provide reason for believing that devaluations are effective in the long run. And in the short run the cost of the medicine in the form of inflation is usually too steep to justify its application.

Inflation, we should recall, came about because policy makers sought to correct the external imbalance. When inflation subsided, the imbalance was still there. Table 11.4 provides the relevant balance-of-payments data, together with the data for 1983, which held the previous deficit record. As the table shows, imports of consumer goods in both 1986 and 1987 topped those of 1983. The table also indicates partly why the huge increase in the deficit did not create the usual run on foreign-exchange reserves. In both 1986 and 1987 (and also in 1985) Israel enjoyed an abnormally high rate of unilateral transfers. First, since 1984 U.S. aid has become an all-grants program. Second, the United States extended special aid in connection with the stabilization program, hence the unusually high grant for 1986.

When economists who study stabilization programs talk of "fundamentals," they usually mean budget deficits and monetary policy—the components of orthodox stabilization. But as we have seen, an inflationary process could be generated entirely by cost-push factors, and budget deficits could then occur not as a cause, but as an effect. Under such circumstances, at least part of the "fundamentals" are not really fundamental. Moreover, we have seen that in an open economy, when the rate of exchange is used to maintain

TABLE 11.4

Balance of Payments Data, Millions of Dollars

Indicator	1983	1986	1987
Excess Imports:			
Total	4,821	3,827	5,627
Excluding Direct Defense and Oil	2,171	1,701	2,007
Consumer Goods Imports	953	1,029	1,337
Unilateral Transfers	2,865	5,382	4,769
U.S. Grants	1,618	3,817	2,981

Source: Bank of Israel, *Annual Report 1989*, pp. 198, 200, 214, 221, 239; *1990*, pp. 208, 218, 226, 248.

export profitability, the central bank may not have much chance to pursue any monetary policy at all. In Israel's case, though, capital was not allowed to move freely in and out of the country. The restrictions applied mainly to short-term capital, so that the Bank of Israel did have an opportunity to target short-term interest rates, those that apply to line-of-credit accounts.

The relevant figures have already been provided in Table 2.1. The salient feature of the table consists of the outlandish short-term real interest rates: almost 94 percent on the average for 1985, and 33 percent for 1986. Yet, real average outstanding short-term credit increased by 11 percent in 1985 and grew by a further 74 percent in 1986.[8]

Probably no business establishment anywhere in the world, let alone in Israel, enjoys rates of return high enough to justify borrowing at these absurd interest rates for any length of time. Yet businesses kept on borrowing nonetheless. The only consideration that could have conceivably led them to such behavior was their belief that, if necessary, the government would rescue them. But even more significant is the fact that the banks were willing to lend at these outrageous rates, despite the enormous loan default risk such rates, taken from the land of loan sharking, imply. The willingness to go on lending can be explained only by the conviction held by the banking system that the government would provide relief in the event of substantial default ratios.

The tools that facilitated the sharp ascent of interest rates were substantially increased reserve ratios and much higher interest rates on the monetary loan. In addition, as Table 11.5 reveals, reserve requirements were changed frequently, making it hard for banks to plan their actions.

The course followed by the Bank of Israel was harmful from the standpoint of both the specifics of the implementation of monetary policy and the effect the action was likely to have on the economy's more fundamental problems.[9] The intense criticism that the Bank's policy generated made the Bank less willing to use interest rates later on, even under circumstances where such use was entirely appropriate.

The abrupt end of an intense inflationary process always generates events that are a delight to economists. Israel's stabilization is no exception. As in other such cases, the end of the high inflation was accompanied by a huge increase in the quantity of money. At the end of June 1985, the quantity of money (defined here as M_1—cash in circulation plus demand deposits) was NIS510 million. By the end of June 1986, it stood at NIS1,574.1 million, an increase of 209 percent. As inflation during the same period was only 58 percent, the implication is that the real stock of money rose by 96 percent; that is, almost doubled.

What is unusual in the Israeli case is that it provides unambiguous proof to the effect that this increase was a consequence of the public's willingness to trust, once again, the domestic currency as a store of value, as fear of its rapid inflationary erosion subsided. When the cost of holding money is no longer so steep, the convenience gained by holding it becomes important again. It is beneficial to the government, too, as it can enjoy once again a measure of seigniorage. The data that verifies this analysis is derived from the evolution of *patam* (foreign-exchange indexed) accounts. At the end of June 1985, the public held almost $4 billion in *patam* demand deposits; a year later this had shrunk to $2.7 billion.[10] The protection indexation to foreign exchange provided was no longer important enough to forego the convenience of being able to write checks, a privilege *patam* accounts did not enjoy.

TABLE 11.5

Reserve Requirements, Percent

Type of Deposit	1984	1985				1986		
	Dec. 6	July 4	July 11	July 25	Aug. 1	Jan. 16	Mar. 13	May 15
Demand	35	35	35	45	50	50	45	38
Time:								
1 week	11	15	30	40	45	45	45	38
2 weeks	9	13	28	38	43	43	43	30
1 month	8	12	23	33	38	25	25	20
2 months	7	11	20	30	35	15	15	15
6 months	7	7	15	25	30	10	10	10
CDs	9	13	28	38	43	43	43	38

*Source: Bank of Israel, *Annual Report 1985*, p. 338; *1986*, p. 311.

The Road Ahead

Stopping galloping inflation was, and had to be, the foremost objective of economic policy. The retreat from inflation of several hundred percent a year saved the economy from collapse. Although inflation at between 15 and 20 percent per year is still an important obstacle to growth, it is not the only one remaining. And as pointed out, the need to grow has become urgent in view of the massive immigration of Jews from the former Soviet Union. By the end of 1991, over 330,000 Soviet Jews had arrived, and another 25,000 had come from Ethiopia. The incorporation of the Soviet Jews into the economy presents a special challenge, because they are highly skilled. Throughout history, the bulk of immigrants came from the less privileged classes. Hence, they could be employed at first for relatively low wages. This made it possible to base on them labor-intensive industries like steel, coal mines and so on. In the case of the Soviet Jews this road to economic integration is blocked, as a sizable proportion of immigrants are professionals—doctors, engineers, technicians, and so on—which means that the potential for economic growth embodied in the newly arrived immigrants is very considerable. The attempts to achieve growth without removing the obstacles on the road leading to it created the inflationary process. To achieve growth, these obstacles must be removed.

Let us consider first the credit and capital markets. As Table 11.6 demonstrates, the most progress has been achieved in bank credit. The government's involvement in the allocation of credit declined considerably since the end of 1985. The degree of government involvement is measured here in terms of the sum of government borrowing and credit extension to the public on government orders, as a percentage of total bank credit. In these terms, the government decreased its involvement by almost 39 percent between 1985 and 1991. When involvement is measured without government borrowing, the progress made is much more pronounced: directed credit (including credit from earmarked deposits) declined from 67 percent of total credit extended to the public at the end of 1985 to only 27 percent at the end of 1991. The decline in the rate of involvement here is by 60 percent.

But even that progress suffered a setback on the last day of 1991, when the minister of finance gave in to populist demands and agreed to reinstate for certain categories of home buyers mortgage loans not fully indexed to the CPI. That is, the government once again agreed to grant subsidies whose amount cannot be calculated in advance, because they are going to be determined by the rate of inflation. It therefore also created once more a group of voters who have a vested interest in the continuation of the inflationary process.

Hardly any progress has been made in other aspects of the capital market. The law for the Encouragement of Capital Investment has yet to be reformed. In fact, it has been extended to include loan guarantees by the state

TABLE 11.6

Degree of Government Involvement in the Credit Market

End of	Bank Credit, NIS Millions				Percent of Credit Controlled by Government
	To Public		To Government	Total	
	Total	Directed*			
1985	20,095	13,490	23,719	43,814	84.9
1989	55,348	21,820	38,902	94,250	64.5
1991	83,383	22,526	43,755	127,138	52.1

*Including credit from earmarked deposits.

Source: BOI, Supervisor of Banks, *Annual Statistics of Israel's Banking System 1984–1988* and *1987–1991*.

under certain circumstances. It has also been used as recently as 1989 to declare specific locations as development areas, so government help could be extended to a particular business that ran into difficulties. A case in point is Or Akiva, where Carmel Carpets is located.

The domination of the capital market by the government has continued with little change. In fact, as Table 11.7 clearly indicates, as far as gross capital raised the situation even deteriorated somewhat: the government increased to over 90 percent its share of capital raised. Admittedly, most of the gross amount raised by the government is used to either retire existing debt or roll it over. This is evident from the net amount raised. In the absence of flow-of-funds statistics, it is difficult to get a picture of how the public's savings have been utilized. Despite the government's continued domination of the capital market, there has been considerable improvement in the way the government borrows. The share of tradable instruments has grown from 53.6 percent in 1987 (already a big improvement over past practices) to 71 percent in 1991. The process of rendering the national debt tradable is slated to continue.

The share of equity and options in total capital raised by the private sector over the three-year period was only 27 percent. More worrisome still, the private sector has resorted to issuing indexed bonds on a relatively large scale. For example, in 1990, 58 percent of the capital raised was in the form of indexed bonds. No unindexed bonds have been issued at all. As we have seen, this is a dangerous strategy, and it thus seems that the private sector still perceives itself as being implicitly insured by the government. It also underlines the importance of the continued fight against inflation.

Developments in the capital market are also related to the government's promise to privatize. So far, precious little has been done. The government did

TABLE 11.7

Equity and Debt Capital Raised

Year	NIS Millions, in December 1989 Prices, by Sector						Percent Raised by Public Sector	
	Private		Public		Total			
	Gross	Net	Gross	Net	Gross	Net	Gross	Net
1987	1,390	204	6,953	-1,465	8,343	-1,261	83.3	—
1989	1,568	-75	13,382	2,102	14,950	2,027	89.5	103.7
1991	1,683	-556	16,540	29	18,223	-527	90.8	—

Source: BOI, Monetary Department, *Developments in the Capital and Financial Markets*, Annual Survey 1991, No. 59, March 1992, pp. 69–70, 72 [Hebrew].

sell its majority holdings in the Paz oil company. It also sold the Jerusalem Economic Corporation, which is really a real estate holding company owning some of the choicest land in the city. The sale was a private one; that is, no bidding took place and, as in the case of Paz, it was made to a foreign investor. The most marked effects on the capital market were produced by issuing stock in some of the bigger government corporations, such as Bezek, the phone company. In all such cases, however, the government retains a majority of the stock. Although the issues were advertized as steps toward privatization, at this point they actually constitute further nationalization of capital, for the public invests in corporations totally run by the government. The haste with which members of the government that lost the elections appointed their cronies to directorships in government corporations prior to their departure from office underscored the importance of barring politicians from patronage opportunities at the expense of business enterprises.

In some areas, however, progress has been made, even if the beginnings are modest. The main achievements concern the weakening of the reliance of the private sector on government largess. The turning point came when Ata, one of Israel's oldest and most venerable textile firms, was allowed to collapse. Since then a wave of bankruptcies have swept the country, and the government desisted from intervening even in development areas.

The most spectacular business debacle by far has been that of Koor. It managed to accumulate a debt of about $1.2 billion, which is estimated to be double the amount that could be comfortably serviced.[11] Although the government did provide some assistance in this case, it imposed a stiff price on the Histadrut, which had to reduce its share in the industrial giant to just over a quarter. Koor has also been pressured into substantial restructuring. This is not an exception: there are other such instances, like Egged, the public-transportation behemoth.

The idea that businesses will survive only if they perform efficiently has definitely sunk in. In many places the labor force was reduced by scores of percent while output stayed the same or even increased. The results are plainly reflected in industrial labor productivity, which has increased by over 20 percent since stabilization.

Another improvement is the decline of the weight of the public sector in the economy. In 1984, government spending constituted 72.2 percent of the GNP, and domestic spending came to 58.8 percent of the GNP. These shares declined to 56.7 percent and 50.3 percent, respectively, in 1990.[12] The first steps toward reforming the energy sector have also been taken. Consequently, two new companies entered the market, although their impact is still confined to special sectors, such as cooking gas.

Changes in attitude toward the infrastructure are also felt. More room has been made in the budget for road construction and improvement. There is also a plan to reform the health system. The first steps were taken on January 1, 1992, when five publicly owned hospitals were declared independent, non-profit organizations. However the workers, excluding the doctors, are fighting the change because they fear that some will lose their jobs as the hospitals become more efficient. Union opposition managed to cause the minister of health to freeze the reform. But the virtual bankruptcy of Kupat Holim, the Histadrut's sick fund, whose accumulated debt is estimated at NIS2.5 billion, highlights the urgency of a fundamental reform of the health system. The Histadrut is resisting such reform, because one of its provisions is the severance of the link between health insurance through Kupat Holim and union membership. If this happens, the Histadrut stands to lose a lot of power.

As the wave of immigration is proving every day, however, the improvements are a long way away from what is needed. Naturally, the consequences of decades of economic mismanagement manifest themselves in the two most crucial areas for immigrants: housing and jobs. Turning to housing first, virtually no serious policy changes have occurred except for the partial exit of the government from the mortgage market. In particular, no privatization of land has taken place, and the Rent Control Law has not been abolished. Worse, no serious consideration is given to privatizing the land. Under the existing circumstances the supply of land is not identical with the stock of land. The Land Authority decides how much of the existing stock will constitute the supply. Hence, land prices are necessarily higher than they would have been if the entire stock could be traded.

As for rent control, the present version is, as has been pointed out, a relatively weak one. But experience shows that it takes a long time—possibly decades—for the residential-construction economy to recover from government meddling in rents. The government must therefore go out of its way to assure prospective builders of its intentions to stay out of the rental market. Instead, it has done nothing.

The twin failures have twin consequences. On the one hand, there is no construction of rental units. Hence, new immigrants must purchase apartments with mortgage loans, even though many of them do not have permanent employment. And because land prices are higher than need be, so are the prices of apartments and hence so are the amounts of loans needed. This could have two sorts of dire consequences. First, thousands of immigrants may face foreclosure, implying a serious social problem. Alternatively, there will be pressure to forgive mortgage debt. The economic consequences are clear: more public spending. But in addition, a new variety of moral hazard will be created, because the possibility of being forgiven will affect people's behavior. This is precisely why partial deindexation of mortgage loans has been reintroduced.

It is still hard to say how the new, Labor-led government, will acquit itself as far as the economy is concerned. Labor's platform is a mixture of old and new, indicating a process of the sort that labor parties all over the Western world are undergoing. Promises to promote exports, taken from yesterday's manifestos, cohabit with words about the urgency of privatization. Like Britain's Labour party, a lot may depend on how much influence the Histadrut will have on the government, particularly as some members of the coalition are Left of Labor in the political spectrum.

As these concluding remarks are written, Israel has secured $10 billion worth of loan guarantees from the United States to facilitate borrowing on the international market to finance immigrant absorption. It stands to reason that this new largess on the part of the United States will deal a blow to the reform process in Israel, for in the absence of an outstanding leader, politicians are not likely to undertake reform if they do not have to and the loan guarantees certainly ease the pressure. Furthermore, the loans obtained on the strength of the guarantees may actually cause harm, unless a way is found to make sure that the money is used exclusively for investment, primarily by the private sector. But because the guarantees constitute an intergovernmental deal, this is a tall order indeed. It should be noted that the loans will increase the national debt. So unless they are used to augment the economy's capacity to produce, they will mean an increased future tax burden.

The preferred alternative is direct foreign investment and direct foreign borrowing by Israeli business enterprises. This will not happen, unless the reforms go much farther than they have. In particular, foreign lenders have to hedge against the possibility of devaluation by charging interest rates that will make foreign borrowing unattractive. Such borrowing has been facilitated in principle by the Bank of Israel's removal of most restrictions on capital movements into and out of Israel. But the threat of devaluation, brought about by continued inflation, prevents these changes from making much of a difference in practice. One more reason for the new government not to relegate the fight against inflation to a position of secondary importance.

In 1991, Israel imported goods and services for $7 billion more than it exported, without raising its international debt one penny. This was made possible by transfers to Israel totaling over $6 billion. It is hard to imagine that, as long as this state of affairs continues, much will be done in the way of reform. From Argentina through Mexico to Eastern Europe and the republics of the former Soviet Union, politicians undertake courageous reforms only when they find themselves managing a bankrupt economy. Margaret Thatcher in Britain was the exception, not the rule. So far, Israel has conformed to that rule.

Appendix

Define the price indexes in 1985 as being equal to 1. Let m denote the component of imported productive inputs in the output, q, and let y denote the share of the product in 1985. Then by assumption

(1) $\dfrac{m}{q} = .4, \quad \dfrac{y}{q} = .6$

Let p_m, p_y and p_q denote the 1991 price levels of imported inputs, the product, and the output, respectively. Then the data in Table 11.2 imply that

$p_m = 2.58$ and $p_q = 3.039$

It follows, that

(2) $2.58m + p_y y = 3.039q$

Dividing both sides of (2) by the righthand side and recalling (1), one obtains

$\dfrac{2.58}{3.039} (.4) + \dfrac{p_y}{3.039} (.6) = 1$

Solving the equation for the product's price yields

(3) $p_y = 3.345$

This means, that the price of the value added has increased by 234.5 percent.

Let the wage index for 1985 be 1 as well and let L and K denote the shares of labor and capital in the product, respectively. Then by assumption

(4) $\dfrac{L}{y} = .6, \quad \dfrac{K}{y} = .4$

Let w and r denote the price indexes of labor and capital in 1985, respectively. In particular, let w stand for the labor cost of a unit of output. Then from the data in Table 11.2 and by (3) and (4),

(5) $3.699L + rK = 3.345y$

Dividing both sides of (5) by the righthand side of (4) yields

(6) $\dfrac{3.699}{3.345}(.6) + \dfrac{r}{3.345}(.4) = 1$

Solving for r yields $r = 2.81$.

The first term of (6) implies that labor's share in the value added has increased to 66.3 percent. This means that capital's share has shrunk to 33.7 percent.

NOTES

Introduction

1. "Competition as a Discovery Procedure," in C. Nishiyama and K. R. Leube, eds., *The essence of Hayek,* Stanford, Hoover Institution Press, 1984, pp. 254–65.

Chapter 1. The Roar That Became a Whisper

1. Henceforth CBS.

2. See, e.g., James M. Buchanan, "Post-Socialist Political Economy," mimeo, 1991.

3. "Sweden's Stock Market Stunner," *The Economist* (December 2–8, 1989).

4. See, e.g., H. Ben-Shahar, "The Israeli Economy—A Time for Reckoning," *Economic Quarterly* 121: 114–23; Y. Yoran, "Economy in Structural Crisis: The Israeli Economy Since the Oil Crisis and the *Yom Kippur* War of 1973," *Economic Quarterly* 131 (1987): 827–54; M. Bruno, "Israel's Crisis and Economic Reform in Historical Perspective," *Economic Quarterly* 141 (1989): 89–113 [all in Hebrew]. Fixing 1973 as the turning point is a novelty in itself. The predominant view used to be that 1977, when Likud ascended to power, constituted the start of the crisis, whereas the years 1975–76 signified the start of a recuperative process. More will be said about this.

5. The detailed data underlying Figures 1.1 and 1.2 is provided in the appendix to this chapter.

6. No figures are available for the period prior to 1960. Source: Central Bureau of Statistics, *Gross Domestic Capital Formation in Israel 1950–1978,* Special Series No. 635 (Jerusalem, Author, 1980).

7. The impression that rates of change of public sector investment swing more wildly than those of the private sector is not just visual: the sample standard deviation for the public sector is 27.82, whereas the sample standard deviation for the rates of change in private housing investment is 17.5. The coefficients of variation are 256.9 and 189.7 percent for the public sector and total construction, respectively.

8. Bank of Israel (henceforth BOI), *Annual Report 1964,* p. 240.

9. CBS, *Statistical Abstract of Israel,* 1964 and 1969.

10. CBS, *Statistical Abstract of Israel: 1964*, Table M/6; *1974*, Table xiv/5.

11. A. Halperin, "The Recession and the Recovery in the Economy," *Economic Quarterly* 56 (1968): 287–97.

12. Arie Bregman, *Industry and Industrial Policy in Israel (1965–1985) (Jerusalem: Bank of Israel, 1986) [Hebrew]*.

13. *BOI*, Annual Report 1972, pp. 106–7.

14. Bregman, *Industry and Industrial Policy in Israel*, p. 25.

15. BOI, *Annual Report 1975*, p. 155.

16. BOI, *Annual Report 1974*, p. 8.

17. BOI, *Annual Report 1973*, p. 138.

18. BOI, *Annual Report 1975*, p. 172.

19. Computed from CBS, *Statistical Abstract of Israel 1973*, Table VI/2. The calculations were made at constant 1964 market prices. It is important to point out that the share of excess imports in investment does not represent the share of foreign investment in Israel, because a substantial share of excess imports has been financed over the years by unilateral transfers from abroad. Much more will be said about this later.

20. The idea that what is perceived as a recession in 1966–67 was engineered, at least partly, by the government, is expressed in, e.g., M. Sandberg, "Economic Independence and Political Independence," *Economic Quarterly* 56 (1968): 269–73 [Hebrew]; Halperin, "The Recession and the Recovery in the Economy."

21. BOI, *Annual Report 1966*, p. 321.

22. Bregman, *Industry and Industrial Policy in Israel*, p. 62.

23. The result is based on a corporate survey, reported in ibid.

24. Ibid., p. 71.

25. Haim Levi, "Capital Structure, Inflation and the Cost of Capital in Israeli Industry, 1964–78," *Bank of Israel Economic Review* 53 (1982): 31–63.

26. Nachum Grosss et al., *A Banker for the Nation in Its Revival: The History of Bank Leumi Le'Israel* (Jerusalem: Massada, 1977), p. 357.

27. BOI, *Annual Report* 1984, p. 122.

28. The daily *Ha'aretz* (December 9, 1959) [Hebrew].

29. *Ha'aretz* (February 26, 1971).

30. According to a report in *Ha'aretz* (March 11, 1966).

31. *Ha'aretz* (October 29, 1967).

32. BOI, *Annual Report 1974*, p. 41.

33. Ibid., p. 90.

34. BOI, *Annual Report 1972*, p. 5.

35. BOI, *Annual Report 1973*, p. 211.

36. BOI, *Annual Report 1974*, p. 41.

37. Data here refer not to the inflation rate during the year, but rather to the increase in the average annual price level. When the rate of inflation is on a continuous rise, the increase in prices during the year outraces the increases of year-on-year averages. The opposite is true when inflation declines. The data are drawn from CBS, *National Accounts,* various years.

38. BOI, *Annual Report 1973*, p. 51.

39. CBS, *Statistical Abstract of Israel,* various years.

40. CBS, *National Accounts,* various years; CBS, *Israel's Balance of Payments 1966–1976,* Special Series No. 549 (Jerusalem, 1977).

41. The sources for these data are as follows: (a) transfer payments up to 1975, BOI, *Annual Report 1975*, p.198; (b) transfer payments for 1976–77, BOI, *Annual Report 1979*, pp.181, 183, 188 (in all cases interest payments on the internal national debt are not included); (c) tax burdens, BOI, ibid., pp. 173, 175; (d) GNP growth rates are the ones published in CBS, *National Accounts,* real growth rates for transfer payments were calculated from the nominal figures, using the consumer price index.

42. Amendment to the Income Tax Ordinance (No. 18), adopted on March 29, 1973; and Amendment to the Income Tax Ordinance (No. 20), adopted on April 2, 1974.

43. BOI, *Annual Report 1974*, p. 254.

Chapter 2. Obstacles to Growth: The Abducted Captial Market

1. Except, possibly, India's. But then India, with its caste system and deep religious animosities, is not exactly a free society in the liberal sense.

2. Translated from the Hebrew in Ministry of Finance, *The Position of the Ministry of Finance in Regard to the Support of Banking Shares* (Jerusalem: Author, 1985): pp. 2–3. The Commission of Inquiry that investigated the supporting scheme, which ultimately led to the collapse of the banking shares in October 1983, agreed with this assessment. See Commission of Inquiry into the Support of Banking Shares, *Report* (Jerusalem: Author, 1986): pp. 56–7 [Hebrew].

3. Much the same approach is taken in Irving Kristol, *Two Cheers for Capitalism* (New York, Basic Books, 1978).

4. BOI, Supervisor of Banks, *Current Banking Statistics*, Table V–7.

5. Haim Ben-Shahar, Shaul Bronfeld, and Alexander Cukierman,"The Capital Market in Israel," in P. Uri, ed., *Israel and the Common Market* (Jerusalem, Weidenfeld and Nicolson, 1971): pp. 257–367. The quotations are from pp. 363 and 367.

6. BOI, *Annual Report 1955*, pp. 194–95. It is worth noting that the 1955 report was the first full report issued by the Bank, which had been established in 1954.

7. BOI, *Annual Report 1957*, pp. 116–17.

8. Nachum Gross et al., *A Banker for the Nation in Its Revival: The History of Bank Leumi Le'Israel* (Jerusalem: Massada, 1977): p. 347 [Hebrew].

9. David Horowitz, *The Economy of Israel* (Tel-Aviv: Massada, 1954): p. 295 [Hebrew].

10. Leora Blum and Sylvia Piterman, "Government Intervention in the Israeli Capital Market—Survey and Reform Outlines," *Economic Quarterly* 131 (1987): 855–64 [Hebrew].

11. Continental-Allied Company, Inc., *Israel Industrial Finances—A Second Look*, Report to the Government of Israel and the U.S. International Cooperation Administration (Washington, D.C.: Author, 1960), p. 50.

12. BOI, *Annual Report 1955*, p. 201.

13. Ibid., pp. 204–5.

14. Ibid., pp. 201–2.

15. BOI, *Annual Report 1957*, p. 174.

16. BOI, *Annual Report 1970*, p. 7.

17. See Meir Heth, *The Legal Framework of Economic Activity in Israel* (New York: Praeger, 1967).

18. *Law for the Encouragement of Capital Investment* (Jerusalem: Investment Center, State of Israel, June 1983), pp. 49–50 [Hebrew].

19. *Brochure for the Industrial Investor* (Jerusalem: Investment Center, April 1, 1986) [Hebrew].

20. Ibid.

21. Uri Litvin and Leora Meridor, "Estimation of the 'Gift' Inherent in the Law for the Encouragement of Capital Investment in Israel," *Bank of Israel Review* 54 (1982): 3–24 [Hebrew].

22. See Daphna Schwartz, "The Effective Incentive Inherent In the Law for the Encouragement of Capital Investment," *Economic Quarterly* 124, (1985): 12–21 [Hebrew].

23. Excerpts from an article by H. Greenbaum in *Israel Export Journal* 11 (November 1950), as published in the monthly *Ha'taassiah* [Industry] (January 1951) [Hebrew].

24. "The Third World, A Survey," *The Economist* (September 23, 1989).

25. See Daphna Schwartz, "The Impact of the Law for the Encouragement of Capital Investment on Industrial Investment in Development Towns," in *Studies in the Economy of Israel 1980* (Jerusalem: Maurice Falk Institute for Economic Research in Israel, 1981) [Hebrew]; and Daphna Schwartz and Daniel Felsenstein, *The Economic Relation Between Plants in Development Towns and the City* (Rehovot: Settlement Study Center, November, 1988) [Hebrew]. See also Arieh Bregman, *Industry and Industrial Policy in Israel* (Jerusalem: Bank of Israel, Research Department, 1986), p. 65 [Hebrew].

26. Horowitz, *The Economy of Israel,* pp. 295, 341.

27. Don Patinkin, *The Israel Economy: The First Decade* (Jerusalem: Falk Project for Economic Research in Israel, 1960), p. 87.

28. BOI, *Annual Report 1956*, p. 93.

29. Patinkin, *The Israel Economy,* p. 88.

30. It should be pointed out that, even among the members of the coalition, there had been no unanimous support for the Israel Corporation Law. Thus, M. K. Yochanan Bader, who over the years battled consistently the expanding government involvement in the economy, both pointed out that discriminating laws are not a sign of good government and mocked the pretension that the shareholders in the corporation were motivated by a desire to help Israel, rather than by the prospects of profit. See *Divrei Ha'Knesset* [Knesset Transcripts], No. 26, Session 401 (May 21, 1969), p. 2666 [Hebrew].

31. BOI, *Annual Report 1956,* pp. 311–12.

32. Marshall Sarnat, *Saving and Investment Through Retirement Funds in Israel* (Jerusalem: Maurice Falk Institute for Economic Research in Israel, 1966).

33. BOI, *Annual Report 1958*, p. 257.

34. For empirical evidence, see, for instance, Theresa van Hoomisen, "Inflation and Equilibrium Price Dispersion: Theory and Empirical Evidence from Israel, 1971–1984," Ph.D. dissertation, University of California at Davis, 1987.

35. Heth, *The Legal Framework,* p. 230.

36. BOI, *Annual Report 1956*, p. 321.

37. Translated from the Hebrew in BOI, *Annual Report 1962*, p. 265.

38. Translated from the Hebrew in BOI, *Annual Report 1967*, p. 460.

39. BOI, *Annual Report 1962*, p. 325.

40. Sarnat, *Saving and Investment.*

41. BOI, *Annual Report 1970*, p. 322.

42. BOI, *Annual Report 1976*, p. 339.

43. BOI, *Annual Report 1961*, p. 300.

44. Ibid.

45. BOI, Monetary Department, *Developments in the Capital Market 1988*, Review No. 56, April 1989, p. 25 [Hebrew].

46. BOI, *Annual Report 1978*, p. 319.

47. Heth, *The Legal Framework,* p. 230.

48. D. Ottensooser, "The Approved Saving Plans," *Bank of Israel Review* 16 (1962): 13–22 [Hebrew].

49. BOI, *Annual Report 1967*, pp. 405–6.

50. Translated from Hebrew in BOI, *Annual Report 1968*, p. 310.

51. BOI, *Annual Report 1967*, p. 448.

52. The data on government debt and financial wealth were obtained from BOI, *Annual Report 1988*, pp. 112, 287.

53. BOI, *Annual Report 1955*, p. 195.

54. Ibid., p. 178.

55. Ibid., p. 188.

56. Continental-Allied Company, *Israel Industrial Finances,* pp. 50–51.

57. BOI, *Annual Report 1955*, p. 127.

58. BOI, *Annual Report 1963*, pp. 5, 277.

59. All data on directed credit were obtained from BOI Supervisor of Banks, *Annual Statistics of Israel's Banking System 1982–1986*, Table IV–6, pp. 96–97.

60. Ibid., Table V–2.

Chapter 3. The Capital Market: The Origins

1. See, e.g., Jacob Metzer, *National Capital for a National Home 1919–1921* (Jerusalem: Yad Izhak Ben-Zvi Publications, 1979), p. 24.

2. Arthur Ruppin, "A General Colonization Policy" [1913], in Arthur Ruppin, *Three Decades of Palestine* (Jerusalem: Schocken, 1936), p. 47.

3. Ibid., p. 59.

4. Arthur Ruppin, "A Colonization Fund" [1922], in ibid., pp. 102–5.

5. Metzer, *National Capital for a National Home,* p. 98.

6. For a description of the debate, see Jacob Metzer, "National Capital in Zionist Thinking 1919–1921: The Creation of the Foundation Fund," in N. Halevy and J. Kop, eds., *Studies in the Israeli Economy 1976* (Jerusalem: Falk Institute for Economic Research, 1977), pp. 50–63 [Hebrew].

7. Louis Brandeis, *The Zealand Memorandum,* August 1920. The document was written on board the steamer Zeeland, hence its name, and submitted as *Statement to the Delegates of the 12th Zionist Congress on Behalf of the Former Administration of Z.O.A.*

8. Ibid.

9. Louis Brandeis, "Self-Help in Palestine" [1923], in Jacob De Haas, *Louis D. Brandeis: A Biographical Sketch* (New York: Bloch, 1929).

10. Chaim Arlosoroff, "The Settlement Funds of the Jewish Agency" [1923], in *The Collected Writings of Chaim Arlosoroff* 2nd ed., vol. 2 (Tel-Aviv: Stible, 1934), p. 157 [Hebrew]. Arlosoroff headed the Political Department of the Jewish Agency prior to his murder in 1933. The description of the attitudes of the political Left is based mainly on his article. Many other, similar expressions from about that time exist as well.

11. Recall the quote from Ruppin, Three Decades of Palestine.

12. Egyptian pounds, which constituted the legal tender in Palestine until 1927 and were virtually equivalent to the pound sterling.

13. The remarks were made in a symposium on "The Question of the National Loan," *Trade and Industry* 7 (1926): pp. 177–84. Other participants were Arthur Ruppin, Z. D. Levontine, and George Halperin.

14. Nachum Gross, "Private and Public Enterprise in the Upbuilding of Palestine According to Z. D. Levontine," *Economic Quarterly* 116 (1983): 488–94 [Hebrew]. Levontine was even more orthodox in his beliefs in private enterprise than Brandeis. Thus, he argued that even the infrastructure could be financed on strict business considerations.

15. Zalman David Levontine, *To Our Fathers' Land: A History of the Work of the Zionist Organization 1915–1927*, vol. 3 (Tel-Aviv: Massada, 1928), p. 32 [Hebrew]. See also ibid.

16. Z. D. Levontine, "The Settlement of Palestine, Its Means and Methods," pamphlet B, December 1935, p. 15 [Hebrew].

17. Abraham Granovsky, *Land Settlement in Palestine* (London: Victor Gollancz, 1930). Granovsky was the chairman of the JNF.

18. Abraham Granovsky, *Land Problems in Palestine* (London: George Routledge & Sons, 1926), pp. 27–28.

19. Eliezer Kaplan, *The Financial Activities of the Executive of the Jewish Agency and the Tasks of the National Capital* (mimeo, Zionist Archives, January 1935) [Hebrew]. Kaplan at the time was the treasurer of the Jewish Agency and was to become Israel's first minister of finance.

20. Abraham Granovsky, "The Jewish National Fund—the Social Instrument for the Upbuilding of Palestine," *Commerce and Industry* 19–20 (October 1924): 551–53 [Hebrew].

21. Granovsky, *Land Problems in Palestine,* 1926, p. 12.

22. The analysis is contained in a circular sent to the regional offices of the JNF on March 23, 1943, which summarized a talk by Joseph Weitz, the head of the Land Department at the JNF.

23. Abraham Granovsky, *Land Policy in Palestine* (New York: Bloch Publishing Co., 1940), p. 115.

24. For a vivid description of the atmosphere that typified the attitude toward private dealers in land, see Dan Giladi, *Jewish Palestine During the Fourth Aliya Period (1924–1929)* (Tel-Aviv: Am Oved, 1973) [Hebrew].

25. Granovsky, *Land Policy in Palestine*, p. 104.

26. Ibid., p. 110.

27. Abraham Granovsky, *Land Problems in Palestine*, 1926, p. 4.

28. Ibid., p. 59.

29. *Report of the Public Commission for the Evaluation of the Objectives of Land Policy* (Tel-Aviv: January 1986). The quotation is translated from the Hebrew.

30. I shall henceforth refer occasionally to the Histadrut economy as *labor economy* and to the socialistically oriented political parties as *Labor*.

31. A. Ulitzur, *The National Capital and the Upbuilding of the Land* (Jerusalem: Foundation Fund, 1939), p. 31 [Hebrew].

32. See Levontine, *The Settlement of Palestine*. His distinction between the two kinds of loans was actually made in the context of criticizing the founding of the Workers' Bank with public funds.

33. Giladi, *Jewish Palestine*, p. 168.

34. Arlosoroff, "The Economic Conditions in the *Yishuv*, in *The Collected Writings* (*Yishuv* was the Hebrew word used to describe the Jewish community in Palestine).

35. Chaim Arlosoroff, "Conclusions," in ibid., p. 57.

36. A. Ulitzur, *The National Capital*, p. 45.

37. Giladi, *Jewish Palestine*, p. 110.

38. Ibid.

39. M. Novomeysky, "Palestine Potash Limited: Memorandum" (New York, January 1951). This and some of the other documents from which the story is pieced together were kindly given to me by Yossi Vardi, whose expertise on the matter comes from years of association with Israel Chemicals, the parent company of the Dead Sea Works, which inherited Palestine Potash. I am grateful to him.

40. A legal opinion to that effect was produced by Mr. Rosen, who served in 1949 as the counsellor of Israel's Foreign Ministry. It is summarized in the report of the Hoofien Committee, see later.

41. As we shall see later on, Mr. Hoofien can be credited with many of the obstacles placed in the way of private enterprise, all this while assuming the image of the champion of economic interests.

42. Novomeysky, *Palestine Potash Limited*.

43. M. Novomeysky, "The Truth about the Dead Sea Concession," *Ha'aretz* (May 1950); M. Novomeysky, "The Dead Sea Concession," *Ha'aretz* (September 24, 1951); "Notes on Meeting Between the Committee of Ministers and Representatives of Palestine Potash Ltd., held on Tuesday, May 30 1950, at the Knesset Building in Jerusalem"; "Government's Conditions for the Continuation of the Dead Sea Concession," English transcript from *Haboker* (a Hebrew daily, now defunct) (October 6, 1949).

44. Not only did the Israeli government rob Novomeysky of his magnificent creation, it also saw to his oblivion.

45. Kaplan, *The Financial Activities*.

46. Ibid.

47. For a proof, see the appendix to this chapter.

48. Ulitzur, *The National Capital*, p. 249.

49. Ibid., p. 260.

50. Anglo-American Committee of Inquiry, *A Survey of Palestine*, vol. 1 (Government Printer, 1946), p. 512.

51. Eliezer Kaplan, "Private and Public Investment in the Jewish National Home," in J. B. Hobman, ed., *Economic Future* (London: Humphries and Co., 1946), p. 112.

52. Excerpts from speeches by David Ben-Gurion, Eliezer Kaplan, and Golda Meirson (later Meir, the fourth prime minister of Israel), in "Sober Statements by the Heads of the Ruling Party," *Industry* (May 1949), pp. 4–7 [Hebrew]. See also the 1949–50 budget speech of Eliezer Kaplan in the Knesset, June 14, 1949, p. 10.

53. H. Greenbaum, "On the Investment Center," *The Israel Export* 11 (November 1950). The writer was the director general of the Ministry of Trade and Industry, to which the Investment Center belonged.

54. Gross et al., *A Banker for the Nation in Its Revival*, p. 347.

Chapter 4. Obstacles to Growth: The Economic Culture

1. The opposite, a high rate of interest for producers (borrowers) and a low one for consumers (savers), is possible without a wedge in the present sense. High reserve ratios imposed on banks will cause a large interest-rate spread.

2. Source of data: International Monetary Fund (IMF), *International Financial Statistics* (IFS) *Yearbook*, 1987. The choice of 1986 as the year for which the comparisons are presented was dictated by the belief that during that year the exchange rate for the shekel was closer to representing purchasing power parity than in 1987 or 1988.

3. CBS, *National Accounts 1990*.

4. CBS, *The Balance of Payments 1990*.

5. Total resources are defined as the GDP at factor prices (that is, GDP at market prices less indirect taxes plus production subsidies) plus total F.O.B. imports.

6. All data are computed from Central Bureau of Statistics, *National Accounts 1985–88*. Ben-Porath gets somewhat different results, but he uses data expressed in real terms. See his "Public Sector Employment and Wages in the Process of Adjustment, Israel 1973–1985," *Economic Quarterly* 131 (1987): 943–61. There is no clear way of deciding which of the two approaches is preferable.

7. O.E.C.D., *Economic Outlook* 42 (December 1987), Table R 12.

8. Ibid.

9. David Levhari, "The Israeli Capital Market" in Alvin Rabushka and Steve Hanke, eds., *Toward Growth: A Blueprint for Economic Rebirth in Israel* (Jerusalem: Institute for Advanced Strategic and Political Studies, 1988), pp. 83–90.

10. Some economists think that individuals do not view government obligations as wealth, because they know that one day they will have to pay more taxes to enable the government to discharge its obligations. In this view, people hold government obligations as a hedge against future taxes. In a long-run equilibrium, where rational expectations may be logically assumed, this may be true. See Robert Barro, "Are Government Bonds Net Wealth?" *Journal of Political Economy* 82 (1974): pp. 1095–1117. Without joining the theoretical debate, I think it safe to observe that in Israel government obligations are definitely regarded as net wealth.

11. Dani Yariv, *The Development of the Public's Financial Wealth in Israel Compared to the World's Developed Countries* (Jerusalem: Research Department, Bank of Israel, 1984), Table 1 [Hebrew].

12. BOI, *Annual Report 1975*, p. 186.

13. See Robert Lerman, "A Critical Overview of Israeli Housing Policy," Discussion Paper No. 15–76 (Jerusalem: The Brookdale Institute, 1976), pp. 10–11.

14. *The Economist* (April 9, 1988), p. 13.

15. *The Economist* (August 19, 1989).

16. BOI, *Annual Report 1988*, pp. 162, 164.

17. BOI, *Annual Report 1990*, p. 164.

18. BOI, *Annual Report 1989*, p. 84; *Annual Report 1990*, pp. 90–91.

19. Israel is not the only country where declining government deficits have been accompanied by declining saving rates. The adherents of rational expectations and the Ricardian paradigm see it as a proof of the assertion that government bonds are not regarded as net wealth. They argue that as government deficits decline, people perceive a decline in future taxation requirements, and so see less need of buying bonds as a hedge against future taxes. This leads to declined saving.

20. BOI, Examiner of Banks, *Israel's Banking System: Annual Survey 1980*, pp. 10–13 [Hebrew]. The examiner of banks surveys are also published in a concise English edition.

21. BOI, *Annual Report 1984*, financial accounts.

22. This has changed since the influx of immigrants from the former Soviet Union began.

23. Computed from the total weekly input of hours and the average number of people employed, as given in BOI, *Annual Report 1987*, p. 78.

24. O.E.C.D., *Main Economic Indicators*, December 1988.

25. Ibid.

26. BOI, *Annual Report 1987*, p. 129.

27. The rate of increase is calculated from a chart in BOI, *Annual Report 1988*, p. 79.

28. Economic Planning Authority, Prime Minister's Office, *Israel Economic Development* (Jerusalem: Author, 1968), p. 297.

29. See, e.g., Jane Jacobs, *The Economy of Cities* (New York: Random House, 1969).

30. BOI, *Annual Report 1962*, p. 178.

31. BOI, *Developments in the Capital Market, Annual Survey, 1985*, Survey No. 53 (Tel-Aviv: Author, 1986), p. 28 [Hebrew].

Chapter 5. The Economic Culture: The Origins

1. His statements on the subject can be found in Moshe Bella, ed., *The World of Jabotinsky* (Tel-Aviv: Defusim, 1972), pp. 232–35.

2. Howard M. Sachar, *A History of Israel* (New York: Alfred A. Knopf, 1979).

3. Arthur Ruppin, *The Agricultural Colonization of the Zionist Organization in Palestine* (Westport, Conn.: Hyperion Press, 1976), p. 1.

4. Sachar, *A History of Israel*.

5. David Ben-Gurion, "The Aim of Labor," *The Palestine Review* (October 1944), pp. 114–15.

6. Arthur Ruppin, "Mass Immigration and Finance," address delivered before the Thirteenth Zionist Congress, August 1923, in A. Ruppin, *Three Decades of Palestine* (Jerusalem: Schocken, 1936), p. 107.

7. At that time the legal tender in Palestine had been the Egyptian pound, which was roughly on par with the British pound sterling. In 1927 it was replaced by the Palestinian pound, which was pegged to the pound sterling at par. Hence, financial figures are comparable despite the change.

8. The facts concerning both population and land prices are quoted from Dan Giladi, *Jewish Palestine During the Fourth Aliya Period (1924–1929)* (Tel-Aviv: Am Oved, 1973) [Hebrew].

9. *The Collected Writings of Chaim Arlosoroff*, vol. 2, 2d ed. (Tel-Aviv: Stible, 1934), p. 29 [translated from the Hebrew].

10. Eliezer Kaplan, *The Financial Activities of the Jewish Agency and the Tasks of the National Capital* (mimeo, Zionist Archives, January 1935), [Hebrew].

11. Z. D. Levontine, *To Our Fathers' Land: A History of the Work of the Zionist Organization 1915–1927*, vol. 3 (Tel-Aviv: 1928), p. 120.

12. Quoted from Bela, *The World of Jabotinsky*, p. 106. The quote is from an article written in 1929.

13. The concept of productivity as occupation in physical production is what underlies the peculiar national accounting in communist economies, where "net material product" replaces "gross national product."

14. In a free economy, this is where takeovers play such a useful role. Their existence facilitates the distinction between failures of individuals and unavoidable failures.

15. Arthur Ruppin, "Tel-Aviv," *Mischar Veta'assia* [Trade and Industry], no. 5 (1925): 148–49 [Hebrew].

16. Ernst Kahn, "How to Reduce Rents," *Palestine Review* (February 26, 1937): 911–12.

17. Selig Lubianiker, "The Tasks of *Shikun*" (mimeo, Tel-Aviv, August 1937) [Hebrew].

18. The reserve and equity ratios were calculated from Nachum Gross et al., *A Banker for the Nation in Its Revival: The History of Bank Leumi Le'Israel*, pp. 180–81.

19. A. Hoofien, chairman of the General Mortgage Bank of Palestine, address to the shareholders' meeting, February 7, 1943 [Hebrew].

20. Milton Friedman and Anna Jacobson Schwartz, *A Monetary History of the United States, 1867–1960* (Princeton, N.J.: Princeton University Press, 1963), Table B–3.

21. Letter by the Landlords' Association to Eliezer Kaplan, April 14, 1944 [Hebrew].

22. Letter of J. M. Tocatly, president of the Central Union of the Palestine Landlords' Association to the chief secretary of the Government of Palestine, February 17, 1944; Letter of Se'adia Shoshany, chairman of the executive of the landlord's organization, to Eliezer Kaplan, treasurer of the Jewish Agency, April 13, 1944 [Hebrew]; Investigation Concerning Subtenants, conducted by the Department of Statistics of the Jewish Agency, April 1944 [Hebrew]. It is important to emphasize that the statistical survey, which was done in connection with an unrelated topic (namely, developments in the cost of living), bears out the contentions of the landlords. The outcome of the investigation was officially sanctioned in Eliezer Kaplan, "Memorandum on House Rents" (Jerusalem, July 4, 1944).

23. Minutes of the Fifth Meeting of the Housing Accommodations and Rents Committee, November 23, 1944.

24. Ibid.

25. Eliezer Kaplan, "Memorandum on House Rents."

26. Meir Heth, *The Legal Framework of Economic Activity in Israel* (New York: Praeger, 1967), pp. 215–16.

27. BOI, *Annual Report 1963*, p. 231.

28. *The Economist* (June 20, 1992), p. 81.

29. Heth, *The Legal Framework*, p. 218.

30. Zvi Sussman, *Wage Differentials and Equality Within the Histadrut* (Tel-Aviv: Massada, 1974).

31. Ibid., p. 19.

32. Ibid., p. 27.

33. "A First Milestone," *Palestine Economic Review* (August 1945).

34. M. Medzini, "Labor Exchanges: A Wrong Approach," *Palestine Review* (August 4, 1939): 253–54.

35. The first violent episode occurred in Kfar Saba where the Histadrut tried to prevent the employment of workers who had not been hired through its exchange. See J. Ofir, *Sefer Ha' oved Ha' leumi* [The National Worker's Book] (Tel-Aviv: Executive of the National Workers Federation, 1959), p. 71 [Hebrew].

36. Ludwig Gruenbaum, "The Public Jewish Labor Exchange in Palestine," July 6, 1943, Zionist Archive File S90/687 (mimeo).

37. Ofir, *Sefer Ha' oved Ha' leumi*, pp. 224–28.

38. M. Ettinger et al., *The Yishuv Economy Book for 1947* (Jerusalem: The National Committee [Va' ad Leumi], 1947), p. 304 [Hebrew].

39. Letter no. 1494/48 by the National Workers' Union to Y. Gruenbaum, head of the Jewish Agency's Labor Department.

40. Heth, *The Legal Framework*, pp. 164, 175.

41. Ibid., p. 177.

42. As an aside, it is interesting to note what was included under the definition of *public sector*. In addition to what is usually perceived as the public sector, the law includes institutions of higher education, air transportation, and the production and distribution of oil, water, and electricity.

43. The exponents of the Histadrut's position were Mordechai Namir, then minister of labor, on March 3, 1958: *Divrei Ha'Knesset* [Knesset Transcripts], vol. 23, p. 1169; Giora Yoseftal, minister of labor, on April 4, 1960: *Divrei Ha'Knesset*, vol. 28, p. 1093; and Moshe Bar'am, minister of labor, on March 15, 1971: *Divrei Ha'Knesset*, vol. 76, pp. 1545–46. The first two objected to unemployment insurance, and the third spoke against legislating a minimum wage.

44. Avraham Ofek and Eliezer Rosenstein, "The Trade Unions and the Institutional Structure of the Histadrut," *Economic Quarterly* 131 (1987): 1021–30 [Hebrew].

45. The use of logarithms is dictated by the fact that the total wage increase is calculated as the product, not the sum, of the various components. Take, for example, 1976: the total wage increase was 43 percent; it consisted of 19.2 percent COLA, 6 percent Histadrut, and 13.2 percent unions; we have

$$1.43 = 1.192 \times 1.06 \times 1.132.$$
$$\log(1.43) = \log(1.192) + \log(1.06) + \log(1.132).$$

The weights (shares) are now computed as $\log(1.192)/\log(1.43)$ and so on.

46. Mancur Olson, *The Rise and Decline of Nations* (New Haven, Conn.: Yale University Press, 1982).

Chapter 6. Obstacles to Growth: The Would-Be Business Sector

1. BOI, *Annual Report 1988*, p. 204; and Shlomo Maoz, "The Hard Sell," *The Jerusalem Post* (August 18, 1989).

2. Arieh Bregman, *Industry and Industrial Policy in Israel* (Jerusalem: Bank of Israel Research Department, 1986), p. 9 [Hebrew].

3. Dun & Bradstreet (Israel), *The Dun & Bradstreet 100* (Tel-Aviv: Dun and Bradstreet, 1984).

4. See, e.g., J. Greenberg, "From Heroic to Rational Economics," *Economic Quarterly* 117 (1983): 577–601; Noah Lucas, *The Modern History of Israel* (London: Weidenfeld & Nicholson, 1975).

5. The source for all data is IMF, *International Financial Statistics Yearbook, 1987.*

6. BOI, *Annual Report 1988*, p. 241.

7. Bregman, *Industry and Industrial Policy in Israel*, pp. 80–81.

8. Ibid., pp. 82–83.

9. *Dun & Bradstreet, 100.*

10. *Hadashot,* a Hebrew daily (September 26, 1989).

11. The data were reported by *Globes,* the country's foremost financial daily (April 9, 1990) [Hebrew].

12. BOI, *Annual Report 1988,* p. 151.

13. Ibid., p. 157.

14. Ibid., p. 158.

15. Data for countries other than Israel: O.E.C.D., *Labor Force Statistics 1965–1985* (Paris: Author, 1987).

16. Institute for International Strategic Studies, *The Military Balance 1986–1987* (London: Author, 1986).

17. Mark A. Heller, ed., *The Middle East Military Balance 1985* (Boulder, Co: Jaffe Center for Strategic Studies, Jerusalem Post, and Westview Press, 1986).

18. Since the end of 1987, as a consequence of the *intifada,* the uprising in the occupied territories, labor input from the West Bank and Gaza has declined considerably. But in 1988, this was reflected less in the number of persons employed, and more in the number of days worked per person.

19. BOI, *Annual Report 1988,* pp. 93, 95.

20. CBS, *National Accounts,* various years.

21. Ruth Klinov, "Israel's Labor Force, 1948–1984," Discussion Paper 86.04, Maurice Falk Institute for Economic Research in Israel, 1986, p. 19 [Hebrew].

22. U.S. Center for Educational Statistics, *Digest of Education Statistics,* Table 150.

23. Translated from the Hebrew in BOI, *Annual Report 1957,* p. 117.

24. Haim Levi, *Government Intervention, Investment Incentives and the Price of Foreign Exchange* (Jerusalem: Department of Business Administration, Hebrew University of Jerusalem, Research Report No. 4/1973 [Hebrew].

25. Haim Levi and Marshall Sarnat, "Investment Incentives and the Allocation of Resources," *Economic Quarterly* 87 (1975): 304–15 [Hebrew].

26. CBS, *National Accounts for 1985,* Tables 5 and 10. The subsidies were computed by combining columns 4, 7, 8, and 9 and subtracting the figure in column 12 of Table 7. These columns contain all the capital and credit-related subsidies, except subsidies associated with directed credit, as the latter is of a short-term nature. See Chapter 2 for details.

27. BOI, *Annual Report 1966,* pp. 51–52.

28. BOI, *Annual Report 1968*, p. 44.

29. CBS, *National Accounts for 1986*, Table 13.

30. BOI, *Annual Report 1980*, p. 115.

31. "Economy-Wide Effects of Agricultural Policies in OECD Countries," OECD Economic Studies No. 13, quoted from *The Economist* (March 31, 1990).

32. All three stories concerning farm-related steps are based on BOI, *Annual Report 1960*, pp. 98, 106–7.

33. BOI, *Annual Report 1959*, pp. 96, 123.

34. Ibid., p. 96.

35. BOI, *Annual Report 1961*, p. 160.

36. BOI, *Annual Report 1978*, p. 354.

37. BOI, *Annual Report 1979*, p. 219.

38. The calculation is based on data concerning the sectoral composition of the GDP, given in ibid., p. 24. These were combined with the actual absolute GDP for 1979.

39. The fact that the government was aware of the distorted incentives created by the various farm-sector rescues is clearly evident from ibid., p. 220.

40. "The Swedish Economy, A Survey," *The Economist* (March 3, 1990).

41. Ibid.

42. BOI, *Annual Report 1968*, p. 149; *1969*, p. 133; *1970*, p. 149.

43. Amira Galin (Goldfarb) and G. Yanai Tab, "The Package Deal—A Turning Point in Israel's Labor Relations," *Economic Quarterly* 69–70 (1971): 106–13.

44. Yossi Margoninsky, "Income Policy: The Israeli Experience, 1970–71," Discussion Paper 87.05 (Jerusalem: Maurice Falk Institute, 1987).

45. BOI, *Annual Report 1985*, pp. 70–71.

46. Strike data: BOI, *Annual Report 1965*, p. 193; employment data: CBS, *Statistical Abstract of Israel*, 1969, Table J/11.

47. B. Avniel, "A New Tendency in the Position of Manufacturers on Strikes," *Hata'assiya* (February 1946).

48. The data on interest rates and working capital were obtained from the following sources: BOI, *Annual Report 1984*, pp. 271, 273; *1985*, p. 281; *1986*, p. 255; and BOI, *Recent Economic Developments* 44 (September 1988): Table 21.

49. Meir Heth, *The Legal Framework of Economic Activity in Israel* (New York: Praeger, 1967), especially pp. 58–59.

50. BOI, *Annual Report 1963*, p. 69, and *1965*, p. 97.

51. BOI, *Annual Report 1985*, pp. 70–71, and *1986*, p. 59.

52. BOI, *Annual Report 1959*, p. 137.

53. The material concerning the Restrictive Trade Practices Law is wholly based on Heth, *The Legal Framework*, pp. 220–26.

54. BOI, *Annual Report 1960*, p. 143.

55. BOI, *Annual Report 1962*, p. 198.

56. BOI, *Annual Report 1960*, pp. 142–3.

57. *Ha'aretz* (September 15, 1989).

58. The details of the ownership structure are based on Ilan Maoz, "The Structure of the Oil Economy and the Need for Reform" (mimeo, April 7, 1987) [Hebrew].

59. Comptroller of the State of Israel, "Report on Inspection at Paz" (January 1986) [Hebrew].

Chapter 7. The Would-Be Private Sector: The Origins

1. See Howard M. Sachar, *A History of Israel* (New York: Alfred A. Knopf, 1979).

2. Arthur Ruppin, *The Agricultural Colonization of the Zionist Organization in Palestine* (Westport, Conn.: Hyperion Press, 1976), pp. 194–95; first published by Martin Hopkinson, 1926.

3. "Industrialization of Palestine: Its Possibilities and Limitations," *Palestine Economic Bulletin* no. 6–7 (1933).

4. Dan Giladi, *Jewish Palestine During the Fourth Aliya Period (1924–1929)* (Tel-Aviv: Am Oved, 1973) [Hebrew], p. 47.

5. Arthur Ruppin, The Agricultural Colonization, pp. 196–97.

6. See, e.g., Anita Shapira, *The Disappointing Struggle: Jewish Labor 1929–1939* (Tel-Aviv: Hakibbutz Hame'uhad, 1977), p. 35 [Hebrew].

7. Editorial in *Trade and Industry,* no. 13–14 (August 1927) [Hebrew].

8. Editorial in *Trade and Industry*, no. 1 (January 1928). It is important to stress that this journal, in contrast to *Hataassiya* [Industry], which represented the views of the Manufacturers' Association, was not a parochial organ.

9. Contract between Arthur Ruppin, representing the Zionist Organization in London, and Ephraim Blumenfeld, Nachum Tversky, and Berl Katzenelson, representing the Histadrut, signed on April 1, 1921 [Hebrew].

10. A. Ulitzur, *The National Capital and the Upbuilding of the Land* *(Jerusalem: Foundation Fund, 1959), Table 38 [Hebrew]*.

11. *See Shapira,* The Disappointing Struggle; and Baruch Kimmerling, *Zionism and Economy* (Cambridge, Mass.: Schenkman Publishing, 1983), p. 13.

12. Giladi, *Jewish Palestine*, p. 151.

13. Arthur Ruppin, The Agricultural Colonization, pp. 2–3.

14. David Ben-Gurion, "Jewish Labor," in *Jewish Labor* (Tel-Aviv: General Histadrut of Jewish Workers in Palestine, 1936). The article was originally published as a series in the Histadrut daily *Davar* in 1932 [translated from the Hebrew].

15. Ibid., p. 25. He also quotes Eliezer Ben-Yehuda, the modernizer of the Hebrew language, as describing such attitudes on the part of the colonists a quarter of a century earlier.

16. "Banking in Palestine," *Palestine and Middle East Economic Review* (January 1933).

17. Ben-Gurion, "Jewish Labor," p. 21.

18. M. Ettinger et al., *The Yishuv Economy Book for 1947* (Jerusalem: 1947), p. 271 [Hebrew].

19. David Ben-Gurion, "To the Rescue of Jewish Labor in the Colonies," *Jewish Labor*, pp. 136–39. The article is based on a speech delivered before the council of the Palestine Labor party (MAPAI) in 1934 [Hebrew]. See also Shapira, *The Disappointing Struggle*, p. 105.

20. See Shapira, ibid., pp. 108, 121; Eliezer Kaplan, *The Financial Activities of the Jewish Agency and the Tasks of the National Capital* (mimeo., Zionist Archives, January 1935), p. 2 [Hebrew].

21. Letter written by the Farmers' Federation to the British Mandate adviser on labor, January 1, 1941 (Zionist Archives Document No. S53/1026).

22. Giladi, *Jewish Palestine*, p. 165.

23. Letter by H. Rosenberg, secretary of the Executive of the National Farmers Organization, dated May 18, 1937.

24. Letter to Eliezer Kaplan, treasurer of the Jewish Agency, by the Agricultural Workers' Organization, dated April 27, 1937. The juxtaposition in time of this and the growers' letter is, of course, not a coincidence.

25. Letter addressed to Eliezer Kaplan, dated November 25, 1942.

26. As earlier, the prefix E£ stands for the Egyptian pound, which served as legal tender until its replacement in 1927 by the Palestinian pound. Both were on par with the pound sterling (£).

27. Eliahu Biletzki, *Solel Boneh 1924–1974* (Tel-Aviv: Am Oved, 1975), p. 81 [Hebrew].

28. Ibid., p. 123.

29. Ibid., pp. 122, 136.

30. Giladi, *Jewish Palestine*, p. 189.

31. Harry Viteles, *A History of the Cooperative Movement in Israel*, Book 1 (London: Valentine-Mitchell, 1968).

32. The daily *Ha'aretz* (September 1, 1941). The sum was quoted in connection with the purchase by the renewed Solel Boneh of the Vulcan Foundries in 1941. See also minutes of a meeting between representatives of the Manufacturers' Association and the executive committee of the Jewish Agency, which took place on January 1, 1936.

33. Naomi Lewitzky, "Koor—Troubles of an Empire," *Koteret Rashit* [a weekly whose name translates as "Headline"] (September 9, 1987) [Hebrew]. Since the article was published the financial troubles of the concern grew to the extent that Mr. Gavish, the executive to whom the quote is attributed, had to resign, and Koor is undergoing restructuring.

34. D. Rosolio, "Alive and Kicking," *Economic Quarterly* 117: 559–62; E. Avneyon, "The Triple Role of Directors in the Companies of Hevrat Haovdim," *Economic Quarterly*: 601–5; G. Gazit, "Hevrat Haovdim and Bank Ha'Poalim," *Economic Quarterly*: 661–6. The title translation of the last of the three articles, as given on the journal's cover, is entirely inadequate. The Hebrew title is very suggestive of the author's views, which is what counts in our context. It actually translates into "Is Bank Ha'Poalim Like Any Other Bank?"

35. Minutes of a meeting between representatives of the Jewish Agency and the Manufacturers' Association. They are undated, but from the context it is clear that the meeting took place some time during 1935.

36. Viteles, *A History of the Cooperative Movement in Israel*, p. 23.

37. A. Zabarsky, "The Workers' Economy, Its Achievements and Problems," *Economic Quarterly* 1–2 (September 1953) [Hebrew].

38. Chaim Arlosoroff, a leading member of the political Left, made the observation during the Fourth Aliya. See Giladi, *Jewish Palestine*, p. 151. Likewise, Meir Dizengoff, the first mayor of Tel-Aviv, observed while trying to explain the causes of

the 1926–29 depression, that the capitalists of Palestine were too weak to counter a labor organization that rivaled its Western counterpart. See ibid, p. 178.

39. Z. D. Levontine, *To Our Fathers' Land: A History of the Work of the Zionist Organization 1915–1927,* vol. 3 (Tel-Aviv: Massada, 1928), p. 120 [Hebrew].

40. For example, David Remez, elected in 1935 secretary general of the Histadrut, in a joint meeting with Kaplan of the Jewish Agency and representatives of the Manufacturers' Association, January 22, 1935.

41. Manufacturers' Association, Circular No. 3/37 [Hebrew].

42. Letter from Y. Merminsky of the executive committee to the Manufacturers' Association, dated March 3, 1937.

43. Communique to the press issued by the cooperative on December 12, 1938.

44. Hillel Dan, *On an Unpaved Road—the Solel Boneh Saga* (Jerusalem: Schocken, 1963), pp. 215–16 [Hebrew].

45. M. Rosen, "What Delays the Signing of the Collective Agreement," *Hataassiya* [Industry] 9 (February 1944).

46. B. Avniel, "To Settle Labor Relations!" *Hataassiya* (April 1944).

47. Eliezer Kaplan, minutes of a meeting between representatives of the Jewish Agency, the Manufacturers' Association and the Histadrut, which took place in the offices of the association on January 22, 1935.

48. M. Novomeysky, *Industry in Palestine* (Tel-Aviv: Corporation for Economic Development in Palestine, 1924).

49. Peter Temin, *Did Monetary Forces Cause the Great Depression?* (New York: W. W. Norton, 1976), Figs. 4, 5.

50. Alexander Landsberg, "Industrial Credit," *Trade and Industry* 16 (1924): 489–90.

51. Nachum T. Gross, "The 1923 Recession and Public Sector Finance in Palestine," Discussion Paper 794, (Jerusalem: Maurice Falk Institute for Economic Research in Israel, 1979).

52. Chaim Arlosoroff, "The Financial Problems of the Building of Palestine, in *Collected Writings of Chaim Arlosoroff,* 2d ed., vol. 2 (Tel-Aviv: Stible, 1934), p. 97 [Hebrew].

53. Chaim Arlosoroff, "The Settlement Finances of the Jewish Agency," in ibid., pp. 97, 162. This article was written earlier than the one quoted in the preceding note. It is only fair and also interesting to point out that, in the later of the two articles, Arlosoroff returned to the idea of an investment trust based on the sale of shares and debentures on international capital markets. Yet this trust, too, had to be at least directed, if not managed, by the Zionist executive committee.

54. "Industrial Bank Credit," *Palestine Economic Review* September 1945), p. 11.

55. Nachum Gross et al., *A Banker for the Nation in Its Revival: The History of Bank Leumi Le'Israel* (Jerusalem: Massada, 1977), pp. 187, 191.

56. Minutes of a meeting of the Banking Committee of the Jewish Agency, which took place on November 21, 1935, at the offices of APB in Tel-Aviv; the data were supplied by Mr. Hoofien, the general manager of the bank.

57. Calculated from Nachum Gross et al., *A Banker for the Nation*, p. 180.

58. Abraham Granovsky, Land Problems in Palestine (London: George Routledge & Sons, 1926), p. 60.

59. Abraham Granovsky, Land Settlement, p. 98.

60. Testimony by A. Shenkar, president of the Manufacturers' Association, in a meeting with representatives of the executive committee of the Jewish Agency. Undated minutes, but apparently 1935 [translated from Hebrew].

61. See ibid., p. 4.

62. "Palestine Economic Corporation," *Palestine Review* (November 27, 1936).

63. The other loans were extended against personal guarantees, bank guarantees, and mortgages on movables.

64. The data concerning the experiment are derived from "Industrial Finance in Palestine," *Trade and Industry* (1932) [Hebrew]; see also *Palnews Annual 1937*, p. 83.

65. Heinrich Margulies, "Medium Term Industrial Credit," *Hataassiya* (August 1937). Margulies was a member of the Advisory Board to the Mortgage and Credit Bank and as such was intimately familiar with its operations.

66. The story was pieced together from balance sheets and documents from the company's file at the Israel Registrar of Corporations in Jerusalem. See also Dan, *On an Unpaved Road.*

67. Ibid., pp. 215–16.

68. Heinrich Margulies, "What Is an Industrial Bank?" *Trade and Industry* 20 (1926) [Hebrew].

69. See, e.g., A. Shenkar, "A Decade of the Palestine Industrial Bank," *Hataassiya* 11 (April 1943).

70. Manufacturers' Association, "Memorandum Submitted to the President of the Nineteenth Zionist Congress in Lucerne," 1935.

71. Minutes of the meeting, May 10, 1936.

72. Manufacturers' Association, "Memorandum Submitted to the President of the Nineteenth Zionist Congress in Lucerne."

73. Minutes of the meeting of the Joint Committee of the Jewish Agency and the M.A., appointed July 28, 1936, which took place on August 1, 1936.

74. Manufacturers' Association, "Memorandum Submitted to the Twenty-First Zionist Congress in Geneva" (Tel-Aviv: Author, August 1939) [translated from Hebrew].

75. "Memorandum Submitted to the Nineteenth Congress."

76. "Memorandum Submitted to the Twenty-First Congress."

77. Ibid.

78. "Industry—to the Twenty-Second Zionist Congress," *Hataassiya* 5 (October 1946).

79. "The Development and Activities of the M.A.," *Hataassiya* 2 (July 1946).

80. "On the Activity of the M.A.," *Hataassiya* (May 1950).

81. Minutes of a meeting between representatives of the Jewish Agency, the executive committee of the Histadrut, and the M.A., January 22, 1935.

82. "Memorandum Submitted to the Nineteenth Congress."

83. "Resolutions of the Joint Committee Appointed by the Jewish Agency and the M.A. on the Basis of the Resolution of the Meeting Convened on July 28, 1936, by the Jewish Agency's Executive," August 3, 1936.

84. "Memorandum Submitted to the Twenty-First Congress."

85. "Industry Demands a Regime of Loyalty to Domestic Produce," *Hataassiya* 2 (July 1946).

86. "The Biannual Meeting of the M.A., Resolutions," *Hataassiya* (November–December 1948).

87. "On the Activities of the Union for Domestic Produce," *Hataassiya* 2 (February 1949).

88. "The Industrial Outlook—Interview with Mr. A. Shenkar, President of the M.A.," *Palestine and Middle East Economic Magazine* (1937): 91, 94.

89. "Industrial Organization—Interview with Mr. H. Margulies, Assistant General Manager, APB," *Palestine and Middle East Economic Magazine* (1938): 110–11.

90. "Industrial Cartels in Palestine," *Hataassiya* (June–July 1938).

91. Krinitzy, the head of the M.A.'s Labor Department, Minutes of the Meeting of July 28, 1936.

92. Horowitz of the Jewish Agency, ibid.

93. Marcus, ibid.

94. H. Margulies, Minutes of the Meeting between Representatives of the M.A., The Jewish Agency, The Histadrut, and A.P.B., August 3, 1936.

95. See, e.g., Horowitz's articulation, Minutes of the Meeting of the Joint Committee, August 1, 1936.

96. "The Activities of Departments and Institutions Associated with the M.A.," *Hataassiya* (November 1940).

97. Ibid.

98. See letter by Krinitzy, then head of the M.A.'s Labor Department, to A Shenkar, the M.A.'s president, on February 1, 1934. In this letter, Krinitzy urges that individual employers refrain from signing labor contracts with the Histadrut.

99. See Goralsky's articulation, Minutes of the January 22, 1935, Meeting.

100. "Resolutions of the 1943 Annual Meeting of the M.A.," *Hataassiya* (November 1943). None of this negates, of course, the possible advantages of centralized wage setting mentioned in connection with the Swedish example.

101. See "Memorandum Submitted to the Nineteenth Congress"; letter by Kaplan to the South Africa Office of the Foundation Fund, May 23, 1937.

102. "Minutes of the August 1, 1936, Meeting of the Joint Committee."

103. "Memorandum Submitted to the Nineteenth Congress."

104. "Industry—To the Twenty-Second Congress."

105. David Horowitz, "The Program for the Industrial Recuperation Fund" (Tel-Aviv: Institute for Economic Research, The Jewish Agency, August 6, 1937) [Hebrew].

106. Department of Trade and Industry, The Jewish Agency, *Report for 1941–42*, pp. 29–31 [Hebrew]. See also David Lichtenstein, *Industrial Development and Finance in Palestine* (Jerusalem: Department of Youth Affairs of the Zionist Organization, 1946) [Hebrew].

107. Office of Public Relations, "Labor Disputes and Department of Labor Mediation Efforts for Their Settlement, August, 1937–May, 1940" (Jerusalem: The Jewish Agency, August 20, 1940).

108. David Ben-Gurion's address to the biannual meeting of the M.A., December 19, 1948, as reported in *Hataassiya* (November–December 1948).

109. Bejerano on planning in the general annual meeting of the M.A., January 29, 1950, *Hataassiya* (February 1950).

110. A. Shenkar, "The State and Industry," *Hataassiya* (February 1948).

111. Letters to the Editor, *Hataassiya* (December 1949).

112. See Michael Michaeli, *The System of Exchange Rates in Israel* (Jerusalem: Maurice Falk Institute, 1968) [Hebrew].

113. See ibid.; and Alex Rubner, *The Economy of Israel* (New York: Praeger, 1960).

114. Ibid.

115. See, e.g., Rubner, *The Economy of Israel*.

116. *Hataassiya* (February 1949).

117. Peretz Bernstein, the leader of the General Zionists, in a speech to the 1950 annual convention of the M.A., as excerpted in "The Annual Convention," *Hataassiya* (February 1950).

118. Paul Johnson, *A History of the Jews* (New York: Harper and Row, 1987), p. 247.

Chapter 8. Obstacles to Growth: The Almighty Weakling

1. BOI, *Annual Report 1988*, pp. 112, 116.

2. BOI, *Annual Report 1990*, p. 164.

3. A summary of data concerning U.S. assistance can be found in, e.g., BOI, *Annual Report 1978*, pp. 160–61; *1982*, p. 201; *1987*, p. 187.

4. GDP data for fiscal years: IMF, *Government Finance Statistics Yearbook*, 1987; data for calendar years: IMF, *IFS Yearbook, 1987*. To facilitate comparisons, all data were converted to a fiscal-year basis by multiplying the calendar-year data by the ratio of fiscal-year GDP to calendar-year GDP.

5. IMF, *Government Finance Statistics Yearbook 1987*, p. 98. All data are expressed in $U.S., and therefore may yield results different from what one would get on using each country's domestic currency to compute proportions.

6. Arie Hecht, "Local Government Finance," Chapter 7 in Daniel Elazar and Chaim Kalchheim, eds., *Local Government in Israel* (Lanham, Md.: University Press of America and Jerusalem Center for Public Affairs, 1988).

7. All the data concerning government corporations are taken from "Symposium on Privatization," *Economic Quarterly* 135–36 (April 1988) [Hebrew].

8. James M. Buchanan and Gordon Tullock, *The Calculus of Consent* (Ann Arbor: University of Michigan Press, 1962).

9. Mancur Olson, *The Rise and Decline of Nations* (New Haven, Conn.: Yale University Press, 1982).

10. Robert Lerman, "A Critical Overview of Israeli Housing Policy," Discussion Paper No. 15–76 (Jerusalem: Brookdale Institute, 1976), pp. 64, 66.

11. BOI, *Annual Report 1988*, p. 97.

12. The daily *Al Hamishmar* (August 1, 1986) [Hebrew].

13. The mayor of Arad has since served as the chairman of the Knesset's finance committee, a powerful position from which to look after the interests of the development towns. He became minister of finance in 1992.

14. BOI, *Annual Report 1957*, p. 164.

15. Moshe Glazman, "Public Transportation in Israel Today: Prospects for Reform," Policy Paper No. 2 (Jerusalem: Institute for Advanced Strategic and Political Studies, 1989).

16. The daily *Ma'ariv* (October 24, 1989).

17. Ministry of Finance, Department of Budgets, *Report of the Commission for Monitoring the Profitability of Industrial Exports Exclusive of Diamonds in 1981–1982*, February 23, 1983 [Hebrew].

18. "Globes," May 15, 1990; quoted in the context of published excerpts from the fortieth report of the comptroller general.

19. Interview on TV, September 25, 1991.

20. Israel Television report of August 1, 1987.

21. A very exhaustive analysis of the water situation is provided by Ran Mosenson, "The Budget of the Water Economy—A General Long-Term View" (mimeo, Jerusalem: Office of the Budget, Ministry of Finance, 1986) [Hebrew]; and in a letter by Ran Mosenson to the Water Commissioner, March 29, 1990.

22. Ibid.

23. Agricultural Center, Economic Department, "On the Problem of Pricing Water for Agriculture" (mimeo, February 1986) [Hebrew].

Chapter 9. The Inflationary Prescription: Institutions and Policies

1. Letter to Kaplan dated July 27, 1936, signed by Granovsky, Schneursohn, and Bromberg; reply by Kaplan to a July 16, 1936, letter by Bromberg, dated July 22, 1936 (both at the Zionist Archives). Despite the fact that the reply by Kaplan is to a different letter than the one cited here, there can be no doubt that the entire exchange revolves around the argument concerning COLA under the circumstances created by the disturbances [Hebrew].

2. Zvi Sussman, *Wage Differentials and Equality Within the Histadrut* (Ramat-Gan: Massada, 1974), p. 66 [Hebrew].

3. Jewish Agency, Information Circular 5/5700, December 12, 1939; Department of Labor, Jewish Agency, *Mediation and Arbitration of Labor Disputes,* the document is undated, but clearly surveys the events of the years 1940–42 [Hebrew].

4. Letter from Grunbaum, head of the Labor Department of the Jewish Agency, to the Manufacturers' Association, dated February 22, 1940 (Zionist Archives) [Hebrew].

5. B. Avniel, "COLA and Wage Increases," *Hataassiya* 8 (December 1941) [Hebrew].

6. Jewish Agency, Information Circular and *Mediation and Arbitration*; report on Manufacturers' Association activities, *Hataassiya* (November 1940) [Hebrew]; B. Avniel, "COLA and Wage Increases."

7. Manufacturers' Association report, ibid.

8. Jewish Agency, Information Circular and *Mediation and Arbitration.*

9. Robert Nathan, Oscar Gass, and Daniel Creamer, *Palestine: Problem and Promise* (Washington: Public Affairs Press, 1946), p. 237.

10. The appendix to this chapter presents the skeleton of a mathematical model within which these effects can be rigorously established.

11. BOI, *Annual Report 1975*, p. 186.

12. BOI, *Annual Report 1982*, p. 38.

13. This breakdown of prices into the import and domestic components was not usually published at the time in this form; see, e.g., BOI, *Annual Report 1973*, p. 158. The breakdown of prices is the result of my own computations, based on the following data: the implicit price index of total resources and the consumer price index are those published by CBS with the national accounts; the price index of imports is the Paasche price index published in CBS, *Foreign Trade Statistics Monthly*. Admittedly, its use in conjunction with Lespeyres price indices for the other components of total resources introduces a certain bias. However, a correction of the bias could reinforce the results. The reason is that the Paasche price index uses current consumption as the base basket. In the face of rapidly increasing import prices, the share of goods with a high import component in the consumer's consumption bundle should be expected to shrink. So, in most probability, if the total price rise had been broken down into the domestic and imported components with the help of a Lespeyres index, the domestic component share would have been even smaller. By 1975 and 1976 the direction of the bias is reversed, but by then domestic inflation was running so much faster than imported inflation that one could hardly attribute the difference to the bias.

14. David Horowitz, *The Economy of Israel* (Tel-Aviv: Massada, 1954) [Hebrew].

15. Moshe Zanbar and Shaul Bronfeld, "Monetary Thought, Policy, and Development, 1948 to 1972, Part 2," *Economic Quarterly* 78–79 (1973): 217–36 [Hebrew].

16. BOI, *Annual Report 1955*, pp. 180–81, 195, 200.

17. David Horowitz, "The Hole Cannot Be Filled with Its Excavated Dirt," *Economic Quarterly* 25–26 (1960): 5–21.

18. Surprisingly, this odd method of going about monetary policy did not elicit criticism from the country's leading economists. For example, see Don Patinkin, *The Israel Economy: The First Decade* (Jerusalem: Falk Project for Economic Research in Israel, 1960), p. 119. He describes the policy without commenting on it.

19. BOI, *Annual Report 1955*, p. 200.

20. BOI, *Annual Report 1956*, p. 23.

21. I. Bar-Yosef, "The Practicality of Israel's Monetary Policy," *Economic Quarterly* 36 (1962): 351–61 [Hebrew].

22. Avigdor Steinberg, "Intermediation of Notes in the Israeli Economy, 1963 to 1967," *Bank of Israel Review* 30 (1968): 3–27 [Hebrew].

23. BOI, *Annual Report 1970*, p. 7.

24. Moshe Zanbar and Shaul Bronfeld, "Monetary Thought, Policy, and Development, 1948 to 1972, Part 1," *Economic Quarterly* 77 (1973): 3–16 [Hebrew].

25. Milton Friedman visualizes a different kind of bank under a regime of 100-percent reserve ratio. See his *A Program for Monetary Stability* (New York: Fordham University Press, 1959).

26. Zanbar and Bronfeld, " Monetary Thought, Part 2," p. 227.

27. BOI, *Annual Report 1972*, p. 301

28. Arnon Gafni, Fredi Vieder and Zalman Schiefer, "Monetary Developments and Bank of Israel Policies: Lessons from the Seventies," *Economic Quarterly* 109 (1981): 95–114 [Hebrew]. Gafni was the governor of the Bank when the article was written.

29. BOI, *Annual Report 1973*, p. 51.

30. The Bank of Israel did not hesitate in making exactly this observation. See ibid., p. 52.

31. BOI, *Annual Report 1974*, p. 12.

32. BOI, *Annual Report 1975*, p. 3.

33. The nominal wage figures were obtained from CBS, *Statistical Abstract of Israel*, 1983, Table XII/35; these were combined with the average increases in the con-

sumer price index, obtained from CBS, *National Accounts for 1984*, to obtain real wage changes.

34. BOI, *Annual Report 1974*, p. 8.

35. Matityahu Herschkowitz, "The Significance of the New COLA Arrangement," *Economic Quarterly* 87 (1975): 270–76 [Hebrew].

36. BOI, *Annual Report 1974*, p. 214; *1975*, p. 9.

37. Recall the refusal of Eliezer Kaplan, in 1936, to accept the position that workers should not be compensated for shocks exogenous to the economy. The situation following the events of 1973–74 is of the exact same nature.

38. BOI, *Annual Report 1975*, p. 176.

39. BOI, *Annual Report 1976*, p. 218.

40. BOI, *Annual Report 1979*, pp. 54, 94.

41. Ibid., p. 47.

42. The nominal amounts of credit subsidization were obtained from BOI, *Annual Report 1979*, p. 183. These were used, together with export data taken from the national accounts, to compute the rates.

43. BOI, *Annual Report 1976*, p. 45.

44. BOI, *Annual Report 1979*, p. 86.

45. Ibid., p. 207.

46. Ibid., p. 7.

47. Ibid.

48. BOI, *Annual Report 1976*, p. 35.

49. See BOI, *Annual Report 1977*, pp. 48–49. The figure of 16 percent that the bank quotes as the decline in investment differs from my 18.5 percent, because national accounts are usually revised slightly for several years after their original publication. Although the bank used the fresh accounts for 1977 when writing its report for that year, I used the accounts for 1980, which contained the revised figures for the period under consideration.

50. BOI, *Annual Report 1977*, p. 33. The figure used for disposable income is the one net of compulsory loans, which are viewed as a tax.

51. See, e.g., Mario Henrique Simonsen, "Indexation: Current Theory and the Experience in Brazil," in R. Dornbusch and M. H. Simonsen, eds., *Inflation, Debt and Indexation Cambridge, Mass.: M.I.T. Press, 1985); Alex Cukierman, "The Effects of Wage Indexation on Macroeconomic Fluctuations: A Generalization,"* Journal of Monetary Economics 6 (1980): 147–70; Edi Karni, "On Optimal Wage Indexation," *Journal of Political Economy* 91 (1983): 282–92.

52. BOI, *Annual Report 1978*, p. 183.

53. Ibid., p. 10.

54. BOI, *Annual Report 1976*, p. 161.

55. *A History of the Jews* (New York: Harper & Row, 1987).

56. Nadav Halevi, "The Impact of Inflation on Exchange Rates: The Israeli Experience," Discussion Paper 7711 (Jerusalem: Maurice Falk Institute, 1977). Note the indicative title: the paper does not discuss the impact of devaluation on inflation.

57. See Michael Bruno and Zvi Sussman, "From Crawling Peg to a Floating Rate: Israel 1977–1979 in Retrospect," *Economic Quarterly* 107 (1980): 359–73, especially p. 373 [Hebrew].

58. BOI, *Annual Report 1975*, p. 12.

59. BOI, *Annual Report 1978*, p. 183.

60. Nadav Halevi, "The Exchange Rate in Israel: Policy and Opinion," Discussion Paper 779 (Jerusalem: Maurice Falk Institute, 1977).

61. See also Y. Yoran, "Economy in Structural Crisis: The Israeli Economy Since the Oil Crisis and the Yom Kippur War of 1973," *Economic Quarterly* 131 (1987): 827–54. His assessment of the welfare developments in the mid-1970s is particularly scathing.

62. Shlomo Yitzhaki, "On Tax Relief Methods for Families with Children" (mimeo, November 1989) [Hebrew].

63. Ibid., and Shlomo Yitzhaki, "Taxation Developments During the Third Decade of Israel," Discussion Paper 83.09 (Jerusalem: Maurice Falk Institute of Economic Research, 1983) [Hebrew].

64. National Insurance Institute, *Annual Survey 1981*, Chapter 5.

65. BOI, *Annual Report 1976*, p. 213.

66. A unit of currency basket was made up of $.35, £.1295, DM.515, FF.6832 and DF.2187. This mix was constructed as a representation of Israel's foreign-trade mix.

67. Ministry of Finance, Department of Foreign Exchange, *Changes in Indirect Tax Refunds by Value Added Categories*, undated [Hebrew].

68. Imri Tov, "The Objectives of the 1977 Reform and the Mode of its Implementation" (unpublished 1987) [Hebrew]. Tov was a senior Bank official when the reform took place. The acceptance of the new government's political agenda without as much as a professional critique is remarkable in itself, because the top administrations of both the Bank of Israel and the Ministry of Finance were inherited from the outgoing Labor government.

69. Gafni et al., "Monetary Developments and Bank of Israel Policies."

70. Computed from BOI, *Annual Report 1976*, p. 282.

71. BOI, *Annual Report 1977*, p. 312.

72. See Yoav Kislev and Yakir Plessner, "Inflation and the Exchange Rate: A Monetary View," *Economic Quarterly* 109 (1981): 137–55.

73. BOI, *Annual Report 1977*, p. 312.

74. BOI, *Annual Report 1978*, p. 270.

75. For 1977 and 1978, see BOI, *Annual Report 1978*, p. 275. The 1976 percentage may not be entirely accurate, as the Bank changed the classification of some credit categories after that year. Hence, strictly speaking, the data are not fully comparable. Still, there is no doubt about the direction in which the credit composition evolved. The data do not include mortgage loans and loans from development banks. Both categories were fully controlled by the government.

76. See R. I. McKinnon and D. J. Mathieson, "How to Manage a Repressed Economy," in *Essays in International Finance* 145 (Princeton, N.J.: Princeton University, 1981), 1–26.

77. See also Yoram Ben-Porath, "The *Mahapach* That Wasn't: Ideology and Economic Policy 1977–1981," *Economic Quarterly* 115 (1982): 325–33.

Chapter 10. Inflation! The Obstacles Gang Up

1. BOI, *Annual Report 1972*, p. 5.

2. BOI, *Annual Report 1970*, p. 155–56.

3. Ibid., pp. 123–24.

4. The data concerning private and domestic public consumption were obtained from CBS, *Statistical Abstract of Israel*, 1974; *Israel's Defense Expenditures, 1950–83*.

5. BOI, *Annual Report 1983*, p. 129.

6. BOI, *Annual Report 1970*, pp. 96–104.

7. BOI, *Annual Report 1971*, p. 8.

8. BOI, *Annual Report 1974*, pp. 12, 41, 82, 84–91.

9. BOI, *Annual Report 1978*, p. 176.

10. Ibid., p. 5.

11. See also ibid., p. 43.

12. Henceforth, all the rates of devaluation are relative to the "new" basket of currencies, instituted formally on August 1, 1986. It consists of 60 U.S. cents, 41.77 German pfennigs, 6.7 English pennies, 33.94 French centimes, and 7.7 Japanese yen.

13. BOI, *Annual Report 1978*, p. 351.

14. Ibid., p. 43.

15. The quarterly I£ figures are reported in ibid., p. 257. These were divided by the average quarterly exchange rates to obtain the dollar figures. The latter may therefore be inaccurate, but the deviations are an order of magnitude smaller than the reported data.

16. BOI, *Annual Report 1979*, p. 5.

17. Ibid., p. 7.

18. Ibid., p. 49.

19. BOI, *Annual Report 1980*, pp. 4, 32.

20. Ibid., p. 33.

21. See Yoav Kislev, "The Monetary Approach to Israel's Balance of Payments," *Economic Quarterly* 96–97 (1978): 37–50; and Yoav Kislev and Yakir Plessner, "Inflation and the Exchange Rate—A Monetary View," *Economic Quarterly* 109 (1981): 137–55 [both in Hebrew].

22. A sketch of a theoretical model within which these results can be established is given in Yakir Plessner, "Inflation in a Small Open Economy: Theory and Evidence from Israel's Inflation" (unpublished, January 1988).

23. IMF, *Iceland—Staff Report,* SM/83/236, 1983.

24. BOI, *Annual Report 1980*, p. 36.

25. The real purchasing power was calculated as

$$\sum_{t=1}^{30} \frac{50}{(1.00318)^t} = 1428.51$$

The resultant sum is 4.766 percent below 1,500. An exact calculation, one that assumes a continuous increase in prices over the month, yields a somewhat different result, which is calculated as follows: let the price level at the beginning of the first day be defined as 1. Then the average price level for the month p, is calculated from

$$p = \frac{1}{30} \int_0^{30} (1.00318)^t \, dt = 1.0498.$$

This means, that the average price level during the month is almost 5 percent above the initial price level, and hence the real purchasing power is $1,428.84, which is only 4.74 percent below $1,500.

26. These increases constitute supplements of 5 percent each, exactly what is needed to offset the excess of the average monthly price level over the price level on the day on which wages are paid.

27. The calculation is IS1 million X (1286.3/986.5).

28. 1268.3/1535.5 = .826.

29. The option of reducing the public work force does not yield budgetary savings in the short term either because of the expenditures involved in such a reduction; for example, in the form of severance payments.

30. This description is compatible with "rational expectations," a theory that concludes that it is impossible to fool the average citizen.

31. BOI, *Annual Report 1981*, p. 75.

32. Ibid., p. 41.

33. See ibid., especially pp. 41–44.

34. Ibid., p. 74.

35. The translation is as faithful to the original as I was able to render it. If it sounds peculiar and even convoluted, this is because the original sounds that way as well.

36. BOI, *Annual Report 1987*, p. 87. These figures differ a little from the ones underlying Table 10.5, because the former are derived from national accounts, whereas the latter are figured from cash flows.

37. BOI, Supervisor of Banks, *Israel's Banking System—1979 Annual Survey*, p. 209 [Hebrew].

38. BOI, *Annual Report 1983*, pp. 98, 100.

39. BOI, *Annual Report 1982*, p. 266.

40. Figured at December 1983 prices and rate of exchange. See BOI, *Annual Report 1983*, p. 253.

41. The details of the "shares arrangement," as it was known, were taken from BOI, *Annual Report 1983*, p. 253.

42. BOI, Research Department, Main Israeli Economic Data No. 084, April 18, 1988, Tables F–1, F–2.

43. The budget deficit is defined here, and everywhere in the sequel, as domes-

tic government revenues, excluding borrowing, less domestic spending, excluding lending and investment. A negative deficit means positive saving.

Chapter 11. Stabilization and Missed Opportunities

1. See, for instance, Rudiger Dornbusch and Mario Henrique Simonsen, "Inflation Stabilization with Incomes Policy Support," paper prepared for the Group of Thirty, New York, October 1986. Other examples are Alex Cukierman, "The End of the High Israeli Inflation—An Experiment in Heterodox Stabilization," in M. Bruno et al., eds, *Inflation Stabilization* (Cambridge, Mass.: M.I.T. Press, 1988), pp. 48–94; Miguel Kiguel and Nissan Liviatan, "Inflationary Rigidities and Orthodox Stabilization Policies: Lessons from Latin America," *The World Bank Economic Review* 2 (1988): 273–98.

2. A description of the plan, the rationale motivating it, and its major components is given in BOI, *Annual Report 1985*, pp. 60–67.

3. Ibid.

4. BOI, *Annual Report 1990*, p. 164.

5. Ministry of Economy and Public Works and Services, "Economic Policy of the Argentine Government" (undated, but circa January 1992; no page numbers).

6. BOI, *Annual Report 1990*, p. 18, and *Annual Report 1991*, p. 20.

7. See, e.g., CBS, *Input-Output Tables 1982–83* [English Edition], Special Series No. 824 (Jerusalem: Author, 1988), p. 33.

8. BOI, *Annual Report 1985*, p. 280; *Annual Report 1986*, p. 255.

9. For a comprehensive description and analysis of poststabilization monetary policy, see Yakir Plessner, "Post-Stabilization Monetary Policy in Israel (1985–1990), Policy Studies No. 9 (Jerusalem: Institute for Advanced Strategic and Political Studies,1991).

10. Supervisor of Banks, *Annual Statistics of Israel's Banking System 1982–1986*, Table III–2. The quoted numbers were arrived at as follows: the NIS figures for demand and time deposits for Israeli residents were added and divided by the end-of-month representative rate of exchange.

11. Based on a conversation with Arnon Gafni, chairman of Koor's board.

12. Bank of Israel, *Annual Report 1990*, p. 164.

INDEX